PROPERTY AND POWER IN SOCIAL THEORY

In social and political theories of class inequality and stratification property and power perform a key role. However, theorists have yet to clearly define these concepts, their mutual boundaries and their scopes of application. Moreover, a 'primacy puzzle' remains unsolved: is power ultimately dependent upon property, or property upon power? Which is primary, which derivative?

Dick Pels seeks answers to the property/power puzzle by undertaking a broad historical inquiry into its intellectual origins and present-day effects. He re-examines the increasingly misleading terms of the debate between property and power by placing the traditional controversy within the framework of intellectual rivalry. He traces the intricate pattern of rivalry between the two concepts through a series of case studies, including:

- Marxism vs. anarchism
- the fascist assertion of the primacy of the political
- social science as power theory
- the managerial revolution
- the knowledge society and the new intellectual classes

Having examined knowledge as property-and-power, Pels elaborates a radical and reflexive theory of intellectual rivalry.

Property and Power in Social Theory unravels the dialectics of social-scientific dichotomies and provides a novel and informative way of organizing twentieth-century social theory. This work makes a valuable contribution to sociological theory and to the history of thought.

Dick Pels is Professor of the Social Theory of Knowledge in the Faculty of Philosophy at the University of Groningen. He is also scholar in residence at the Amsterdam School for Social Science Research.

ROUTLEDGE STUDIES IN SOCIAL AND POLITICAL THOUGHT

PROPERTY AND POWER IN SOCIAL THEORY

A study in intellectual rivalry

Dick Pels

London and New York

First published 1998
by Routledge
11 New Fetter Lane, London EC4P 4EE

Simultaneously published in the USA and Canada
by Routledge
29 West 35th Street, New York, NY 10001

Typeset in Garamond by Routledge
Printed and bound in Great Britain by Biddles Ltd,
Guildford and King's Lynn

British Library Cataloguing in Publication Data
A catalogue record for this book is available from the British Library

Library of Congress Cataloging in Publication Data
Pels, Dick, 1948–
[Macht of eigndom?. English]
Property and power in social theory: a study in intellectual rivalry/Dick Pels.
Originally written as a dissertation at the University of Amsterdam and
published in Dutch translation in 1987, "it has been thoroughly revised, to
such an extent as to effectively become new."
Cf. Pref.
1. Power (Social sciences) 2. Property. 3. Knowledge, Sociology of.
4. Intellectual life – History. I. Title.
HM136.P54313 1998 98–23828
306.4'2–dc21 CIP

ISBN 0–415–18780–X

CONTENTS

ILLUSTRATIONS

FIGURES

TABLES

Tsjalling Swierstra was important in rendering the Introduction more accessible.

I have long felt that, if I were to dedicate this study to anyone, it could only be to the memory of Alvin W. Gouldner. More than anything else, it was his towering presence in Amsterdam in the mid-1970s that was decisive for my sense of direction (and perhaps also of mission) in the busy metropolis of modern social thought. Although the present book speaks critically about some of his work, Gouldner's spirit evidently colours even this critique. More than a set of ideas or a form of craftsmanship, it was a way of life and a kind of person which I recognized as perhaps also my own. In a strange and emotionally ambiguous manner, conversation with Gouldner did not cease after his sudden death in December 1980. As his posthumous publications began to appear, I was often jealous to come across superb and powerful formulations of what I thought I had arrived at independently – and I confess that at times I was rather glad that he was gone and could not surprise me once again. I persuade myself that he might have liked this book, which is written in a language which in more than one sense is his.

Amsterdam
October 1997

PREFACE

Rather than for truth's sake and the world at large, books are usually written for some people and against some others; the present author himself belongs in both categories at once. Every book is a fight for personal identity as much as for communicable clarity, attained by both identifying with and counteracting the example of significant others. Certainly, it is an attempt to persuade, but I need not persuade *all* others, just those whose judgement is significant to me. Moreover, I must persuade *myself* as much as them, not simply of the justice of my intellectual intuitions but also of the justice of my existence and ambitions as an intellectual – which is somewhat different from the impersonal and procedural work of justification which is commonly accepted as the hallmark of scientific practice. I confess I have never been much at home in those intellectual lifestyles which repress rather than utilize the committed presence of the observer in the object observed, and which easily forget about the essentially contested nature of all scientific postures and propositions.

If scientific work answers to a logic of significant others, let me name some of those whose judgement I especially sought and appreciated. This book was originally written as a dissertation under Derek Phillips' and Louis Boon's supervision at the University of Amsterdam. It was published in a Dutch translation in 1987. But I could not resign myself to the prospect that it would not reach the broader audience that it was actually written for (and against). Over the years, I have become fully instructed about the systematic blockages – which are inseparably linguistic, psychological, and social – which prevent intellectuals from outside the centre from conversing (and doing battle) with the dominant as equal partners. Hence I am grateful that, after a decade or so, the book has finally made its appearance beyond the flatlands and the dykes. Meanwhile, it has been thoroughly revised, to such an extent as to become effectively new. That it has taken this improved shape is also due to the encouragement of a few people who backed me at crucial points in time. I have long cherished Lolle Nauta's friendship. Steven Lukes, Steve Fuller, Bill Lynch, Nico Stehr, and especially Stephen Turner have given vital support. The insightful criticism of Rokus Hofstede, Baukje Prins, and

INTRODUCTION
The problem of intellectual rivalry

> This is a habit we all share, of relating an inquiry not to the subject-matter itself, but to our opponent in argument.
>
> Aristotle

PROPERTY AND POWER

In everyday speech, we are both serviced and deceived by our most common-place concepts: we have grown into their usage to such an extent as to forget that *they* are actually using *us*. Their functions appear self-evident, and their rules of reference remain largely implicit. Even in more disciplined discursive fields such as the historical sociology of ideas – which forms the subject of this study – such deceptive utensils proliferate in great quantity. The genealogy of 'master concepts' such as property and power offers no exception to this rule. As summary notations for fundamental building blocks of social life, they manifest the familiar translucency which comes from uninterrupted, mindless daily usage.

Axial terms in the Western repertoire of social thought, power, and property have been central concerns of political theory, jurisprudence, sociology, history, and political economy. They have played a pivotal role in theories of social inequality and class formation, identifying nodal points around which secondary, derivative inequalities were most likely to accrue: chances to participate in different lifestyles, to enter and operate social networks, to gain access to education, or to acquire social prestige. Both are also conceptual crossroads at which different currents in classical and modern social theory have met and interbred.

Despite this axial character (or rather, because of it), both concepts present a notorious source of embarrassment to modern academic social science. Property and power exuberantly illustrate Karl Kraus's experienced observation that 'the closer one looks at a word, the further it recedes in the distance'. The disciplinary partitions of twentieth-century social thought have cut up the analytical field into sociological, legal, historical, economic, and politico-scientific slices which, taken by themselves, provide too narrow an analytical platform for the broader and longer view which issues of property and power evidently require.

Jurists and political economists are often absorbed in definitory conflicts over the precise demarcation between detention, possession, and property; the juridical theory of property is itself parcelled out over disparate technical branches such as the law of realty and the law of persons, family law and public law. Political philosophers and political historians still do not talk much to sociologists and economists, while the latter have long remained imprisoned in sociologically weak theories of distribution. Critical sociologists have duly signalled the 'common neglect of property institutions' in their discipline (Gouldner 1958: 9), complaining that the contemporary sociology of property presents 'an extremely fragmented appearance' (Hollowell 1982: 18).[1] In the case of power, concentrated and comprehensive multidisciplinary studies appear less sparse, although some version of MacIver's observation that there exists 'no reasonable adequate study of the nature of social power' (1947: 458) is echoed by many modern students of society and politics.

It is correct to say that politically committed strands of theorizing have more successfully resisted this risk of fragmentation than mainstream academic thought. Marxism, for example, has consistently presented the property question as the pivotal question of political economy and the revolutionary movement, while the anarchist tradition has similarly fastened upon power or authority as the alpha and omega of its theoretical and practical efforts. But, as the latter-day cliché runs, socialists have often been too impatient to change the world to await its careful interpretation. As a result, concepts such as property or production in classical Marxism have been swept along in a vortex of ambiguities, and perplexity has reigned about what precisely the abolition or supersession of private property could be taken to mean. A similar perplexity has been fomented by classical anarchists, for whom the 'abolition of government' has likewise acted as a close equivalent of the Apocalypse.

But there is more to the problem of property and power than the false transparency of their everyday usage, or the fragmented and ambiguous character of their more technically articulated definitions. It is a rudimentary idea of the present study that they are also *interrelated* in peculiar fashion, and that it might be profitable to explore the unkempt border area of their definitional distinctions and overlaps from a new and somewhat unusual perspective. The two master concepts of property and power, I am convinced, are tied together by so many historical threads that definitional problems on either side remain insoluble unless they are studied as a conceptual doublet. Indeed, despite the apparent ease with which property and power are routinely distinguished from one another – a distinction which basically reduces to a dichotomy between the disposition of physical *things* and command over the actions of *persons* – they are often defined in terms of one another or as mutual opposites, elliptically, without an independent definition of either. The common-sense distinction itself, if subjected to further enquiry, appears to turn upon a more deeply rooted cleavage between 'material production' and 'organization' (or between 'economic' interactions between humans and nature and 'political' interactions amongst humans themselves), which is often correlated with an equally venerable dichotomy between civil society and the state (in their classical binary conceptualization).

As I shall demonstrate, this set of collateral distinctions, though often presented as a timeless configuration which reflects the natural articulation of the world, ontologically 'freezes' what is manifestly a transient and reversible ideological conjuncture. Property and power, or economics and politics, or civil society and the state, only acquire independent status in an extended process of conceptual fissure which, after long historical gestation, reaches its deepest cleavage in the classical systems of political liberalism and liberal political economy – a process of differentiation, moreover, which does not stop at its point of largest amplitude, but is being reversed with accelerating speed as we approach our present time. Indeed, both the concept of property and that of power have recently been implicated in drives for *generalization* which have made them simultaneously vaguer and more similar to one another – to the point of developing into virtual synonyms. The major puzzle, as Chapter 1 sets out to demonstrate, is therefore to be found less in the notorious variability and vagueness of both master concepts taken in isolation, than in the peculiar pattern of divergence and convergence which characterizes their long-term historical relationship.

The liberal dualism of 'propertyless' power vs. 'powerless' property, in other words, does not reflect a logical essence or a timeless fact of nature, but marks a provisional culmination of a long process of semantic polarization, which increasingly splits the inclusive feudal conception of *dominium* or *domain* into political and economic compartments. As rights of property are defined in a more absolute and exclusive manner, they are ever more clearly demarcated from and profiled against rights of sovereignty, which are subjected to a process of concentration and substantialization which mirrors in its essential features the parallel fortification of property rights. However, this splitting movement does not halt at the node of largest amplitude, as Whiggish liberal narratives would insist, but is 'toppled over' and reversed – a secular process which roughly begins in the middle of the nineteenth century but accelerates considerably in the course of the twentieth. In what appears like a concerted attempt to undermine the divide from both sides, the two vocabularies are once again interfused and collated. In a long historical perspective, we are therefore approaching a new comprehensive theory of dominion (or as I shall call it, *disposition*) in which many traits of the original feudal conception are recognizable anew. This movement of fission and fusion can be visualized in the diamond pattern shown in Figure 1.

THE PRIMACY PUZZLE

Moreover, as soon as the nature of such historic linkages between property and

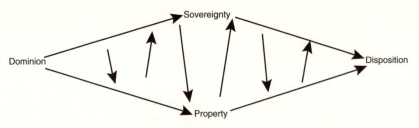

Figure 1 The diamond pattern

power is questioned in an explicit manner, two mutually exclusive answers are likely to emerge, which have long settled in two rivalling master repertoires of social ontology. In one tradition, power is routinely presented as the grounding concept and property as its derivative, while the alternative tradition has undertaken to *reverse* this order of logical and generative priority. This 'eco-nomic' tradition has consistently rejected an allegedly 'groundless' or 'abstract' notion of power in order to locate this absent ground in property, albeit in the 'last instance', whereas the 'political' tradition has stood matters on its head, arguing that property was itself in need of a grounding, since it ultimately constituted a form or function of power. In an essay on the rise of political sociology, Runciman has traced this dilemma to the emergence of the 'essential distinction, unthinkable in the Middle Ages, between society and the State':

> Once . . . the distinction begins to be realized, it should be possible to ask the question: which determines which? Is it, as sometimes implied by Machiavelli, the State (or rather, the statecraft of the prince) by which society is moulded, or is it, as explicitly stated in Marx, society which determines the form and nature of the State?
> (Runciman 1963: 22–3)

Bottomore has likewise drawn attention to this gradual polarization between the social and the political, as originally formulated in the contrast between civil society and the state. Against this backdrop, the central problem of the age becomes 'the relation between the sphere of production, property and labour on one side, and organized political power on the other'. This remains a focal point of controversy 'in which Marxist theory . . . is broadly opposed to those theories which are more exclusively concerned with the independent effects of political institutions' (Bottomore 1979: 8–9, 12).[2] The concurrence of such rivalling options therefore gives rise to a peculiar primacy puzzle or dilemma of reduction: is power a function, an articulation of, or otherwise dependent upon property? Or is it the other way around? This is the question which Dahrendorf, the sociologist of conflict, has also paradigmatically asked of Marx: is property a special case of authority, or vice versa, authority a special case of property (1959: 20–2)?

One important aim of the present study is to clarify why we cannot be partisan to either strategy of reduction, since power and property, and the broader socio-political vocabularies which they animate, are also deeply enmeshed in the politics and morals of *intellectual rivalry*. Concepts such as power and property themselves constitute *means of power* which supply the weaponry of intellectual polemics, or *items of property* which perform as stakes in bids for intellectual competition. As competing theoretical favourites, they continually rise and fall with the ideological tide. Such tidal changes show a definite oscillatory pattern. The 1970s, for example, witnessed a grand sweep 'from Marx to Nietzsche', which also involved a marked shift from a master narrative of property and economics towards one of power and politics. The 1980s, by contrast, massively reverted to the economizing metaphors and individualistic behavioural models of neo-liberalism and rational choice theory. On the face of it, then, the 'long political decade' of the 1960s and 1970s was succeeded by a decade (and a half) of economistic rationality, efficiency, commercialism, and privatization, which reached its provisional culmination in the anti-statist and pro-market revolutions of 1989–90 in Eastern and Central Europe.

But the grand polemic between political and economic metaphors is far more intricate than this, and features some unexpected continuities and duplicities. It is arguable, for example, that the Marxian theorem about the 'last instance' determination of the economy precisely functioned to legitimize something like a 'first instance' prerogative of the political, i.e. the political voluntarism of revolutionary intellectuals who offered themselves as *spokespersons for* the iron laws of the capitalist economy. The neo-liberal marketeers, on the other hand, in reacting against this not-so-hidden interventionist agenda, appropriated the formula for their own contrary ends, claiming ontological primacy for a market logic which this time 'objectively' demanded a major roll-back of state power. It only adds to our confusion if we notice that, after the dramatic 'credibility loss' suffered by Marxism and other left-wing ideologies, the most vigorous criticism of such neo-liberal economism, and the most insistent claim for the primacy of the political, no longer issues from the left but from an increasingly vocal (and intellectual) New Right. Such contrapuntal melodies and performative double games at least awaken us to the relative *arbitrariness* with which the idiom of power and politics is often preferred over that of property and economics – or the other way around.

The 'rivalry perspective' which is advanced here inevitably modifies our attitude towards that core dispute in classical and contemporary social theory which is still (too) often introduced in terms of the 'correct' division of labour or the 'natural' boundary line running between economic society and the political state. As the historical record demonstrates, such boundaries have continually shifted from one context and locale to another, and require incessant 'boundary work' by those who are interested in ascertaining an autonomous identity (and the productive status of their line of work) over others who dominate the field and wish to consolidate their positions of primacy against such newcomers' claims. In this boundary work, both the sharpness with which demarcation lines are drawn and the hierarchy among the domains and activities separated by them are continually at stake and open to negotiation. The survival of 'last instance' ontologies of the political or the economic, and of the grand polemic between them, cannot therefore be exhaustively explained by reference to objective economic or political realities which they supposedly reflect, since such arguments simultaneously 'act upon' these realities in order to shift the balance of forces, e.g. to stabilize a particular boundary and a particular hierarchy between fields and types of productive activity. In addition, these arguments also act upon each other, since they are implicated in a compelling figuration of rivalry which has a determinate logic of its own, and which condemns them to oscillate between fixed conceptual points.

Chapter 2 begins to focus upon the recurrent vocabulary switches and primacy battles between the 'master sciences' of property and power, as they unfold within the expanding and contracting space of the diamond pattern. After tracing early manifestations of the priority dispute in the Roman Law school, it charts the gradual polarization which develops between an 'Aristotelian' tradition of political philosophy and a 'Smithian' tradition of political economy, which increasingly fixes the contrasting profile of their core notions of sovereignty and property. While philosophers such as Bodin, Hobbes, and Montesquieu followed Aristotelian premises about the grounding and encompassing nature of power and politics, Lockean liberalism and Scottish–French political economy departed from the opposite premise about the infrastructural character of property and economics – a vocabulary switch which was subsequently re-enacted in Marx's dramatic 'overturning' of Hegelian idealism. On both sides of the rivalry, the master concepts were defined so broadly as to permit a continual 'dialectical' slippage from part to whole, which implied that the object boundaries of these rivalling master sciences could be drawn as widely as possible. Starting from opposite ends (politics or production), both the Aristotelian and the Smithian master sciences hence manifested a pervasive imperial drive, and strategically hesitated between the modest study of the part and the intellectual annexation of the whole.

Chapter 3 proceeds with a detailed investigation of the rivalry between Marxism and anarchism, and especially of the dispute between Marx and Bakunin, whose ideological opposition has been taken as a case of paradigmatic significance by many students of intellectual competition. This dispute once again centred in considerable degree upon the different priority which the antagonists assigned to property or power as generative 'last instances' of social reality, and upon the opposite order of abolition (state first, then capital, or the other way around?) which summed up their political projects. Even though the late twentieth-century twilight of the Grand Narratives has boded decline for both ideologies and for their sibling rivalries, the old opposition has by no means died out, as is amply confirmed by the polemics conducted by the French Althusserian school, the more recent antics of 'rational choice Marxism', and the critical work of modern 'ecological' anarchists such as Bookchin. In addition, new movement ideologies such as feminism and ecologism prolong ritualized debates in which this heritage of rivalry between Marxism and anarchism and their originary vocabularies of property and power are repeated in attenuated but still recognizable form.

Chapter 4 continues this inventory by focusing upon the historic confrontation between fascism and Marxism, in light of the radical-right conviction that politics should take priority over economics, and that the power question was more fundamental than the question of property. To take fascism seriously as an intellectual system still remains a hotly contested 'revisionist' approach which many students of right-wing ideology consider dangerously close to gainsaying political irrationalism and evil. However, fascist ideology was not simply nihilistic and power-sick, but departed from a genuine revolutionary idealism, and offered reasonably coherent solutions to intellectual dilemmas which were left standing by rival ideologies – among which Marxism was routinely singled out as the most formidable competitor. In their totalizing conceptions of power and the state, right-wing ideologists tended to repeat a cognitive pattern which characteristically beset the more respectable intellectual systems they were attempting to reverse: the dialectic of the 'last instance'. Carl Schmitt's influential conception of the political perhaps offers the most clear-cut example of this reversal of ontological priorities. The recent reinvention of 'the ubiquity of the political' on the political left therefore paradoxically recycles many of the critical arguments which were previously advanced against Marxist and liberal economism by intellectuals of the prewar political right.

The three chapters that follow are together devoted to a comprehensive analysis of the rise and development of academic social science in terms of the power–property dilemma, ranging from early demarcations of the sociological object up to present-day analyses of the 'knowledge society'. Chapter 5 begins by raising doubts about 'the discovery of society' as emerging through a constitutive demarcation from the state – and about the autonomy of social science as traditionally demarcated against classical political philosophy. Counteracting the tendency to homogenize social theory's past from an overly 'Anglo-Saxon' or liberal image of its early history, it offers a triadic, 'knowledge-geographical' tableau of interpretations of the social object, all of which were much more closely aligned with political ideologies than is normally acknowledged in academic disciplinary history, and most of which resisted a clear-cut delineation in state vs. society terms. In the tripartite space of emerging social science, the French and German–Italian branches stuck significantly closer to the political and *staatswissenschaftliche* tradition than the Anglo-Saxon branch, and exemplified not so much a rupture with as an innovatory *continuation* of

Aristotelian political philosophy, extending and generalizing its scope of analysis from state sovereignty towards a more inclusive theory of the generation and distribution of social power.

This approach introduces a new specification both of the unity and the diversity of the sociological object/project. It highlights the ambiguous position of emerging social theory as simultaneously weighed down by the historic antagonism between 'power theory' and 'property theory', and as striving to clear a *third* location which claims to supersede it. This ambition is especially marked in the tradition of French positivism, in its dual rupture from political philosophy and political economy and its repositioning of the social object *in between* state and economic market (and of the project of societal corporatism as a third way between individualism and socialism). This elusive object/project can perhaps be redescribed as that of *knowledgeable organization*. It defines at once the classical promise and the classical *hubris* of the sociological tradition, according to which positive social science would be capable of laying a firm groundwork for the comprehensive engineering of social change. In this fashion, budding social science issued an early (and quite self-interested) prediction about the 'knowledge society' and the rise of a new 'knowledge class' of sociologically educated intellectuals.

THE NEW CLASS THESIS

When looking at the property–power dilemma across a range of theoretical traditions, we are therefore not only intrigued by the peculiar structuring effects of intellectual rivalries on conceptual profiles and styles of thought; we are also, and inevitably, pulled towards the big issue of social class. Property and power, we noted, have traditionally performed as axial concepts in different, often opposite, theories of social stratification, and it is no doubt in this domain of social enquiry that their competitive relationship has wrought the most pernicious results. Different socialist and social-scientific traditions, in their own house and in rivalry with each other, have fuelled an interminable dispute in which some currents focused on the concept of class and defined it in terms of property, while alternative currents embraced the concept of elite, usually defining it as grounded in power. In this regard, Marx's contention that all history (so far) was the history of class struggles perfectly mirrored Pareto's less familiar dictum that history was nothing but 'a graveyard of aristocracies'. Of course, the current relationship between property/class and power/elite theory is far more complex: oppositions such as the one that rallied Pareto against Marx have long been overtaken by attempts to synthesize the two viewpoints – as is conspicuous in the writings of, for example, Mills, Dahrendorf, Gouldner, Giddens, and Bourdieu. However, although such efforts have become the rule rather than the exception, many mediating attempts still tend to fall back upon one of the two conceptual alternatives.[3]

8

Chapters 6 and 7 of this study contend that the dilemma of reduction, and the liberal dichotomy upon which it historically turns, increasingly reveal themselves as discursive anachronisms which stand in the way of an adequate analysis of contemporary developments in the social division of labour and the distribution of social rewards. The theory of class and stratification must no longer be torn between the property and power vocabularies. This contest is the more unfortunate because there is broad agreement that the most significant developments over the past century have precisely been the following:

1   A progressive (though not linear or geographically even) process of *inter-twinement* or *osmosis* of the spheres of civil society and the state, and the institutionalization of an intermediate zone of connecting associations.
2   A new spurt in the secular process of rationalization or intellectualization, which is drawing the contours of an emerging 'knowledge society', and which progressively imposes something like an 'intellectual' logic and habitus upon non-intellectual societal domains.
3   The concomitant rise of new strata of 'knowledge professionals' who typically prosper at this 'reflexive' intersection between polity and economy, and increasingly infiltrate the old economic and political classes – if they do not posit themselves as their historical successors.

Despite such epochal realignments in social structure, the conceptual challenges posed by them are still often met in discursive terms which are imprinted by the stereotypical distinction between property and power, and by a premeditated view of the order of priority which governs them. While the modern sociology of stratification, for example, treats the gradual shift *from* property *to* power as dominant stratificatory axis as a virtually uncontested theoretical baseline, it is confronted by an equally vigorous tradition of neo-Marxist inquiry which takes the erosion of property by no means for granted, and continues to work from a generalized vocabulary of production, capital, and class. Chapter 6 illustrates this persistent opposition (but also the growing convergence between the two camps) by re-examining the controversies centring upon Mills' *The Power Elite* in the 1950s and Dahrendorf's power theory of social class in the early 1960s, the polemic between New Left critics and mainstream sociologists in the 1970s, and the more recent positionings of 'analytical' Marxism, neo-Weberian 'closure theory', and the field theory developed by Bourdieu. This dual pattern of rivalry and osmosis is further traced through the prism of the 'managerial revolution' debate, where the competition between a property and a power analysis has induced a curiously repetitive game of classificatory expansion and contraction. This debate also usefully refocuses my concern with the problem of 'knowledgeable organization', since managers may be typified as a new organizational intelligentsia, which displays some typical closure practices and legitimation strategies of a new 'knowledge class'. What is the specificity of such a class's holdings or assets, of its havings-and-doings?

As the congruence between polity and economy advances, the dilemma of reduction already loses the little meaning which it may possibly retain for sociologically identifying 'old' property-based classes or power elites. But it forbids the more thoroughly an understanding of the peculiar stratificational situs of such *new* strategic elites because their holdings constitute new configurations of dispositional chances which together make up something *less* than exclusive, heritable material property but also add up to something *more* than political or bureaucratic power, and hence form a composite whole which is not quite equal to the sum of its parts. The point is not so much that vast hierarchies of control and surveillance have been superimposed upon the disposition of physical means of production, but that new dispositional configurations have arisen which integrate different productive resources (external material goods and tools, divisions of labour and leadership roles, incorporated cultural assets), and various modalities of disposal (collective or bureaucratic control over physical means of production and human labour, direct individual disposition of cultural capital), which are formally divorced from inheritance through kinship and are active at one and the same time. Because the new strategic elites which emerge in the 'societal state' (Kraemer 1966) most immediately embody the productive force of 'knowledgeable organization', their dispositional identity is complex, but the main thing appears to be that their access to the exercise of material property (which is not privately but institutionally held) and their access to political or bureaucratic hierarchies is increasingly mediated and dominated by the closure mechanisms and inheritance patterns of personally held *cultural* capital.

Hence the need for a more head-on confrontation with the issue of intellectual disposition and closure, as it is reposed in terms of this emerging logic of 'reflexive modernization'. Following Bourdieu's classification of forms of cultural capital, which is slightly modified by insights acquired from Mills, Collins, and Parkin, Chapter 7 outlines a provisional model of intellectual closure, the 'spinal cord' of which is formed by the disposition over non-material incorporated goods, which strongly conditions the appropriation of other relevant resources, both material and immaterial. It is interesting to note, in this context, that current controversies surrounding culture, knowledge, and technical skill as forces of production and factors of distribution already evidence an advanced state of fusion of the property and power repertoires. However, ultimate semantic preferences still remain divided, and a complete fusion between both hegemonic metaphors has so far not been achieved. Recent contributions either elaborate a 'political economy of culture' through a generalization of the vocabulary of investment, property, and capital, or generalize the idiom of political theory in the direction of a theory of cultural or symbolic power. The first strategy typically issues in a notion of 'cultural capital' such as advocated by Gouldner or Bourdieu; the second one is bound to arrive at something like Foucault's master idea of *pouvoir/savoir*. However, if we wish to account for the true complexity of the havings-and-doings of the new 'knowledgeable organizers', we need to mix and synthesize the connotations which are historically transmitted by the two rivalling vocabularies: the static or 'residential' connotations of property and the 'active' or 'performative' ones of power. Rather than generalize from one or the other alternative, we had better circumvent the residual effect of the dilemma of reduction altogether, and propose new bridging terms such as 'disposition', 'competency', and 'closure', which I presume are less burdened by deceptive historical connotations.

DYNAMICS OF INTELLECTUAL RIVALRY

In undertaking to analyse the various phases of this particular reduction puzzle, light may be thrown upon a characteristic feature of the mode of intellectual production itself – which, as sociologists of knowledge from Mannheim to Bourdieu have claimed, is simultaneously a game of intellectual distinction, in which competitors–producers attend as much to what their rivals say as to 'reality out there'. If the agonistic field is surveyed as a whole, we may attain a clearer view of the commonality of interests which binds intellectual rivals who can only see themselves as diametrically opposed, and who hasten to accentuate mutual difference rather than admit mutual kinship. Usually, investment in a particular discursive tradition and investment in a particular rivalry are two sides of the same intellectual coin. Priority disputes such as that about property vs. power are to some extent *cherished* conflicts, the logic of which is adopted by all and which penetrates deeply into the infra-structure of the contesting theories. An investment in one particular doctrinal option represents an investment in the entire configuration and, logically, a minimal but important investment in the adversary's game. Following Bourdieu, such theoretical alternatives may be identified as epis-temological–sociological *couples ennemis* which express objective relation-ships between adversaries who are at the same time accomplices, who, 'through their very antagonism, demarcate the field of legitimate argument, excluding as absurd, eclectic, or simply unthinkable, any attempts to take up an unforeseen position' (1981: 282). Habitualized rivalries close off the field of dispute, precisely because the polemical content of the competing viewpoints is underplayed or denied. The doctrinal opposition is maintained from both ends as a permanent one, and is routinely taken to reflect the natural state or deep structure of reality itself. A theory of intellectual rivalries, by searching out the combative, critical aspects of scientific propositions and concepts, could then show that much of what intellectuals offer as solid principles which are strongly supported by facts, are rationalized *inversions* of the viewpoints taken by their adversaries, and do not carry much intellectual weight beyond the battleground of polemics itself.

The doctrinal contest which is examined here therefore represents a larger set of conflicts in which the contestants are simultaneously unwitting accomplices. The rivalry between such master repertoires illustrates a transversal logic which can also be discerned in other *summae divisiones* of the intellectual field. It is not unlikely that disputes between consensus and coercion theorists, actionists and structuralists, or idealists and materialists offer primacy puzzles and dilemmas of reduction quite similar to the one which I have presently selected for review. To investigate whether, or to what extent, these various divisions parallel, fortify, or intersect one another cannot be the task of the present book. What I hope to accomplish, rather, is to follow the historical unfolding of one of these intellectual antinomies, to trace how it is perpetuated and perfected through many intellectual generations, how vocabulary switches enable newcomers to oppose the established without treading outside the logic of the game, and to fathom the intellectual politics which suggest difference and originality by defocalizing the common cadre within which the contest is enacted. By thus throwing light upon the 'powerful' or 'proprietary' character of particular scientific claims, it is hoped that we can move somewhat nearer to a sociology of professional intellectuals and of the glittering prizes they are seeking.

In the social theory of knowledge, the study of intellectual rivalries may prove fertile because it brings out the sheer *complexity* of the difficult and often gratuitous notion of the 'existential determination' of thought, and helps to focus its various meanings more clearly. More specifically, it strikes a middle course between a materialist theory about the 'reflection' of external economic or political interests (as deriving from a vulgar Marxism or elitism) and an idealist theory of disinterestedness (cf. the conventional image of science as value neutral) by inserting the intermediary level of *intellectual* interests, and by undertaking to weigh their independent effect upon the formation of social and political ideas (their capacity to 'refract' external interests) (Mannheim 1952; Bourdieu 1993a: 180–2; Bourdieu and Wacquant 1992: 69). Far from returning to the classical fold of the history of ideas, my veritable aim is to turn the perspective of the sociology of knowledge back upon itself, by trying to learn how ideas succeed in finding their human bearers through the rise and fall of many generations; that is, to account sociologically for the remarkable stability of intellectual inheritances and the equally remarkable persistence of rivalries among long-established currents of thought. Although it is a basic intuition of the present study that much *more* of the (supposedly rational) content of concepts and arguments in social theory is accountable in terms of non-rational 'existential' causes than is ordinarily supposed (cf. Mannheim 1952: 192–3), the reduction undertaken is of a special kind, in so far as privileged attention is given to the specific autonomy of interests which escape easy classification in terms of an external–internal division, since they arise from the relations of production and competition which intellectuals are necessarily subject to as soon as they enter specific discursive fields.

At this point, there arises an interesting reflexive loop, because a radical interest theory of knowledge is most fruitfully explored by making the most of two familiar, competing metaphors – which are none other than those of property and power. Modern social studies of science residually repeat the terms of the old rivalry, in so far as, for example, Bourdieu's 'capitalist' analysis of scientific competition is polemically countered by Latour's favourite slogan that science is a form of politics 'conducted by other means'. To some extent, therefore, the instrument of critical analysis is corrupted by the same opposition which it seeks to analyse and rectify. It is precisely because of this threatening circularity that the property–power rivalry presents no ordinary case study, but is in more than one sense critically relevant to my scenario of explanation. My earlier point was that, minimally, we need to mix these metaphoric connotations if we wish to make sense of the 'heterogeneous engineering' of things, humans, and symbols which is characteristically undertaken by members of the new knowledge class. Their havings-and-doings simultaneously display the relative 'hardness' of embodiments and objectivations and the relative 'softness' of performative definitions and struggles for recognition. Now that we have identified what is at stake in struggles for intellectual property and power, this recommendation can be reflexively applied to the theory of intellectual rivalry itself.

Here we also see more clearly that the upkeep of the dilemma of property and power may be ideologically profitable on both sides of the competitional fence. The vicious circularity is that the study of the dispositional capacities of intellectuals – what determines their autonomous stratificational place – is obstructed precisely because intellectuals themselves still often reason from one of the two alternative vocabularies. Both property theory and power theory, however, offer ample opportunities for *suppressing* the existence and independent impact of intellectual interests, because neither of these idioms is quick to portray the intelligentsia – which is neither an economic property class nor a political power elite – as a sociological category in its own right. This oversight gives rise to what might be called the 'metonymic fallacy of the intellectuals', who can hide as 'absent' spokespersons behind an essentialized economy or an essentialized state, and advance 'last instance' ontologies which channel their own ambition to act as 'first instances' of social reconstruction. As a paradigmatic example of 'antagonistic complicity' in Bourdieu's sense, the property–power rivalry has made it easier for intellectuals on either side to conceive of themselves as a free-floating, impartial party, and to miss the logic of their own behaviour as owners-in-competition or as power-getters in a quasi-political struggle of interest.

In this way, intellectuals have stood historically opposed as property theorists and power theorists, and are still so opposed, because they (often unwittingly) deploy their concepts and theories as quasi-capital or as conveyor belts of a will to intellectual power. An endearing example of this is provided by Proudhon, who prudishly assumed that the definition 'Property is Theft' constituted his only piece of property on this earth, but also considered his invention more valuable than the Rothschild millions, and the most important event that graced the reign of Louis Philippe (1846 II: 254).[4] Since their most characteristic and inalienable capital is formed because intellectuals *invest* in their theories (an investment which is simultaneously epistemological, political, and social), they link their identity and their holdings according to an old 'Lockean' code of appropriation. However, because intellectuals simultaneously tend to ignore that they hold knowledge as capital or as a 'power pack', they are easily prevented from seeing how they maintain traditional disciplinary fences, engage in traditional domanial struggles, and perpetuate rivalries which separate them from traditional opponents – who are intellectuals much like themselves.

It is this radical 'rivalry perspective' which offers both the point of departure and the point of return for the present study. Chapter 8 accordingly sets out to reclaim the radical nature of Karl Mannheim's early work on intellectual competition, who already intriguingly mixed the metaphors of property and power in order to articulate his central intuition about the existential determination of social and political thought. It briefly traces the history of the idea of intellectual competition in Mannheim's right-wing contemporaries (such as Schmitt) and in Merton's sociology of science, up to the recuperation of 'Mannheimian' themes in the constructivist science studies movement of the 1970s and 1980s. It further reconsiders the question of the specificity of intellectual havings-and-doings in terms of a radical notion of reputational prestige or credibility which, through its peculiar mixture of 'hardness' and 'softness' (or objective stability and subjective fragility), asks us once again to combine the thinglike or 'residential' connotations of property and the actionist or 'performative' ones of power.

LIMITATIONS AND PROVISOS

In consequence, this study ambitiously installs itself on the boundaries of three fields of enquiry whose intercourse is essential to the success of my project: the historical sociology of ideas, the social theory of intellectuals, and the sociology of social class. The problem of intellectual rivalry naturally brings along that of the specificity of intellectual holdings, which in turn invites the still wider issue of the productive force of knowledge and culture and that of the possible rise of new intellectual strata at the structural crossroads of civil society and the state. In each of these problem areas, the peculiar conceptual relationship between property and power, and more deeply, that between the master sciences of political economy and political theory, defines the centre of analytic gravity. That is why I am convinced that the problems which motivate this study will continue to elude us unless these three disciplinary perspectives are pulled together more closely.

These ambitions should be balanced by some cautionary remarks about the limitations of the present study. First of all, let me repeat that my theoretical recovery of the power–property antinomy does not claim an ultimate determinative significance for it over other intellectual conflicts, but aims at upgrading and highlighting a relatively neglected axis of discussion. It serves to relativize the taken-for-granted preponderance of other such conflicts to which it is often subordinated, e.g. the ones that have locked micro-ists and macro-ists, idealists and materialists, consensus and coercion theorists, or objectivists and subjectivists together in similar antagonistic complicities. In this manner, the property–power problematic acts as a searchlight which illuminates part of a complex intersection of intellectual coordinates rather than a single dominant axis.

A second proviso concerns my description of the historical fissure between the property and power concepts, which is only encountered in ideal–typical form in some classical writers of the liberal age. The dual axiom of the 'propertylessness of power' and the 'powerlessness of property' rather acts as a prism for other distinctions which are laterally connected to it. As I have suggested, it variably overlaps with the state–society split or that between an 'ideal' superstructure and a 'material' infrastructure, and is often generalized towards a broader distinction between human–nature relationships (the realm of production and labour) and relationships between human and human (the realm of organization and politics). Although these various phases of the liberal dichotomy are certainly interconnected, we should be careful not to suggest complete symmetry, since some of these distinctions are defocalized or even absent in individual authors, whereas still others deliberately attempt to escape from (some of) them.

A third string of qualifications must be affixed to the suggested explanatory function of the rivalry perspective itself, i.e. the influence which intellectual competition exercises upon the pattern of theoretical fission and fusion which I will shortly begin to sketch, and its connection with the supposedly more 'solid' historical background of developing economic and political rationalities in Western systems of democratic capitalism. The structuring impact of intellectual competition and the refraction of 'external' by 'internal' interests is not a historically invariant feature, but 'gains weight' with the progress of rationalization and the increase in autonomy of the intellectual field itself. Although 'overdetermination' of economic or political by intellectual interests marks the entire period which is covered by the diamond pattern, it gradually develops from a thin overlay into a historical factor of major importance, which gathers its own momentum and increasingly frees itself from its subservience to the logic of the two other fields.

Far from simply dismissing the property–power dichotomy and its substitutes as ideological artefacts, we must therefore account for the way in which they simultaneously express and 'enact' the developing structural bifurcation of economy and polity, in such a manner as to preserve both the constraint of historical reality itself and its performative 'distortion' by interested theoretical interpretation. The 'dictate' of historical reality and its representation in theoretical discourse intermingle in so many intricate ways that it is impossible to separate them out or rely on simple judgements of reflective adequacy. If representations of reality are invariably 'contaminated' by interests (including interests which are peculiar to the work of representation itself), and 'pull and push' reality rather than merely reflect it, the performative presence of intellectuals 'in' the phenomena they describe must not be accounted a mere liability; rather, it is the *lack of awareness* of this inevitable performance which tends to reify the reality of which the intellectual is always in part also the creator.

In view of the above, another cautionary footnote must be attached to my 'solution' of the dilemma of primacy itself. Concepts such as disposition, capacity, competency, or closure first of all act in a negatively sensitizing manner, as a 'point zero' or temporary stop in between the disaggregation of the traditional bundles of property and power and their reallocation in new sociological combinations. Of course, one may be satisfied to mix the two vocabularies and refrain from introducing mediating neologisms. In principle, there is no objection to this, because the terminological resolution of the dilemma is less important than a full recognition of the theoretical constraints and options which are dictated by it. Whatever idiom one wishes to adopt, however, it had better be relatively innocent *vis-à-vis* traditional discursive connotations (which, to be sure, does not imply value-neutrality nor absence of polemical intent).

But perhaps a more pressing need for developing a new set of terms is that, even if purposively mixed or fused, the idioms of property and power are still incapable of accounting for the specific configuration of 'knowledgeable' holdings, which typically include embodied, 'residential' properties which are simultaneously performative powers to act. Cultural holdings tend to blur the distinction between ownership of productive capital (*Eigentum*) and property as a personal characteristic (*Eigenschaft*), and in this particular sense restore Locke's famous claim that 'every man has a property in his own person'. As a capacity or disposition to act which is actualized in, but not exhausted by, its exercise (cf. Ball 1988: 98), cultural competences both partake of human individuality and supply means of power over other humans. A theory of competency, disposition, and closure is needed precisely in order to chart this simultaneously hard *and* soft, corporeal *and* institutionalized, private *and* collective, thinglike *and* relational, objective *and* fiduciary character of intellectual holdings-and-powers. In this light, a mere mixing of the metaphors may still inhibit a full grasp of that most elusive 'thing in the middle'.

This ambition to erase all residual traces of the property–power binary finally highlights a crucial epistemological feature of the diamond scheme, which does not attempt to dodge its own performative rules, but also acts upon and advocates what it has seemingly set out 'merely' to describe and

16

explain. It offers a *retrospective* model which is only imaginable and operable from a specific 'knowledge-political' position in the contemporary intellectual field. The diamond scheme hence claims the virtue of being self-reflexive and self-consciously performative, in so far as it normatively advocates the same semantic closure which it simultaneously captures in historical description. Its true origin and source of intellectual energy are therefore not to be found at the beginning (in the far west) but at the very end (in the far east) of the scheme, in a virtual location which is only reached by extrapolating the double converging movement towards its point of final closure. The entire movement of fission and fusion is then reconstructed, in conscious circularity, from its end result. However, as I hope to demonstrate in the pages that follow, this circularity is taken to be a *virtuous* one.

1

THE LIBERAL DICHOTOMY
AND ITS DISSOLUTION

FALSE TRANSPARENCIES

If we wish not to be used by the words we use, we must be prepared to rein-spect our tacit language routines, in order to be able to preserve or desert them in a rationally controlled manner. However, as soon as we probe further into the daily grammar of property and power, both concepts instantly demateri-alize. 'Power, like love', says Roderick Martin, 'is a word used continually in everyday speech, understood intuitively, and defined rarely: we all know what the "power game" is' (1977: 35). In the entire lexicon of sociological concepts, Robert Bierstedt complains, 'none is more troublesome than the concept of power. We may say about it in general only what St. Augustine said about time, that we all know perfectly well what it is – until someone asks us' (1970: 11). 'Power', considers R. H. Tawney, 'is the most obvious characteristic of organised society, but it is also the most ambiguous' (cit. Lynd 1968: 103). And Daniel Bell tersely concludes: 'Power is a difficult subject' (1968: 189).

The everyday notion of power more or less coincides with what several writers refer to as the 'simple' or 'primitive' notion, which in turn does not differ dramatically from the average dictionary definition. According to Steven Lukes, 'the absolutely basic common core to, or primitive notion lying behind "power" is that A in some way affects B in a non-trivial or significant manner' (1974: 26). To Dennis Wrong, power is basically the capacity to produce an effect of some sort on the external world (1979: 1). This is not far from Bertrand Russell's familiar definition of power as 'the production of intended effects' (1940: 35), which in turn recollects Thomas Hobbes' equally general view ('The Power *of a Man* [to take it Universally] is his present means, to obtain some future apparent Good') (1968: 150). The *Penguin English Dictionary* adheres to the same generality: power is 'ability to do some-thing; strength, force, vigour, energy; ability to control and influence others, ability to impose one's will'. Power is the 'ability to do or act', an 'active prop-erty' (*Concise Oxford Dictionary*), 'vermogen om iets te doen' (*Van Dale*), 'possibilité d'action d'une personne, d'une chose, droit d'agir, capacité de produire certains effets' (*Lexis/Larousse*), 'faculté, possibilité, propriété, possi-

18

bilité d'agir sur qqnn, qqch' (*Petit Robert*), 'ability to compel obedience, capability of acting or producing an effect, faculty, talent' (*Webster's New Third International Dictionary*).

As such a summary review makes apparent, the primitive notion of power does not yet distinguish clearly between the positive or 'developmental' dimension (ability to do, to act) and the dimension of repression or constraint (ability to compel obedience). The latter aspect is emphasized by Robert Dahl, whose 'intuitive' idea of power is this: 'A has power over B to the extent that he can get B to do something that B would not otherwise do' (1969: 80). This, of course, is the traditional, more restricted scope of Max Weber's celebrated definition: 'Power is the probability that one actor within a social relationship will be in a position to carry out his own will despite resistance, regardless of the basis on which this probability rests' (1978: 53). At this level of generality, we do not yet separate power from close cognitive relatives such as control, influence, or authority; nor is there room for debate on the instrumental vs. the relational quality of power, its 'residential' or 'performative' nature, the consensual/productive vs. the conflictual/distributive view of it, the differential depth and width of power relations, the immense structural variety of 'power houses', or the equally limitless variety in the identity of their residents, the power-holders. In other words, we have still not moved very far beyond true but definitionally empty assertions that there is no society without the regulation of power, that power is many-sided and ambiguous, and that it is some sort of active property or capability of being able to control or influence others.

What, on the other hand, is property? Proudhon's celebrated question is answered by experts and dictionaries in the same variegated manner. The deceptive transparency of the common-sense notion is possibly even greater than in the previous case. Just like epistemology studies all utterances which contain the copula 'to be' in order to question their truth value, the theory of property rights spans the entire range of Mines and Thines, in order to examine the validity of a multicoloured spectrum of claims in the possessive mode. 'Ownership', says Lawson, 'would seem to the layman to be a simple notion. It is a simple question of *meum* and *tuum*. If the thing is mine I own it, if it is not, I do not' (1958: 6). The classificatory genitive appears sufficient for all purposes. But R. H. Tawney is again quick to censure the layman:

> Property is the most ambiguous of categories. It covers a multitude of rights which have nothing in common except that they are exercised by persons and enforced by the State. Apart from these formal characteristics, they vary indefinitely in economic character, in social effect, and in moral justification.
>
> (1920: 56–7; cf. Waldron 1988: 28)

Proudhon's question is taken up by the dictionaries as follows: property is a 'quality or trait belonging to a person or thing; special power or capability; something that is or may be owned or possessed; wealth, goods, exclusive right to possess, enjoy and dispose of a thing' (*Webster's*), 'droit d'user, de jouir et de disposer d'une manière exclusive et absolue sous les restrictions établis par la loi; bien-fonds possédé en propriété; qualité propre' (*Petit Robert*). As in the case of power, we are saddled with truisms which are more sensible than enlightening. Human life, it is repeated, is impossible without disposition over material goods, and every society regulates this disposition and determines the scope and duration of their tenure. Karl Renner has restated this position with comprehensive clarity:

> Whatever the social system, disposal of all goods that have been seized and assimilated must be regulated by the social order as the rights of persons over material objects. Only thus can the continuous and undisturbed process of production be ensured. Every stage of the economic development has its regulations of goods as it has its order of labour. The legal institutions which effect this regulation, subject the world of matter bit by bit to the will of singled-out individuals, since the community exists only through its individual members. These legal institutions endow the individuals with detention so that they may dispose of the objects and possess them.
>
> (Renner 1949: 73)

Pitched at this level of generality, ownership is still indistinguishable from disposal, detention, or possession (terms variably preferred by Renner, Proudhon, Duguit, and others) and may cover any sort of relationship between humans and individually or socially acquired objects. There is as yet no room for distinction between physical possession and enforceable claims or rights, as there is no ideological contest between developmental or productive property (Locke) and distributive or exploitative property (Marx). The borderline between what I call my own and what belongs to others may be seen as easily passable or as relatively obstacled, excluding specific parties or specific claims. Owners may be individuals, kinship groups, cliques, corporations, states, or supranational bodies; objects owned can be tangible or intangible, separable or non-separable from the person; property can embrace the object in its entirety, or be divided up into a scatter of partial rights. In its most general sense, then, ownership is about the allocation of 'values' to specifiable persons, and the object of the law of property is to provide security in the acquisition, enjoyment, and disposal of such 'valued things'.

Both property and power, in sum, denote bundles of chances, competences, or rights which, if we may borrow Hobhouse's phrase, admit of 'variation in several distinct directions'. In view of such protean flexibility, we do not advance very far if we proclaim their sociological or anthropological ubiquity 'side by side' as it were, without worrying too much about logical compatibility. If property or power arrangements are loosely defined as social universals, necessary to any conceivable ordering of society, we have a double truism on our hands which is neither definitionally helpful nor, for that matter, ideologically innocent. As may be gathered from some of the previous definitions, property and power display various conjunctions and overlaps, but also tend to be demarcated in tensionful opposition – which together makes for an intricate play of distinction and identity, *rapprochement* and divergence. Our major definitional puzzle, I therefore suggest, does not so much arise from a simple addition of the indeterminacies of both concepts, but rather from their unclarified, taken-for-granted *reciprocal relationship*. This implies that problems of definition on either side will remain difficult to resolve unless the two sets of issues are brought face to face; or otherwise put, unless the concepts of property and power are analysed as *Siamese twins*.

For a start, we may note the sheer difficulty of drawing a proper line of distinction between property and power as they are conventionally described. They have a curious habit of reappearing in each other's definitions, and are often characterized in terms of one another without an independent definition of either. Property, for instance, is frequently designated as a power or a bundle of powers, a form of domination or *Gewalt*, whereas power is regularly identified as a property (in the sense in which one 'has', 'possesses', or 'wields' power). This blurring of definitional boundaries is enhanced by the fact that, in many languages, property has retained the dual meaning of 'right to things' and 'faculty' or 'trait' (property is from the Latin *proprius*), whereas power in its most general sense is indiscriminately made to refer to persons and objects. In this respect, terms such as 'capacity', 'faculty', 'competency', 'disposition', *Eigenschaft*, or *Vermögen* offer points of confluence of the historical connotations of both concepts.[1]

Property and power, however, also regularly officiate as each other's limiting cases or points of negative demarcation. Power is often circularly defined as 'that which is not property', as something less than the fullness of command which is commonly associated with rights of ownership. Many modern theorists of power contrast an acceptable view of power-as-relation with a non-acceptable one of power-as-property (Lasswell and Kaplan 1950: 75; Easton 1953: 143; Foucault 1980: 88–9, 198; Clegg 1989: 207). The metaphorics of power, on the other hand, often serve to indicate that private property relations have been progressively hedged in by social and political prescriptions or have disappeared altogether. Many modern theorists of social stratification for example observe that, across the last century, the axial determinant of social inequality has shifted *from* property *to* power, which in this case is often taken as broader in scope than the mere title to dispose of materially productive assets. In this context, managerial power or economic control is usually identified as the core element of property: this is what is left when the property bundle is stripped of secondary incidents such as beneficial enjoyment or heritability.[2]

The heart of the complexity produced by such overlaps and cross-demarcations seems to be that property and power are principally considered as 'domanial' media, which most primitively relate to tenure of *things* or action towards *people*, and are hence taken to organize distinct types or fields of social behaviour (e.g. economics vs. politics), while they also have a larger metaphorical application that transcends these connotations and fields, and severs the double linkage between property/things and power/people. Different actions and tenures can themselves be described in property-like or power-like terms, in so far as controversy arises with regard to their essentially thinglike or residential vs. their relational or performative nature – a conceptual opposition which is often expressed in terms of 'static' possession vs. 'dynamic' action (or power exercise). Anticipating part of the argument of this and the following chapter, this complex interference between the domanial references of property and power and their metaphorical extensions may be visualized in the four-square layout given in Table 1.

THE SPLIT WORLD OF LIBERAL THEORY

Given this intriguing simultaneity of definitional overlaps and contrasts, it is imperative to explore further the demarcation line between property and power and the theoretical no man's land through which it is drawn. As we may begin to see, the majority of technical definitions show the rudiments of a fundamental *prima-facie* distinction, which is even more forcefully present in everyday usage, where it has hardened into an almost ineradicable stereotype. This venerable dichotomy axiomatically sets the logic of power at right angles to that of property, and separates their areas of jurisdiction as a matter of ontological course. It can be summarized most simply as the *'propertyless' nature of power and the 'powerless' nature of property*. This deep structure dualism, which is partly descriptive of a real historical configuration but is simultaneously fictional and performative, constitutes a grounding principle of liberal social theory in its classical eighteenth- and nineteenth-century form. With due precaution, it can be taken as partly coincident with the much-disputed

Table 1 Static and dynamic theories of property and power

	Thinglike (property-like)	*Relational (power-like)*
Property	Locke, Blackstone	Marx
Economics	Code Civil 1804	Macpherson
Power	Hobbes	Foucault
Politics	Elite theory	Elias

sectoral cleavage between the domains of state and civil society – in the classical bipolar view according to which the former is interpreted as the superstructure of political organization and the latter as the infrastructure of economic production or market relationships (cf. Keane 1988; Cohen and Arato 1992).

Although expressed most uncompromisingly in classical liberalism, the contours of this bipolar division were already manifest in many of its ideological precursors. Long before prepared, it marked a provisional culmination of a century-long process of theoretical fissure, which was initiated by the eleventh-century rediscovery of Roman jurisprudence and the subsequent revival of Aristotelian political philosophy at the newly founded universities and clerical schools of the West. In the course of an extended process of semantic decomposition – which we shall trace in sufficient detail later – the inclusive feudal conception of *dominion* or *domain* gradually split up into a political and an economic compartment. As rights of property were defined in a more absolute and exclusive manner, they were ever more clearly demarcated from and profiled against rights of sovereignty, which were subjected to a process of concentration and substantialization which mirrored in its essential features the parallel institutional fortification of property rights. The scalar, parcellarized structure of feudal dominion gave way before a polar regrouping of power relationships in the narrower sense of public authority over citizens, and of property relations in the narrower sense of the exclusive detention of things (Anderson 1974: 19–27). At the culminating point of this largely synchronous process of divergence, classical liberal theory came to embody the self-evident conviction that exercise of power and disposition over material goods constituted distinct domains and different concerns, and that there existed a natural line (and law) of demarcation to separate them (Figure 2).

This modern distinction between property, the rule over things by the individual, and sovereignty, the rule – as it was originally conceived – over all individuals by the prince, was absent from the doctrines of the church fathers, whose conception of dominion still reflected the highly fragmented, stratified, and interfused system of personal obligation and land tenure which had developed after the economic contraction and political disintegration of the Roman world. The essence of a theory of dominion, McIlwain has written, is a

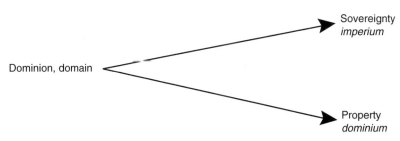

Figure 2 The fissure

23

hierarchy of rights and powers all existing in or exercisable over the same objects or persons, and the fundamental relationship of one power over another in this hierarchy is the superiority of the higher to the lower, rather than a complete supremacy in any one over all the others.
(McIlwain 1932: 355; Anderson 1974: 19–20)

No one within the feudal compass could claim to exercise the concentrated, 'pointlike' sovereignty which became a familiar conception only at a later period; no one could claim to own the land in the typically Roman sense of holding property as an absolute and exclusive privilege against all the world. Everyone, from the king down to the meanest peasant, exercised a portion of dominion over it, without anyone holding it in full severalty, i.e. as a walled-in area forbidden to all others.

But since the legists of Renaissance Bologna first rebuilt the edifice of Roman law, and reanimated the typically Antique distinction between *dominium* and *imperium*, property and sovereignty were characteristically relegated to discrete realms of factuality and seen as governed by essentially dissimilar principles. With amazing regularity and concord, political thinkers came to repeat Seneca's maxim that 'to kings belonged authority over all, to private persons, property'. Bartolus, Du Moulin, Bodin, Grotius, and numerous others reappropriated this motto. Francis Bacon recognized 'a true and received division of law into *ius publicum* and *ius privatum*, the one being the sinews of property, and the other of government' (cit. Lawson 1958: 90). Montesquieu likewise affirmed that men had acquired liberty by political, and property by civil, laws, and warned that one should not decide by the laws of liberty, which were 'the empire of the city', what could only be decided by property law. Political law should in no way impinge upon civil law, the 'palladium of property', since no public good was greater than its undisturbed maintenance (1969: 262–3).

Both the English Civil War and the French Revolution reflected and dramatized the extent to which, at least conceptually if not in actual fact, the realms of property and sovereignty had become disjoined; both revolutions, in the course of extended political and ideological battles, also established a decisive superiority of the former over the latter. A famous decree issued by the Constituent Assembly in 1789, which envisaged the 'complete destruction' of the feudal regime, went on to abolish all traces of personal servitude, seigneurial rights and jurisdictions and all judicial or municipal venal offices (Goubert 1973: 5–6). Whereas the feudal chain of vassalage had involved a close federation of landownership and political or jurisdictional sovereignty, this decree drove a final wedge between *iura in personam* and *iura in rem*. The same fiction of a natural dualism between *dominium* and *imperium* and a natural contraposition of individual proprietor and state subtended the revolutionary attempts at suppressing the professional corporations (Tigar and Levy 1977: 249–50; Renner 1949: 82–3).

The revolutionary constitutions and codes, by legally completing the 'separation of the condition of men from the condition of estates' (Goubert), thus crowned a development which had set in from the earliest stages of the *Ancien Régime* itself. The Code Napoleon of 1804 consecrated property as an unassailable, absolute right of exclusion, and turned the exercise of political power chiefly into a proprietor's privilege. Portalis, one of the jurists who authored it, differed not from Seneca, Bodin, Grotius, or Montesquieu: 'to the citizen belongs property, to the sovereign the realm of Empire'. The Code, he went on to argue, finally re-established the 'true' relation between property and empire which had been 'confused' by the feudal regime (Schlatter 1951: 234). His co-author Maleville added that 'the idea of co-propriety by the sovereign of the wealth of the territory is false; it is contrary to the rights of property'. Even the Emperor solemnly announced to his Conseil d'État: 'Property is inviolable. Even Napoleon himself, notwithstanding the numerous armies that stand at his disposal, cannot seize a single field' (Lévy 1972: 84–5, 94).

It has become rather commonplace to insist that this conceptual opposition between property and sovereignty served a concertedly descriptive and adhortative purpose. Not only did liberal theory attempt to chart the fissure which had been developing between the two institutional realms under the old regime, it simultaneously sought to *promote* the distinction and carry it to its (socio)logical completion. As is evident from Portalis's words, it was an essential ambition of liberals to establish a 'true', 'just', or 'natural' dividing line between civil society and the state, and to reconstruct political life so as to approximate it to the ideal dichotomy which was thought already resident in the deep structure of reality. The feudal or patrimonial modes of fusion of sovereignty and property constituted a logical confusion in the eyes of the true liberal – as does the totalitarian fusion of both principles and realms for liberals of our own day.[3] This is how John Locke already criticized Filmer, the royalist:

> Some men have been apt to be deceived into an opinion that there was a natural or Divine right of primogeniture to both 'estate' and 'power', and that the inheritance of both rule over men and property in things springs from the same original, and were to descend by the same rules. Property, whose original is from the right a man has to use any of the inferior creatures for the subsistence and comfort of his life, is for the benefit and sole advantage of the proprietor, so that he may even destroy the thing that he has property in by his use of it, where need requires; but government, being for the preservation of everyman's rights and property, by preserving him from the violence or injury of others, is for the good of the governed.
>
> (Locke 1975: 65; cf. Tully 1980: 55ff.)

This supposedly natural distinction between property and sovereignty, it is now widely recognized, enhanced bourgeois self-emancipation by carving out for private property and civil society an autonomous sphere of discretion, in forcing back the irritating confusion of state interference and monopoly. Simultaneously, property and civil society were considered as 'foundational' and infrastructural over against public power, which was increasingly contrasted with the latter in terms of parasitism and leisure vs. productive work. In this fashion, the conceptual split both dramatized and certified the urge for independence and for social recognition of the rising classes of merchants and private entrepreneurs. A clean switch of vocabulary was required which not only defined property and civil society as sharply different from and essentially primary over against sovereignty and the state, but which also naturalized both the distinction and the order of primacy. In this fashion, property and civil society turned into euphemistic substitutes or sublimated self-designations of the aspiring bourgeoisie itself, or more specifically, of its intellectual and political spokesmen (cf. Keane 1988: 65).

THREE DIMENSIONS OF DIFFERENCE

Residues of this liberal heritage are still with us today. In common parlance and in many technical theories a categorical split is retained between the logics of power and property, which is often taken for granted as expressive of a natural cleavage or dichotomous articulation of the real world itself. It is also increasingly acknowledged, however, that this disjunction between 'property-less' power and 'powerless' property is not enshrined in ontological immobility, but should be taken as an anachronistic survival of a unique and transient ideological configuration. The ontological 'naturalness' of the split (and of the liberal priority sequence) cannot be taken as an explanatory point of departure but is precisely the thing to be explained. As argued below, historical analysis indeed reveals that the identifying characteristics typically ascribed to power or property relations (which simultaneously act as criteria of mutual distinction) are essentially unstable and reversible, and vary in an intriguing semantic interplay of expansion and contraction. In order to carry this argument further, it will first be necessary to investigate the constitutive terms of the liberal dichotomy in a more detailed manner. If we reinspect the basic distinction, it appears to include three closely intertwined dimensions, which can be succinctly characterized as follows:

1   Power exercise is (active) *doing*, while property exercise is (static) *having*.
2   Power is about *persons*, while property is about *things*.
3   Power is *shared, multiple, and limited*, while property is an *absolute* and a *zero-sum*.

In the following subsections, I will briefly chart each of these dimensions of difference.

Dimension 1

Power is usually taken to denote activity, process, performance, 'the production of intended effects' (Russell), whereas property is primarily represented as a static condition, a *Zustand* or 'state of allocation' of objects to persons (Jakobs 1965: 26–8).[4] The possession of things, Simmel has remarked, does usually not appear as movement but as a stationary and virtually substantial condition that relates to other dynamics of life just as 'being' relates to 'becoming' (1990: 303–4). While the logical kernel of property thus appears to be the static relationship between subject and object or person and thing, the concept of power displays a larger affinity with more dynamic subject–subject relationships. This finds expression in the long tradition of political and social thought in which power has been closely aligned with a model of agency. Prefigured in classical seventeenth-century philosophy, this connection is reproduced right up to the sociological accounts of power which have dominated the late 1970s (Ball 1978; 1988; Clegg 1989).[5] In Giddens' view, for example, power is logically tied to action, and defined very generally as 'the capacity of the agent to mobilise resources to constitute the "means" necessary to achieve outcomes'. It is only another word for the 'transformative capacity' of human action (1976: 110–12; 1979: 88ff.). Steven Lukes has likewise identified agency with the exercise of power, in critical rejection of the structuralist tendency to view powerful actors as mere 'bearers' of powerful structures: 'To use the vocabulary of power, is to speak of human agents who significantly affect the thoughts and reactions of others' (1974: 52ff.). Foucault has similarly placed power in the context of action theory, defining it as a mode of acting upon the actions of others (1983: 220). Sociologists such as Crespi (1992), political philosophers such as Young (1990), constructivists such as Knorr-Cetina (1981b), and 'actor–network' theorists such as Callon (1986), Latour (1986), and Law (1991b) have further strengthened this close association between power and agency, often arguing against the appropriative or distributive logistics of the vocabulary of 'having' (e.g. Young 1990: 15ff.; Latour 1986). But the basic configuration is already present in Hobbes, who thus distinguished between Dominion and Authority:

> For that which in speaking of goods and possessions, is called an *Owner*, and in latine *Dominus*, in Greeke *kurios*; speaking of Actions, is called Author. And as the Right of possession, is called Dominion; so the Right of doing any Action, is called AUTHORITY. So that by Authority, is always understood a Right of doing any act.
>
> (Hobbes 1968: 218)

Dimension 2

The power vocabulary, it is thus commonly thought, focuses upon relationships of dependence among persons and defocalizes the world of objects, whereas the commonplace notion of property tends to defocalize interaction and to foreground the connection between *persona* and *res*. Virtually all definitions of power, Max Weber's celebrated one not excepted, are about what actor A can do to actor B, regardless of the specific resources which create A's power credit and secure B's deficit. On the other hand, ordinary usage usually identifies property with things (Ackerman 1977: 99–100; Grey 1980: 69; Munzer 1990: 16). And although most theoretical languages conceive of property as the legal title or *right* to the thing, the gulf which separates everyday usage from the philosophy of law proves less wide than expected (Honoré 1961: 128). As Jakobs argues, no one denies that property is also a social relationship between persons, but this aspect is secondary as compared with the subject–object relationship and is not constitutive for the conceptualization of property as such (1965: 28). Both Martin (1977) and Wrong (1979) put restrictions upon the all-inclusive notion of power precisely in order to differentiate control over nature from control over men.

That power is about persons and property about things remains in greater or lesser degree an unexamined, subliminal presupposition of both lay and professional speech. Thus, the repertoire of power easily sounds odd or anachronistic when reference is made to control over material objects: one is transported back to a dark age of exorcism and black magic, where things in the external world are thought to be but projections of the wills of good or evil spirits, and in which objects are deemed in possession of powers of magical control which can be mastered by ritual. Magic, Ruth Benedict has argued, invariably employs false analogies between the animate and the inanimate world, since it imposes a supernatural world of *power* upon the world of natural causation. Like other forms of religion, it 'employs towards a personalized universe all the kinds of behaviour that hold good in human relations' (Benedict 1935; Gurevich 1977: 9; Weber 1978: 422ff.). Animistic behaviour, like totemism or witchcraft, introjects causal principles of a quasi-personal nature into objects or animals: by way of false analogies, amulets are thought to 'have' power; fetishes are treated essentially as if they were human.[6]

Correspondingly, it has become one of the pillars of modern liberal sensibility that persons cannot be owned (Becker 1977: 37; Honoré 1961: 130; Reinhold Noyes 1936: 419); it is one way of translating the familiar Kantian maxim never to use man as mere means. Sir John Holt, the English judge, phrased it as early as 1707: 'By the common law no man can have a property in another'. The essence of slavery, Martin recalls, 'was the non-human status of the slave, his transformation into an object' (1977: 61). Slavery, according to Davis, constituted 'a kind of ultimate limit in dependence and loss of natural freedom . . . that condition in which man most completely approximates the status of a thing' (cit. Martin 1977: 60). A Jamaican slavery act of 1674 simply identified bondslaves with goods and chattels. Slaves were their master's slaves in the literal possessory sense, items of property whose legal personality was entirely absorbed in their master's own.

In the great debate on slavery in nineteenth-century America, Southerners therefore argued that interference with slavery was interference with property, and that abolitionists should hence be combated as a dangerous breed of socialists. The abolitionists countered that men were born free and equal, and that natural law clearly forbade turning men into property. Interestingly, the major difference between the Northern and Southern parties did not concern a defence or rejection of the sanctitude of property itself: both agreed to the principle that, as it was phrased in the 1857 Kansas Constitution, 'the right of property is before and higher than any constitutional sanction'. The difference of opinion instead was about the *kind* of 'things' which could become property, i.e. could accede to the total domination of individual owners.

Indeed, the theoretical crux of the abolitionists' rejection of the ownership of persons was the Lockean conviction that every man was inalienably the owner of his own person. 'Every man', the Anti-Slavery Convention of 1833 stated, 'has a right to his own body . . . and to the produce of his own labour'. This ownership of one's life and labour constituted the only form of ownership of persons which the canons of classical liberalism considered legitimate. This proprietary concept of natural liberty (which, to be sure, referred to the independent male producer and householder, and excluded women, children, servants, and alms-takers) universalized the idea of legal personality without completely discarding the vocabulary of property in human beings. From the Levellers' pamphlets during the English Civil War up to Adolphe Thiers' *De la propriété* (1848), self-ownership was considered foundational for the exercise of exclusive private rights. The most significant of these concerned the ownership of material objects, which was seen to hold good against all the world.[7]

Dimension 3

Property is therefore taken as the most complete form of control which is permitted by a mature system of law. It is the greatest possible legal interest in a thing, and constitutes an all-embracing right of domination (Honoré 1961: 108; Friedmann 1972: 99; Römer 1978: 210). Ownership, to Renner, conveys an absolute legal power:

> The right of ownership, *dominium*, is a person's all-embracing legal power over a tangible object. It is a right, i.e. a power conferred upon a subject (person) by the law. This right is absolute, the imperatives upon which it is based are addressed to all persons without exception and claim their respect. Its content is the power to dispose of the object, and this power is all-embracing. . . . Ownership is not, therefore, an

29

aggregate of individual rights, it implies unlimited possibilities of disposal.

(1949: 81)

Dominium accordingly contains the element of eternity as a matter of principle; an estate which is limited to the life of a person or to a fixed period does not constitute property (ibid.: 93). This adds up to the typically modern or bourgeois view of property as an exclusionary right which is unencumbered by social obligations or functional demands, which primarily accedes to natural individuals, and which is preferably exercised over physical objects. This 'official' liberal view was already enunciated by Blackstone who, in his widely influential *Commentaries on the Laws of England* (1765–9) circumscribed property as 'that sole and despotic dominion which one man claims and exercises over the external things of the world, in total exclusion of the right of any other individual in the universe'.[8] And such was also the definition which entered into the centrifugally important Code Civil of 1804.

As we shall see below, this fortification of bourgeois property into a virtually unlimited set of rights gradually transformed it into the same unitary, pointlike substance which had characterized the earlier emergence of the absolutist conception of sovereignty. Less and less property was seen as a *bundle* of component rights, as an inventory of incidents into which the whole was ultimately resolvable. In its bourgeois conceptualization, property was increasingly thought of as one and indivisible, as an essence which transcended its several parts, or a substance which remained complete and equivalent to itself even when a number of subordinate rights were seceded from it. Its corollary of *plena in res potestas* meant that the thing was either mine or yours unqualifiedly and admitted of no difference in degree. Property, as the utopian socialist Charles Hall critically put it, had come to be a 'plus or minus affair'.

By contrast, power increasingly came to be conceived as relational and divisible, and was less comfortably coerced into the strait-jacket of a zero-sum conception. After the institutional break-up of the fullness of absolutist sovereignty into a *trias politica* and the establishment of constitutionally representative political regimes, public authority was more naturally pictured as distributed by degree or stratified throughout the polity in a continuous manner. As Lefort has lucidly suggested, the locus of power in modern democracies has become an 'empty place', preventing governments from 'appropriating' power for their own ends and growing consubstantial with it (1986: 279; 1988: 17, 27–31). Habermas has likewise argued that (popular) sovereignty should no longer be viewed as an incorporated substance, but as 'procedural' and 'communicatively dissolved' (1992). In the world of Western democracy, power is now typically viewed as delegated, dispersed, and decomposed; as a collection of chances or rights which are shared out among a variety of titulars or tenants, and which by their very nature are socially obligated and circumscribed.

For the many modern writers who defend such a relational and gradualist conception, the metaphorics of appropriation routinely describe the negative limiting case. 'Power is defined relationally, not as a simple property', Lasswell and Kaplan write (1950: 75), while Easton has argued that 'power is a relational phenomenon, not a thing someone possesses' (1953: 143). Dennis Wrong has adopted a similar notion:

> Unfortunately, power lacks a common verb form, which in part accounts for the frequent tendency to see it as a mysterious property or agency resident in the person or group to whom it is attributed. The very use of words such as 'influence' and 'control', which are both nouns and verbs, as virtual synonyms for power, represent an effort (not necessarily fully conscious) to avoid the suggestion that power is a property rather than a relation.
>
> (Wrong 1979: 6)

Authors as bewilderingly diverse as Russell, Friedrich, Poulantzas, Lukes, Giddens, Foucault, Bourdieu, Coleman, Young, Barnes, and Latour are of one mind in combating the older essentialist view. Elias therefore focuses what is now a major consensus:

> We say that a person possesses great power, as if power were a *thing* he carried about in his pocket. This use of the word is a relic of magico-mythical ideas. Power is not an amulet possessed by one person and not by another; it is a structural characteristic of human relationships – of *all* human relationships.
>
> (Elias 1978: 80)[9]

THINGS AND REIFICATIONS

As already intimated, however, the liberal dualism of 'propertyless' power vs. 'powerless' property does not reflect a logical essence or a timeless fact of nature, but should be taken as a complex historical and knowledge-political construct and explained accordingly. The classical composition of the property and power bundles (the specific summation of their respective incidents) does not exhibit the ontological necessity which is still routinely ascribed to it; instead, their identifying characteristics are contingently and contextually distributed. It is my basic hypothesis throughout this study that such contingencies and contexts become more readily discernible as soon as property and power are analysed concertedly, rather than as self-contained and static conceptual universes. I have already noted that their differential scope and content were initially determined through a gradual process of cellular fission which parted the feudal notion of dominion 'right through the middle', generating separate bundles of political and economic rights. As the rift between the two widened and hardened into a natural fact, so also sovereignty and property were increasingly fixated into reified, natural essences.

But sovereignty arrived there first, both in concept and in practice, and property largely emulated this first reification, while being polemically raised against the sovereign absolutism which was demanded by the already-established political regimes. This implies that the three marks of difference listed above were initially distributed in inverse order. Historically, a possessory, thinglike, all-or-nothing character was first ascribed to the concept of sovereignty, while ownership continued to be seen as naturally limited, fragmented, and socially obligated as long as this essentialist notion of sovereignty prevailed. Long after the decline of feudal tenures, property was considered partial and limited in nature, circumscribed both by the eminent domain of the sovereign state and by the large number of variously protected rights which could coexist in the same piece of land. A multitude of estates and the simultaneous detention of several parties was conceived as the normal condition. Concepts such as usufruct, *dominium utile*, seisin, or *ius in re aliena* all indicated dependent and derivative forms of ownership; the same piece of land, for example, could support several seisins of a different nature. This doctrine of limited, reserved property remained a cornerstone of Aquinian and Renaissance Christian philosophy, and was continued by the prophets of the Reformation and the defenders of royal absolutism.

It found its logical counterweight in a theory of unreserved, monistic state sovereignty. As Jean Bodin first classically defined it in the late sixteenth century, sovereignty meant supreme, transcendent, and perpetual state power, unlimited in extension as well as duration, and unaccountable to anything on earth (Bodin 1962: Bk 1, ch. VIII). Because sovereignty was thus 'singularized' into an impartible, untranslatable right, the idea of a cascade of domains, i.e. of manifold and partial claims superimposed upon one another, ceded before a dichotomous, zero-sum separation between Rulers and Ruled.[10] Unlimited and indivisible public authority presupposed limited and partible ownership. Absolute property rights were in turn incompatible with absolute sovereignty but tended to enforce the latter's partition and functionalization. Hence when liberal thinkers counterposed an absolutist definition of property to the absolutist notion of sovereignty, property gradually 'took over' the static, thinglike and zero-sum connotations which had long been reckoned essential features of its opposite number.

As soon as they were launched upon their tangential course, sovereignty and property, while consolidating themselves in their separate domains, therefore also tended to expand and contract according to a distinct pattern of *inverse variation*. In this perspective, the rise of constitutional liberalism can be interpreted as a gradual turnover process, dramatically accelerated in the course of the liberal–democratic revolutions, in the course of which a number of decisive legal incidents were constitutionally transferred *from* the domain of state sovereignty *to* that of private property. It was this displacement of incidents which largely prompted the ultimate de-reification of the idea of public authority, while it simultaneously furthered a progressive reification of the concept of property.

The 1789 Declaration, for example, consecrated property as an inviolable and sacred individual right. Sovereignty, on the other hand, although still defined as 'one and indivisible', was now thought to reside essentially in the Nation, which formally transformed all political offices into delegations. The 1791 Constitution expressly considered the royal power as 'delegated in hereditary succession to the ruling race'. Of all other public offices, its preamble stipulated, there was to be 'neither venality nor hereditability'. One year after the National Convention had solemnly abolished royalty and five months after the regicide, the Jacobin Constitution of 1793 could hence proclaim as a matter of principle that 'public functions are essentially of a temporary nature; they cannot be considered as distinctions nor as recompenses, but must rather be performed as duties'. The 1795 Constitution likewise affirmed that equality did not admit of any distinction of birth or any hereditary transfer of powers. While emphasizing that 'the cultivation of the soil, all manner of production, all instruments of labour, and the entire social order' were predicated upon the maintenance of properties, it warned that public functions could not become the property of those who exercised them (Godechot 1970: 35, 38, 82, 101–3). Unequivocally, the revolutionary constitutions thus denied to public authority those powers of free alienability and hereditability which by the same stroke were allocated to the exercise of property rights.

One important corollary of this reallocation of transfer rights was the gradual reification of property into a concept of thing–ownership. As Macpherson has noted, this idea resulted from a series of narrowings which first transformed the medieval concept, which had still mixed communal with private rights, into an early modern idea of private individual ownership which included life and liberty as well as material estate; to be narrowed once again to a right to use material things or revenues, and ultimately confining it to the right to alienate as well as use material goods (Macpherson 1979: 3). Until the seventeenth century, property was still primarily conceived as a right *in* something rather than the thing itself. The great bulk of property was in land and was generally limited to certain uses, often excluding the right of free alienation, while another substantial segment of property consisted in corporate charters, monopolies, tax-farming rights, and the incumbency of various political and ecclesiastical offices. All of them were in some measure limited, shared, or delegated rights rather than tangible things.

It was only with the replacement of these limited rights in land, revenue, or office by the virtually unlimited rights required by the capitalist market that an unequivocal distinction appeared between freely disposable material objects and limited rights to political roles and functions. The concentration of property rights in the post-feudal West was thus doubly predicated upon the individualization of the owning subject and the extension of the scope of ownership itself, which came to include not only rights of use and benefit, but also rights of transfer by bequest and sale:

> In fact the difference was not that things rather than rights in things were exchanged, but that previously unsaleable rights in things were now saleable; or, to put it differently, that limited and not always saleable rights *in* things were being replaced by virtually unlimited and saleable rights *to* things.
>
> (Macpherson 1973: 128)[11]

In this fashion, the liberal (and commonplace) conception of thing–ownership expressed and consolidated a view of the world in which a major split had occurred between 'horizontal' human–human and 'vertical' human–nature relationships, or between rights *in personam* and rights *in rem* (cf. Renner 1949: 267). This great divide emerged both in materialist theories such as Locke's, who affirmed that rightful property resulted from the mixing of an individual's labour with unclaimed nature, and in idealist theories such as propounded by Kant or Hegel, who saw property as originating from a subjective act of individual appropriation, and thus as an extension of individual personality over part of the material world. Pocock recalls that this distinction between persons and things increasingly gained in prominence, and that property, instead of being a mere prerequisite to political relations between persons, turned into a system of legally defined relations between persons and things, or between persons through things (1985: 104). Mannheim has similarly interpreted this alteration as producing both an impersonal relationship to the world of things themselves and a more abstract relationship to other persons (1982: 154–5, 162–3, 260–1).[12]

The resulting confusion between the legal interest appertaining to the physical object and the object itself derived from the definition of *iura in rem* as rights which were defensible against all other persons, and which could be transferred or alienated at will by their possessor (Reeve 1986: 15–16). Hence, what was in fact a matter of *intensity* of disposition, i.e. a contrast between limited and unlimited rights, was represented (and simultaneously occluded) as an opposition between 'immaterial' subject–subject relationships and relationships obtaining between subjects and material objects. It divided the world of goods or resources (material and immaterial, human and non-human) into material objects which could become property, and immaterials which could not (other individuals, skills, knowledge, social relationships, political and human rights). The reification or substantialization of the ownership relation was thus contingent upon the definition of rights as 'good against all the world'. In reverse, a thinglike status could readily be conferred upon all items that permitted sovereign completeness of title and absence of temporal limitation in its exercise.

That this reifying tendency is not restricted to material objects but may touch any kind of relationship was already confirmed by the examples of slavery and of the early modern conception of political sovereignty. It receives further corroboration by the persistent survival of essentialist and dichotomous conceptions of power and sovereignty both in the languages of everyday life and those of social and political science. One example is Michael Korda's former bestselling manual *Power! How to Get it, How to Use it* (1975), which is sufficiently evocative of Aladdin's lamp, the Philosopher's stone, or a crude pecuniary metaphor, to discourage more detailed study. However, similar thinglike or possessory notions of power have been shared by a phalanx of more academically reputed writers who have staked out a simple dichotomy between a powerful elite and a powerless mass. For founders of elite theory such as Mosca, Pareto, and Michels, power was not spread along a distributional curve, but displayed a simple opposition between those who had it, the governing elite, and those who had none, the governed masses. In this respect at least, the elitist tradition in political sociology (cf. also Lasswell 1936) continued the older essentialist conception of power which had struck a virtual analogy between unitary sovereignty and 'Roman' exclusive property. A modern sociologist such as Aron has echoed this by conceiving of power relations as 'essentially' asymmetrical and inegalitarian, while Dahrendorf has contrasted the allegedly gradualist distribution of wealth with the dichotomous, polar character of power or authority relations (Aron 1986; Dahrendorf 1959).[13]

Hence the concept of ownership is not definitionally dependent upon the physical externality, self-sufficiency, or materiality of the object owned, but rather upon the relative fullness of command which specified rights convey at a specific historical conjuncture over specified resources. This is why sovereignty tended to be seen as a *form of* property by patriarchal absolutists such as Filmer, and why liberals such as Locke were so much concerned to draw a principled *distinction* between the two concepts and their domains of application (cf. Tully 1980: 56).[14] Hobbes significantly maintained that elective princes who did not dispose of the succession did not have the sovereign power 'in propriety' but in use only (1968: 248). For Paine, on the other hand, state power was essentially delegated and on trust; no particular group or institution was therefore 'possessed of' government, in obedience to the more basic principle that 'man has no property in man' (1969: 64). In the idiom of natural rights philosophy, it was indeed possible to enjoy property of one's own self – but precisely because subjective rights were conceived as naturally innate and inalienable, even when a portion of the self was temporarily alienated in exchange for a wage. What the 'propertylessness of power' meant was precisely this legal absence of rights to sell and to bequeath. Complementarily, the free disposal or fullness of rights which was thought distinctive of private property indicated the presence of such saleable and heritable rights.[15]

In sum, there exists no ontological affinity or logically necessary association

35

between property and things or, for that matter, between power and persons. The idea of thing–ownership results from a reification of social relationships which occurs as a corollary of the exclusive and absolute nature of classical bourgeois property rights, which convey *plenitudo potestatis* or fullness of command (cf. Clegg 1989: 207).[16] As Marx, Simmel, and many other social theorists have argued, appropriation must be viewed as processual and relational rather than stationary; possession should be grasped as an action, not as a substance (cf. Simmel 1990: 303–4). Physical tangibility or intangibility are of no great consequence: the nature of property is to be found in institutionally defined rights, not in the physical externalities of the object (Davis 1970: 455; Grey 1980: 70). 'It is public opinion', Durkheim has concurred, 'that makes some objects regarded as liable to appropriation and others not; it is not their physical nature as natural science might define it, but the form their image takes in the public mind' (1992: 138). Indeed, the demarcation line between what is considered human, quasi-human, or non-human and the attendant ascription or withholding of independent rights of agency remains an ever-negotiable and contested one, and is continually being redrawn in different historical and moral contexts (cf. Haraway 1991; Latour 1993). In this sense women (and particular species of domestic animals) have crossed (or are presently crossing) the border area which separates the world of things from the world of persons; a line which had been crossed before by emancipated slaves, serfs, and proletarians (cf. Eckersley 1992: 44). Many objects of magic, on the other hand, such as fetishes, totems, and effigies, have crossed this boundary in the opposite direction: they have gradually been stripped of their personal *anima* in order to turn into unobtrusive, passive things.

THE DIAMOND PATTERN

So far, our forays into the definitional wilderness of property and power have driven home one important lesson. At least they have established the irrevocable necessity of analysing the chequered careers of the two concepts as a unified project, since they appear coupled in a complex manner and participate in a peculiar game of overlap and distinction, symbiosis and competition. Not only do they emerge as ideological twins in a secular (but chronologically uneven) process of duplication which splits the concept of dominion into a sovereignty part and a property part, but they also appear to *exchange* incidents in a slow movement of inverse variation which, at specific peaks of historical drama, is intensified into something like a 'changing of the guard': property 'dethrones' sovereignty in order to usurp its majestic place.

If this already constitutes sufficient reason why classical liberalism's great divide cannot be looked upon as a fact of nature which is enshrined in ontological fixity, there are additional ones which perhaps go deeper. Foremost among these is the common observation that the bifurcation of sovereignty and property, which reached its maximum amplitude in eighteenth-century liberal theory, is increasingly reversed – a secular process which roughly begins in the middle of the nineteenth century but accelerates considerably in the course of the twentieth. In what appears like a concerted attempt to undermine the divide from both sides, the two vocabularies are once again interfused and collated. In a long historical perspective, we are approaching a new comprehensive theory of dominion (or as I shall call it, disposition) in which many traits of the original feudal conception are recognizable anew. That is to say that the process of differentiation does not stop at the node of largest amplitude, as Whiggish liberal narratives would insist, but is 'toppled over' and reversed, resulting in the diamond pattern shown in Figure 3.

Indeed, even before the nineteenth century drew to a close, qualifications and restraints of all kinds once again began to erode the unassailable 'Roman' quality of ownership, reverting to the older juridical tradition in which property was conceived as a social trust or function. The robust unitary conception of ownership dissolved into a more shadowy 'bundle of rights', while the necessary connection between property rights and things was gradually eliminated (Hohfeld 1978; Grey 1980: 69).[17] The social institutionalization of ownership and the ascendancy of public law resuscitated not only the 'medieval' practice which permitted several persons to enjoy simultaneous rights *in rem* of equal rank, but also that of an incomplete separability of rights to rule and to possess. This 'new feudalism' in the theory of property gradually restored not only the idea of partible ownership, but also that of functional commitment and stewardship (cf. Reich 1978).[18] The 1919 Weimar Constitution already declared: 'Property obliges, and should be made to serve the common good'. The principle was retained in the present German Constitution, and found its way into those of many other democratic states (e.g. Huber 1966).[19]

The philosophy behind it was already clearly outlined by Ihering in *Das Zweck im Recht* (1877), and received extensive elaboration around the turn of the century in the sociological functionalism of historically minded jurists such as Gierke, Renner, Hauriou, and Duguit. Duguit's account of property as a social function in turn distinctly influenced the authors of the Soviet Civil Code of 1923. Art. 1 of this Code stated that 'the law protects private rights except when they are exercised in contradiction to their social and economic

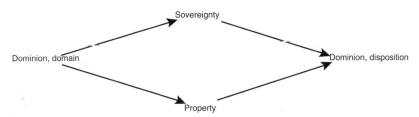

Figure 3 The diamond pattern: from domain to disposition

purposes'. Arts. 4–6 granted legal capacity (the capacity of having private rights and obligations, e.g. rights to acquire and alienate property within the limitations established by the law) to individuals 'for the purpose of the development of the productive forces of the country' (Gsovski 1948: 69–70). The 'Western capitalist' fission between civil and public law was explicitly discarded. Legal textbooks from 1934 to 1935 commonly celebrated the supersession of the 'contradiction' between private and public law and between civil society and the state through the advent of socialized property (Jakobs 1965).

Since then, modern jurists have generally abandoned simple dichotomous models of ownership and have returned to a conception of property as multiple, dispersed, and relational. 'It is indeed possible', Karl Renner observed, 'to carve out of the universal right of disposition selected powers of disposal and beneficial enjoyment and to constitute them as separate *iura in rem*. This is what is happening again in modern times' (1949: 80–1). Essentially divisible, complete property then turns into 'a mere concept of totality rather than an actual phenomenon. Property is a complex which is divisible into many assortments of the component rights, rather than an integer' (Reinhold Noyes 1936: 302). Becker has described property rights as 'typically aggregates of different sorts of rights and right-correlatives', following the influential example of Honoré, who has split the property compound into no less than eleven legal incidents (Becker 1977: 21; Honoré 1961: 113). Harper's formula that property is 'by its nature' something that exists in parts or pieces, shows how 'natural' this new construction has become (1974: 18).[20]

In our longer perspective, the new resolve to functionalize property and to 'put it in the plural' can therefore be interpreted as a faithful repetition of earlier efforts by liberal thinkers of the classical age to de-absolutize the theory and practice of political sovereignty. The classical liberal attack on the pointlike, monistic conception of public power, which asserted its essential partibility and functionality, is presently paralleled and supplemented by a wide-ranging critique of the classical countermodel of absolute and impartible property. Even if twentieth-century utopias about the socialization of property have been far from immune to conceptual absolutism – often including a myth of 'popular property' (*Volkseigentum*) as a recondite, impartible essence which is quite comparable with (if not identical to) a substantialized notion of popular sovereignty – the idea of fragmentable and limitable rights has generally been gaining momentum on both sides of the ideological fence.

This double fragmentation has produced a converging movement which has progressively broken down the demarcating fence itself. In recent times, both the concepts of property and power have become subject to movements of metaphoric generalization and 'confusion' which together constitute a secular process of *synonymization*. They tend to converge towards an inclusive concept which is both dynamic and relational, which does not dramatically divorce the rule over humans from the detention of things, which is functionally limited, and which admits of differences in degree. In our technology-driven world, the conceptual divide between human–human (or subject–subject) and human–nature (or subject–object) relationships is increasingly subjected to pressure (cf. Haraway 1991; Latour 1993; Law 1991a). In all three dimensions of the liberal dichotomy, sharp distinctions appear to be melting down, and there is an increasing, although still incoherent, awareness that property and power constitute species of one genus and can be included in a single order of 'mastery' or 'disposition'.

In so far as modern definitions of property still retain a residual reference to tangible or material benefits (cf. Brandt 1974: 12; Hollowell 1982: 8; Waldron 1988: 33ff.), this lingering emphasis appears unnecessary, and can be replaced by a more general notion of 'values', 'rewards', or 'goods' which embraces *all* conceivable means of a fully human life, rights to persons not excepted (cf. Arneson 1992). The venerable juridical cliché that severs real from personal relations then cedes before the idea that rights both real and personal may vary according to the number and quality of persons and things affected and the scope and duration of the rights involved. Both property and power are then made to refer to the allocation of 'valuables' to specifiable persons – which may include the acquisition, enjoyment, and disposal of other persons as well.

Evidently, this converging movement creates its own peculiar tangles, if only because both concepts tend more and more to invade each other and become vaguer as the intertwining process advances. The property idiom is ever more freely employed to denote intangibles such as shares of stock, bank accounts, welfare benefits, goodwill, patents, copyrights, and jobs, and is stretched even further in order to encompass sets of social relations, organizational power, cultural accomplishments, and political or human rights. The concept of power has similarly outgrown the restricted scope of political sovereignty, to be tendentially broadened into a concept which indicates the moulding force of all human relationships. Both therefore develop in the direction of a conceptual totalism which is increasingly devoid of the demarcative specificity which still obtained in their earlier state of sectoral opposition. Clearly, this produces a major conceptual quandary, because the two generalizing strategies inevitably intersect and collide, and are ultimately incompatible with the motive to retain either property or power as the privileged explanatory axis of social order and social inequality.

THE GENERALIZATION OF PROPERTY

This tensionful process of generalization will now be (illustratively rather than exhaustively) traced in a number of modern theories, starting at the property end. Let me begin by observing that the work of 'sociologizing' jurists such as

Renner, Duguit, or Friedmann already exemplifies an advanced state of convergence between the analytics of property and power, although their basic thesis that property has an important 'power aspect' still implies a measure of distance between the two. This distance is virtually annulled in more radical proposals by, for example, Morris Cohen, R. H. Tawney, and C. B. Macpherson, who have variously argued that property is ultimately a *political* relation between persons. Cohen's celebrated lecture on 'Property and Sovereignty' (1927) paved the way for this interpretation. Since the essence of private property was the right to exclude others, it in fact constituted a sovereign power which compelled service and obedience:

> the owners of all revenue-producing property are in fact granted by the law certain powers to tax the future social product. When to this power of taxation is added the power to command the services of large numbers who are not economically independent, we have the essence of what historically has constituted political sovereignty.
>
> (Cohen 1978: 160)

This tendency to identify property and power, conceived as a right to demand a certain kind of behaviour, is enhanced in Macpherson's more boldly conceived 'political theory of property'. From about the middle of the twentieth century, he noted, property rights were once more conceived as rights to a revenue or income rather than as rights in specific material things. Investors and beneficiaries of the welfare state found their main property to lie in dividends, allowances, pensions, unemployment benefits, and access to free or subsidized services, while managers, employees, and workers claimed rights to a job, i.e. rights to use their labour and skill in order to earn an income. Against this background, Macpherson argued, the concept of property needed to be liberated from its historical confinements and assimilated to a broad right of access to the accumulated resources of society. Since it defined a right to a kind of society which enables individuals to live a fully human life, the right to share in political power perhaps became the most important kind of property. Such a broadening of property towards 'a revenue of enjoyment of the quality of life' or 'a right to participation in a satisfying set of social relations' explicitly revived the older idea that the means of living a good life constituted the main object of property, including, as did the seventeenth-century conception, a right to 'actions' as well as 'goods', to 'life and liberty' as well as to 'estate' (Macpherson 1973: 136–40).

This generalization of the property discourse, which reanimates the broad scope of seventeenth-century 'propriety' but inevitably also inherits its vagueness, is equally evident in other intellectual currents, such as 'anarcho-libertarian' political philosophy and the school of 'New Property' economists. Departing from a strong justificatory notion of 'self-ownership', libertarians such as Nozick, Rothbard, and Narveson have argued in favour of treating all rights as property rights (Nozick 1974; Narveson 1988; cf. Ryan 1994). Furubotn and Pejovich, the editors of a programmatic anthology in the 'new property' economy, similarly enlarge the notion of property as covering the 'sanctioned behavioral relations among men that arise from the existence of goods and pertain to their use', while expanding the term 'good' to indicate 'anything that yields utility or satisfaction to a person . . . to exclude some people from free access to a good means to specify property rights in that good' (1974: 3, 8). Other contributors to the volume, such as McKean, Demsetz, and Alchian, likewise tend to identify property rights with 'rights in general' pertaining to objects or resources, while the scope and identity of the latter are not clearly circumscribed.

If property rights are thus extended to cover all kinds of enforceable claims, a dilemma arises, since analytic preferences for the idiom of property or that of power become increasingly arbitrary. Macpherson's justification for identifying property rights as human rights, for example, expressly built upon the presumed *prestige* of the property concept as it derives from the liberal ethos:

> We have made property so central to our society that any thing and any rights that are not property are very apt to take second place. So I think that, given our present scale of values, it is only if the human right to a full life is seen as a property right that it will stand much chance of general realization.
>
> (Macpherson 1973: 138; 1977: 77)

It is rather doubtful, however, whether a neo-Marxist extension of the concept of property which veers so closely towards arch-liberal defences of capitalism and private property adds up to a convincing case. Worse perhaps, the new property rights are effectively coincident with Macpherson's own conception of what should belong to a human's developmental *power*, i.e. the ability 'to use and develop essentially human capacities' or 'to get what one wants', which includes access to the means of life and labour – the extent and distribution of which are in turn set by the institution of property. Macpherson himself did not systematically confront this difficulty: he liberally translated property and power into each other, without relinquishing the conviction that property was ultimately basic, comprehensive, and prior, and that class analysis somehow still constituted the basic science of society (cf. Svacek 1976: 407–9).

In this respect, Macpherson's conceptual strategy summarized and prefigured the long-term 'politicizing' drift which has become a characteristic feature of neo-Marxist theorizing about the contemporary entwinement of culture, polity, and economy. In classical mid-century works such as Burnham's *The Managerial Revolution* or Djilas's *The New Class*, which radicalized the managerialist thesis concerning the separation of ownership and control and the Trotskyite critique of 'bureaucratic collectivism', the span of property was already sufficiently enlarged to include positional, formally non-heritable rights in the exercise of bureaucratic power – which rescued the idea that managers, political bureaucrats, and intellectuals could in some sense be identified as new property classes. Both works noted the osmosis of political relations or administrative and managerial monopolies and relations of ownership, as well as the rise of a new exploiting class which had anchored itself on new, institutional forms of property.[21] Burnham typically extended the ownership criterion towards that of 'corporate control', circularly defining it as the 'ability to prevent access by others to the object controlled (owned)' (1945: 53–4). Since then, this surreptitious displacement from the repertoire of appropriation/exploitation towards that of domination/oppression has been in continual evidence in disputes about the significance of the 'managerial revolution' and the fate of 'really existing' socialism. Nowak's (1983) generalization of historical materialism towards the idea of a 'double class of rulers-owners' is only one among a plethora of recent examples.

While it is already discernible in the classical writings of revisionist social democracy, Sorelian syndicalism, and the early Frankfurt school, the generalizing gesture and the discursive shift have surfaced more definitely and acutely in post-1968 currents such as Althusserian structuralism, feminist historical materialism, Anglo-Saxon 'cultural materialism', and the school of 'analytic' or 'rational choice Marxism' (see further Chapter 3). It is also manifest in recent sociological accounts of the new stratificational weight of cultural assets and political power, and of the possible emergence of new classes based upon such 'superstructural' goods. In theories such as those of Gouldner, Collins, or Bourdieu, which represent consanguine attempts to outline a political economy of culture, metaphors of property and capital are liberally applied to the tenure of social positions, disposition of cultural and educational assets, and access to sets of social relations. Gouldner's prediction of the rise of a new class of intellectuals which capitalizes on its control over valuable cultures is anchored in an expansive notion of 'capital' as *any* income-producing resource or utility (Gouldner 1979; Szelényi 1982). Collins adds 'political' to 'productive' labour in order to highlight the importance of organizational alliances and the definitory construction of positions; in his conception, such 'position-shaping' opportunities constitute the most immediate form of property (1979: 50–4). In the programmatic writings of Bourdieu, the metaphor of capital is widely proliferated in order to denote cultural, social, political, scientific, linguistic, bodily, and symbolic resources. Although in his work the property and power repertoires are more consciously interchanged, since cultural capital is freely identified with symbolic power, and cultural, linguistic, and scientific competences are treated as powers as much as goods, Bourdieu's project remains ultimately geared towards the elaboration of what is called a 'generalized economy of practices', or a 'political economy of symbolic violence' (1980; 1993a,b; 1994; Bourdieu and Wacquant 1992).

THE GENERALIZATION OF POWER

But if for neo-Marxists such as Djilas, Burnham, Macpherson, or Nowak 'all roads lead to property' (Macpherson 1973: 121), they all lead to *power* in the eyes of another large constituency in modern social and political thought. Here we may encounter sociologists such as Elias, Dahrendorf, Giddens, and Beck, postmodern philosophers such as Lyotard, Deleuze, and Foucault, constructivists such as Knorr, Callon, and Latour, eco-anarchists such as Bookchin and Dobson, feminist authors such as Harding, Butler, and Haraway, and 'New Right' ideologues such as Mohler, Maschke, and De Benoist. With the work of Lukes and Giddens in particular, Clegg argues, the concept of power has graduated from the restricted arena of political theory proper in order to become 'the single most important concept' for contemporary sociology, perhaps even 'one of the central concepts of the social and human sciences *per se*' (1989: xviii). This expansionary drift closely parallels and complements that of the property trend outlined above. It likewise liberates the idea of power from its historical confinement to *public* authority over *citizens* (while property was narrowed to *private* disposal over *things*), and enlarges it in order potentially to cover all conceivable life chances and life situations, not excepting access to material property – although, once again, the converging movement does not preclude the retention of power or authority as the more original and comprehensive social variable.

Examples are legion; again my listing is suggestive rather than comprehensive. During the 1970s and 1980s, both the Nietzschean and the anarchist approaches to power have been widely resuscitated as mutually reinforcing ideological alternatives to an increasingly battered Marxism. In Paris, 'old' philosophers such as Castoriadis and Lefort, 'new' philosophers such as Lévy and Glucksmann, postmodernist philosophers such as Lyotard, Deleuze, and Foucault, and (what some would like to call) 'premodern' philosophers such as De Benoist, collectively channelled the disillusionment with the property and class language of classical Marxism into a general 'defection' to power theory. Swept along by the subliminal political drift in neo-Marxism itself, certain believers found it relatively easy to shift allegiances from Althusser to Foucault, and ride with the new fashion.[22] Anarchism, for its part – surely the least spoilt and contaminated of the grand political narratives – likewise returned rather spectacularly to the political and theoretical scene, after having roamed in the ideological desert for more than a decade, dictating its themes to the agenda of new social movements such as feminism, ecologism, the squatters' movement, and the campaign against nuclear energy. The resultant pressure to enlarge the scope of the political has been especially manifest in feminist theory, as exemplified in Kate Millett's early and influential *Sexual Politics*, whose comprehensive notion of power (1969: 43) was applauded by an anarchist in the following terms:

> On this model . . . we may conceive of the politics of production and consumption, the politics of education, the politics of race, the politics of religion, the politics of art, the politics of age – and the politics of every social sphere, the conventionally political included, in which a group or class or caste dominates others, or some institutional complex rules the lives of people.
>
> (Wieck 1975: 30)

In this perspective, the much-vaunted paradigm shift from 'modernism' to 'postmodernism' across the broad disciplinary range of philosophy, sociology, political theory, cultural studies, and feminism is to a large extent condensed in the cognitive leap 'from Marx to Nietzsche' and the concurrent displacement of a grounding ontology of property by an equally grounding ontology of power. The most influential messenger of this discursive landslide has no doubt been Michel Foucault, whose genealogy of modern disciplinary technologies promoted the most radical generalization of the power concept so far undertaken – a generalization, moreover, which developed in explicit critical distanciation from previous liberal (but also Marxist) monistic, thinglike conceptions of state sovereignty. Sovereignty, Foucault insisted, should not be conceived as the generative essence or central point from which all other social powers emanated and derived, but rather as the 'terminal' form which power adopted as it developed upwards from below. In his conception, power constitutes an omnipresence which lacks a particular anchorage; it is a diffuse and multidirectional ensemble of relations of force

> produced from one moment to the next, at every point, or rather in every relation from one point to another. Power is everywhere; not because it embraces everything, but because it comes from everywhere . . . power is not an institution, and not a structure; neither is it a certain strength we are endowed with; it is the name that one attributes to a complex strategical situation in a particular society.
>
> (Foucault 1978: 92–5)

The political, in this view, does not remain confined to a specific instance, sphere, or field but traverses the entire social body. The accelerated advance of the technologies of individual and social discipline – the bipolar emergence of an anatomo-politics of the human body and a biopolitics of the population – has created a 'disciplinary society' in which technologies of power invest and colonize all the major institutions. Discipline, in other words, cannot be understood as a function of relations of production or property but takes analytic precedence: power surpasses the limits of production and operates as a constitutive element at the very heart of production relations themselves. It is intriguing to note, in this context, that Foucault's discursive tactic virtually mirrors that of Bourdieu in liberally mixing the tropes of political economy and political theory, while ultimately reverting to 'power' as his master concept. Once again, the confederation of both vocabularies is most conspicuous in the analytic region of (embodied) knowledge, language, and culture, where Foucault speaks about the 'economy' of discourses, the 'production' of truth, and the 'politics' of knowledge without apparent discrimination. However, his ultimate thesis is not cast in the generalized idiom of appropriation but in that of *pouvoir/savoir*, and emphasizes the switch from an 'economics of untruth' towards a 'politics of truth' (Foucault 1978: 73; 1977: 304ff; 1980: *passim*).

As we progress in our study, we will realize that Foucault's celebration of the power theme is the logical terminus of a generalization process which originates in classical political philosophy but only reaches its high-water mark in twentieth-century sociology – which in more than one respect must be seen as its effective heir. The theme of disciplinary authority is already a central one in the classical systems of Weber and Durkheim (cf. O'Neill 1986; Lacroix 1981), while a generalized theory of power arguably constitutes the common underpinning of virtually all contemporary theories of social stratification (Mann 1986: 10). Some influential grand narratives in modern historical sociology, such as those of Elias and Mann, are centrally organized around it. The Beck/Giddens approach to 'reflexive modernization' is explicitly presented as a 'political epistemology of a self-critical modernity' which is geared towards a 'reinvention of the political' (Beck 1993: 56; Beck *et al.* 1994: 17–18). Nikolas Rose and his associates have inventively applied Foucault's notion of 'governmentality' to a comprehensive analysis of neoliberal governance (cf. Barry *et al.* 1976). The modern sociology of science has likewise enlarged the vocabulary of politics, in conscious generalization of Foucault's microphysics of power to the stabilization of scientific facts, material techniques, and machines (cf. Latour 1986; 1993). Beyond sociology proper, modern feminists and ecologists have widened the frame of reference of the political even further to encompass the personal, the human body, and the non-human natural world (for the latter, see e.g. Dobson 1993).

At first sight, then, the past decades appear witness to another grand vocabulary switch and a correlative exchange of master concepts and 'last instances' of social determination. However, the widespread revival of liberal market rationality during the 1980s, and the simultaneous resurgence of economizing metaphors across a broad range of social studies, should warn us against oversimplifying the picture. The rise of 'economizing' theories of collective action, democracy, and public choice, of 'rational choice' paradigms in sociology and psychology, and of lively currents of 'analytic' and 'cultural' Marxism, sufficiently demonstrate that 'property theory' is nowhere easily defeated. Indeed, if there are many circumstantial factors which may explain the 'postmodern' repertoire switch, there are perhaps few *intrinsic* conceptual reasons why property theory cannot map the modern stratificational order as comprehensively and adequately as power theory can. We have noted before how the idiom of appropriation was historically applied to immaterial goods such as knowledge claims, the possession of women in marriage, paternal *dominium* over children, servants, and apprentices, and the closure practices of professional corporations. Modern theorists once again freely speak in terms of 'cultural capital', 'job property', or 'property rights in persons'. Indeed, the main point I have been making is that both the span of property and that of power can be (and are) extended so liberally that the choice for either one becomes increasingly arbitrary. If this is indeed the case, why does the synonymization of property and power remain unachieved?

This intellectual knot can only be untied, I claim, if we realize that property and power are also deeply enmeshed in the politics and morals of *intellectual rivalry*. In the intellectual field, concepts such as power and property themselves constitute *means of power* which supply the weaponry of intellectual polemics, or *items of property* which function as stakes in intellectual bids for competition. As a result of their polysemic capacity for extension and contraction, both property and power may feed traditional rivalries for pride of place as grounding variables of social stratification or as basic determinants of social structure and social development, a contest from which neither has so far emerged victorious – nor does it appear likely that one will.

2

INSIDE THE DIAMOND

Rivalry and reduction

VOCABULARY SWITCHES

In the previous chapter I have sought to demonstrate that the ideological stereotype which sets the logic of property and civil law at right angles to that of power and public law naturalized a fragile and transient conjuncture in the genealogy of Western juridical and political philosophy. But the ontological distance which was perceived between the realms of property and power – the differential sharpness with which the line of demarcation was drawn – is not the only variable present. The liberal dichotomy, as was intermittently noticed, simultaneously presumed a definite *order of causal priority*, which established the realm of production as infrastructural and basic, and set up property as an unlimited right of exclusion which could not be infringed by the public power. Although likewise presented as a natural fact, this sequence of causal and productive primacy turned out to be equally contextual and historically fragile as the idea of the divide itself. Indeed, it constituted a reversal of an older sequence in which the sphere of politics was characterized as most decisive, and in which sovereignty was depicted as a radiating substance from which property rights ultimately depended and derived.

This reversal of theoretical priorities should not be interpreted as a singular and definitive occurrence which sharply demarcated the political and legal philosophy of the *Ancien Régime* from that of the subsequent liberal era. The great watershed of modern political thought was not marked by a once-and-for-all switch of last instances, but was both preceded and followed by many lesser alternations, which were repeated at regular intervals within the diamond-shaped pattern of conceptual fission and fusion which was schematically outlined above.[1] In order to grasp the relevant details of this complex intellectual dialectic, it is therefore essential to observe a measure of distance between the two constituent variables which liberal theory itself normally tended to conflate. Liberalism immediately identified the ontological separation between property and power with the claimed natural primacy of the former over the latter. As will be shown, however, the question of differentiation and the question of priority are much more loosely interconnected and manifest a much more varied interplay, although of course they remain to some extent logically interdependent.

Indeed, despite the outward appearance of secular continuity in two separate discursive realms, the diamond pattern is in a sense constituted by vocabulary switches which become more dramatic as the conceptual gap widens, and manifest a tendency to 'ease off' when the point of greatest amplitude is passed. These vocabulary switches reverse the order of causal primacy and substitute a proprietary last instance for a political one – or the other way around. Locke's criticism of the patriarchal system of Filmer (and by implication, of the political philosophies of Bodin and Hobbes) and his switch from sovereignty to property was, though extremely influential, not at all an isolated example. As we shall see below (Figure 4), a similar inversion defined the reception of Montesquieu's political system by the founders of Scottish moral philosophy and classical political economy, while the most celebrated of these vocabulary switches has probably been Marx's attempt to set Hegelian idealism 'back upon its feet again'. The order of priority postulated by Lockean liberalism, Smithian political economy and Marxian historical materialism was in turn uprooted by many later intellectual systems which developed through critical distanciation from them, which included classical anarchism, revisionist social democracy, intellectual fascism, and some major schools of classical and modern sociology. Property and power, in brief, have regularly exchanged places in the hierarchy of foundational concepts; they have retreated and advanced in an intricate conceptual *chassé*.

As a result, two broad intellectual traditions have emerged, one of which has been inclined to consider power as a secondary function of property, whereas the other preferred to see property as a special instance of power. Both currents of thought attempted to reduce what was considered secondary and derivative to what was thought primary and formative, and by offering opposite and logically exclusive answers concertedly raised a tenacious *reduction dilemma*: was property logically and factually prior to power, or did power precede property? Did 'power follow property', as the Scottish Enlighteners maintained, or was it the other way around? 'Property theory' and 'power

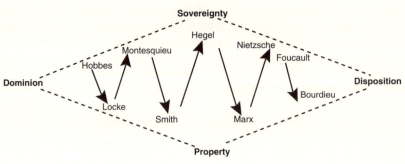

Figure 4 Vocabulary switches

theory', thus conceived, long presented themselves as a virtually inescapable choice of conceptual alternatives. In antagonistic complicity, these master vocabularies contrived to dominate a vast field of dispute by establishing themselves as privileged argumentative poles to which all conceptual efforts were invariably attracted, so much so that critics of the one position found themselves irresistibly drawn towards the other. In this way, 'property theory' and 'power theory' became encased in a complicitous configuration which tied the two rivals to such an extent as to exhaust all legitimate alternatives, and to force all dispute into the ready mould of the reductionary dialectic.

If we wish to account for the survival of this dilemma in the face of the tendencies towards convergence and synonymization touched upon before, it is vital to delve more deeply into its historical conditions of origin. In doing so, we shall confirm our supposition that the grand narratives of property and sovereignty did not simply develop along a dual track of linear articulation from union to divorce, but from their very moment of fissure were implicated in a structural rivalry which progressively grew more acute as the conceptual gap was widened. Precisely because of this prior *dis*connection, theories could emerge which proclaimed the essential reducibility of the one to the other. The more the fissure evolved, the more dramatic this cadence of rivalling last instances became, since the two conceptual clusters were increasingly defined as grounding absolutes or prime ontological movers of larger theoretical systems. The unitary or substantialist conceptions of sovereignty and property were thus forged along a double gradient of intellectual divergence *and* intellectual competition, and increasingly bore the mark of this competition through their very articulation as opposite 'last instances'.

The parallel reification of sovereignty and property, and the reification of the demarcation line which ran between them, is therefore not exclusively accountable to the double polemical deployment of these novel concepts against the feudal dispersion of rights and the feudal (con)fusion of polity and economy. To the partisans of state absolutism, the 'bundle of rights' conception of public authority was equally repulsive as the 'bundle of rights' conception of ownership subsequently became for political liberals. Both the state and, subsequently, civil society had to be emancipated from the stratified web of coterminous property/power relations; hence both absolutists and liberals consecutively rejected the relational and functional view in favour of a more thinglike, pointlike paradigm of absolute rights. But, as we saw earlier, this double process of semantic closure developed unevenly. Property rights had also to be liberated from an already entrenched conception and practice of political sovereignty. As a result, the historical relationship between the two concepts evidenced a complex pattern of inverse variation, of rivalry-induced expansion and contraction, in the course of which property finally came to absorb some crucial incidents from the bundle of sovereignty.

This is also to suggest that it was not simply the emerging *Realdialektik* of state formation and market capitalism which performed as the principal catalyst of this two-tracked semantic transformation. The new monistic concepts of sovereignty and ownership simultaneously evolved in response to an intricate and relatively autonomous logic of intellectual rivalry. Intellectuals, I hypothesize throughout, do not approach their subject matter in straightforward or undiluted fashion, but through a knowledge–political filter which is largely shaped by their polemic with significant rivals in the intellectual field. Since intellectuals monitor one another as carefully as they monitor 'reality', their analytic construction of the world is inevitably overdetermined by a cognitive–strategic surplus which is the product of interested intra-intellectual competition. What is intriguing, therefore, is that both the concept of sovereignty and that of property became carriers of an imperialistic drive which was not only connected to specific political class projects, but simultaneously expressed the 'politics of theory' of rivalling groups of *intellectuals* which acted as spokespersons for the different class parties. The very definition of sovereignty and property as pointlike, absolutist, radiating essences not only exemplified the legitimation needs of new political and economic classes, but also answered to the relatively independent interests of intellectuals who were organically tied to these classes, but nevertheless threw in their specific sociological weight as 'cultural capitalists' or as political managers of the symbolic.

Both the classical theory of sovereignty and that of property were fuelled by a desire to magnify the political and economic claims of either Crown or People, but the specifically reified profile which these theories came to adopt was influenced in significant measure by 'additional' claims to *intellectual* power and by efforts at intellectual *self*-magnification on the part of the professional lawyers, political theorists, and political economists who emerged as spokespersons for either of the two great political causes. The (onto)logical opposition between property and power was to an appreciable degree an opposition between *(onto)logicians* speaking not simply in the name of larger property and power interests but also in their *own* interest as competing symbolic experts, and thus as owners of knowledge and rulers of science. It was this self-regarding motive which, by superimposing itself upon broader political partisanships, gave a much sharper (indeed, ontological) edge to the dispute about primacy.[2]

DIALECTICS OF SOVEREIGNTY AND PROPERTY

It would be going too far afield to enter upon a detailed account of this zigzag movement as it can be reconstructed from histories of political and constitutional thought and histories of civil jurisprudence and political economy. But it is valuable to recapitulate it at least in brief outline, if only to confirm the remarkable stability of the secular trend itself and the equally remarkable constancy with which familiar rules of dispute were reproduced without major alteration across the span of several centuries: from the first reception of Roman law in eleventh-century Italy through the rediscovery of Aristotle's *Politics* in thirteenth-century France right up to the classical statements of Hobbes and Locke in seventeenth-century England.

There is one important setback which complicates attempts to trace such patterns of intellectual co-variance. The disciplinary partition which has governed traditional political and social theory has tended to dissociate the historiography of constitutional thought and public law from that of property theory and private law, so that the story of their development is still often related in a partial and disintegrated manner. Histories of the concept of sovereignty such as those of Merriam (1900) and Cohen (1937), of political theory by Droz (1948) or Sabine (1968), and of the property concept by, for example, Schlatter (1951), Lévy (1972), Kiernan (1976), or Ryan (1984) tend to uncover not more than half of the picture, which is only fully revealed when the common filiation and the essential interdependence of both concepts are more seriously taken into consideration. This unfortunate division of labour is less pronounced in older contributions to constitutional and civil history by jurists such as von Gierke, Pollock and Maitland, or Duguit, while it is also absent in the Harvard school of constitutional historiography which originated in the work of McIlwain and his pupils (McIlwain 1932; Gilmore 1967; Church 1941). In more recent works by Macpherson (1962), Anderson (1974), and Skinner (1978) the two lines of conceptual development are once again drawn together and analysed in mutual correlation. These modern contributions stand closer to the spirit of Duguit's early programmatic insight that 'sovereignty and property . . . have the same origin and march as a pair' (1920: 153).

Combining various materials from the above sources, I have attempted to visualize this paired march in the following diagram (Figure 5), which interconnects a few names, dates, and places in a summary view of the historical process of differentiation, rivalry, and reduction with which we are already familiar. It starts off when the 'umbilical cord' between property and sovereignty (Anderson) is already broken, inaugurating the long drift towards a double antithetical concentration of powers and rights. As Gierke put it, the sovereignty of the state and the sovereignty of the individual steadily became the two central axioms from which all theories of social structure would proceed, and whose relationships to each other would henceforth be the focus of all theoretical controversy (1958: 87).

As the previous chapter has already briefly laid out, the twelfth century saw the germ of a doctrine of state sovereignty which tended to exalt a single ruler to an absolute plenitude of power. The content of this plenitude 'needed no explanation, its substance was inalienable, impartible, and proof against prescription, and all subordinate power was a mere delegation from it' (Gierke 1958: 35). This exaltation of sovereignty as a *suprema potestas* implied an altered view of the relation between social Part and social Whole. If the feudal

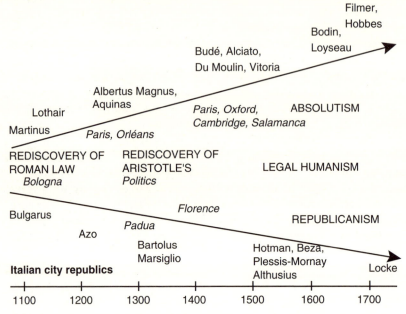

Figure 5 The fissure of sovereignty and property

polity was still conceivable as a graded articulation of partial bodies which corresponded with a federalistic distribution of rights and powers, the modern idea of indivisible public authority introduced the notion of an *emanative* or *dialectical* relationship between part and whole. Because sovereign authority was focused in a single point (Hobbes, among others, emphasized its 'perfect singleness'), subordinate political offices and magistracies could only be conceived as mere *commissions to use* the power of the prince or of a more abstract state power, which remained in substance one and untransferable. In the early modern view, all public offices were precarious holdings, mere delegations of the sovereign power, and the partial authority which was incident upon office was thought to revert to its generative source as soon as the office was vacated.

This emanative theory of magistracy was gradually perfected along the intellectual road which I conducted from Aquinas to Bodin and Hobbes. If earlier thinkers still tended to view sovereignty as an agglomeration or mosaic of different rights, and compiled lists of such 'marks' of sovereignty (e.g. the right to act as supreme judge, the right to exterminate heretics, the right to coin money, the right to hold a parliament), subsequent ones exchanged this additive view for a 'nuclear' or 'solar' conception in which the title was conceived as one and indivisible. If, at the beginning of the sixteenth century, Chasseneuz advanced that all offices and dignities issued from the prince as from a fountain (*tamquam a fonte*), it was clear that in his view the crown preserved the ultimate title, and that all governmental officers were regarded as constituted agents – or even more literally, as embodied in the royal person. Bodin, who was the first to define the right of sovereignty as an undifferentiated plenum of power, explicitly derived the different regalian rights from this original whole rather than constituting the whole from an assemblage of partial rights. His idea of an ultimate unity of power manifestly implied that every 'mark' was somehow contained in the central power of legislation, and that possession of the latter implied a claim to all the rest. Le Bret, in a treatise on the sovereignty of the king (1632), likewise held that it was 'equally indivisible as the point in geometry'.[3]

The development of property rights is directed by a similar teleology, from the resuscitation of the Roman idea of *dominium* by the first Civilian doctors through Bartolus and the Huguenot and republican writers up to John Locke and classical liberalism. Here as well the scalar or partible idea of ownership was gradually supplanted by an essentialist notion which included an emanative connection between partial rights and the whole from which they were thought to derive as from a fountain. Property became an irreducible nucleus, a *residuum* from which all other rights in the totality were derived, upon which they remained dependent, and to which they automatically returned when liberated (Reinhold Noyes 1936: 302; Renner 1949: 23; J. Coleman 1988: 611–12). An important staging post on this road was Bartolus's celebrated definition of private property, which was transferred almost intact from the fourteenth century to the Code Civil of 1804, and which included not only the element of absoluteness but also that of materiality (*Quid ergo est dominium? Responde: est ius de re corporali perfecte disponendi, nisi lege prohibeatur*) (Woolf 1913). This essentialist definition of property was increasingly harmonized with the natural law conception of the inherent and inalienable rights of individual men. The natural right to *dominium* was ever more clearly conceived as a resident, thinglike quality, because it was thought to issue directly from the fountain of subjective rights (to life, liberty and estate, as Locke was to say) which constituted each individual in his simple capacity as a human being.

In this fashion, two axial and complementary questions emerged in political and social theory which, in this particular phrasing, were previously unthinkable: 1. *Where is Sovereignty?* 2. *Who is the Owner?* The problem of the precise *seat* or *locus* of sovereignty and property could of course only be posed in such terms because both were now interpreted as concentrated, procreative Wholes which somehow also remained present in their derivative Parts, and therefore invited a logic of ultimacy and an either/or distribution of attributes. Hobbes' basic intuition that 'there must be an absolute sovereignty somewhere in all commonwealths' set the terms of debate not only for defenders of the eminent right of the king, but likewise for those (such as Bartolus, Marsiglio, the republican writers, and later Rousseau) who rather saw the people as represented in its various communal and parliamentary bodies as the ultimate depository of all public authority. As a perfect parallel to this search for the true sovereign power in the realm, disputes about the distribution of property rights came increasingly to be dominated by the question: where resides the true owner?

EARLY PRIORITY DISPUTES

Naturally, these twin questions did not emerge as simply parallel, since a particular answer to the one narrowed down the range of possible answers to the other. Although the line of division between sovereignty and property was drawn with increasing determination by *all* thinkers, royalists, and republican liberals alike, it was clear from the outset that the two totalizing conceptions could coexist peacefully only to a limited extent, because they embodied a political and intellectual contradiction which was soluble only if the balance was tilted in favour of one or the other. The question of the precise locus of sovereignty or property was never clearly separable from the question of ultimate precedence. An emphasis upon private property as a unitary and unconditional right, grounded in natural law, logically precipitated a notion of *popular* sovereignty and a theory of rulership and public office which focused upon its fiduciary, derivative, and thus revocable character. This was already the theory of Bartolus and Marsiglio in the fourteenth, that of the so-called Monarchomachs in the sixteenth, and of the Levellers and Locke in the seventeenth century.

If, on the other hand, the case was made for the unconditional unity and supremacy of sovereignty, the normal corollary was a kind of retarded 'feudalism' in the theory of property rights. These were often denied a natural origin and interpreted as products of convention, i.e. as ultimately constituted by the public power and therefore limited in scope and subject to recall. This tended to be the basic theory of all monarchist political writers from Alciato and Du Moulin through Bodin and Loyseau to Filmer and Hobbes. Chasseneuz and Du Moulin, for example, retained a theory of property which recognized a series of varying and superimposed rights – although both also tended to see allodial property which could be owned completely as a more distant ideal.

Both writers also reaffirmed the basic sectoral distinction of private and public law, as it was typically expressed in the sixteenth-century maxim that *fief et justice n'ont rien de commun*. The king, in other words, was not the owner of all real property in the realm, but acted as supreme overlord and administrator in the political sense (Gilmore 1967: 39–40; Church 1941: 158, 174–5, 181–3). For Bodin, private property likewise set the most important limitation upon sovereign authority. Invoking Seneca's familiar rule that authority belonged to kings but property to private persons, he maintained that the prince was bound by both divine and natural law and was therefore limited in his fiscal and economic rights: 'Since the sovereign prince has no power to transgress the laws of nature, which God, whose image he is on earth, has ordained, he cannot take the property of another without a just and reasonable cause' (Bodin 1962: 204, 210, 707; Franklin 1973: 23–6, 84–5; Church 1941: 225, 234). This coupling of the practical inviolability of private property and the overarching right of the absolute sovereign produced somewhat of a logical difficulty of which Bodin himself remained largely unaware.

The reduction problem itself had long been familiar to political theorists and doctors of the law in Bodin's age. The disputes between the Politiques and the Huguenot republicans in sixteenth-century France largely copied those which had absorbed the legal humanists of Alciato's school and the Bartolists in the fifteenth century, and reached back in turn to the famous differences among the Roman lawyers of the Bologna school. Two of these disputes need a brief mention, because their terms are so similar, and because they served as complementary theoretical matrices for many subsequent disputes far into the seventeenth century. The first one dated from the first half of the twelfth century and opposed Bulgarus and Martinus, the two most celebrated of the four doctors from the second generation of the Bolognese glossators of the Roman law. The second controversy erupted almost a century later within the same school, and was widely known and cited as the dispute between Lothair and Azo (Vinogradoff 1961; Skinner 1978 I: 127–9; Gilmore 1967: 15ff.).

When the lawyers of Bologna attended the Diet of Roncaglia in 1158, where the emperor Barbarossa proclaimed his sovereignty over the whole of the *regnum italicum* and his right to tax the wealthy cities, they broadly favoured the emperor's claims without agreeing upon the precise limits of the imperial prerogative. A famous anecdote relates that when Frederic was riding one day with Bulgarus on his right side and Martinus on his left, he asked them whether the emperor was not by right *dominus* of everything that was held by his subjects. Bulgarus courageously answered that he was lord in the political sense but not in the sense of an owner; Martinus instead concurred with the emperor. The controversy was recalled much later by Bartolus, who recorded that his predecessors of the Glossator school overwhelmingly sided with Bulgarus, adopting the latter's view that the emperor's supremacy did not interfere with private ownership also as his own (Woolf 1913: 22–4, 46; Skinner 1978 I: 51ff.; Carlyle and Carlyle 1909: 72–3).

The second classical debate was conducted about a century later between Azo and Lothair on the concept of *merum Imperium* in Justinianus's *Codex*. The anecdote was the same one of riding with the emperor (Henry VI this time). Azo's answer to his query to whom the *merum Imperium* belonged was that, although it belonged to the emperor *par excellentiam*, it also belonged to other magistrates. Opposing him, Lothair maintained that the emperor was the sole depository of public authority in the realm. Four centuries later the dispute was reported by Loyseau in his *Cinq Livres du droit des offices* (1610), who also mentioned that, while at first Azo's opinion had enjoyed dominance among the Roman lawyers, Alciato had reverted to Lothair's view, followed by Du

Moulin and Bodin. Lothair's notion about the basic integrity and indivisi-bility of *imperium* therefore exercised a permanent attraction upon the long succession of legal theorists who wished to strengthen the prerogatives of the crown. Azo's conception of divisible *imperium* instead strengthened the legiti-mation of the institutions of republican city government, and resonated well with the defence of a naturalistic view of property such as could also be encountered in Bartolus and Marsiglio. Bartolus's reorientation of the theory of *imperium* canvassed the idea that, although *de iure* the emperor alone wielded sovereign power, the cities *de facto* possessed the *merum imperium* in themselves. This early conception of popular sovereignty was compatible with the view that the public domain was divisible across a hierarchy of magistratures, whose powers were essentially limited and revocable.[4]

Although the early Civilians remained ambiguous with respect to the natural or conventional character of ownership, a global connection persisted between the conventionalist idea of property as a creation of the law and an abso-lutist emphasis upon the eminent domain of the sovereign, as was evident in Martinus, Placentinus, or Lothair. A similar connection held between the idea of property as an institution of natural law and Bulgarus's denial, subsequently reaffirmed by Azo and Bartolus, that the sovereign was also the supreme owner of the goods of the realm. In the preceding Augustinian or feudal tradition, the priority question had not commanded much attention, since government and property were blended and were both seen as divine remedies for human weak-ness; neither were to be found in the state of innocence but arose from human convention. As soon as the Civilians had rediscovered the Roman distinction and the Roman idea of property as deriving in principle from *naturalis ratio*, there was once again room for dispute about logical and factual precedence. Along the stretch of six centuries which separated the first Romanists from Hobbes and Locke, this dispute tended to focus upon the dilemma of whether or not sovereignty or property were conventional or natural in origin. If sovereignty was accorded primacy through natural or divine institution (e.g. through an irredeemable original alienation by the people, or by direct investiture by God), property tended to be seen as a grant by the sovereign power which was essentially revocable. If property, in turn, was located in the state of nature preceding any social compact, sovereignty was rather seen as a temporary commission which could be retracted at will or renegotiated in a new contract between ruler and people (cf. J. Coleman 1988: 614).

But even if sovereignty was thought to derive from immediate divine authorization and conceived as a personal right to the entire *chose publique*, civil law still placed definite limitations upon its discretion. Although Bossuet, in his *La Politique tirée de l'Ecriture sainte* (1679), went much further than Bodin or the *Politiques* in affirming the immediate divine investiture of absolute royal authority, he admitted the existence of fundamental laws which protected the liberty of persons and the inviolability of properties. Even a proud advocate of royal absolutism such as James I Stuart (*Trew Law of Free*

Monarchies, 1598) felt himself obliged to recognize that the law of God had ordained private property, and that the king should at least have a just occasion for disinheriting his subjects. Hence Filmer the royalist, against whom John Locke was to marshal his powerful polemic wit, could defend the theory of divine right as a most reasonable and safe theory of property: the owner enjoyed greater security of possession when his title was based on a royal grant than when it derived from a conventional agreement or from a natural right which Filmer saw as fictitious (Schochet 1975; Tully 1980).[5]

Another champion of unconditional sovereignty – though not of divine right and not necessarily of absolute *monarchy* – was Thomas Hobbes. If we contrast his complementary theories of sovereignty and property with those of his great liberal counterpart John Locke, we once again witness the familiar reversal of last instances, their alternative grounding in nature or convention, but also the retention, despite this switch of master concepts, of a similar theoretical essentialism in both. In Hobbes' state of nature, before the institution of the commonwealth, there is 'no *Propriety*, no *Dominion*, no *Mine* and *Thine* distinct; but only that to be every mans, that he can get; and for so long, as he can keep it'. Property rights are only established by the sovereign and his 'Lawes civill'; since they are a creation of the state, it follows that the rights of ownership are not valid against the sovereign: 'Propriety therefore being derived from the sovereign power, is not to be pretended against the same'. Although Hobbes defined property in the characteristically modernist or bourgeois sense as an individual right 'that excludes the Right of every other Subject', it could never exclude the sovereign power, without which the commonwealth would not even exist (Hobbes 1968: 188, 234, 296–7, 367–8, 384; Goldsmith 1966: 197–9).

The key idea of liberal contractualism, on the other hand, was that the agreement which introduced private ownership preceded the institution of the sovereign power, and that governments were basically established in order to protect the unconditional exercise of property, not to interfere with it. Though anticipated by Althusius, Grotius, and the Leveller democrats in the period of the English Civil War (Woodhouse 1938; Hill 1974), this liberal contract theory was perfected by Locke in his classical *Two Treatises of Government* (1690). Locke's central concern was to establish individual, exclusive property on the unshakeable ground of natural right, and to justify limited government by consent, including a guarded right of resistance and even deposition of the ruling sovereign. Absolute monarchy was inconsistent with civil society, and hence could be 'no Form of Civil Government at all'. It was not social convention which had created the right of ownership; the social contract was only agreed upon in order to provide natural and pre-existing rights with the additional guarantee of human institution. The right of ownership was one of those innate and inalienable rights which accrued to the individual in his natural state, which was a state of perfect freedom and exclusive disposal over both one's own person and one's material possessions. No longer was freedom, as with Hobbes and other absolutists, something which depended upon 'the silence of the law'. Man in the natural state was 'absolute lord of his own person and possessions, equal to the greatest and subject to nobody' (1975: 129–41, 179–90; Buckle 1991: 125ff.; Waldron 1988: 137ff.).

The derivation of property from innate liberty was effected by the interposition of a crucially important middle term: the appropriation of nature by individual *labour*. In a celebrated paragraph in the *Second Treatise* Locke developed the metaphor of the embodiment of external nature:

> Though the Earth and all Inferior Creatures be common to all Men, yet every Man has a *Property* in his own *Person*. This no Body has any Right to but himself. The *Labour* of his Body, and the *Work* of his Hands, we may say, are properly His. Whatsoever then he removes out of the State that Nature hath provided, and left it in, he has mixed his Labour with it, and joyned to it something that is his own, and thereby makes it his *Property*.

This notion of natural self-propriety fortified the individual property right to an unprecedented degree. First, it was withdrawn from the inconstancy of human convention and hence made virtually unconditional upon the performance of social functions. Second, its beneficiary was only answerable to the public body in so far as he delegated specific discretionary powers to it, retaining his most essential innate liberty. Sovereignty should therefore ultimately retreat before property rights:

> the Supreme Power cannot take from any Man any Part of his Property without his own Consent. For the Preservation of Property being the End of Government, and that for which Men enter into Society, it necessarily supposes and requires that the People should have Property.

In the priority dilemma, Hobbes and Locke therefore stood as polar opposites. Over against the former's all-encompassing notion of power as including command, honour, wealth and knowledge (1968: 150ff.), the latter entertained an equally broad notion of property as a right to 'life, liberty and estate'. And even though Hobbes also saw property as including a right to 'actions' as well as 'goods' (1968: 234), and the demarcation between the two master concepts remained slippery and vague, both Hobbes and Locke reaffirmed the overall distinction and, more interestingly, an inverse order of constitutive priority.[6]

TWO MASTER SCIENCES: POLITICAL THEORY VS. POLITICAL ECONOMY

So far, I have argued that the development of the pointlike, emanative conceptions of sovereignty and property is incomprehensible if we do not reckon with the context of progressive theoretical polarization which enveloped and partly defined them. Sovereignty and property gradually adopted the form of sublimated absolutes which could coexist only in a state of logical tension even if they were set up in their own house, i.e. were relegated to the separate institutional realms of the state and civil society. This in effect amounts to saying that social and political tensions (between economic or political classes) were translated to the level of *logical* tensions between *concepts*, and that two partisan projects of political dominance (of the royal or statal prerogative vs. that of the people as gathered in parliament) were universalized and provided with an unshakeable epistemological foundation in the nature of things. This process of theoretical articulation therefore included a specific form of dissimulation, a politics of legitimation which solidified a partisan project into indubitably natural or divine principle.

However, monistic property and sovereignty constituted much *more* than interested myths in the customary sense of being ideologically serviceable to external political interests, because in form and content they also expressed the strategic, competitional interests of the intellectual spokespersons themselves – even if these were still largely subordinate to those of more powerful strata than their own. The true functional complexity of the essentialist, dialectical notions of sovereignty and property becomes visible only if one views them also as vehicles of a politics of *theory* or as stocks of *theoretical* capital, and recognizes their implication in historically stable configurations of intellectual polarization, rivalry, and reduction.

The persistent polemic between such master concepts, I am suggesting, does not issue from a predestined inclination of free-floating theories to overstep their limits and engage in contradiction, but are only intelligible sociologically as forms of expression of knowledge-political rivalries between groups of intellectuals who compete for hegemony both in the scholarly or educational and in the organizational and political field; intellectuals, moreover, who are likely to dissimulate their own partiality through the invention of reified essences which appear to be energized by an innate polemical drive. Master concepts such as sovereignty, property, state, civil society, production, polity, and economy do not simply describe entities or instances in the real world, or serve the legitimation needs of the individuals or classes which intellectuals are hired to glorify, but also and simultaneously serve the legitimation needs of the legitimators themselves. They are hiding places for intellectual ambition, laudatory substitutes with which intellectuals identify themselves, but through which they also hide their will to power and their desire for the certainty of irrefutable dogma. The absolutism and holism of such concepts are one form through which the universalizing and conquering impulses of intellectuals are externalized, who discover fixed and firm principles of natural or divine law and then, in deceptive modesty, set themselves up as privileged mandatories of these self-created idols.

If sovereignty and property are master concepts in this sense, they are also organizing centres of two larger theoretical systems which stand in a similar position of symbiotic antagonism, and in which the same strategies of intellectual capitalization can be studied anew. These two master sciences, as I will call them, are likewise structured by a dialectical interchange of part and whole. By manoeuvring their core concepts into the position of privileged 'last instances', they claim precedence both in the hierarchy of the sciences and in terms of an exclusive 'property' of scientific truth. Their theoretical imperialism comprises two demarcative efforts: to stake out the largest possible intellectual *territory*, and to stabilize *certainty* of methodical grounding. The (partial) domains of state and civil society may both be magnified into originary and grounding social wholes, so that the *sciences* of state and society may also offer themselves as rivalling *Grundwissenschaften* which imperially subordinate the lesser human sciences, and pose as exclusive depositories of scientific truth. This dialectic of parts and wholes, as crystallized in the causality of last instances, therefore produces a typical ambiguity with respect to their territorial expanse, since it enables them to enlarge their partial *object* into a totalizing *project*. In this fashion, the dialectic becomes a vehicle of a politics of theory which is simultaneously made to disappear in the articulation of the object itself.

Reporting back to our historical scheme, we may observe that the uneven process of bifurcation of sovereignty and property was paralleled by the rise of two basic discourses about social and political reality, which even in their relatively inconspicuous thirteenth-century beginnings displayed a marked difference of emphasis. The split did not develop in linear progression but in a discontinuous manner, through lags and advances which were interspersed with reductionary disputes such as we have previously summarized. The first phase was inaugurated by the Civilian school of Bologna, which began a careful restoration and an initially timid but increasingly audacious work of glossation of the Roman law corpus. Since the reception of Roman law developed in the 'anachronistic' atmosphere of a commercial revolution and the emergence of an archipelago of free, prosperous communes, the emphasis initially fell upon the restoration and contemporary adaptation of Roman civil jurisprudence and commercial law. This 'civil science' was the first one to be exalted as a master science in the modern secular sense, i.e. as an independent branch of human study, but also as the apex and self-evident foundation of all other branches of human learning. In this capacity, the Roman codex enjoyed an incomparable prestige among many generations of law doctors, and was celebrated as *ratio scripta* far into the sixteenth century.

However, as soon as the study of Roman jurisprudence spread to the cities of Languedoc and Catalonia, and from thence to Orléans and Paris, a gradual shift of emphasis occurred. The law began to be studied with a different eye, because it was now revived within the contrasting atmosphere of a developing national state, and was soon made serviceable to the ambitions of a new type of temporal rulers. From at least the reign of Saint Louis (1226–70), the lawyers–bureaucrats trained at Montpellier, Orléans, Toulouse, and Paris grouped themselves around the sovereign and developed theories of public law which legitimized the gradual emancipation of temporal authority from the authority of the church and the centralization of all dispersed powers in the hands of the prince. A new class of educated officials or *literati* emerged which staffed the developing institutions of monarchical power. They were recruited from the bourgeois middle strata and from the lesser nobility, and had received a humanist education at the new universities of the realm (Tigar and Levy 1977; Vanderjagt 1988).

The Aristotelian renaissance of the second half of the thirteenth century in many ways enhanced and accelerated this recuperation of Roman law. Arriving by a different channel, through the great universities of Moslem Spain, it founded its first Western bulwark at the University of Paris, which became a point of dissemination from whence it spread in reverse direction to the Italian cities. In this novel confluence of Aristotelianism and Roman jurisprudence, the initial and decisive emphasis was upon a naturalistic theory of politics and public authority. After centuries of oblivion, the idea was revived that political philosophy constituted a separate discipline which was worthy of being studied in its own right and could lay claim to a distinct, relatively autonomous object. Not only was politics once again interpreted as a self-contained autonomous sphere of human activity; the *communicatio politica* was simultaneously valued as the highest form of community, so that political science positioned itself at the apex of the scientific pyramid. Already for Latini (c. 1220–94), who taught as a Florentine exile in France and might be considered the first political 'scientist' in the above sense, politics constituted 'the noblest and greatest of all sciences', as he thought Aristotle had proved beyond controversy (Skinner 1978: 349–50; Canning 1988: 360–1; Viroli 1992b: 26–8).

In Aristotle's *Nicomachean Ethics*, the science of politics was indeed introduced as the study which exercised 'most authority and control over the rest' (1977: 26–7). Political philosophy, as was clear from the opening paragraphs of the *Politics* itself, was the study of human association, and especially of the supreme association which embraced all the others: the city or state, to which both households and villages tended as their natural model of perfection. The state enjoyed priority over the households as the whole enjoyed priority over the parts (1979: 21, 25ff.; Wiseman 1972; Frisby and Sayer 1986). Book 1 of the *Politics* already contained the principal ingredients of what I have called the master science of politics. First, the ambiguous demarcation of the field of enquiry, through the familiar identification of *social* man as a *political* animal; second, the moral elevation of the state and the presumptively natural ubiquity of the ruler–ruled relationship; third, the instrumental and limited character of property and wealth, which were considered necessary preconditions for virtuous citizenship; and crowning the edifice, a *dialectics* of statehood which Hegel was able to adopt almost ready made. Notwithstanding their many differences, for Aquinas, Alciato, Bodin, Hobbes, and other champions of the Aristotelian conception, the list of priorities and the sequence of deductions remained effectively the same.

It is crucial to bear in mind that, in speaking about an 'Aristotelian' master science, I am referring to the reception and reworking of Aristotle by early Western political thinkers rather than to the original texts themselves. For thirteenth-century political theorists, it was of course not the small *polis* but the large sovereign state, not the amalgam of civil and political relations but their developing separation (and the maintenance of primacy of the political over the civil–economic) which commanded all analytic attention. As Runciman has reminded us, the crucial distinction in Aristotle was not between state and society but between *polis* and *oikos*, or between the undifferentiated political-cum-social realm and the private household (1963: 25). It was only much later that economics, which in Aristotle remained subordinate not so much to the polity but to household management, became visible as a *social* activity in its own right (Polanyi 1957; Tribe 1988: 22–3). If, therefore, Aristotelian political science appeared to argue the primacy of the political over property (Mathie 1979: 17, 29), this formulation was clearly informed by its thirteenth-century reorientation to the novel problem of the sovereignty of the national state vs. modern market liberty.

This recovery and critical reception of Aristotelian political theory effectively began around the middle of the thirteenth century, when Albertus Magnus and his pupil Thomas Aquinas lectured at the University of Paris. The early 1260s also saw the first integral Latin translation of the *Politics* by Willem van Moerbeke (Viroli 1992b: 30ff.). Aquinas's writings were thoroughly Aristotelian in at least a threefold sense. First, by marking a distinction between rulership and ownership, contrary to their amalgamation in the writings of Ambrose, Augustine, and other fathers of the church. Second, by denying that property and political authority were necessary evils and the product of original sin, and claiming instead that they were natural instruments of the good life and of well-ordered society. And third, by affirming the emergent claims of political sovereignty over against property, by virtue of the originary character of the state as embodying the 'perfect community'. It was the legislator, Aquinas held, who was ultimately responsible for distributing and regulating private property for the common good. On all three points of doctrine, the philosopher's authority was expressly invoked (Schlatter 1951; Parel 1979).

It is intriguing to observe that, as Aristotelianism travelled to the Italian city-states, its theoretical emphasis was once again deflected. Political theory was disseminated through direct contact with Paris (Aquinas, Marsiglio) as well as through the lawyers of the Bolognese school, of whom Bartolus had been an early example. But the 'Italianization' of Aristotle by Bartolus, Ptolemy of Lucca, and Marsiglio of Padua also entailed a critical distanciation from Aquinas's apology of royal sovereignty and his idea that rulers should always be *legibus solutus*. Bartolus and Marsiglio rejected Aquinas's assumption that monarchy was always the best form of government, and defended a form of popular government as most fitting and productive for free cities. Whereas Aquinas maintained (as all advocates of absolute sovereignty would do after him) that the institution of the sovereign power was an act of original alienation or forfeiture on the part of the people, Bartolus and Marsiglio held that the body of citizens retained the power of legislation ultimately in their own hands; public authority was only assigned by temporary delegation. Thus a difference arose between the original Aristotelian notion of state sovereignty and that of the Italian defenders of republican *libertas*, which never acquired the supremacy which was ascribed to the former. Marsiglio, for that matter, chose the term *civitas* as his translation of Aristotle's *polis*; Moerbeke's translation rendered Aristotle's 'political' as 'civil' (cf. Gewirth 1956: lxvii, lxxx).[7]

Nevertheless – or perhaps because it permitted such ambiguities to persist – the grammar of Aristotelian political theory long reigned supreme as the highest order of knowledge and tended in all respects to absorb and surpass the study of Roman jurisprudence. Its century-long domination left little room for the development of a science of 'civil society' outside of the Aristotelian framework, and the cycle of political bureaucratization and progressive 'monarchization' of the city-states left too little time for the development of an independent economic science in the modern sense of this term. Although Bartolus's theory of private property was reproduced as a matter of course through the ages, and the *quattrocento* even saw the first inklings of political economy in the writings of humanists such as Bruni, Poggio, Palmieri, and Alberti, there remained a large chronological gap between Bartolus and Locke which was filled by Aristotelianism, so that all relevant controversies tended to be conducted in the hospitable vocabulary of political theory. Although the idea of the natural origins of property and its priority as a principle of social organization was gradually perfected, the idea of a sphere of civil society which was autonomous from the political commonwealth only emerged in vague outline in the writings of Locke. Locke's notions about labour, property, and civil society, however, offered only the first premonition of what would be established a century afterwards as a veritable science of political economy in the writings of the Physiocrats and the Scottish Enlighteners. Only in Adam Smith do we see the articulation of a scientific project which was comparable in scope and purpose with the Aristotelian one. It was only at that period, when a new and more comprehensive commercial revolution had consolidated a new type of world economy, and property had scored its first political successes against sovereignty, that the second master science veritably came of age.[8]

The lawyers of the Bolognese school had not developed a sharply delineated theory of civil as distinct from political society, despite the fact that they revived the Roman distinction between *imperium* and *dominium* and placed considerable emphasis upon the civil law. The Aristotelians, on the other hand, while advancing the same distinction, also tended to identify political and civil society, so that the sphere of property exercise was conceived as an independent though subordinate creation of the sovereign power. What Bodin called 'civil science' was a comprehensive and universal jurisprudence which was to some extent emancipated from its dependence upon Roman legal sources, and was closely inspired by the framework of the *Politics* (Franklin 1973: 107). The aim of 'civil science', Hobbes reaffirmed in his Preface to the *Philosophical Rudiments*, was 'to make a more curious search into the rights of states and duties of subjects'. Civil society, the object of this encompassing civil science, was thought coincident with the body politic, which in turn was identical with the commonwealth more generally (Hobbes 1841: 69; Frisby and Sayer 1986: 17; Viroli 1992a: 475–6). For Montesquieu, the distinction between the *état politique* and the *état civil* still referred to two aspects of the political organization of the state (Montesquieu 1969: 54–6; Riedel 1975). And for De Bonald, to cite a 'late' example, civil society was still coterminous with 'superstructural' politico-religious society: 'Civil society is the reunion of intellectual or religious society and political society' (cit. Therborn 1976: 156).

POWER FOLLOWS PROPERTY

If it is true that philosophers such as Bodin, Hobbes, and Montesquieu proceeded upon the Aristotelian master science of political theory, Scottish and French political economy, when it came of age in the writings of Hume, Millar, Smith, Turgot, and Quesnay, connected back to the theoretical preferences of Lockean liberalism. The vocabulary switch from Hobbes to Locke was comparable, in broad outline, with that which separated Montesquieu from Smith and other Scotsmen, and was re-enacted in Marx's critique of Hegel. That is to say that the materialist or productionist bias of Marxism, and its emphasis upon the infrastructural character of relations of production and property, was a direct heritage of that proud seedling of 'bourgeois' social theory, the Scottish Enlightenment, although it also extended backwards to the Lockean tradition of natural law, of which the Scottish utilitarians were both the critics and the continuators. For Adam Smith, civil society was something quite other than the Hobbesian commonwealth or the Aristotelian *politeia*: it was the groundwork of 'subsistence' or 'production' upon which the political realm itself rested and by which it was economically maintained. Not the universal 'quest for power after power', the grounding human urge postulated by Hobbes, but the equally foundational tendency 'to truck, barter, and exchange one thing for another' now occupied pride of motivational place. Political economy, as the science of subsistence, was thus not simply proclaimed independent from politics but tended to replace it as a *scientia scientiarum* which concentrated the entire field of human studies (Hont and Ignatieff 1983).

The new master science, while introducing new foundational concepts such as subsistence, production, labour, and property, added the crucial axiom that 'power follows property' – as first stated in Sir John Dalrymple's *Essay towards a General History of Feudal Property in Britain* of 1757 and more or less implied in Lord Kames' *Historical Law Tracts* of the following year (Wilsher 1983; Rendall 1978: 140–1; Lehmann 1971: 203; Cropsey 1957: 56–64; 1975); it clearly resonated in the political theories of both Blackstone and Bentham (cf. Long 1979). Although it is customary to identify Adam Smith's lectures of the mid-1750s as the original source (Meek 1976: 99; 1967), a better case might be made in favour of Francis Hutcheson, Smith's teacher, whose *System of Moral Philosophy* (1755) already contained the maxim

> That property, and that chiefly in lands, is the natural foundation upon which power must rest, though it give not any just right to power. . . . When power wants this foundation, the state must always be restless, fluctuating, and full of sedition, until either the power draws property to itself, or property obtains power.
>
> (cit. Rendall 1978: 92)

This might also be read as a handsome abbreviation of Harrington's much older economic interpretation of the English Civil War, which emphasized the idea of a necessary correspondence of the form of government with the distribution of property (Macpherson 1962: 160ff.). Moreover, when Adam Smith claimed that civil government was instituted for the security of property ('Till there be property there can be no government, the very end of which is to secure wealth, and to defend the rich from the poor'), this was in fact only a more realistic rehearsal of Locke's view, who had set the acquisition of property both chronologically and normatively prior to the institution of civil government.

But if Dalrymple thought in 1757 that 'there is no maxim in politicks more generally true, than that power follows property', it is simultaneously evident that no maxim in the materialist canon was more taken for granted than this one. Surprisingly, the logical precedence or unique causal weight of subsistence, production, or property was never really argued for – not counting down-to-earth assertions modelled after Mandeville, who opined that 'the Cement of civil Society' is simply that 'every Body is obliged to eat and drink' (Mandeville 1970: 350). But then, of course, there existed only a negligible difference between this statement and a much more famous but equally specious derivation of materialism: that men should first be in a position to live in order to be able to make history (Marx and Engels 1974: 48).

Adam Smith, Adam Ferguson, and John Millar, all of them ardent admirers of Montesquieu, stood their master on his head, just as Feuerbach and Marx would at a later date admiringly overturn Hegel. Extending Montesquieu's method of analytical historiography, they simultaneously stepped out of the long and venerable tradition of which Montesquieu was such a great representative; rejecting his 'superstructural' interest in the historiography of forms of government, they were among the first to attempt a general history of 'modes of production'. The destruction of the Legislator Myth, i.e. the myth of the primacy of the state or politics to which Montesquieu still paid his respects, thus constituted 'perhaps the most original and daring *coup* of the social science of the Scottish Enlightenment' (Forbes 1966: xxiv).[9] Ronald Meek notes that there is no indication in *The Spirit of Laws* that Montesquieu regarded the mode of subsistence

> as being in any sense the key factor in the total situation. . . . There is indeed a great deal about the mode of subsistence in Book XVIII; but there is very little about the mode of subsistence – and a great deal about climate, government, etc. – in the other thirty books.
>
> (Meek 1976: 34; cf. Aron 1965: 62)

John Millar's summary of Adam Smith's course on Moral Philosophy is cited here because, even while invoking Montesquieu, he caught the very spirit of what Montesquieu *failed* to do, and what was undertaken with so much vigour and ingenuity by Smith and Millar themselves:

> Upon this subject (Smith) followed the plan that seems to be suggested by Montesquieu; endeavouring to trace the gradual progress of jurisprudence, both public and private, from the rudest to the most refined ages, and to point out the effects of those *arts* which contribute to *subsistence*, and to the accumulation of *property*, in producing *correspondent improvements or alterations in law and government*.
>
> (cit. Meek 1976: 109; cf. Meek 1967: 36–7)

And the following are some notes which Millar (or one of his students) jotted down when lecturing (or being lectured) on Government:

> The first object of mankind is to produce subsistence. To obtain the necessaries, the comforts, the conveniences of life. Their next aim is to defend their persons and their acquisitions against the attacks of one another. . . . Property is at the same time the principal source of authority, so that the opulence of a people, not only makes them stand in need of much regulation, but enables them to establish it. By tracing the progress of wealth we may thus expect to discover the progress of Government.
>
> (cit. Meek 1976: 165–6)[10]

The primordial significance of the mode of subsistence also found expression in the 'four-stages theory' which was common conviction to the Scottish philosophers: the idea that society naturally or normally progressed through four consecutive stages, each corresponding to a different mode of subsistence, which were defined as hunting, pasturage, agriculture, and commerce. Several main ideas of this stadial theory were anticipated in the early writings of Turgot, and by the end of the 1750s they had been diffused to the works of Quesnay, Helvétius, and Goguet. Dalrymple's four-stages theory was mainly oriented towards the problem of property; the same applied to Millar, for whom the stadial theory constituted the 'guiding principle throughout' (Meek 1976: 161ff.). Also and more famously for Smith, history was to be narrated as a succession of four materialist tableaux, which were qualitatively distinct 'in that they featured different types of productive activity, different modes of earning subsistence, and different forms and arrangements of property' (Skinner 1970: 31).[11] Smith's main classificatory criterion in distinguishing these types of social structure was the form taken by the institution of ownership; the advent of property in a permanent form gave rise not only to patterns of authority and subordination but also to government properly so called. Although in Ferguson's *Essay on the History of Civil Society* (1767) we look in vain for the Smithian periodization – which was otherwise generally adopted by the school – his major historical division was between a state of society in which private property was unknown and one in which it was introduced (Ferguson 1966: 81ff., 133–4). The Scottish philosophers also closely approached the sophisticated Marxian position that the economy asserted itself as the *ultimate* rather than the *sole* determining factor (Skinner 1975: 175).

But this causal proposition, like the materialist ground rule itself, rested upon an unexamined core axiom which was upheld by a logical sleight of hand. The identification of the mode of subsistence as the key factor was not supplemented by clear definitions of its logical extent. As in the case of production, labour, and property, continual shifts were operated between a broad, anthropological definition and a narrower or sectoral one; it was never clear whether subsistence, production, or labour were categories of *historical* origin, whether they expressed a *logical*, *sociological* or *ethical* primacy, a household truth, or all of these things at one and the same time. This was reflected in the persistent ambiguity of the term 'civil society' which, as in Robertson, coincided with the 'state of society' in general, whereas Smith, Ferguson, and Millar designated it as the infrastructure of economic or market relationships – the modern sense in which it found its way towards Hegel, von Stein, and Marx. As suggested, these vacillations were precipitated as much by the difficulties of conceptualizing the novel and dominating realities of the market and the nascent capitalist division of labour, as by the conquistadorial purposes of the new master science of political economy itself – which could never decide whether it was about the Part or about the Whole. Political economy was thus born with a central dialectical ambiguity.

THE MARXIAN REVERSAL

There is no particular exaggeration in saying that the relationship between property and power constitutes the holiest of historical materialism's holy places of interpretation; it opens the heartland of its promises, pretentions, and most obstinate contradictions. Classical Marxism, to put it briefly, postulated the ontological correlation of property and power on at least three distinct levels of explanation. First, it emphasized the power differential which inhered in modern concentrated private property, i.e. its exploitative class nature. Second, it posited relationships of production and property as foundationally prior to political and ideological relationships, even if this priority only persisted in the 'last instance', working through a complicated framework of reciprocal causalities. And third, it interpreted the split between civil society and the state in terms of an objective historical contradiction which would be superseded in a future state of identity, and thus abolish both the realm of production and the realm of state power as alienated and isolated domains.[12] In this final section, I will successively examine each of these postulates from the perspective of intellectual rivalry which informs this chapter as a whole.

The axiom that property equalled power over people was immediately borrowed from the early utopian socialists who, being for the most part Smithians, had radicalized their master's suggestion that private property, especially capital stock, conferred upon its owner a specific 'power of buying', or more precisely, a power to dispose of labour and the products of its work. When Marx first took up Adam Smith in his *Economic-Philosophical Manuscripts* of 1844, he had no difficulty in introducing property, which after all was the product of alienated labour, as essentially relational (a *gesellschaftliches Produktionsverhältnis*) and power infused, since alienated labour not only severed the relationship between man and (the product of) his own life-activity, but also constituted a relationship of domination and subjection which had estranged man from man. This analysis was applied not only to 'vertical' appropriation under mature capitalism as subsequently examined in *Capital*, but also to the 'horizontal' division of labour and exchange which was inherent in the germinal stage of simple commodity production, which still constituted Smith's main preoccupation.[13] This is clear from Marx's *Excerpts from James Mill*, which date from the same period as the *Manuscripts*, but it is equally valid for the famous treatment of the fetishism of commodities in *Capital*.

If John Locke therefore still upheld the dual axiom of the asocial, 'powerless' nature of appropriation and the concomitant 'propertyless' character of public power, Karl Marx proceeded to undermine the liberal dichotomy on both counts, and continued upon the road of fusion between the property and power vocabularies which was initiated by the utopian radicalizers of Enlightenment political economy. Nevertheless, a crucial ontological distinction between politics and economics was retained, as well as an all-important sequential order of constitution and causality. Here as well Marx began by retracing Smith, who had drawn the distinction against Hobbes in the following manner:

> Wealth, as Mr Hobbes says, is power. But the person who either acquires, or succeeds to a great fortune, does not necessarily acquire or succeed to any political power. . . . The power which that possession immediately and directly conveys to him, is the power of purchasing; a certain command over all the labour, or over all the produce of labour, which is then in the market.
>
> (Smith 1976: 48)

In Marx's work, however, the institutional distinction between these two types of command (economic and 'extra-economic') was much more clearly conceived as a provisional stopping-place in an ongoing process of historical fission and fusion. In the *Manuscripts*, as in the earlier critiques of Hegel, feudalism was characterized as a stage of social development in which political and proprietorial domination were still blended, one aspect of the gradual autonomization of state and civil society *vis-à-vis* one another being the progressive depoliticization and depersonalization of property relations (Marx 1981: 319).

It must be noted that Hegel had already expounded this dualism of state and civil society, not simply as a secular process of historical fission, but simultaneously as the unfolding of a logical contradiction which would of necessity be superseded in a higher order of fusion. The split between the sphere of the particular (civil society) and the sphere of the universal (the state) was interpreted as a dual articulation of *Geist* which, in doubly incarnating itself institutionally, also remained divided against itself. One of the composite terms of this *Entzweiung des Geistes* was celebrated as the locus where the contradiction would ultimately be resolved. The state, in fact, embodied the highest form of objectivation of mind, 'the divine idea as it existed on earth', and hence expressed the general will as a matter of definition. It constituted an 'ethical whole' in which the individual could realize his own freedom as part of the community, effecting a reconciliation between the subjective will and the dictates of universal reason. Hence the distinction which Hegel drew between civil society and the state served the more clearly to focus the state as 'the actuality of the ethical Idea' (Kolakowski 1981: 71–3; Colletti 1973).

As Avineri has shown, Hegel's description of civil society bespoke an early acquaintance with Steuart and Smith, and closely approached the classical economists' model of the free market. Unlike the economists, however, who posited the causal primacy of the newly discovered realm of production and exchange, Hegel remained heir to the Aristotelian tradition. Civil society presupposed and depended upon the 'reasonable' state; as the clash of inimical and ego-centred social forces, its universality was only apparent and had to be transcended by the true universality of political *Geist*. The primacy of the political thus asserted was pertinently dialectical: the state was simultaneously whole and part, and remained present in the other parts as their ultimate end, in the form of a potential self-consciousness that was coming-to-be (Avineri 1972: 181).

At this point Marx, while retaining this historical dialectic of fission and fusion, effected the materialist reversal:

> the family and civil society make *themselves* into the state. They are the *driving force*. According to Hegel, however, they are *produced* by the real Idea; it is not the course of their own life that joins them together to comprise the state, but the life of the Idea which has distinguished them from itself.
>
> (Marx 1981: 63)

In a lesser-known passage of *The German Ideology*, the reversal was also formulated in the course of a (once again quite Smithian) polemic against political philosophers such as Hobbes, who construed power as the basis of all rights:

> The material life of individuals . . . their mode of production and form of intercourse, which mutually determine each other – this is the real basis of the State and remains so at all the stages at which division of labour and private property are still necessary. . . . These actual relations are in no way created by the State power; on the contrary they are the power creating it.
>
> (Marx and Engels 1974: 106)

In this fashion, historical materialism effected a switch of constitutive priorities which ran parallel to previous Scottish criticisms of the Legislator Myth, in according primacy to the sphere of civil society and property, and in drawing a line between a productive base and a superstructure of allegedly non-productive statal and ideological relations. Standing Hegel on his head, Marx redirected his thought from political theory to political economy, and began to argue 'from civil society to the state'. This materialist inversion of predicate and subject was directed both against Hegelian idealism itself and against the idealism of young Hegelians such as Bruno Bauer, who shared their master's providential notion of the ethical state; in subsequent polemics, Marx would equally wield it against the etatism of Rodbertus and Lassalle and the anarchism of Proudhon and Bakunin.

Although designated as the 'true source and theatre of all history', the concept of civil society remained structurally ambiguous, sharing this elusiveness with close cognates such as production, labour, and property. 'Civil society' appeared to capture an original *movens* which, while remaining itself, simultaneously articulated itself in secondary or superstructural manifestations which were nevertheless constitutive of its self-development. The shifting imagery of part and whole and the dialectics of constitution are both sufficiently captured in the following passage:

> Civil society embraces the whole material intercourse of individuals within a definite stage of the development of productive forces. It embraces the whole commercial and industrial life of a given stage and, insofar, transcends the State and the nation, though, on the other hand again, *it must assert itself* in *its* foreign relations as nationality, and inwardly *must organize itself* as State. The word 'civil society' emerged in the eighteenth century, when property relationships had already extricated themselves from the ancient and medieval communal society. Civil society *as such* only develops with the bourgeoisie; the social organisation evolving directly out of production and commerce, which *in all ages* forms the basis of the State and of the rest of the idealististic superstructure, has, however, always been designated by the same name.
>
> (Ibid.: 57; all italics mine)

This intricate structure continually reappeared in the mature Marx's statements on the logic of production, most notoriously perhaps in that eternal dialectical puzzle, the *Einleitung* to the *Grundrisse*, where production was described as articulating itself in distribution, exchange, and consumption, which were simultaneously identical to and separate from it, while 'production' still remained the true antecedent and the underlying motive force (Marx 1973: 83ff.). By taking over the chameleon role of the state in Hegelian idealism, the productionist reversal did not touch the heart of the dialectic itself. Production, in the Marxist sense, ambiguously referred both to the whole and the part, quite like the Hegelian state which, as the part of parts, simultaneously included the whole as the sum of its own articulations. While Hegel thus formally perfected the Aristotelian tradition of political ontology by projecting its long-standing imperialist claims into the structural ambiguities of the dialectic, the Marxian dialectic of production quite similarly formalized and perfected the competing imperialism of Smithian political economy.

Political economy's ambiguous delineation of its own subject matter was therefore intimately correlated with its aspiration to be self-sufficient and self-grounding, to reach beyond the mere study of the 'ordinary business of life' (Marshall's definition of economics) in order to gain the venerated title of *mater scientiarum* or new fountainhead of all the sciences of man. Smith's *Wealth of Nations* already reached out across the entire spectrum of the then-known human sciences; Marx's *Capital* was likewise designed to lay a sufficient foundation from which the other human sciences could be reconstructed in

71

integral fashion. This grandiose project was boldly announced in *The German Ideology*, where historical materialism was assigned the formidable task of

> expounding the real process of production . . . as the real basis of all history, and to show it in its action as State, to explain all the different theoretical products and forms of consciousness, religion, philosophy, ethics, etc. etc., and trace their origin and growth from that basis; by which means of course the whole thing can be depicted in its totality (and therefore, too, the reciprocal action of these various sides on one another.
>
> (Ibid.: 58)

Gouldner has in like manner accentuated the generative (but oppositional) dialectic of part and whole in Hegelian cultural and Marxian economic holism. Every grand theory, he has fruitfully suggested,

> is involved in a precarious dialectic between (1) its effort to provide a comprehensive picture of the totality and (2) its wish to accent only a limited part of the totality that it takes to be a precarious, cognitively underprivileged bit of reality – i.e. in danger of being forgotten, neglected, or underestimated.
>
> (1985: 284)

As opposite 'doctrines of recovery', both Hegelianism and Marxism foster a permanent elision between sector and totality. However, whereas for Hegel the whole is integrated by the common spirit, Marxist materialism asserts the unity of the world through the controlling substance of the economy; the topography of the Hegelian structure is retained even while inverting it. Viewed more reflexively and critically, however, the factor of unification which is the subject of such recoveries is always theoretically defined, by scholars who are interested in justifying their originality and to demarcate their own contributions from others, which easily induces them to overemphasize the ontological weight of the part with which they associate themselves (ibid.: 289–90). Hence Goethe's dictum, 'What spirit of the time you call, is but the scholar's spirit after all', reflects as critically upon the Marxian privileging of the economy as it does upon the Hegelian privileging of *Geist*.[14]

While Gouldner therefore recognizes that intellectuals may perform as 'functionaries of the totality' in the above sense, his view of the dialectic of recovery and holism loses some of its critical edge when he judges that, ideally, such tendencies must balance each other out, and that rational social theory requires the maintenance of a delicate balance between holism and recovery (1985: 293). Even though he recognizes limits to the rationality of each, Gouldner remains guardedly sympathetic to holistic analysis, and hence fails to establish a sufficiently critical link between such part–whole oscillations and the knowledge politics which is made to act through them. This means that he still undervalues the risk of intellectual spokespersonship, both on the level of cognitive recovery and on that of constitutive holism itself. It prevents him from fully acknowledging that any recovery of cognitively precarious and underprivileged *factors* to some extent euphemizes the ambition of intellectuals to recover *themselves* as privileged *actors*, and that all attempts to reconstitute the whole from a causally privileged part channel an implicit drive for universalism and exclusivity of representation. Grand theories such as Hegelianism and Marxism are typically patterned by such dialectical leaps from part to whole; indeed, their much-contested 'grandiosity' is precisely defined by this dialectic's success in 'aggrandizing' the theorist by subtly transforming him into a spokesperson for the totality.

From this perspective, both the Aristotelian and Smithian master sciences clearly manifested a pervasive but cognitively sublimated imperial drive. Starting from opposite ends (politics or production), they remained strategically ambiguous about the logical expanse of their respective objects/projects, and continually but effectively hesitated between the modest study of 'their' part and the intellectual annexation of the whole. The problem of parts and wholes was therefore virulently present from the very moment of their inception. In the Aristotelian view, politics tended to be conceived in the limitless sense of 'knowledgeable organization' or 'immaterial activity', providing a close synonym and model for what sociologists would subsequently call 'interaction'. The Lockean and Smithian tradition advanced the equally unbounded idea of 'labour' as anthropogenesis, as a vehicle of the fulfilment of the capacities of (individual or social) man, and as a uniquely productive form of social activity. Together, but from opposite points of departure and driven by rivalling ambitions, they reaffirmed the grand conceptual divide between the domain of interaction, which included relationships between subjects and subjects, and the domain of production, which constituted relationships between subjects and objects, which became such a basic matrix of dispute in the following centuries, and remains so far into our own.

3

MARXISM VS. ANARCHISM

My power am I myself, and through it am I my property.

Max Stirner

RIVALLING REVOLUTIONARIES

In the preceding chapters, I have prepared my ground by offering a synopsis of the historical emergence and consolidation – through a secular process of severance and polarization – of the paired ontological conceptions of property and sovereignty and the master sciences which they animate. I now proceed to analyse their survival, and that of the dialectic of reduction to which they have jointly given rise, in some major debates and traditions in modern social and political thought. For this purpose, the survey chart of modern social and political theory might be redrawn by crossing two dichotomies. The first one distinguishes the tradition of power theory from that of property theory (or the master narrative of politics and domination from that of production and exploitation), while a second, transversal one marks off empirical and explanatory social 'science' from normatively committed political 'ideology'. The resulting fourfold classification repartitions the field of the grand narratives as given in Table 2.

Table 2 The field of the grand narratives

	Fact-oriented science	*Value-oriented ideology*
Property theory	Classical jurisprudence	Utopian socialism
Economic philosophy	and political economy	Marxism
Power theory	Comtean positivism	Anarchism
Political philosopy	Elite theory	Fascism
	Weberian sociology	

74

This tabulation has the virtue of de-emphasizing the traditional binary opposition between academically detached and empirically grounded social science vs. value-committed and 'volitional' types of thought, which is still upheld as a matter of principle by a great many practitioners of both. Instead, it brings out the bipolar continuity of intellectual inheritance and of inherited rivalry through power and property lineages which run at right angles to the former division. It helps to refocus our attention towards transversal contradictions which internally divide schools of social science and currents of political ideology, and emphasizes important affinities and continuities between apparent rivals. The previous chapters have already provisionally brushed in the top boxes of the table; the chapters that follow are designed to fill in its lower boxes in a more detailed fashion.[1]

First, I will critically examine some motives and modules of rivalry in Marxism and anarchism, whose ideological antagonism has been interpreted as a case of paradigmatic significance by many students of the socio-logic of intellectual competition. The dispute between Marx and Bakunin, more especially, has become an attractive analytical resort not least because it has offered an almost perfect historical example of the 'logic of mutual objectivation', which induces ideological rivals to lay bare one another's weaknesses, while being unable to rise to a comprehensive view of the structural configuration which envelops them, and which forces them to repeat terms and convictions which are as much *products* as they are *causes* of their mutual antagonism. Since Mannheim's early lecture on cultural competition, which touched upon the Marx–Bakunin dispute only in passing (Mannheim 1952), this paradigm case has not ceased to intrigue modern social theorists of knowledge. Mannheim's intuition has in recent times been followed up by Bourdieu and Sloterdijk, and has received broader articulation in works by Thomas and Gouldner (Bourdieu 1993b: 59; Sloterdijk 1983: 189ff.; Thomas 1980; Gouldner 1985).[2]

The shared moral of their stories is that the existential fact of rivalry was much more causally decisive for the inner structure of concepts, definitions, and trains of argument on either side than has traditionally been recognized. One overall effect of this competitional configuration has been to produce artificial differences and to minimize similarity between opponents – which of course represents the inveterate temptation of all political (and knowledge–political) discourse. Marxism and anarchism, indeed, have long insisted upon their mutual incompatibility as theories and political practices, a dispute which has centred in considerable measure upon the different priority which was assigned to property or power as generative master concepts, and the different order of abolition (state first, then capital, or the other way around?) which summed up their political projects. It will be argued, however, that these two 'categories of origin' were also vehicles for the expression of doctrinaire certainty claims and the monopolization of intellectual territory, and that their elusive performance as ontological 'last instances' was accountable to a large extent to the structure of intellectual and political competition in which they were encased.

For a century or more, Marxists have indeed been tempted to defame and deride anarchists, while the latter have been quick to return the compliment. Marxists have slighted anarchists as irresponsible Bohemians, petit-bourgeois idealists, preachers of disorder, or traitors to the Revolution, while anarchists have not hesitated to denounce Marxists as mundane materialists, lovers of authority, self-serving intellectuals, or similarly, as traitors to the Revolution. Since the goddess of Revolution herself has not deigned to conclude the dispute – although, in the course of a long revolutionary century and a half, she has extended more worldly favours to the followers of Marx than to those of Bakunin – the war of words has been prolonged well into the 1970s and 1980s, even though the spectre of another Kronstadt or another Barcelona has turned increasingly dim. The recent bankruptcy of state communism and the universal *Dämmerung* of the grand narratives has of course boded decline for both Marxism and anarchism and mitigated their sibling rivalries, although anarchism, easily the least contaminated of the nineteenth-century ideologies, has been able to survive better than its traditional rival in new political habitats such as feminism and ecologism. But, as we shall illustrate later on, feminist and, more recently, Green political theory have likewise indulged in ritualized debates in which the rivalling heritages of Marxism and libertarian socialism, and their originary vocabularies of property and power, were critically balanced against each other.

One shared article of faith which has long been common currency to both parties, predisposing them towards mutual hostility, was that Marxism and anarchism, as theoretical and practical doctrines, constituted 'truly basic alternatives' (Wieck 1975: 33). As *Golos Truda*, organ of the Union for Anarchist Propaganda, predicted right before the *moment suprême* of October 1917, the final stage of the revolution would entail a contest 'between two principles which have been battling for pre-eminence for a long time: the Marxist principle and the Anarchist principle' (Voline 1974: 116). After the fact, Voline's *The Unknown Revolution*, that classic of *engagé* historiography, canonized it in terms of an inevitable struggle between two 'Opposing Conceptions of the Social Revolution', one of which had succumbed to the other after a heroic clash of principle.[3] Such notions still find echoes today, as for example in a distanced and reflective work such as Paul Thomas's *Karl Marx and the Anarchists*, which is guardedly sympathetic towards the Marxian position:

> Marx's contemptuous dismissal of Bakunin was matched only by Bakunin's contemptuous dismissal of Marxism. The dispute between the two in the First International has its place not only in the history of socialism but also in the history of invective, a history that would not be stretched unduly if it also included Marx's earlier disputations with Max Stirner, in *The German Ideology*, and with Pierre-Joseph Proudhon, which culminated in *The Poverty of Philosophy*. The personal antagonism and pronounced tactical differences separating

Marx from Bakunin were symptomatic of a far more fundamental division between Marxism and anarchism (which were rival ideologies, and were perceived as such by their bearers), a division which later historical events have done nothing to bridge.

(Thomas 1980: 14)

Although the distinction is in a sense incomplete, since both schools wish to liquidate the state in its present form, the area of agreement 'is in the nature of a penumbra, an overlap . . . and not a convergence' (ibid.: 11).

If, however, one moves to a position equidistant from both contenders and takes their self-perceptions as seriously as they take one another's, the balance of difference and similarity is subtly redrawn. From a more symmetrical perspective, Marxism and anarchism seemed implicated in a conspiracy of silence which *played down* convergences, while simultaneously distinction and otherness were accentuated with all the tools of persuasive rhetoric. At the very least, ideologists from both camps professed a quite similar urge to *be different* from one another, so that their major concepts and propositions did not simply pronounce upon the order of things, but also bore the stigmata of mutual envy and competition. The stakes in this demarcation game were always set higher than the mere assertion of truth and its triumph over error. While the antagonists themselves routinely derived their mutual enmity from pre-existing doctrinal differences, much of their doctrinal opposition actually sprang from knowledge-political attempts to legitimize previous competitive drives – bids for power and prestige within the institutional settings of Internationals, revolutions, or civil wars. Both Marxists and anarchists, to be sure, were *intellectuals* who competed for hegemony in the same theoretical and organizational fields – intellectuals, moreover, who were easily given to subsume their own interests under larger and seemingly weightier causes than that of their own advancement in the world. Their theories and certainty claims partly served to distinguish them from their enemies, to draw lines of solidarity, to separate ins from outs and friends from foes according to ancient warlike ritual.

This is also how Alvin Gouldner described the long sequence of conflicts which Marx conducted with rival intellectuals such as Weitling, Gottschalk, and Schapper, of which the last and most bitter was fought with Bakunin and his adepts for intellectual and political control of the First International. All of these battles, Gouldner implied, exhibited both the intellectual's love for sound theory and his hatred of 'ideology' *and* his will to gain organizational power and to purge rivals from key positions. The quest for power, therefore, was intimately conjoined with the urge to implement the 'right' ideas. Like many others, the conflict between Marx and Bakunin

was furthered partly by their doctrinal differences, but, in turn, these are also partly due to their conflict. . . . What they take to be their

77

principles, doctrines, ideologies, or theories are, in some part, ante-
rior convictions that genuinely generate the contention; but in some
part they are also *post bellum* rationalizations of an involvement fueled
by other forces.

(Gouldner 1985: 145–6; 1980: 381)

This was also evident in the earlier disputes which ranged Marx against
Stirner and Proudhon, although from the 1860s on the stakes were raised
considerably by the multiplication of institutional settings in which the battle
was fought and the prodigious growth of the supporting political armies.
Whereas the debates with Stirner and Proudhon still exemplified the Marxian
and anarchist will to power in embryonic and personalized form, the conflict
with the Proudhonists was already largely institutional in character, and was
acted out at the Geneva and Lausanne congresses of the First International.
The advent of Bakuninism, finally, brought the battle to a pitch, and finally
split the International from top to bottom (cf. Thomas 1980: 249ff.).

ANARCHIST INVERSIONS

A major *theoretical* issue dividing Marxism and anarchism, which concentrated
a number of derivative disputes and opened up many others, of course
concerned the relative status of power or property as ontological primitives,
residing spider-like at the centre of their respective theoretical webs. Property
and power not only functioned as conceptual axes around which Marxism and
anarchism organized their different sequences of causal explanation, but also
as *Fahnenwörter* or banner concepts around which they deployed their mutual
rivalry, i.e. their attempts to outshine and reduce one another on the ideological and political battlefield. Accordingly, Marxist theory consistently defined
power as a derivative function of property, whereas anarchist theory preferred
to understand property as a special instance of power. Enter once again the
intractable dilemma of reduction: was property (onto)logically and empirically prior to power, or did power precede property? Which was governing
and which was governed?

   In the previous chapter, we have already emphasized the crucially constitutive function of the property concept in the Marxian conceptual system, as a
focus for condensing the entire question of bourgeois relations of production
and class division. The property question, the authors of the *Communist
Manifesto* notoriously proclaimed, constituted 'the pivotal question of the
movement', while communist theory could be fairly summarized in the single
phrase: 'abolition of private property' (Marx and Engels 1848: 493, 475). It
was always the direct relationship of the owners of the conditions of production, Marx insisted, 'which revealed the innermost secret, the hidden basis of
the entire social structure, and with it the political form of the relation of

sovereignty and dependence, in short, the corresponding specific form of the state' (Marx 1894: 799–800). As already noted, however, it would be inaccurate to imply that, for Marx and Engels, power was *reducible* to property in any linear or short-cut fashion. As early as the 1844 *Economic-Philosophical Manuscripts*, 'power over people' or command over alien labour formed an integral constituent of Marx's conception of capitalist private property, so that property and power were analytically fused at the point of production itself. Moreover, the determination between economic and political instances was never thought of as unidirectional and simple: economic contradictions were invariably viewed as overdetermined by political and ideological ones, so that, as Althusser once excusingly phrased it, 'the lonely hour of the last instance' would never arrive (1976: 113). Property was hence considered constitutive of power both directly and indirectly, in an intricate double play of formal separation and practical collation.

In an early critique of Karl Heinzen, for example, Marx did not hesitate to incorporate both under the more general heading of force or *Gewalt* (1847: 377). This brief polemical essay is of more than passing interest, because it provides early evidence of the awkwardness of the primacy puzzle, and anticipates the contours of a polemic that would resurface in Marx's and Engels' subsequent strictures against anarchists such as Proudhon and Bakunin and state socialists such as Dühring, Lassalle, and Rodbertus. A year before this exchange, Heinzen had penned a spirited critique of both anti-statist and anti-capitalist currents in communist thought, in which he wedded a prescient critique of despotic tendencies in projects to 'supersede' both property and the state to a welfarist optimism that a redistributing *Rechtsstaat* would be able to mitigate class inequality (Heinzen 1846). The democratic state, in his view, was a moral institution that embodied the collective conscience and represented the pinnacle of rational human association; its communist dissolution would only entail that the existing 'property and moral police' would be replaced by a 'work police'. Communists misdirected their energies, Heinzen implied, in so far as they picked *Gewalt* as the lesser evil and *Geld* as the primary one. The bankruptcy of Money would not in itself restrain Force, whereas the bankruptcy of Force would simultaneously and necessarily harness the power of Money. There could be no doubt that the struggle against Force was more imperative than the struggle against Money, and that Money, in so far as it was not geared towards abuse, could be mustered as an ally against Force (1846: 87–8).

Joining the fiery exchange which developed between Heinzen and Engels in the *Deutsche-Brüsseler Zeitung* in the fall of 1847,[4] Marx lost no time in censuring his opponent for maintaining that force dominated property and that 'the injustice in the relations of property were only perpetuated by force'. Although he conceded that property was also a species of force, an assertion like Heinzen's eternalized what was only a transient relationship of the German bourgeoisie, which had not yet constituted itself *politically* as a class, to the German state power. In fully mature bourgeois conditions the order of priority would be different:

> The 'injustice in the relations of property' which results from the modern division of labour, the modern forms of exchange, competition, concentration, etc. is in no way produced by the political domination of the bourgeois class, *but in reverse*, the political domination of the bourgeois class issues from these modern relations of production, which are proclaimed necessary and eternal laws by the bourgeois economists.
>
> (Marx 1847: 337; emphasis added)

In Marx's view, it was sheer tautology for Heinzen to assert that *Geld* and *Gewalt*, *Eigentum* and *Herrschaft*, *Gelderwerb* and *Gewalterwerb* were dissimilar things. In locating their essential difference, Heinzen failed to see the simultaneous unity, the fact that property could be transmuted into political power, that it could be united with political power (1847: 337–9).

While preserving this partial blending of the analytic of power and that of property, the anarchist tradition has nevertheless diametrically opposed itself to the Marxian order of social constitution. From early founders such as William Godwin through the revolutionaries of 1917 and 1936 up to the present day, it has been government, the state, sovereignty, and power rather than property or wealth which were singled out as the primary producers of moral degeneration and inequality, including inequality of an economic kind. Anarchism thus simply – if we may simplify in turn – reversed the sequence of determination. 'I came to recognize', Louise Michel said, returning from Communard exile in 1881, 'that power, of whatever kind, must work out to be a curse. That is why I avow anarchism.' 'No one should be entrusted with power', Michael Bakunin had concluded some time before, 'inasmuch as anyone invested with authority must, through the force of an immutable social law, become an oppressor and exploiter of society' (cit. Berman 1972: 37, 39). Inclusive cognates such as 'authority', 'sovereignty', and 'government' were similarly placed under a negative sign. All of them were considered equally responsible for Man's fall from Grace, although normally the state, the great enemy of liberty, spontaneity, and creative ingenuity, was singled out for special treatment:

> Every State is a *despotism*.
>
> (Stirner 1845)

> Where the State begins, individual liberty ceases, and vice versa.
> (Bakunin 1867, cit. Berman 1972)

> Human society marches forward; the State is always the brake.
> (The Worker's Federation of the District of Courtelary 1880, cit. Berman 1972)

Anarchism's conception of the state, then, was perhaps less a conception than a form of *horreur* – the word is Guérin's (1965: 17).[5]

In Bakunin we not only find expressed the view (which was shared by Marx who departed from the opposite analytical end) that political power and wealth were inseparable, but also the more significant idea that the state instead of property was the original:

> The doctrinaire philosophers, as well as the jurists and economists, always assume that property came into existence before the rise of the State, whereas it is clear that the juridical idea of property, as well as family law, could arise historically only in the State, the first inevitable act of which was the establishment of this law of property.
>
> (cit. Berman 1972: 51)

In full agreement, Proudhon emphasized the invariable tendency of society 'to constitute itself first of all as a political body; to produce externally, under the name of *magistrates*, its organs of conservation and centralization, before developing itself internally as a centre of production and consumption'. That the political order preceded the creation of the industrial order appeared to him a 'grande loi d'histoire' (Proudhon 1982, V: 379, 387, 421).[6] For the anarchists, this order of historical primacy normally also decreed an 'order of abolition' (and of subsequent 'withering away') which meticulously reversed the Marxian scenario of the abolition of property and the 'withering away of the state'. As Berkman argued, 'It follows that when government is abolished, wage slavery and capitalism must go with it, because they cannot exist without the support and protection of government' (cit. Berman 1972: 51). And right on target, the inevitable Bakunin, after censuring Marx's neglect of the 'evident retroaction of political, juridical, and religious institutions upon economic conditions', elaborated this view in the following terms:

> [Marx] says, 'Economic misery produces political slavery, the State', but he does not allow this to be turned around to say, 'Political slavery, the State, reproduces in its turn, and maintains, misery as the condition of its own existence; so that, in order to destroy misery, it is necessary to destroy the State'.
>
> (Bakunin 1972: 834)

An illuminating reversal of this charge is found in Engels who, at the height of his and his companion's struggle against the anti-authoritarian tendency in the First International, wrote to T. Cuno in the following manner:

> Bakunin has a peculiar theory of his own, a medley of Proudhonism and communism. The chief point concerning the former is that he does not regard capital, i.e. the class antagonism between capitalists

and wage workers which has arisen through social development, but the *state* as the main evil to be abolished. While the great mass of the Social-Democratic workers hold our view that state power is nothing more than the organisation which the ruling classes – landowners and capitalists – have provided for themselves in order to protect their social privileges, Bakunin maintains that it is the *state* which has created capital, that the capitalist has his capital *only by the grace of the state*. As, therefore, the state is the chief evil, it is above all the state which must be done away with and then capitalism will go to blazes of itself. We, on the contrary, say: Do away with capital, the concentration of all means of production in the hands of the few, and the state will fall of itself. The difference is an essential one: Without a previous social revolution the abolition of the state is nonsense; the abolition of capital *is* precisely the social revolution and involves a change in the whole mode of production.

(Marx *et al*. 1972: 69, 172)

In this fashion, Marx's earlier condescending comment on Proudhon ('he thinks he is doing something great by arguing from the state to society') was repeated nearly intact by Engels against Bakunin; but the charge was returned without much ceremony, since Marxists were incessantly accused by anarchists of committing precisely the opposite fallacy. Modern anarchists such as David Wieck therefore renew old commitments when they contend that 'For those who suspect that power rather than wealth may be the root of oppression, and that power may be the more comprehensive concept, anarchism offers a framework of explanation' (1975: 35; cf. 1978: 229–30).

If classical anarchists thus cast state and government as the chief sources of social coercion and oppression, their modern successors, while preserving the canonical order of priority between power and property, have characteristically sought to broaden their conceptual framework from a focus upon the political in the narrower, domanial sense towards a more widely encompassing theory of social domination and institutional hierarchy. In furthering this generalization, they have articulated a cognitive potential which was already contained in the diffusive and originary conceptions of state and government as enshrined in the classical tradition.[7] David Wieck, for example, has recently understood anarchism 'as the *generic* social and political idea that expresses negation of *all* power, sovereignty, domination, and hierarchical division, and a will to their dissolution. . . . Anarchism is therefore far more than anti-statism . . . [it] is anti-political . . . in a comprehensive sense' (1975: 30–1). And Murray Bookchin, easily the most influential among modern anarchist thinkers, has advanced a wide-ranging theory of social hierarchy which is doubly contrasted with traditional Marxist class analysis and anarchist 'state analysis', since its emergence is viewed as historically and ontologically prior to the rise of both economic and political stratification. As recently as the

1960s, Bookchin has noted, terms like hierarchy and domination were only rarely used by orthodox socialist radicals; Marxists still spoke almost exclusively in terms of class and material exploitation, while orthodox anarchists placed most of their emphasis on the state as the ubiquitous source of social coercion: 'Just as the emergence of private property became society's "original sin" in Marxian orthodoxy, so the emergence of the State became society's "original sin" in anarchist orthodoxy.' But hierarchical phenomena, i.e. the cultural, traditional, and psychological systems of obedience and command which define oppression of the young by the old, of women by men, masses by bureaucrats, body by mind, or nature by society and technology, are definitely prior to and determinative of both private property and the state, and may easily continue to exist in both stateless and classless societies (Bookchin 1982: 2–4, 162).

Bookchin's intellectual itinerary is intriguing because it replicates a classical vocabulary switch from orthodox Marxism through Trotskyite leanings towards anarchist power theory, against the novel backdrop of efforts to salvage and revise the nineteenth-century grand narratives in the light of their corrosion by the ecological problematic. Bookchin's solution has not been to generalize Marxism in the direction of an 'eco-Marxism', but to elaborate an impressive synthesis blending the anarchist thematic and ecological thinking into what he has termed 'social ecology' (cf. Marshall 1992: 602ff.). His *Post-Scarcity Anarchism* (1986 [1971]) already carried a comprehensive and fierce polemic against Marxist economism, pinning down its 'particularization of the general', i.e. its tendency to neglect the fact 'that exploitation, class rule, and happiness are the *particular* within the more *generalized* concepts of domination, hierarchy, and pleasure' (1986: 195ff., 247ff., 265). Subsequent critical essays went on to identify this confusion of the general and the particular as identifying a fundamental split within socialism as a whole. The ability of a theory based on class and property relations to explain history and the modern crisis was judged to be severely limited. The ubiquitous phenomena of hierarchy and domination could not be subsumed by class rule and economic exploitation, but were indicative of more deep-seated conflicts which long antedated the history of class struggles. The revolutionary project should therefore shed Marxian categories from the very beginning and fasten upon more fundamental ones: 'It is no longer simply capitalism we wish to demolish; it is an older and more archaic world that lives on in the present one – the domination of human by human, the rationale of hierarchy as such' (1980: 208–10, 242–3). Social ecology accordingly aimed at a radical reversal of the equation of human oppression, which would broaden its scope enormously (1990: 45–6).

In another of his pitiless polemics, this time directed against Gorz's effort to environmentalize Marxism, Bookchin rehearsed his view that the real conflict facing the left was not between a specious form of bourgeois ecology and socialist politics but between a libertarian form of social ecology and an economistic, technologically oriented form of socialism – in short, Marxism (1980: 219ff., 292). Even though Gorz, Bookchin charged, promiscuously (but clandestinely) pilfered Kropotkin, Goodman, and other anarchist theorists for his eclectic notion of 'political ecology', he eventually did not escape the corrosive alternatives of centralized power vs. decentralized coordination, market economy vs. mutualism, state vs. society, or Marxian orthodoxy vs. a consistently libertarian theory. This contest for advantage in defining the ecological crisis has also mobilized other anarchists against well-intentioned neo-Marxist efforts to supersede traditional productivism in order to account for the human subjugation of nature (cf. Lee 1980; Routley 1981; Clark 1984; 1989; Carter 1993). Eckersley's (1992) synoptic work on Green political theory, for example, is largely organized as a fine-tuned assessment of the continuing hold which is exercised upon modern ecological thought by the Marxian and anarchist heritages as distinct alternatives. Although she views anarchist political philosophy as perhaps most easily compatible with an ecological perspective, she remains critical of Bookchin's residually anthropocentric focus upon *social* hierarchy as root cause of *natural* exploitation, while also remaining sympathetic towards the eco-socialist view that a democratic state is not coercive by definition but may even facilitate ecological emancipation.[8] In this context, Eckersley rephrases a classic critique when arguing that the weblike, horizontal decision-making structure of an eco-anarchist society 'has no built-in recognition of the "self-management" interests of similar or larger social and ecological systems that lie beyond the local community' (Eckersley 1992: 151ff., 172–7).

IN THE LOOKING-GLASS

As a consequence of reasoning from opposite 'categories of origin' and reversing each other's analytic foundations, classical Marxism and classical anarchism came to mirror each other both in their strengths and their weaknesses. While Marxist political economy long maintained a fateful silence on the subject of the state and the specificity of the political – which has only recently been breached by the combined efforts of authors as different as Miliband, Poulantzas, Offe, Therborn, Laclau, Przeworski, and Elster – anarchism has traditionally produced an even more resounding silence about the causal impact of economic factors. Proudhon (ineffectually) conceded in his correspondence that 'political economy is not my strong point, and it will be most unfortunate if I have not given it up by the time I am forty'; his sprawling *Système des Contradictions économiques* duly perplexed even an accomplished dialectician such as Marx. Bakunin expressed his full accord with the economic 'part' of Marx's writings, to which he had little to add, while Kropotkin's economics virtually coincided with the somewhat naïve moral philosophy which was outlined in *The Conquest of Bread*. Conversely, as can be gleaned from a work such as Lenin's *State and Revolution*, Marxist political theory initially offered little more than sweeping statements concerning the repressive class nature of the state, romantic vistas about the dictatorship of the proletariat, and diffuse generalizations based upon the experiences of the Proudhonist-inspired Paris Commune of 1871 – an undead corpse which for more than a century has been the object of unsavoury proprietary struggles between Marxists and anarchists.[9]

Anarchists, of course, were among the first to attempt the – by now traditional – *démasqué* of Marxism as an unself-conscious fighting ideology of revolutionary intellectuals, and confidently predicted the rise of bureaucracy and statism as unintended outcomes of the politics of proletarian liberation. Simultaneously, they uncovered systematic linkages between the rise of the Stalinist Leviathan and Marxism's tendency to externalize and define away the threat of internally generated power. Marxism, anarchists repeated over and over again, was unfit to provide a solution to the problem of power, because it worshipped the same god as its authoritarian enemies, without recognizing that it did so (cf. typically Bookchin 1980: 209).[10] The anarchist tradition accordingly appeared to offer better vantage points for the analysis of political bureaucracies, of the political role of intellectuals, and of the politics of scientific knowledge – more especially, of Marxist bureaucracies, Marxist intellectuals, and the Marxist High Enlightenment self-image as the *summum bonum* of 'scientific socialism'.[11] It also suffered less from Marxism's traditional embarrassment about ethical and psychological phenomena and the study of intimate relations: even before the breakthrough of Freudo-Marxism, Stirnerian 'anarcho-psychology' substantively anticipated many insights that were subsequently developed by Nietzsche and Freud – turning Marx's vehement rejection of Stirnerian individualism into an interesting case of self-effacement and self-evasion (Carroll 1974).[12] David Wieck's claim, then, was not altogether without substance:

> It may be anarchism that implies the more complete view of *anthropos* because it does not by abstraction obscure and ignore the psychology and the now so important sociology of power. And it may be not anarchism but Marxism, with its econocentrism, its controlling dialectic of technology and property, that is simplistic and naive.
>
> (Wieck 1975: 34)

In all, anarchism appears to move more easily than Marxism in the Foucaldian realms of *pouvoir/savoir* and *pouvoir/désir*. Anarchism's negatory fascination with power, however, has engendered its own pathologies, which Marxists have in turn fastened upon with natural relish. First of all, the neglect of property, or as Marx would phrase it, of an analysis of the 'economic conditions of the revolution', led many an anarchist to overstate the power of the revolutionary will to lift the inertia of objective conditions. Second, a destructive contradiction was spotted between anarchist professions of anti-authoritarianism and equally anarchist practices of vanguardism and conspiracy.[13] On a more general level (as already expressed in Marx's indignant marginal notes to Bakunin's *Staatlichkeit und Anarchie*), anarchists attracted suspicions that their political abstentionism and their urge to flatten all relations of authority necessarily implied a return to an individualistic state of nature and the liquidation of all organized social life. Despite eloquent assertions to the contrary, such as those of Proudhon, Bakunin, Voline, and Berkman, the anarchist tradition has never been able to lay this ghost to rest.[14] Its adversaries lost no opportunity to hammer home the truism that social organization is necessarily vertical, and hence includes unequal degrees of power and a hierarchy of command.[15]

Perhaps anarchists clung so unrepentantly to their levelling critique because their anti-power antennae quickly sensed the surplus meaning lurking behind the truism about the natural ubiquity of authority in all organized social life. Indeed, not the smallest of the ironies involved in this *débat encadré* is that the decriers of the evils of property often turned into defenders of the power principle, whereas those who aimed to abolish all authority found themselves restating the functional nature of private property. Congruently with theory, the strategies of Marxist movements were strategies for the seizure of power, strategies of affirmation of politics rather than of its dissolution (Wieck 1975: 33–4; Bookchin 1986: 301). Especially when castigating Proudhonists and Bakuninists, Marx and Engels thought fit to embrace an authoritarianism of an almost military nature, since in their view the anti-capitalist war required a militant apparatus geared to the seizure of state power and the institution of a proletarian dictatorship. In letters to Terzaghi and Cuno from 1872 (the first of which contained the notorious phrase: 'I know nothing more authoritarian than a revolution') and in his brief essay *On Authority*, Engels not only truistically insisted upon the indispensability of authority to any form of collective action but, more ominously, went on to assimilate 'organization per se' to *fighting* organization and 'authority per se' to *imperious* authority.[16] This centralist inclination, of course, was considerably enhanced in the theory of the revolutionary vanguard as set down in Lenin's *What is to be Done?* In this regard, the Marxian formula of revolution was concentrated in the following maxim: in order to drive out Property, one required centrally organized Power.

Alternatively, although both Marxism and anarchism professed to abolish state and property in their present guises, anarchists never fully shared the principled suspicion that Marxists extended towards the latter. With a special eye to Proudhon, Marx routinely earmarked the anarchist position as petty-bourgeois, since it refused to dispense with property altogether and 'merely' wished to reform it. Anti-authoritarians, for their part, chose to defend a (socially obligated) form of private ownership precisely because it appeared the most effective prop of individual liberty and the most formidable bulwark against an all-encroaching state; such at least was the common sentiment of

Stirner, Godwin, and Proudhon. Stirner's radical generalization of the idea of ownership to self-ownership or individual authenticity (*Eigenheit*) not only rendered it coextensive with a widely inclusive notion of (individual) power, but also supported an aggressive egoism which remained suspicious of all forms of organized social life – his own proposed 'Union of Egoists' not excepted (Stirner 1845: 61–2, 157, 185ff.). Since state and society were never clearly distinguished, the insurrection of the 'owner' also sufficed to destroy the state, the sole purpose of which was to 'limit, tame, subordinate the individual'. If it was true that only might decided about (proprietary) right, it was the state which should presently be considered the only proprietor. Under the state's dominion there was no property of mine, and *der Einzige* had nothing: 'therefore *I* am the deadly enemy of the State' (ibid.: 252–5). Presciently, this notion of 'unique' property-as-power was turned against revolutionary communism, which was accused of a doctrinal subjection of individual liberty to the demands of a metaphysically defined collective well-being. Property, therefore, could not and should not be abolished; it had to be torn from the ghostly hands of the collective in order to become *my* property (ibid.: 227, 257–9).[17]

For William Godwin, the analysis of private property was equally crucial, even though it was subordinate to the disclosure of the evils of government (that 'brute engine' that constituted 'the only perennial cause of the vices of mankind'). In a celebrated chapter of his *Enquiry Concerning Political Justice* (1793) property was described as 'the great barrier to the institution of justice' – which, as the title of the book casually exhibited, was otherwise conceived to be primarily *political* in nature. This did not prevent Godwin from defining property more sympathetically as

> all those things which conduce, or may be conceived to conduce, to the benefit or pleasure of man, and which can no otherwise be applied to the use of one or more persons, than by a permanent or temporary exclusion of the rest of the species,

thus pioneering the idea of the subordination of exclusive property to the demands of social utility, and anticipating a distinction between (evil) property and (benign) possession which was subsequently elaborated by Proudhon and his followers (Godwin 1976: 702, 710ff.; Clark 1977: 248; Pels 1977: 492–3).

For Proudhon, finally, Property was not simply Theft, as tradition has it, but rather more abstrusely, 'the sum of its abuses'. The much-maltreated aphorism with which he answered his own celebrated question was rather concerned, as Thomas explains, to polarize exploitative and non-exploitative kinds of private property: Proudhon never really disapproved of personally acquired property that could be seen as a direct extension of the owner's being (Thomas 1980: 188). The twists and turns in the Proudhonian argument, which meandered continually from *Qu'est-ce que la propriété?* (1982 IV) to his posthumous *Théorie de la propriété* (1866) were all dialectically preserved in the following intricate statement drawn from the latter work:

> Property, if one takes it by its origin, is a vicious principle in itself and anti-social, but also destined to become, by its very generalization and the concurrence of other institutions, the pivot and the great resort of the entire social system.
>
> (Proudhon 1866: 208)

As in Godwin's case, the critique of private property effectively coincided with a critique of income unearned by labour, the *droit d'aubaine*, which included a right to receive rent, profit, and interest. Similarly to Godwin, the liquidation of such 'rights to abuse' left a socially approved individual right to use which Proudhon called *possession* and which was celebrated as 'a condition of life itself' (1982, IV: 345–6; X: 132–3). In *Système des Contradictions économiques* and *Théorie de la propriété*, Proudhon could therefore qualify his former battlecry by suggesting that it was *property*, but not *possession*, which equalled theft (cf. 1866: 15). And once again shifting his ground, he concurred with Stirner and Godwin in maintaining that property constituted the natural and necessary counterweight to political power, and that civil property rights erected a countervailing force to the reason of state. Where property was absent, where it was replaced by slave-like possession or the *fief*, there was despotism in government, and instability in the system as a whole (1866: 196).[18] Communism remained wedded to the governmental idea, following the false analogy between family and society to its logical end in dictatorship, which was 'the most exaggerated form of government'. Although it declared against property, communism actually elevated the 'proprietary prejudice' to a new level by making the community the proprietor not only of the goods, but of the persons and wills of its members (Proudhon 1982, IV: 325–7; cf. 1923 II: 223ff., 258, 293ff.). The anarchist formula, therefore, could be truthfully condensed as follows: in order to drive out power and keep it out, we should preserve some kind of private property.

THROUGH THE LOOKING-GLASS

In earlier chapters, I have begun to explain the survival of reductionary dilemmas along the property–power axis by pointing towards the persistence of deeper and more venerable rivalries between the two historic master sciences of 'Aristotelian' political philosophy and 'Smithian' political economy. Each of these master sciences consolidated its claim for independent scientific status by carving out for itself a cognitive terrain which overlapped but did not coincide with that of its rival. Both enclosures – 'politics' and 'production' – were therefore constituted in an ideological ambiance which promoted systematic ambiguities with regard to their precise extension: considered on the one hand as parts of a larger totality, as spheres, levels, or instances, they were simultaneously ready to substitute for the whole itself. We have now encountered this diffuse and dialectical quality of 'politics' and 'production' in our comparison of the two socialisms: both Marxism, as heir of the master repertoire of political economy, and anarchism, as critical inheritor of the master science of political theory, typically constructed their grounding concepts in the form of 'total parts' or 'partial wholes'. While conserving the constitutive emphases and ambiguities of classical political economy, Marxism did for property and production what anarchism, extrapolating the tradition of the *Staatswissenschaften*, did for power and politics: it changed the moral and functional prefix while preserving the inherited order of causal determination.[19]

Accordingly, there is something to be said in favour of a 'political psychology' (or perhaps a 'cognitive economics') of 'last instances', which focuses more intently upon the independent contribution of the intellectual mandatories who profess to speak in their name. Since the dialectic of last instances enables a dialectician to dissimulate his or her own presence and occupy the position of 'absent cause', the dialectician may derive both intellectual certainty and knowledge-political privileges from his or her communion with a self-created idol. Intellectual spokespersons hence typically behave in the manner of Stirner's 'involuntary egoist', 'who serves only himself and at the same time always thinks he is serving a higher being'; the egoist is 'possessed' by a sacred essence which in turn hallows its reverer, since by worshipping it the egoist becomes a saint (1982: 36–9). The constitutive ambiguities of the dialectic conveniently cover and seal off the 'metonymic fallacy' of the intellectuals. They provide a cognitive vehicle which effectively conceals their moral and material presence and their double imperial claim (directed both against rival intellectuals and commoners) to identify with, and thus exclusively diagnose and remedy, the 'root cause' or 'fundamental principle' of social evil. This applies as much to Marxian 'production' or 'economy' as to the Hegelian dialectic of 'statehood', which has set its stamp so indelibly upon anarchist conceptions of state, government, and power.

Whatever else they were, the Marxist and anarchist 'objects' of property and power were therefore also *projects* to further the ideal and material interests of particular groups of intellectual spokespersons. Featuring a similar grammar of substitution of part and whole and of externalization of (symbolically costly) private or group interests, they classify as similar modalities of intellectual politics, establishing the legitimate presence of theorists *vis-à-vis*, or within, state apparatuses or social movements, and arguing their indispensability in the face of old elites, or in the face of new elites formed by their intellectual rivals. They entailed cognitively distinct, but sociologically identical, strategies of accumulation of 'scientific capital', which derived their effectiveness as capitalizing moves precisely from successful attempts at epistemological and social demarcation, from closely related efforts to establish scientific certainty, and hence to enjoy a monopoly of force in a distinct theoretical territory.

However, beyond the possible yield of a political psychology of 'last instances' or a sociology of intellectual rivalries such as initiated by Thomas or Gouldner, we may also profit from something like a *social geography* of knowledge, since we still need to explain why it is that one group of intellectuals chose to confer causal and formative priority to the ideo-political superstructure and turned 'civil society' into a governed instance, while a different group assigned primacy to 'civil society' and the forces and relations of economic production. This structural–geographical dimension, which appears closely linked to the historical variability and displacement of distinct 'agents' of politico-economic modernization (private entrepreneurs in the paradigm case of British capitalism, financial institutions and/or the state in comparatively more retarded or peripheral areas) (cf. Gerschenkron 1962; Moore Jr 1966; Chirot 1977), is not focally addressed in the present study; nevertheless it is possible to indicate a broad direction of analysis.

As is evidenced by their short-lived matrimony in the First International, Marxism and anarchism demonstrated differences of doctrine and temperament which could ultimately flower only in distinct historical and geographical settings. As an intellectual product of advanced capitalism, classical Marxism tended to exaggerate the maturity of proletarian self-consciousness, the bearer of which was still numerically inconspicuous in semi-peripheral countries such as Italy, Spain, and even France. Here the Bakuninist faith in the revolutionary potential of the 'declassed' people as a whole, and more especially of the *educated déclassés*, offered a more relevant strategy.[20] In such semiperipheral settings, where a state aspiring to strength confronted relatively weak property classes (which, Marxian predictions notwithstanding, were little inclined to initiate a liberal revolution), the anarchist theory of power and its 'inverted etatism' identified, if not the most likely direction of social development, then at least the real enemy: the modernizing, entrepreneurial state and its desire to carry through a nationalist and productionist 'revolution from above'. In this restricted sense, the anarchist project had a rational background. This is also borne out by the fact that Marxism, moving as a practical politics into regions where the proletarian revolution was least expected, turned itself inside out in a theoretical sense, and was forced to exchange its materialist and economistic tenets for some of the central convictions of power theory. Indeed, as early as the Leninist programme, Marxism was itself transfigured into a strange amalgam of anarchism and etatism, with the etatist element forcibly on the rise.

Another dramatic illustration of the salience of this historico-geographical factor is provided by the rise of fascist power theory, which stated openly and initially what Leninist and Stalinist Marxism adopted unwillingly and late, and with much dialectical gesticulation. If, as d'Agostino claims, Bakuninism represented 'a kind of summary of the historical circumstances of the revolutionary movement in Eastern and Southern Europe' (1977: 69), we should also acknowledge that the home ground of anarchism swiftly turned into the Wagnerian theatre of successful fascist 'revolutions from above'. Fascist ideology, emerging from a unique confluence of anarcho-syndicalist and radical nationalist ideas, rehearsed major elements of the anarchist critique of Marxism, in emphasizing the primordial importance of politics, power, and the state over against property, of the revolutionary will over against economic determinism, and of the importance of the *lumpenintelligentsia* and the peasantry over against the proletariat, even though it negated the internationalism which classical anarchism and Marxism shared and reaffirmed the beneficent nature of authority, strong leadership, and an all-transcendent state. If, follow-ing d'Agostino, we may characterize Bakuninism as a kind of 'Machiavellism from below', fascist ideology squarely set Machiavelli back upon his feet again.

It is this etatist tradition to which anarchism, as its 'negative' image, still remained heavily in debt.[21] If anarchist intellectuals summoned the people or society to bring down the state, they in the first place spoke for the *powerless* rather than the *propertyless*: for peasants and *déclassé* intellectuals against landlords and bureaucrats, rather than for proletarians against capitalists and the capitalist state. But in the case of anarchism, too, it is important to recognize the relatively autonomous weight of intellectual interests and the logic of the intra-intellectual struggle, the crucial 'addition' which it made to the struggle of those whom anarchist intellectuals claimed to represent, and the essentialist surplus meaning which it injected into their master concepts. Like their Marxist opponents, anarchists tended to universalize a problematic and to dogmatize a structure of causality from experiences which were both socially and geographically restricted. It was perhaps this knowledge-geographical variable which largely determined the choice of the 'instance' which, on both sides, was so vehemently promoted as the 'last' one.

BEYOND MARXISM AND ANARCHISM

In these concluding paragraphs I shall survey, even if somewhat selectively and abruptly, how Marxism and anarchism have fared in a world which is increasingly dominated by problematics (of culture, technology, nature, gender, and race) which, in their present urgency, would be barely recognizable to the founding fathers of both ideologies, and which (or so it can be argued) tend to erode the common understanding which has traditionally framed their mutual contestation. New incongruous 'things' or 'puzzles' have emerged (the 'embarrassment' of the middle classes, the 'knowledge society', the rise and fall of 'really existing socialism', the ecological crisis, the challenges of feminism and ethnic diversity) which impertinently interrogate all the surviving ideologies, which vitally need to articulate and theorize them on penalty of being sentenced to the scrapheap of the master narratives. Predictably, the grand 'isms', which are carried forward by their own socio-cognitive momentum, first attempt to incorporate such anomalous 'its' by expanding their analytics and stretching their terms. But such intellectual gymnastics also elicit suspicions of artificiality and sterility, of the old and articulate attempting to domesticate the new that cannot yet speak coherently for itself – and which, if it did, would quickly detonate some of the binaries which run across the established intellectual arena.

As noted before, the constitutive ambiguities of the dialectic have facilitated expansionist moves from, in the anarchist case, the critique of state and government proper towards a more encompassing critique of social power, or in the case of Marxism, from the critique of class inequality towards more general theories of exploitation which, while departing from economically defined constraints, reached beyond them to include various other dimensions of oppression and inequality. In past decades, conceptual broadening strategies such as those initiated by Bookchin, Wieck, and other anarchists were paralleled by, and to some extent merged with, Foucault's influential genealogy of power, feminist extensions of the political to the personal, and ecological talk of a 'politics of nature'. Neo-Marxists, in their turn, have stretched their analytical framework by variously extending the core conceptions of production, property, class, and exploitation in order to accommodate non-material resources, political and cultural criteria of stratification, and the domination of nature. As intimated before, both the Frankfurt school of critical theory and the 'Gramscian' departure of the Althusserian school pointed the way towards more balanced theoretical elaborations of the specificity of political and cultural determinations. More recently, 'analytical' Marxists such as Roemer, Wright, Elster, and Van Parijs have in various ways enriched and extended the repertoire of exploitation and class by importing the generalized economics of rational choice theory.

In keeping pace with one another, these broadening moves have appreciably hastened the convergence between the two master repertoires and lessened the competitional tension which was inherited from the classical systems. The closure between the semantic zones has become tighter, and the oscillatory movement has proportionally diminished. Since the 1960s, moreover, new social movements have emerged which variously ignored, pleaded indifference to, or consciously worked to supersede the reductionary dilemma – even though they did not fully succeed in breaking the hold of the traditional binary. The New Left and the counterculture movements of the 1960s and 1970s, for example, initially took their theoretical cues with equal nonchalance from libertarian socialism as from its Marxian countermodel. They directed their resistance with equal animus against Western welfare capitalism and the Eastern bureaucratic state (conceptually merged into 'The System' or 'The Establishment'), and solicited revolutionary recruits less among the traditional working class as among the 'lumpenproletariat' of alienated students, blacks, women, and unemployed (cf. Marshall 1992: 539ff.). Cohn-Bendit, the most prominent leader of the French student rebellion, characteristically described himself as a Marxist 'in the way Bakunin was', while Dutschke, his more orthodox German counterpart, called for a student–worker alliance to overthrow both capitalism and the state.

The theoretical landscape configured by these approximations and stereoscopic expansions shows a complex and ambivalent pattern which must be carefully sorted out. The gradual convergence of the two repertoires and the closure of the reductionary gap have not put a definitive stop to all contestatory traffic. Despite the secular drift towards power theory and the progressive mixture of the semantics of exploitation and domination which one may discern in all revisionary schools of neo-Marxism, its economizing framework still demonstrates a remarkable power of absorption in the face of new theoretical challenges, and sharply draws its lines of demarcation whenever power theorists are suspected of imperialistically overstating their claims. However, such normalizing boundary work appears somewhat more representative of intellectual currents which have remained absorbed in the classical issues of class theory (such as the 'contradictory' situation of the middle classes, the social identification of managers and intellectuals, or the threat of statism and bureaucratic centralism). It is less characteristic of new ideologies such as feminism or ecologism which, although they have had their share of disputations across the property–power binary, also manifest a larger indifference towards it, and to some extent escape the constraints of the pendulum swing. Let me illustrate this complex situation by highlighting some features of the more traditionally framed 'repair job' which is attempted in a few strands of neo-Marxism, and of the more novel ventures of theoretical feminism and political ecology.

Althusserian 'scientific' Marxism of the mid-1960s and 1970s, as we saw before, had already mounted the attack upon economism and class reductionism, relaxing and complicating the more orthodox structuration of causal determination in order to accommodate the relative autonomy of the political and other superstructural factors. The debate conducted between Poulantzas and Miliband in the early 1970s was paradigmatically staked on the degree of relative autonomy which was attributable to the capitalist state, or more generally, to the 'specificity of the political' as it was framed by 'last instance' economic determination.[22] A core element in the Gramscian approach was the acknowledgement of the primordial presence of political and ideological relations in the actual constitution of relations of production and exploitation, over against 'externalist' accounts which tended to confine them to the sphere of reproduction. Pressing the Gramscian notion of hegemony even further, Althusser introduced a conception about the 'ideological state apparatuses' which extended the space of the state to ideology-producing establishments such as churches, the educational system, media networks, and the cultural apparatus more generally, irrespective of whether they formally belonged to the state or retained a private juridical character (Althusser 1971: 127ff.; Poulantzas 1978: 28ff.). Several commentators justifiably heckled the looseness of the concurrent definition of the state as 'the instance that maintains the cohesion of a social formation'; one of them perceptively targeted the 'subtle transposition' which led from this expansive definition of the state to the assertion that *everything* that contributes to the cohesion of a social formation pertains, by definition, to the State'. No longer an instance, it was simply a quality which pervaded all the levels of a social formation (Laclau 1975: 100–1).[23]

This inflationary conception of the political already dangerously corroded the structure of the Althusserian causal argument from the inside, since the state tended to eclipse the economy as primordial instance, and the last instance ontology could only be salvaged by means of formalistic distinctions between 'structure' and 'conjuncture' or 'determination' and 'domination'. Nevertheless, the lines of battle were firmly redrawn in the face of a further and more decisive dismantling of the economic scaffolding. Here Foucault's post-Marxist, Nietzschean conception of power served as point of polemical attraction, drawing much of the fire which was formerly concentrated upon anarchist political theory. Given the strong politicizing drift of the structuralist paradigm itself, it was somewhat ironic to see Poulantzas mount a fierce polemic against Foucault's 'peculiar caricature of Marxism' and his transcendental or inflationary conception of power (1978: 146ff.). Power, for Poulantzas, always had a 'precise basis', which was fundamentally though not exclusively determined by exploitation, whereas for Foucault the power relation never appeared to have any other basis than itself. This absolutization led 'irresistibly to the idea of a Power-Master as the prime founder of all struggle-resistance' in the manner of the 'new philosophers'. The reproach that Marxism failed to provide a general theory of power and the political was firmly resisted: it was precisely one of its merits to 'thrust aside the grand metaphysical flights of so-called political philosophy – the vague and nebulous theorizations of an extreme generality and abstractness that claim to lay bare the great secrets of History, the Political, the State, and Power' (1978: 20).

Poulantzas's campaign set the tone for a barrage of similar criticisms, coming especially from modern cultural materialists such as Said, Jameson, Williams, Spivak, and Anderson, who have all singled out Foucault as the dark genius of the new power metaphysic.[24] Quite representative of this cluster is Said's objection to Foucault's 'curiously passive and sterile view' of how and why power is gained, used, and held onto, and his inadequate reduction of the notions of class and class struggle to the status of 'superannuated 19th century conceptions of political economy'. Foucault's eagerness not to fall into Marxist economism, and his theoretical 'overtotalization' of the concept of power, causes him 'to obliterate the role of classes, the role of economics, the role of insurgency and rebellion' (1983: 221–2, 244–6). Likewise reacting against Foucault's and Deleuze's totalizations, Spivak ironically speaks about a 'race for the last instance' which is presently run between economics and power (1988: 274, 279). Jameson similarly ridicules a 'faddish post-Marxism' which has foregrounded 'that shadowy and mythical Foucault entity called power' in order to enter a 'Nietzschean world of micro-politics'. Regretting the unfortunate 'melt-down of the Althusserian reactor', and the collapse of the notion of structural totality 'into a rubble of autonomous instances without any necessary relationship to each other whatsoever', Jameson rather peremptorily defends this notion and that of capital as a 'totalizing' concept, without which a properly coherent socialist politics is considered impossible (1988: 349, 354). Anderson, finally, repeats the same critical pattern against Mann's historical sociology of power, which in his view extends 'the character-istic modern confusion that simply equates power and culture' such as is especially promulgated by Foucault (1992: 82–3).[25]

A conceptual tactic quite different from that taken by cultural materialism or Marxist cultural studies is elaborated in the school of what has aptly been called 'analytic' or 'rational choice Marxism' (cf. Carling 1986).[26] Even though this intellectual tradition stays closer to the classical concerns of Marxist class theory, it once again exemplifies the sheer elasticity of grounding concepts such as property, class, production, and exploitation, which are swept along in a veritable race for extension, resulting in an almost unstoppable proliferation of forces of production, asset bases, and grounds for exploitation. Departing from Cohen's (1978) neo-functionalist defence of the primacy thesis (i.e. the priority of forces over relations of production) and the base–superstructure thesis, theorists such as Roemer, Wright, Elster, and Van Parijs have concertedly sought to vindicate the consistency of historical mate-rialism's most basic claims by importing elements of style and substance from the rational choice paradigm.[27] Their various solutions of the 'primacy puzzle', however, while generally retaining the fundamental principle of explanatory asymmetry and of the priority of material forces of production (cf. Cohen 1978: 278; Elster 1985: 267ff., 398ff.; Van Parijs 1993: 9ff., 20ff.),[28] tend to stretch the notions of materiality and productivity to a faraway point where we are no longer sure whether we are still travelling through Marxist territory, or have already entered the borderlands of Nietzschean or Foucaldian power theory.

Discarding the labour theory of value, Roemer has made a comprehensive attempt to rephrase the Marxian concept of exploitation more clearly in terms of the priority of property relations, conceived as unequal access to society's alien-able means of production (Roemer 1982a, b; 1994: 13, 37ff.). This supplies the basis for a more general taxonomy of property and exploitation, which includes feudal exploitation founded upon unequally distributed ownership of people; capitalist exploitation, which rests upon ownership of means of production; and socialist or status exploitation, which is the distributive effect of the marginal distribution of skills (i.e. all assets that cannot be detached from their bearers). This extension of the resource list to include non-alienable alongside alienable productive assets is further extrapolated by Wright, who includes organizational assets next to labour power, physical means of production, and skills, and separates organizational exploitation (based on control of the technical division of labour by managers or bureaucrats) from skill-based exploitation which is exercised by experts and professionals (1985a, b). The problem of ownership with regard to organizational assets is solved by means of a quite traditional extension of the concept towards effective economic control, which can also be collectively exercised by managerial or bureaucratic elites (1985b: 80–1). Despite this slippage towards power theory, Wright strongly maintains the explanatory centrality of class, property, and exploitation over against domination-centred conceptions, which in his view legitimate a confusing plurality of oppressions, none of which enjoy explanatory priority over any other (1985b: 96–7; cf. Scott 1996: 172ff.).

An even bolder step along the same slippery road is Van Parijs's attempt to generalize the already generalized Roemer–Wright approach to exploitation and class (1987, in 1993), which likewise meets a limit where 'property theory' and 'power theory' become virtually synonymous. First, Van Parijs refuses to follow Wright in analytically privileging exploitation over domination since, in his view, the extension of the class concept effectively covers both income and power. Second, the list of material assets is once again expanded beyond income rights, ownership rights over people, organizational access, and skills, towards what is called 'job property' or 'job exploitation', which is defined as the major stake of the new class struggle which is presently emerging under welfare-state capitalism (1993: 126ff.). Third and predictably, a difficulty arises in demarcating material assets from power chances, since the expanded list includes ownership rights over people, control over the state, and organizational assets which admittedly 'bear a close relation to the problem of authority and hierarchy'. This problem is circumvented (rather than solved) by means of a rather strained distinction between titles or rights and the material advantages derivable from them, or otherwise, between the asset itself (organization) and the way in which it is controlled (through authority). Fourth and finally, while reverting to the view of organizational exploitation as a special case of skills exploitation, Van Parijs also reanimates Roemer's notion of 'status exploitation', only to expand its scope of application towards distributive advantages associated with race, sex, and citizenship. The net result of such additions is the rather extreme proposition that there exist as many class divides as there are factors systematically affecting the distribution of material advantages, attaching 'race exploitation', 'sex exploitation', and 'citizenship exploitation' to an already long list (ibid.: 119, 142–3).

FEMINISM AND ECOLOGISM

In feminist discourse, although it had its initial share of reductionary quarrels, the competition between the analytic of (re)production and property and that of politics and power has always seemed less relevant than their potential collaboration in elucidating the mechanisms of patriarchy and gender oppression (subjects of study which almost naturally attract fusion of the two repertoires). Ecological thought, in like fashion, has been somewhat less interested in rigorously identifying the primacy of capital or the state as sources of ecological risk than in analysing the productionist politico-economic–cultural 'System' which collectively and integrally threatens to exhaust natural resources (Dobson 1990: 175ff.). The practice of mixing rather than polarizing the metaphors of property and power thus appears more congenial both to feminist analyses of the embodiment of gender exploitation and to ecologist analyses of the exploitation and domination of nature. In this respect, the old dialectic between the master narratives of property and power, as handed down by the Marxist and anarchist traditions, may finally be approaching a state of saturation and depletion, and contests for purity of expression between spokespersons for the primacy of class or that of state power may be increasingly seen as irrelevant rearguard actions. Do the stretched vocabularies of appropriation and domination not run together in the same conceptual void when attempting to incorporate feminist analyses of gender? Will post-scarcity Marxism and post-scarcity anarchism survive the ecological crisis?

Since the case of ecology as a site of intellectual rivalry (and as potential spoiler of the game) has already been briefly treated in terms of the Bookchin–Gorz controversy and similar disputes between eco-Marxists and eco-anarchists,[29] I will presently restrict my narrative to some recent developments in feminist theory. I do wish to maintain, however, that the intellectual tactics deployed are in essential respects similar, and similarly tend to slow down the swing of the pendulum, since both mix their expansionary moves (from economic production to cultural, sexual, and natural reproduction, from class exploitation to patriarchal domination and the exploitation of nature) with a fair amount of unconcern about the conceptual rigour which is invested in (and jealously guarded by) paternal vocabularies such as Marxism and anarchism. This remains true even if anarchist power theory seems at first sight better equipped to sort out the new problematics of gender, technology, and ecological risk – as is also suggested by parallel generalizations of the political in Latour's (1993) analysis of techno-scientific hybrids and the nature–society split, in Beck's (1992; 1993) notions about the risk society and reflexive modernization, or in Dobson's (1990; 1993) attempts to reintroduce the non-human ecological world into the political arena. I consider it also to hold for feminist theorizing, even if in past decades it has massively migrated from the idiom of a political economy of sex towards that of a (discursive) politics of gender.

In feminist studies, as elsewhere, the turn from modernism to postmodernism has implied a paradigmatic shift 'from Marx to Nietzsche', or in updated language: from a generalization of neo-Marxian political economy towards the generalized power analytic which has been (re)introduced by Lyotard and Foucault. Feminist historical materialism of the early 1970s, taking its cue from foundational texts such as Firestone's *The Dialectic of Sex*, enlarged and radicalized the Marxist analytic of production and class towards sexual reproduction, sexual appropriation, and 'sex classes', claiming to uncover the psychosexual substratum of the historical dialectic which remained invisible through the Marxian economic filter (cf. Firestone 1970: 4–5). A closely related attempt to enlarge the materialist account was Rubin's influential 'The traffic in women: notes on the political economy of sex' (1975), which similarly interpreted the sex/gender system as a sexual property system, and the exchange of women as an originary form of commodity exchange. The vocabulary of the 'economics of reproduction' and the 'sexual division of labour' also marked other important Marxist–feminist contributions, such as O'Brien's *The Politics of Reproduction* (1981), or works by Meulenbelt (1975), MacKinnon (1982), and Haug (1982). As Haraway sums up: while traditional Marxist approaches failed to produce a political concept of gender because of their tendency to naturalize the sexual division of labour and to theorize economic property relations as the ground of the oppression of women, the Marxist–feminist debate tended to turn on a progressive problematization of the category 'labour' itself, or its various extensions towards theories of reproduction, in efforts to include women's active agency and status as subjects in history (1991: 131, 140, 158).

However, the critical analysis of patriarchy as a blended economic–political structure of ownership (of female bodies, naturalized in terms of 'sex') has also from the very beginning drawn on the opposite idiom, mediating to some extent the combative polarity between the discourses of appropriation and domination, and circumventing the vexed priority question (sexual property or sexual power?). We have already cited Millett's early *Sexual Politics* (1969), whose comprehensive notion of power came in for praise from an anarchist such as Wieck (1975: 30). We might also adduce the example of French feminist materialism (Wittig, Delphy, Plaza), which, on the one hand, followed the familiar path of extension in proclaiming women to be a social class constituted by the hierarchical relation of sexual difference, but which was simultaneously marked by the distinctly 'politicizing' metaphorics of literary deconstruction and Lacanian psychoanalysis. Wittig's conception of the class struggle between the sexes is for instance liberally meshed with the idiom of (linguistic) politics; language is considered to be 'another order of materiality' which is intimately connected to the political field (1990: 55).

Feminist 'standpoint theory', as it has evolved from Smith, Rose, and Hartsock towards Harding and Haraway, once again demonstrates the simultaneous enlargement of the Marxian analytic of production and property and the secular drift towards theorizations which focalize Nietzschean terms of power. Although deriving its initial impetus from the Marxian and Lukàcsian logic of the proletarian standpoint, feminist social epistemology has increasingly departed from its paternal discourse, in order to engage itself more seriously with postmodernist critiques of scientific knowledge which presume the ubiquitous presence of a 'politics of theory'. Hartsock's feminist historical materialism is more traditional in expanding Marxian political economy beyond the work of 'males in capitalism' towards an account of 'phallocratic domination' in general, and in extrapolating proletarian standpoint theory to structural positional differences between women and men. Feminist standpoint theory, to be sure, is claimed to be 'deeper going' (since for instance female reproduction actualizes a unity with nature which goes beyond the proletarian interchange with nature), which suggests a causal reversal of the Marxian relationship between capitalism and patriarchy – and of the correlative vocabularies of appropriation and domination (1983: 283, 290, 293, 305).[30] Harding similarly opposes the privileged causal connection between sexism and class domination, in order to take women and men fundamentally as 'sex classes', and not merely or even primarily as members of economic classes (1991: 136). But she also directs feminist standpoint theory more radically beyond Marxist epistemological assumptions, in more openly adopting the Foucaldian postulate that science is 'politics by other means' (1991: 10–11, 146). Haraway concurs in this view by maintaining that all knowledge 'is a condensed node in an agonistic power field' (1991: 185).

In this fashion, the keynote slogan of the feminist movement about equating the personal and the political is more definitely politicized, in the sense of a switch from an 'economics of sexual difference' towards a 'politics of gender difference', which also introduces new theorizations of the discursive ubiquity of the political itself. Another clear illustration of this discursive switch is to be found in Young's 'defection' from feminist historical materialism and its distribution-oriented analytic towards political philosophy and its generalized theory of social power. A 1981 debate with Hartmann on the 'unhappy marriage' of Marxism and feminism and the 'dual system' of patriarchy and capital still showed Marxian systematics firmly in place (cf. Sargent 1986).[31] Young's *Justice and the Politics of Difference* (1990), however, places itself at some remove from this in staging a wide-ranging critique of the 'distributive' paradigm of justice, which has focused too much on the allocation of material goods (things, resources, income, wealth) or the distribution of social positions (e.g. jobs), and has ignored social structures and institutional contexts, especially those of decision-making power, of divisions of labour, and of culture.[32] In her conception, the metaphorical widening of the concepts of appropriation and distribution ultimately cannot accommodate non-material goods such as power, opportunity, and self-respect, since these are still tendentially represented as static things. This overextension of the vocabulary of distribution and appropriation is considered especially damaging in talk about power. Its reificatory drift can only be neutralized by switching to the more radically relational vocabulary of domination and oppression such as is exemplarily suggested by Foucault. The conception of justice should accordingly be defined much wider than distribution, as coincident with an inclusive sense of the political (1990: 9, 15ff.).

The feminist turn from modernism to postmodernism, then, implies a double refiguration from an economics towards a politics of difference, which is also an epistemological shift from 'sex realism' to 'gender constructivism' in which questions of representation and discursivity are much more intensely foregrounded. Little wonder that Foucault's alluringly enigmatic doublet of *pouvoir/savoir* has become a focus of immense attraction in the encounter between feminism and postmodernism (De Lauretis 1990; Harding 1991; Nicholson 1990; Butler and Scott 1992). In repeated reference to Foucault, theorists such as Scott, Butler, Alcoff, De Lauretis, and Braidotti have thematized gender as a network of discursively constituted power relations, drawing on a shift in the terms of the political which resists its foreclosure to a specific domain, but rather experiments with radical intuitions about its coextensivity with the social and the discursive. To McClure, such feminist extensions of the political are commensurate with 'the broader unsettling of the political in our time', and confirm 'the modern political sensibility that casts "the political" as coextensive with the organization and management of a system of social relations' (1992: 351).

Arguably, postmodernist feminism's fine point (and its most corrosive indigenous paradox) is precisely concentrated in this magnetic notion of a 'politics of theory', which puts increasing pressure upon lingering realist or ontological accounts which suggest the primacy of gender as axis of oppression (Harding 1991; Butler and Scott 1992; Butler 1992; Braidotti 1994). Alcoff and Potter have suggested that recent feminist reframings of the problematics of knowledge, although heterogeneous and diverse, at least share a common commitment to unearth the 'politics of epistemology'. In their view, such an acknowledgement of intrinsic connections between values, politics, and knowledge cannot remain restricted to gender issues, but potentially informs the entire cluster of social markings, including race, class, sexuality, culture, and age. Hence the feminist project should be framed more inclusively and address the full spectrum of forms of domination (1993: 3–4). In this manner, feminist 'politics of knowledge' has reflexively turned from the critique of masculinist knowledge power towards the totalizing and reductionist elements in its own grand narrative of gender, which threatens to break up the grand dualism and tends to reduce gender difference to one difference among many. However one may assess such 'gender-scepticism', which for some is liberatory (Butler 1989), but for others forebodes a taming of feminism's visionary and critical energies (Bordo 1990), it manifestly results from a critical enlargement of the political as intrinsically coding all forms of theoretical classification.

4

FASCISM AND THE PRIMACY OF THE POLITICAL

> Karl Marx may have discovered profit, but I have discovered *political* profit.
>
> Carl Schmitt

THE FASCIST EQUATION

One of the core convictions informing radical right-wing thought has notoriously been that politics should take priority over economics, and that the power
question was more fundamental than the question of property (cf. Lebovics
1969: 219; Herf 1984: 2, 4, 227; Vincent 1992: 167). With the purpose of
resolving the economic and cultural crisis, fascists and national socialists
typically demanded a restoration of the primacy of the political and a repoliticization of economic life, which both liberal and Marxist theory had
illegitimately promoted to the status of an ontological 'last instance'.
Speaking in March 1933, at the nervous height of the political *Gleichschaltung*
following the January coup, Hitler was characteristically straightforward
about his intentions: 'Wir wollen wiederherstellen das Primat der Politik'. In
Mein Kampf of 1924 he had already pleaded a reversal of the relationship
between economics and the state, advising that 'industry and commerce
recede from their unhealthy leading position and adjust themselves to the
general framework of a national economy of balanced supply and demand'.
Capital was to remain 'the handmaiden of the state' and not fancy itself 'the
mistress of the nation'. A strong state was needed to act as 'intelligence' and
'organizer' of national production; economics was only one among its instruments, and could never be its cause or aim (1969: 127, 137, 190; cf.
Sontheimer 1978: 138).

Mussolini and Gentile, in their famous 1932 encyclopedia article 'The
Doctrine of Fascism', likewise asserted that 'everything is in the State, and
nothing human or spiritual exists, much less has value, outside the State'. In a
broadside against both liberalism and historical materialism, they added that
it was absurd to maintain that 'economic improvements' sufficed to explain

101

human history to the exclusion of all other factors. It was the totalitarian state, embodying the conscience and ethical will of all citizens, which was called upon to organize the nation, and thus logically also 'claimed for itself the field of economics' (in Lyttleton 1973: 39ff.). Gentile's neo-idealism, while advocating a reversal of Marx to Hegel, both delineated the all-powerful state as highest embodiment of citizens' ethical consciousness, and economic activity as essentially subordinate to this ethical force. While liberals and Marxists had accepted economic principles as abstract, universally applicable laws, only fascist corporative economists had recognized that they should be controlled and regulated from a higher ethical–political point of view (Harris 1966: 46–9, 234, 235).

This self-image has to some extent been ratified by outside observers, both neutral and inimical. The postwar political sociology of totalitarian regimes has characteristically operated from the assumption, here expressed in Talmon's words, that totalitarianism 'recognizes ultimately only one plane of existence, the political', and tends to widen the scope of politics to embrace the whole of human existence (1970: 2). Neo-Marxist theories of fascism, in relaxing the rigid hold of the reductionary 'iron guard of capital' interpretation, have likewise acknowledged the primacy of the political in fascist regimes, although under the sign of an expanded conception of economic determination in the last instance. In an early (1941) analysis of the national socialist regime as a form of state capitalism, Pollock, the Frankfurt school Marxist, argued that the Third Reich was presently constructing a new economic order 'in which market was replaced by command' (1981: 118).[1] Poulantzas's subsequent (1974b) elaboration of the Marxian model of 'Bonapartism' similarly emphasized the enhanced autonomy of the political *vis-à-vis* the economic sphere. In an equally influential work, Mason typically explained the political disenfranchisement of the propertied classes and the ensuing primacy of politics in national socialist Germany as necessarily ensuing from the incapacity of 'capital' to bring about the recovery of the economy and the reproduction of civil society, which required a strong government that could forge a new social and economic compromise (Mason 1969, in 1995).

In previous pages, I have already hinted at some curious continuities-in-opposition obtaining between anarchism and fascism (characterized earlier as Machiavellian power theory 'set back upon its feet'),[2] while I have also implied that both ideologies demarcated themselves from Marxist economism by their shared insistence upon the primacy of the political. After having reviewed some aspects of the intellectual rivalry between these two 'legitimate' socialisms, I now intend to provide a closer analysis of the intellectual stature and structure of a third, 'illegitimate' socialism, which cannot be ignored if we wish to obtain a more comprehensive picture of the ideological field of contests which are deployed across the property–power axis. To take fascism and national socialism seriously as intellectual systems, however, let alone to take seriously fascist professions of continuity with specific varieties of socialism, still remains a hotly contested 'revisionist' view which many students of the radical right consider dangerously close to euphemizing a politics of irrationalism and radical evil. Traditionally, fascist ideologues could not be taken 'at their word', since even the smallest suspicion of their alleged 'rationality' engendered revulsion and unease; that fascist movements were anti-spiritual, that their sparse ideas were only negative, and that, on balance, ideology did not carry much weight, long remained common conviction to both laypersons and expert historians (Griffin 1991: 14; Pels 1993b: 77–8).[3] In our specific context, this long-standing conviction easily translates into the claim that the 'primacy of the political' did not constitute an intellectual conviction worthy of substantive analysis but constituted no more than the specious signature of an irrational and inexhaustible scramble for power.

Since the early 1960s, however, 'revisionist' political historians such as Stern, Nolte, Gregor, and Sternhell have begun to recognize that fascism did indeed feature a complex, systematic, and coherent ideological doctrine, which reflected a respectable historical ancestry and was strongly directive of practical politics. Fascist ideology, to these observers, was not nihilistic, but was founded upon authentic forms of intellectual idealism; it was not conservative, at least not in the traditional sense, but represented an authentic revolutionary impulse (Griffin 1991: 46–8). Intellectual historians are also increasingly prepared to admit that fascism provided reasonably coherent answers to evident weaknesses, gaps and paradoxes in rival ideologies such as liberalism and socialism, the latter especially in its Marxist and anarchist variants. Perhaps this critical relationship has been especially close with Marxism, which fascist and national socialist thinkers consistently targeted as the most formidable competitor in the realm of contemporary radical politics. Apart from elaborating an extended critique of Marxist scientific rationalism, fascist ideologues also cornered defects in its theory about the role of political elites and cultural leadership, and criticized the silences and biases in its conceptualization of social class (specifically concerning the position of the alienated middle classes and the peasantry), in its theory about national sentiment, and in its conceptions of political power and the state. So far, however, fascism has hardly been given a serious hearing as a theoretical competitor of Marxism, or as an ideology which was pitched at an intellectual level comparable with its rival. It is still rare, in this context, to acknowledge the intellectual failures of socialism and Marxism themselves, and the concomitant attractions which were exercised by the counter-ideology of fascism.

Writing in 1933, both as a former syndicalist Marxist and as the most prestigious political scientist of the Mussolini regime, Robert Michels outlined the relationship between Marxism and fascism in the following terms:

> Fascism cannot be comprehensively understood *without an understanding of Marxism*. This is true not only because contemporary phenomena cannot be adequately understood without a knowledge of

the facts that preceded them in time (and with which they are linked dialectically), but also because of the points of contact which, in spite of everything, remain. That which, to its advantage, distinguishes Italian Fascism from German National Socialism, is its painful passage through the purgatory of the socialist system, with its impressive heritage of scientific and philosophical thought from Saint-Simon through Marx and Sorel.

(cit. Gregor 1979a: 1)

Leading thinkers of the 'Conservative Revolution' in Weimar Germany chose to picture their indebtedness to Marxist thought in more agonistic terms. Moeller van den Bruck, author of the prophetic *Das dritte Reich* (1923), claimed to counter internationalist, democratic, and proletarian socialism by a truly 'German' socialism which was to be nationalist, elitist, and authoritarian in inspiration. It would 'begin where Marxism ended' in order to eliminate all traces of liberalism in the spiritual history of humankind (Sontheimer 1978: 276; Schüddekopf 1972: 35). Hans Freyer, well-known sociologist and author of the influential pamphlet *Revolution von Rechts*, suggested that the very demise of the revolution of the left was presently creating room for a revolution from the right; this *völkische* revolution, directed by the state as its consciousness and organizational vanguard, would finally emancipate the state from its century-long entwinement in societal interests (Freyer 1931: 55, 61). In the preface to his synoptic pro-Nazi work *Deutscher Sozialismus*, Werner Sombart, while recommending an intimate knowledge of Marxism as an 'ineluctable demand' for any participant in politics, considered it his duty 'to direct the apparently strong forces that work for a completion of the national socialist idea in its socialist aspect' (1934: xiii, xvi).

In Weimar Germany, as in France and Italy before the First World War, revolutionary conservatism thus partly developed through a critical confrontation with and digestion of Marxist socialism, which one way or the other counted among the most significant cultural roots of fascist ideology. From this viewpoint, fascism can be truthfully described as socialism's 'dark side' (Pels 1993b). Anticipated by Burnham (1945) and Hayek (1944: 124ff.), this thesis about the peculiar parentage between Marxism and fascism is encountered in contemporary historical disputes with different shades of emphasis. For Nolte, fascism represents a radical counter-ideology which in its 'hostile proximity' remains deeply indebted to its polar opposite. In his familiar definition, fascism is

anti-Marxism which seeks to destroy the enemy by the evolvement of a radically opposed and yet related ideology, and by the use of almost identical and yet typically modified methods, always however, within the unyielding framework of national self-assertion and autonomy.

(1965: 40)

For Gregor (1969; 1979a,b), fascism represents not so much a reversal of Marxism as a radical *heresy* emerging from crisis-ridden classical Marxism, which 'was sufficiently vague and porous to accommodate all the theoretical elements later put together by Mussolini and the first Fascists to fashion their revolutionary ideology'. Young Mussolini, like many others in his political environment, was a Marxist intellectual heretic who should be taken seriously in that capacity; indeed, fascism itself should be taken seriously as 'a variant of classical Marxism' rather than as its metaphysical opposite (Gregor 1979a: xi).

Sternhell has carved out a position which interestingly mediates between the opposite exaggerations of Nolte and Gregor. In his conception, fascism neither constitutes the 'long shadow' or mirror image of Marxism, nor can it be simply seen as one of its heretical branches. The 'fascist equation' instead emerges from the *synthesis* of a specific anti-rationalist and anti-materialist revision of Marxism (the anarcho-syndicalist school of Sorel, Lagardelle, Michels, and Berth) and of a newly developed 'integral' and revolutionary *nationalism*, elaborated in France by Barrès, Maurras, and Valois and in Italy by former syndicalists such as Labriola, Panunzio, Corradini, Michels, and Mussolini. In this respect, a *revision* of Marxism in a revolutionary syndicalist direction (or a 'revolutionary revisionism', as Michels termed it) formed at least *one* of the two crucial tributaries to ideological fascism (Sternhell 1986; Sternhell *et al.* 1994). This 'revolutionary revisionism' considered itself anti-bourgeois, anti-parliamentarian, and anti-party, glorifying in a revolutionary spirit of combat without privileging the proletariat as world-historical actor. It embraced socialism less as an outcome of objectively determined economic revindication than as a matter of ethical choice, and it squarely acknowledged the 'authoritarian' fact of leadership by political intellectuals, grounding its utopian expectations upon a novel union between this radical managerial intelligentsia and the broad ranks of the 'people' or 'nation'.

Fascist ideology thus emerged at least in part from a novel confluence of Marxism and anarchism, or put more precisely: from an anarcho-syndicalist revision of Marxist orthodoxy which increasingly distanced itself from the latter's economistic, deterministic, and egalitarian premises. French revolutionary syndicalism always placed more emphasis upon the role of ethical sentiment and political will, on myth and intuition, and on the autonomy of intellectual and political elites. Its Italian counterpart, drifting away even further from classical anarchist principles, gradually accentuated authoritarian notions about revolutionary organization, discipline, and vanguard leadership, while simultaneously exchanging traditional internationalist views for a closer recognition of the irrepressible fact of nationality. In the first decade of the century, syndicalists such as Panunzio, Olivetti, and Michels, invoking Engels' familiar remarks on the necessity of authority for all types of social organization, came to describe revolutionary syndicalism as essentially authoritarian in character, and the syndicalist elite as a new aristocracy which was charged with the historic mission of educating the passive working masses towards a new moral and political consciousness. In 1909, Michels advanced the notion of an 'iron law of elites', which arose from the necessity of organizing for group and class conflicts, especially of a revolutionary nature (Gregor 1979b: 47ff.). In the same vein, Mussolini called Pareto's theory of elites 'perhaps the most ingenuous sociological conception of modern times', and went on to describe himself as an authoritarian and aristocratic socialist (Gregor 1979a: 47, 57).

In a further development, dominated by the experiences of war and economic crisis in an industrially retarded nation such as Italy, the syndicalist accent upon the role of revolutionary elites substituting for an absent or immature proletariat was blended with a growing emphasis upon the priority of developing the forces of production within the national framework. This emphasis, if stamped with the revolutionary urgency which was constitutive of syndicalist ideology, logically tended towards a reinforced nationalization and etatization of its framework of analysis, which finally overturned what still remained of anarchist anti-authoritarian principles. Italy, to the syndicalists, was a 'proletarian nation' which had first to traverse the stage of industrial development, and throw off the tutelage of the more advanced capitalist nations, before it was able to complete something like a Marxian revolution. What was presently needed was a strong 'developmental' state which would harmonize the classes and organize a productionist revolution from above (Rosenstock-Franck 1934: 16ff.; Gregor 1979b: 83ff., 113ff.). Pioneered in Italy by Corradini, Panunzio, and Michels, this 'proletarian nationalism' or 'state syndicalism' proclaimed an end to the disruptive class war and sought the 'total mobilization' of all productive forces in the nation under the guidance of a dynamic, innovatory, and entrepreneurial state. This set of ideas subsequently re-emerged both in conservative-revolutionary and national Bolshevik thought in Weimar Germany and in that of Belgian and French *néo-socialisme*. In claiming the sovereignty of state politics over economic production, national socialism, in this specific 'developmental' conception, explicitly affirmed the primacy of the political and the essentially secondary nature of the property question (cf. also Klingemann 1996: 277ff.). Property rights were henceforth defined as socially functional and contingent upon the demands of state-directed economic development. Not surprisingly, fascism's comparative 'leniency' towards private property was precisely the master criterion which its Marxist adversaries required in order to 'prove' its essentially reactionary nature as a handmaiden of capitalism.[4] Anarchism, we recall, had been dismissed as a 'petty-bourgeois luxury' on precisely the same grounds.

'GERMAN SOCIALISM' AS POWER THEORY

In the following paragraphs, I will embark upon a more detailed analysis of the primacy question as it has haunted the curious ideological triangle connecting Marxism, anarchism, and fascism. However, I will first note a remarkable anticipation of this basic issue in one of the canonic texts of historical materialism itself. In passing, I have already touched upon the parallelism between Marx's rejection of anarchist anti-etatism and of the state socialism of Rodbertus, Lassalle, Wagner, and others: both strands of thought, Marx insisted, violated the core premise of historical materialism about the explanatory primacy of economic production. Now it is a curious coincidence that one of the most detailed and influential polemics penned against state socialist views by the founders of historical materialism can be plausibly read as an anticipatory critique of the national socialist affirmation of the primacy of the political. This polemic was directed against the 'German socialism' of Eugen-Karl Dühring, and written by Engels in 1877–8 in order to combat the growing influence of the former's ideas in the socialist movement of his day. Dühring, a Berlin philosopher and economist who had turned into a private scholar, combined a defence of free competition with the notion of creating a strong national state which was expressive of the general will of the German *Volk*, which would establish an autarky-oriented political economy and supervise a nationalized culture built on class harmony. This 'German socialism' was strongly contrasted with the 'Jewish' socialism of Marx and his associates (cf. Michels 1987: 128–9; Mosse 1981: 71, 131–2, 277).

Dühring, of course, is one among the select array of thinkers who seems solely remembered today because Marx and Engels at one time considered it worth their while to consign them to the scrapheap of intellectual history.[5] While major figures such as Stirner and Proudhon have successfully shaken off this Marxian shadow, minor ones (such as Heinzen) remain captive under it, while Dühring is still almost exclusively known through the abbreviated title of Engels' exhaustively and consistently malevolent *Herr Eugen Dühring's Umwälzung der Wissenschaft*. For my own purposes, his views are only briefly reanimated here because his vision of a nationalist and state-directed 'German' socialism largely anticipated the lineaments of revolutionary–conservative thinking as it emerged from the ordeal of the Great War and the intellectual ferment of the Weimar 1920s and early 1930s. In the wartime and postwar writings of Plenge, Sombart, Spengler, Jünger, Freyer, and Schmitt, the debate with Marxism was once again largely condensed in the analytical dilemma about the super- or subordination of the political *vis-à-vis* the economic. A considerable part of Engels' polemic was likewise devoted to a critical dissection of Dühring's 'theory of force', seeking to reverse his idea that the constitution of political relations was historically fundamental, and that economic dependencies were only an effect or a special case and hence invariably constituted 'facts of secondary importance'. Some of the newer socialist systems, Dühring stated, had totally reversed the order of priority by deriving political phenomena from economic conditions. Although such secondary, retroactive effects were indeed visibly present, the primitive fact had to be located in immediate political force and not in indirect economic power. The original 'fall from grace', when Robinson enslaved Friday, from which all subsequent history took its departure, was an act of force, and all property was therefore *Gewalteigentum*, since it rested upon this original act of political subjection (Engels 1878: 147).

Dühring's own example, however, Engels riposted, clearly demonstrated that force was only the means, while economic advantage (the surplus labour extracted from Friday) constituted the end, which made the economic aspect of the relationship historically more fundamental than the political one. In order to enslave Friday, Robinson had to dispose of the tools and material objects of labour as well as the means for the slave's own subsistence, which presupposed a certain level of productivity and distributive inequality. In this fashion, Dühring stood the entire relationship on its head. Everywhere private property emerged from changes in relations of production and exchange in which the role of force did not enter. The entire movement towards monopolization of the means of production and subsistence in the hands of a restricted class, and the attendant demotion of the vast majority to the status of propertyless proletarians, could be explained from purely economic causes without having to invoke phenomena such as theft, force, state action, or any other kind of political involvement (ibid.: 148–52; 166–71). *Die Gewalt* remained universally dependent upon *das Geld*, which could only be generated by economic production; it was the economic situation which ultimately furnished force with the equipment it required (ibid.: 154–5).

If Dühring, as Michels later reported (1987: 129), was temporarily 'buried alive' by Engels' massive polemic, it would not last long before ideas closely resembling his *völkische* socialism caught the imagination of an entire generation of German 'anti-intellectual' and anti-Marxist intellectuals. From around 1910, but especially spurred by the outbreak of hostilities in 1914, authors such as Sombart, Plenge, Spengler, Jünger, Van den Bruck, Freyer, and Schmitt were to crystallize similar ideas into what became known as the 'German socialism' of the 'Conservative Revolution'. Roughly a decade after the incubation period of Italian national syndicalism, the 'conservative revolutionaries' reinvented and deepened in all important respects its conceptual merger of intransigent nationalism and radical anti-capitalism. The 'primacy of the political over the economic' stood out as one major common theme (Lebovics 1969: 219; Herf 1984: 36–7; Breuer 1993: 59ff.).[6] In *Die Juden und das Wirtschaftsleben* (1911), for example, Werner Sombart, already renowned as a left-wing sociologist and historian of capitalism, expounded the view that the primacy of the economy over all other spheres of social life had been the special contribution of the 'Jewish spirit'. The capitalist domination of money and abstraction was Jewish in its essence; Jews represented everything that was universal, rootless, international, and abstract in contrast to all that was local, rooted, nationalist, and concrete. Two souls, in fact, lived in the breast of the capitalist entrepreneur: the German one of dynamic risk taking and rational planning of production, and the Jewish one of calculating for financial gain. While the German entrepreneur was an inventor, organizer and leader, 'a hero of production', the Jewish merchant was exclusively interested in commercial profit and remained indifferent to the product itself (Herf 1984: 136–7; Lenger 1994: 187ff.).

Sombart's wartime pamphlet *Händler und Helden* (1915) extrapolated this opposition between the spirit of commercialism and the spirit of organization – and between the exemplary types of economic and political man – to the national contest between Germany, a nation of social order and political hierarchy, and England, the historic guardian of the merchant capitalist spirit. English commercial civilization had to be countered by the 'German idea of the state', as pioneered by Fichte, Lassalle, and Rodbertus, which requested subordination of individual interests to the higher interests of the *Volksgemein-schaft* (Lenger 1994: 246; Hayek 1986: 126). The outbreak of the war had triggered a broad stream of patriotic polemics revolving around what Johann Plenge, a neo-Hegelian sociologist, had influentially styled the 'Ideen von 1914'. Both 1789 and 1914 symbolized the two grand principles in the history of political thought which were presently battling for pre-eminence: the ideal of individual freedom, which was the essence of liberal capitalism, and the ideal of social organization, which constituted the essence of socialism. Whereas the nineteenth century had been an atomized, critical, and disorganized century, the twentieth century was to be dominated by the idea of 'German organiza-tion', which was commissioned to establish the *Volksgemeinschaft* of a national socialism. In *Der Krieg und die Volkswirtschaft* (1915) Plenge, like Sombart, extra-polated the opposition between capitalism and socialism to the war of the West against Germany; first realized as a war economy, German socialism would consolidate a state-regulated *Volkswirtschaft* after the inspirational example of Fichte's 'closed commercial state'. It was high time to recognize that 'socialism must be power policy, because it is to be organization. Socialism has to win power, never blindly destroy it' (cit. Hayek 1986: 127–8).

Spengler's *Preussentum und Sozialismus* (1919) was perhaps the most stirring conservative-revolutionary call to arms issuing from this wartime intellectual ferment. Like Sombart and Plenge, he divined an implacable opposition between the 'English' liberal spirit of *Gesellschaft*, profit and competition, and the 'Prussian' instinct of order, *Gemeinschaft*, hierarchy, duty, and labour. This opposition had unfolded into a heroic life-or-death clash between two domi-nating 'world ideas': the dictatorship of money and that of organization, which defined the world alternatively 'as Booty or as State, Wealth or Authority, Success or Profession'. Would in the future, Spengler rhetorically asked, 'Commerce govern the State or the State govern Commerce?' (1919: 69, 103). To decide this issue, German socialism had to be liberated from Marx, who had merely invented a kind of 'inverted capitalism', in order to install an authoritarian socialism, a socialism of the civil servant and the organ-izer, which was prepared to use to the full the economic authority of the state (ibid.: 47–9). The essence of socialism did not reside in the opposition between rich and poor, but in the fact that rank, performance, and competence would rule life. In Spengler's projected state corporatism, property would not be seen as private booty, but as a procuration of the entire community; not as an expression and means of personal power, but as a trust or fief for which the proprietor owed accountability to the state. Socialization, in this respect, was not so much a matter of nominal possession but of technique of administration (*Verwaltungstechnik*) (ibid.: 92–5). Socialism, in brief, meant 'power, power, and yet again power. Plans and thoughts are nothing without power' (ibid.: 105).[7]

Three other texts are selected as worthy of attention here, since they together consolidated the intellectual framework of German socialism as a theory of power rather than property: Freyer's *Die Bewertung der Wirtschaft im philosophischen Denken des 19. Jahrhunderts* (1921), Jünger's *Der Arbeiter* (1932), and Sombart's *Deutscher Sozialismus* (1934). Freyer's *Habilitationsschrift* fleshed out ideas about the commercial and marketing spirit of the nineteenth century, adopted from his teachers Plenge and Sombart, in a broadly conceived intellectual history of the 'naturalization' or autonomization of the 'economic' frame of mind. Liberal political economy and the socialist tradition shared the same basic conception of the abstract lawlike autonomy and the primordial value of economic life, which Marx had even elevated into an ontologically grounded essence, a 'cause of causes' in the interplay of cultural moments (1921: 75–6, 94; cf. Muller 1987: 81ff.). With the avowed purpose of reframing this economic rationalism in a new communitarian ethics and politics of the *Volksstaat*, Freyer invoked the Romantic tradition of *Nationalökonomie*, especially Adam Müller's *Elemente der Staatskunst*, whose idea of a corporatist *Volkswirtschaft*, in which each function partook of 'the spiritual whole of the politicized economy', had received further elaboration at the hands of authors such as List, Rodbertus, Hildebrand, and Schäffle. 'Economic life', Freyer summed up, 'is not necessarily the commercial contest of atomized interests, which it is at present. It is a spiritual concern of the statal community' (1921: 37ff., 51). Recently this tradition of historical, ethical (and truly political) economy had tended more strongly in a state socialist direction. Extrapolating this trend, Freyer harmonized this tradition's shared neo-Hegelian conception of the ethical state with that of *völkische* political nationalism by identifying it as 'der Spitze, in der das Volk geschichtlich wird' (119), both anticipating his subsequent laudation of the state as the ultimate perfection of spiritual development in *Der Staat* (1926), and his ringing expression about the state as 'das politisch werdende Volk' in *Revolution von Rechts* (1931).[8]

Following closely in the footsteps of Spengler and Sombart, Ernst Jünger, at the beginning of the 1930s, developed a spectacular metaphysic of war, discipline, and total mobilization which has accurately been designated as a 'conservative anarchism' (Schwartz 1962). Jünger's portentous essay 'Die totale Mobilmachung' (1930) and his book *Der Arbeiter. Herrschaft und Gestalt* (1932) – which carried a memorable dedication to Spengler – became foundational for national Bolshevik tendencies such as formulated by his friend Niekisch, for younger conservative revolutionaries grouped around the journal *Die Tat*, and for the left-wing national socialist tendency represented by the young Goebbels and the Strasser brothers within the NSDAP. Developing earlier suggestions found in Plenge and Moeller van den Bruck, these circles saw the insurrection of 'young', 'proletarian' nations such as Soviet Russia and Germany against the 'old' capitalist powers as requiring a national and autarkic 'war socialism' geared towards a total mobilization of all human and material resources of the nation. Germany's military defeat, Moeller van den Bruck had argued after Versailles, should be exploited as an educational challenge. Since, like the proletariat, Germany now possessed little more than its chains, it should not fear the coming world revolution, but could spearhead the war of liberation of the expropriated nations against the world bourgeoisie (Schüddekopf 1972: 35). Jünger, Niekisch, Edgar Jung, the *Tatkreis* intellectuals, and the Strasserites within (and soon to be drummed out of) the NSDAP all echoed this alarming conversion of the Marxist idea of the economic *Entfremdung* of the proletariat into that of the spiritual–political *Überfremdung* of the nation (id. 254).[9]

Reversing Rathenau's dictum that, in the modern world, not politics but economics had acquired the force of fate, Jünger outlined a universal trend towards state-directed mobilization and planned organization of economic life, which forced everybody and everything into the harsh mould of an all-enveloping logic of power.[10] It was instructive to notice, for example, that in the Soviet planning experiment the economic mode of thinking had superseded itself and evolved into an unmitigated deployment of power. The world war had essentially been a gigantic labour process, fusing the type of the Warrior and that of the Worker into a single *Gestalt*, which sharply contrasted with that of the Bourgeois, the typical representative of liberal disorganization (1930: 132, 140). Editors of *Die Tat* such as Fried and Wirsing likewise emphasized this inevitable drive towards state organization of economic life in terms of an autarkic *Planwirtschaft*, which was prefigured in the war economy, but remained imperative in order to shield Germany from the havoc of a collapsing world economy. By pressing the economy into its service, the state would simultaneously 'grow together' with the working masses, and in fusing state and people would realize the perfection of democracy. In this new frame of things, the place of economic science would once again be taken by the *Staatswissenschaften* (Fried 1931: 23).

Jünger's *Der Arbeiter* of 1932 further detailed his figuration of the Worker–Soldier as archetypical 'political man' and torchbearer of a totalitarian industrial dictatorship, over against the liberal and Marxist conception of the Worker as 'product of industry' and a merely 'economic quality'.[11] The emancipation of the labourer from the economic world implied his subordination to a higher law of struggle; it signified that the pivotal point of the Worker's insurrection was neither economic freedom nor economic power, but power as such. In contrast with the security-minded Bourgeois, the Worker enjoyed 'a new relationship with the elementary, with freedom and power'; the will to power was the truest representation of his *Gestalt* (1932: 28, 34, 70). Property and labour power stood under state protection, and hence were essentially limited in their freedom of movement. Indeed, 'in terms of an investigation of the Worker' the question of private property was much less interesting than current ideology presumed. Different from the world of liberal economy, it did matter much less in the world of labour whether property was considered moral or immoral; what exclusively counted was whether it could be included into a general *Arbeitsplan*. More important was the manner in which the state instituted and circumscribed property as a subordinate fact; its value would rather be assessed in terms of its contribution to the realization of total mobilization, or what Jünger synonymically referred to as *Arbeitsmobilmachung* (1932: 246–7, 274–5, 284).[12]

Speaking around the same time at the Fascist Congress of Corporations at Ferrara, Werner Sombart once again summed up what had become the central credo of the Conservative Revolution: that the previous century had been the century of economics, in which economic interests weighed heavier than all other factors of culture, but that we were presently entering the political epoch, in which politics would once again reign supreme (cit. Manoïlescu 1934: 42). Sombart's *Deutscher Sozialismus*, published one year after the Hitler coup, was once again written as a comprehensive indictment of the *Primat der Wirtschaft* as the most essentially negative characteristic of our time. Repeating and systematizing all the major themes developed over a decade by himself and other writers of the radical right, Sombart insisted that economic rationalization had conjured up the triple disease of intellectualization (*Vergeistung*), objectification (*Versachlichung*), and uniformity (*Ausgleichung*). Bourgeois class formation, the proletarian class struggle, and hence also proletarian socialism were actually 'true children of the economic age': Marx's metaphysics of history incorrectly generalized this particularity of the economic into a defining characteristic of human history. Meanwhile the 'idea of the state' had gradually faded away and finally disappeared. German socialism was therefore nothing other than 'the renunciation of the economic age in its totality'. Because it targeted the *Gesamtgeist* of this age, it was far more radical than other movements; while proletarian socialism was only 'capitalism with a minus sign', German socialism was truly anti-capitalist (Sombart 1934: 20–1, 24, 43, 112, 160).

After much definitory footwork, Sombart went on to identify socialism as a 'social normativism' set over against the 'social naturalism' of economizing thought, explaining that obligatory norms originated from the general reason which was rooted in the political community as represented by its state. Socialism was hence not confined to the economy, but had to be understood as 'die Gesamtordnung des deutschen Volkes', a total ordering of all sectors of culture born from a uniform spirit and issuing from a single centre. Because this *volkstümlicher Sozialismus* realized itself within the national framework, the only powers which were able to carry it through were the statal powers. Invoking the heritage of Fichte, Schleiermacher, Hegel, Rodbertus, and Lassalle, Sombart consequently insisted upon the need for a strong state which would govern a corporative, organic, and hierarchical order which recognized the primacy of the political (1934: 219ff., 224). The planned economy of German socialism would be at once comprehensive, single-minded, and differentiated. The private economy would not need to be liquidated, as long as it was incorporated in a larger meaningful whole, which was directed by the popular will embodied in the state. The property question, Sombart stipulated, was indeed 'not an independent issue' for German socialism; the bitterly embattled alternative of private vs. communal property did not exist for it. Private property was not unlimited in scope, but remained socially committed after the model of feudal tenure (*Lehnseigentum*).[13] The kernel issue was that property rights no longer determined the foundations of economic activity, but that the (political) foundations of economic activity henceforth determined the scope and species of property rights (ibid.: 324).

DIALECTICS OF THE POLITICAL

In their totalizing conceptualizations of power, the political, and the state, ideologists of the radical right hence tended to rehearse a cognitive pattern which characteristically beset the intellectual systems which they attempted to reverse: the dialectic of the 'last instance'. While the anarchist thinkers, as argued previously, concentrated their abhorrence of the all-enveloping nature of political oppression in ontological conceptions of the political which permitted a strategic shifting from part to whole, the authoritarian thinkers, in setting this 'inverted etatism' back upon its feet and placing power and the state under a more benevolent sign, generally left intact these concepts' systematic slippage between the particular and the general. Through another inversion across another theoretical divide, that between 'property theory' and 'power theory', the radical conservatives likewise retained the formal epistemological structure of liberal and Marxist assumptions about the causal determination of the economy 'in the last instance'. The subtle Marxist scenario of overdetermined reciprocity remained in place, resulting in a dialectic of constitution which similarly articulated the social whole into relatively autonomous spheres, even if the status of ontological 'category of origin' now befell the political. Curiously, this reversed dialectic derived as much from a politicized recapitulation of the Hegelian notion of the ethical state, interpreted as the point of culmination of the entire tradition of idealist philosophy, as it was nourished by a duly collectivized and nationalized version of the Nietzschean *Wille zur Macht*. If the Conservative Revolution was virtually unthinkable without Nietzsche (Mohler 1972: 29, 87; Aschheim

1992: 128ff.), the work of Spengler, Freyer, and Sombart – and, in the Italian context, that of Gentile, Spirito, Panunzio, Olivetti, and Michels – was there to verify the enduring legacy and converging influence of the accredited father of the dialectic.

Appropriated by Moeller van den Bruck in his pioneering article 'Nietzsche und der Sozialismus' (1919), the Nietzschean metaphysic of power also fully infiltrated Spengler's *Preussentum und Sozialismus* (1919) and its call for 'hardness', for a class of 'socialist mastermen' and for 'power, power, and yet again power' (Aschheim 1992: 195–8). If Spengler could affirm, in the first part of *Der Untergang des Abendlandes* (1918), that 'das ganze Leben ist Politik', politics was again taken in the unbounded, transcendental Nietzschean sense and closely identified with 'life', 'action', and 'war', while his conception of the 'state' tendentially encompassed the totality of human activity, the connecting tissue of its living whole, in the long tradition that connected Müller to Fichte and Hegel. For his part, Gentile, the Italian neo-Hegelian philosopher, was clear about adopting Mazzini's inclusive conception of the political 'in that overall sense which is indistinguishable from morality, religion, or any other conception of life'. As a totalitarian doctrine finding its centre of gravity in political affairs, fascism was therefore not simply concerned with the political order in the strict sense but reached out to encompass the 'will, thought and feelings' of the nation. As supreme creator of rights and liberties, the power of the *stato etico* was coextensive with the social order and constituted the true moral reality of the individual; state and individual should accordingly be considered 'inseparable terms of an essential synthesis' (1934, in Lyttleton 1973: 301–2, 306–7; Harris 1966: 236).

Freyer's *Der Staat* (1926) laid out this political dialectic in terms of a world-historical progression of three stages directed by the development of objective *Geist*, which he described as *Glaube*, *Stil*, and *Staat*. The final stage, in which Spirit took a 'political turn', represented the ultimate telos and perfection of cultural development. Here Spirit realized its ultimate objectification in the State, which would henceforth politicize all elements of culture; it was truly 'Der Geist am Ziel' (1926: 20). The stage of Style, although it had profilerated the manifold expressions of human creativity, had not been capable of unifying them; the essential quality of the State, by contrast, was its ability to forge living humanity with all its forces of production into unity through a political act. The world could only be changed through power, which remained 'one of the integrative and formative forces of the human world'. It was *Macht* which created form out of the flux of life, and which moulded the individual into 'a necessary link in the exalted whole of the Reich' (Freyer 1926: 143; Muller 1987: 111). The totalizing sociological concepts of *Macht* and *Herrschaft* which Freyer set to work here found a clear resonance in Jünger's *Der Arbeiter* (cf. 1932: 70) and many other writings of the radical right (cf. Breuer 1993: 96ff.).

In subsequent works, such as the 1933 essay *Herrschaft und Planung*, Freyer not only repeated his criticism of the Marxist tendency to 'shift the fact of domination towards the economic' and interpret it as a mere form of exploitation, but also explicitly drew upon Max Weber's 'realistic' account of the ubiquity of domination in all types of social organization (Freyer 1987: 31–3, 65–6). In this essay he also specified that, opposite to classical liberal (and one would presume, Marxist) thought, structural differentiation and stratification could well originate from the state, which could even actively create new estates or classes with functions of domination, such as the *noblesse de robe* or a proprietory bourgeoisie (ibid.: 36–7). This emphasis was repeated in somewhat different form in 'Das Politische als Problem der Philosophie' (1935), which lamented nineteenth-century philosophy's dogmatic 'neutralization' of the political, pleading philosophical recognition of the fact that the political belonged to the essence and destiny of humankind, that it signified no less than humankind's 'second creation'. Virtually reversing the Marxian dialectic of economic constitution, Freyer intoned that the political was the true soil from which culture grew, adding in Hegelian fashion that the state constituted the 'totality of the systems of the objective spirit', the sum of its own social articulations. These systems were 'not just regulated or protected or historically represented by it, but *constituted* and brought into existence as its moments, even in their capacity as autonomous spheres' (1987: 62–3).

So far, I have been somewhat reticent in introducing a major intellectual figure whose vastly influential conception of the political (cf. the respectful references in Freyer 1921: 118; 1987: 24; Sombart 1934: 171) perhaps offered the clearest example of this reversal of ontological terms.[14] Indeed, Carl Schmitt's vivid defence of the autonomy of the political against liberal and Marxist 'neutralizations' and 'depoliticizations'[15] notoriously slipped into a far more offensive claim about the political as first and last constitutive instance, which acted as a totalizing force, even while the specificity of alternative instances was to some extent preserved. The political was essentially autonomous, not in the sense of marking out a new object area which was laterally positioned *vis-à-vis* others (such as morality, culture, economics, or religion), but as a self-revealing essence which was not reducible to any one of them but could operate in all. Because it was oriented towards the *Ernstfall* or the state of exception, the specifically political distinction, that between friend and enemy, marked the highest degree of intensity of a social association or dissociation. As a matter of tension rather than extension, it had no substance of its own; the specifically 'political' extremity might be reached from all areas as soon as their indigenous conflicts were fuelled into a high degree of polarity. The political logic was hence always foundational, and the political entity always the decisive entity, sovereign in the sense of being determinant in the decisive instance (*die im entscheidenden Fall bestimmende Einheit*). The state was therefore the determinant condition of a people, 'its status as such', the *societas perfecta* of this nether world (Schmitt 1996: 19–22, 26–7, 44; 1988: 186; cf. Sombart 1934: 171). In a democratically organized community, state and society mutually penetrated and fused, inaugurating the 'total state' of the 'identity between state and society', in which politically neutral areas cease to exist. Even if 'state-free' societal spheres were reconstituted, they were conditionally demarcated by the total-izing and functionalizing state (cf. Schmitt 1932: 93).[16] As Schmitt declared, one should acknowledge not only that 'the political' was 'the total', but also that the decision about whether something was *unpolitical* invariably entailed a *political* decision (Schmitt 1922: 6; 1935: 17).

Such theoretical preferences lent a peculiar significance to Schmitt's *aperçu*, in *Der Begriff des Politischen*, about what he described as the '19th century German tension of state and society, politics and economy'. As backdrop to a rather specific critique of Oppenheimer's liberal sociology of the state, which emphatically reversed the Hegelian order of evaluation, this insight also appeared to have wider validity for interpreting similar reversals by anarchist, syndicalist, and Marxist thinkers. While Hegel, as Schmitt explained, set the state as the realm of ethical perfection and objective reason high above society, Oppenheimer's radical liberalism instead privileged economic society as the sphere of peaceful justice and equal exchange, degrading the state as a region of violent immorality, 'extra-economic' force, thievery, and conquest. While the roles were reversed, the apotheosis remained (1996: 76–7). Despite such unusual perceptiviness about 'knowledge-political' rivalries between founda-tional concepts and intellectual systems, Schmitt himself, however, did not reflexively withdraw from the grand polemic and the grand binary, but mani-festly reinforced them by once again celebrating a grand apotheosis of the political.

Whereas, for Oppenheimer as for radical Marxists, the state would wither away and everything would become 'societal' or 'economic' – since both the liberal and the communist state coincided with the associated producers – everything would turn political in Schmitt's homogeneous people's state. The sovereignty of the economy (and of political economy as master science) was once again exchanged for the sovereignty of the political (and of political philosophy). This structural affinity effectively turned Oppenheimer, Marx, and Schmitt into 'last instance' theorists with comparable ambitions: spokesmen who permitted themselves to be carried by 'their' instances and by the science which lent them a socio-ontological primacy. Indeed, if a specific instance is claimed to be 'sovereign', 'decisive', or 'inescapable', this is metonymically valid for the theory and the theorist that cultivate it as such.

Next to Freyer, the neo-Hegelian sociologist, it was perhaps Schmitt, the Hobbesian jurist and political philosopher, who was most intensely conscious about extending and building upon the long heritage of Aristotelian political philosophy. In his earliest works, he explicitly retraced the path of Machiavelli, Bodin, and Hobbes in order to recuperate their essentialist, pointlike conception of sovereignty, in immediate prefiguration of his own conception of the political as a 'limit concept' which was geared towards the emergency case. The truly impressive character of Bodin's definition, he noted, resided in its either/or quality, in the presumption of indivisible unity of a supreme decision-making power which remained free from all normative constraints (1922: 14, 19). This idea of a monopoly of ultimate decision was likewise applauded in the political philosophy of Hobbes and Rousseau; the latter's doctrine of the general will vividly illustrated to Schmitt that the democratization of the concept of sovereignty did not endanger its pointlike, identitarian essence (1922: 44–5; 1923: 20). A 'truly consistent democracy', Schmitt postulated, required national and cultural homogeneity and exclusion or even annihilation of the heterogeneous; it signified the closest identity of rulers and ruled, state and people, representers and represented (1923: 14ff., 34–5). The Bolshevik and fascist dictatorships, while being definitely anti-liberal, were therefore not necessarily anti-democratic. The liberal doctrine of the separation of powers and other pluralist conceptions of the state had to be dismissed for denying 'that the plenitude of state power may be concentrated at one point', and hence for resisting this democratic presumption of identity and absolute unity (1923: 47, 51).[17] This conflict between identitarian democracy and pluralist liberalism was also defined as running parallel to and resulting from the grand opposition between 'political' and 'economic' thinking (1988: 110).

Reviewing similarly dictatorial conceptions of sovereignty in anti-Enlightenment philosophers such as De Maistre and Donoso Cortes, Schmitt also thematized the curious intellectual 'conspiracy' between their authoritarian conceptions of state power and anarchist convictions about the essential corruptibility of all government, a complicitous rivalry which seemed to offer 'the clearest antithesis in the entire history of political ideas'. Following Donoso, who heartily despised liberals but anxiously respected anarchists such as Proudhon as his most deadly enemies (1922: 79–80; 1923: 81ff.), Schmitt likewise tended to admire the political intransigence of 'inverted etatists' such as Sorel and Bakunin. While Marx still remained spiritually dependent upon his adversary, the bourgeois, a thinker such as Sorel, despite his lingering economism and proletarian class enthusiasm, had liberated himself from political rationalism, evolving towards an appreciation of the irreducibility of the political and of the persistence of the national myth, which for Schmitt possessed far greater energy than the myth of the class struggle (1923: 88–9; cf. Wolin 1992: 435–8).

INTELLECTUALS' SOCIALISM OF THE RIGHT

If 'the political', for many intellectuals on the radical right, performed as a dialectical category of origin, allowing a permanent slippage between partial, domanial conceptions and more totalizing and foundational ones, it also opened up vast possibilities for committing what has been termed the 'metonymic fallacy' of the intellectuals. As radical spokespersons for the higher interests of state sovereignty, national homogeneity, and cultural identity, the political intellectuals of the right consistently insinuated their partial concerns into their missionary definitions of the 'general will' and the world-historical project of the nation. The identitarian dialectic of power reflected their aspiration to emerge as the 'part' that would empower the 'whole'; it enabled them to read their own desired fate (to be prime movers and final causes of social action) into the objective hierarchy and causality of the world. The logic of substitution, according to which the *Volk* was defined as coming to reflexive self-consciousness in its state, also reflected a politics of knowledge through which the intellectuals moulded both people and state after their own missionary self-image. Their oscillatory, 'emanative', systematically over-flowing conceptions of sovereignty, domination, and the state silently suggested that intellectual spokespersons were legitimately everywhere and could substitute for all other interests. The claim about the ontological primacy of the political performatively but obliquely supported a more subterranean claim about the political primacy of the intellectuals themselves.

As an initial illustration of this knowledge-political double play, we may call attention to the obverse side of the right-wing intellectuals' politicization of the intellect, which was consistently balanced with distinctly *spiritualist* or *intellectualist* definitions of the state and the political themselves. Extrapolating the long lineage of idealist philosophy and Romantic historiography which culminated in the Hegelian idea of Objective Spirit, the state was preferably circumscribed as a 'geistige Gestalt', a *Vernunftstaat* in which the people became a subject-for-itself, attaining reflexive self-consciousness about its moral will and historical mission. The Hegelian ethical state was not only the moralizing but simultaneously the reasoning or rational state, the 'social brain' which would act as a dynamic unifier and mobilizer of all human and physical resources. Gentile's neo-idealist statism was equally spiritualist in its conception as was that of Freyer, who eulogized the state early on as the 'geistig beauftragtem Subjekt der Geschichte' (1921: 119) and as 'Der Geist am Ziel' (1926: 20), carefully stipulating that only those who knew the true direction of *Geist* had a right to historical action. Adding to a theme which had already attained prolific dimensions on the radical right, Freyer also portrayed political action as a creative act and the political leader as a creative artist, who gave form to his *Volk* as an artist lent form to his work of art (1926: 109). The 'political turn' of *Geist* was hence consistently accompanied by a 'spiritual turn' in the definition of the political itself; the newly projected synthesis of reason and power, far from implying a linear reduction of the former to the latter, simultaneously represented a bid for a spiritualized politics and a bid for power on the part of the 'spiritual men' themselves.

As we have seen, the core notion of a knowledgeable, moralizing, and entrepreneurial state also included an ambition towards the *Vergeistigung* of economic life, once again to be taken in the triple sense of rationalization, moralization, and politicization. This cluster of virtual synonyms focused what became one of the most persistent thematics in the discourse of the intellectual right: the contrast between the Germanic 'spirit of organization', which was inherently partial to rational planning and socialism, and the un-German (English, Jewish, or generically foreign) spirit of capitalist individualism and disorganization. While the Italian fascist idea of the state as supreme consciousness and universal will of the nation could in this respect build upon the tradition of political syndicalism, the Hitlerian conception of the strong state as 'intelligence' and 'organizer' of national production extended and repeated what was already fully contained in the 'Ideas of 1914'. These had dramatized the world-historical contest between the 'idea of money' and the 'idea of organization' and prophesied the coming rule of 'the socialism of the civil servant and the organizer' (Spengler 1919: 47). This Saint-Simonian *Gestalt* of the intellectual organizer also moved upfront in the 'developmental', mobilizing regimes as they were projected in the planning utopias of the Italian syndicalists or those of Jünger, Freyer, and the *Tatkreis*.[18] The total mobilization of the *Arbeitsplan*, to Jünger, was clearly suggestive of the novel power of organizational thinking (1930: 140). His type of the *Krieger-Arbeiter*, moreover, was evidently metonymic for the political technician or the 'organizing' intellectual (such as Jünger himself), whose existential condition and missionary aspirations had also inspired the (equally self-referring) profile of the class-conscious proletarian fighter according to Marx. In a broader intellectual context, indeed, the national syndicalist and conservative-revolutionary conceptions of a state-directed 'organization of labour' were definitely reminiscent of and parasitic upon left-wing socialist conceptions, as formulated much earlier by, for example, Proudhon and Blanc.

Predictably, this idea of the 'organization of labour' also encircled a persistent theme in corporatist thought, both in its more etatist and its more democratic 'societal' versions (cf. Schmitter 1977). As Manoïlescu phrased it in his influential *Le siècle du corporatisme*, the economically defined dominance of labour and capital was presently fading into the past, while political organization was emerging as a novel autonomous force, inaugurating a regime of order, unity, and competence. In the new functionalist order, authority would dominate property, which was essentially a *fermage* in the general interest, to be guarded by a dynamically innovating and coordinating state. Appealing to Saint-Simon as an inspiring precursor, and emphasizing the radical differences which separated the corporatist project from both liberalism and communism, Manoïlescu foregrounded the organizer as the true prototype of the coming corporatist state (1934: 44–5, 102–3, 361). Similar conceptions about a corporatist technocracy and a 'new aristocracy' of technicians and political intellectuals were current in the writings of Italian syndicalists and nationalists such as Michels, Rocco, Spirito, and Panunzio (Rosenstock-Franck 1934: 16; Gregor 1979b). They also resonated in German Romantic utopias about an organically articulated *Volkswirtschaft*, in which all occupations would be defined as civic duties, and in which a *Leistungselite* of engineers, industrialists, and *völkische* intellectuals would institute rational order within the framework of the national community.

Everything said so far fortifies the suggestion that there existed a significant right-wing, national socialist variant of the traditionally left-identified, Saint-Simonian vision of the political calling of a new managing or organizational elite, and that the significance of fascist ideology cannot be fully grasped unless this specific elitist claim is given due weight. The history of this multifaceted, politically diversified 'socialism of the intellectuals', even if it was promoted by self-styled 'anti-intellectual intellectuals' who were critical of Enlightenment values, at least sensitizes to some peculiar aspects of the still widely tabooed intellectual proximity between radical left and radical right, whose shared technocratic ideals sometimes offered a bridgehead for mutual intellectual exchanges and even crossovers from one side to the other of the political landscape. The viability and ubiquity of this shared 'technocratic dream' were perhaps nowhere more clearly demonstrated than in the fateful itinerary of such 'crossover' intellectuals, a type exemplified by Mussolini, Michels, Lagardelle, and other Sorelians in early-century France and Italy, represented more rarely in Germany by thinkers such as Sombart, and epitomized perhaps most dramatically by Marcel Déat in France and Hendrik De Man in Belgium in the middle and late 1930s. Before concluding the present review, I will briefly profile the latter two cases, in order to enrich my perspective of the claimed 'primacy of the political' by tuning in to some obvious parallelisms between Déat's *néo-socialisme* and De Man's *planisme* and 'national socialist' thinking as so far discussed.

'Crown princes' both of their respective parties, the SFIO and the BWP, and influential revisionists of the orthodox type of Marxism embraced by their *patrons* Blum and Vandervelde, Déat and De Man, in the course of the 1930s, slowly drifted towards a set of intellectual premises and a political tactic which approximated notions about the strong state, a 'national socialism', a state-directed economy of planning, and the rule of an intellectual technocracy which were also current at the other end of the contemporary political spectrum. Opposing Blum's 'economistic' and 'fatalist' policies in the summer of 1933, Déat and his associates capped their defence of a radically activist *néo-socialisme* with the ringing slogan 'Order, Authority, Nation', pleading a shift from class policy to national policy and the necessity of first organizing the economy within the national framework. De Man's Plan of Labour, enthusiastically adopted by the BWP at its Christmas Congress in the same year, similarly propounded a novel doctrine of socialization, according to which national implementation (or 'socialism in one country') was to take priority over the shady prospect of internationalism. In a far-reaching reversal of terms and tactics, the essence of socialization was located less in the transfer of ownership than in the transfer of authority, which implied that the issue of control now took precedence over that of possession (cf. Pels 1987: 221ff.). Anticipating Burnham, Berle, and other managerialists, both De Man and

Déat theorized that property and power were in the process of separating in the modern shareholding economy, which transformed the problem of socialism into one of organization and management rather than property in the means of production. Déat, in *Perspectives socialistes* (1930), explicitly over-turned the Marxist scenario by proposing to tackle first the *power* (*puissance*) of capitalism, subsequently to take over capitalist *profit*, and finally to socialize capitalist *property*. To be sure, the idea that socialization was no longer a question of nominal possession but of 'technique of administration', as a result of the developing fissure between *Besitz* and *Betrieb*, could already be encountered in conservative revolutionaries from Spengler (1919: 95) up to Fried (1931: 142ff.), and is traceable even further back towards French and Italian syndicalism.[19]

In the late 1930s, the embryonic conception of the *état fort* shared by neo-socialism and planism, which presumed at least some degree of autonomy of the political *vis-à-vis* the economic, gradually evolved into a fully fledged doctrine of state primacy and 'authoritarian democracy', according to which the political state was to carry through a socialist revolution 'from above' against the powers of capitalist finance, and institute a corporatist regime to be run by an elite of intellectual technicians. Distancing themselves ever further from liberal parliamentarian politics, both Déat and De Man came to distinguish between what the latter called a 'true, social, and proletarian democracy' and a 'false, only parliamentary and formal bourgeois democracy' (Pels 1987: 226). After the Nazi victory in early 1940, they both stood convinced that the demise of capitalist democracy was final, and that the war inaugurated a revolutionary period which offered new promises to socialism. In a notorious manifesto of June 1940, De Man advised his fellow socialists to join 'the movement of national insurrection' in order to realize 'the sovereignty of Labour' under the guidance of a single party and a totalitarian state. Somewhat later, he acknowledged German national socialism as 'the German form of socialism' and pleaded cooperation with the Reich 'within the framework of a unified Europe and a universal socialist revolution' (cit. Pels 1993b: 89–90). Like De Man, whose collaborationist adventure was compara-tively brief, Déat in 1940 disposed his considerable powers of intellect in the service of the national socialist revolution, and entered the collaborationist regime of Vichy (cf. Grossman 1969; Goodman 1973).

REINVENTING THE POLITICAL

Half a century after the defeat of the fascist regimes, our intellectual horizon is in many respects dramatically altered. Precisely as a result of the indissoluble association between the heritage of the radical right and the agonizing memo-ries of the Holocaust, 'fascism' has become a universal term of political abuse, eclipsing its ideological stature and pedigree, and censuring its intellectual content as being unworthy of serious analysis. Given the persistence of this ideological void on the right, radical assertions about a 'primacy of the political' in the postwar period tended to originate from the left side of the political spectrum, and were often clad in the confusingly indirect Marxist vocabulary of the 'primacy of the economic'. As suggested previously, however, some major new schools of Marxist theorizing that emerged in the early 1960s permitted a secular, if initially subterranean, conflation of the two vocabularies, following from an increasingly explicit 'Gramscian' recognition of the specificity if not primordiality of political and cultural causation, which pressed against the limits of extension of the logic of 'last instance' economic determination. While theorists such as Althusser and Poulantzas already stretched the Marxian logic of causality to its breaking point, post-Marxists such as Foucault, Deleuze, Lefort, the 'new philosophers', and Laclau and Mouffe extrapolated this tendency even further, ending up by emphatically reinstating the political at the centre of critical attention. As we have noted, their efforts were paralleled by the massive 'defection' of feminist theorists from a Marxist-inspired 'political economy of sex' towards generalized notions about the 'politics of the personal', 'the politics of (gender) identity', and the 'politics of discourse'. Other intellectual currents, such as ecology or constructivist science and technology studies, similarly abandoned the apparent constrictions of economic repertoires in order to clear the field for a 'politics of nature' and a 'politics of things'.

There is a coldly ironic, disquieting aspect of *déjà vu* in this novel omnipresence of the political on the political left, which to some extent exhibits an involuntary 'return of the repressed', in so far as it actually recycles many of the critical arguments previously advanced against Marxist and liberal economism by intellectuals of the prewar political right. Some theorizations, indeed, come rather close to reinventing the 'conservative-revolutionary' reversal of priorities, by substituting ontological conceptualizations of the political for previous conceptions of the economic that continue to resemble the transcendental mechanics of the 'last instance'. Three such examples may be briefly cited here, as collectively exemplifying the latter-day paradox of a right-inspired search for a new left-oriented political paradigm. Many are also sufficiently impressed, especially by Carl Schmitt's razor-sharp critique of traditional liberalism, to honour him with recalcitrant or inverse readings of his political theory. The journal *Telos* has long stood in the forefront of this critical acclamation.[20] Introducing a special issue on the French New Right, for instance, its editor Paul Piccone identifies the 'bureaucratic centralism' of the former Soviet Union and Western 'liberal technocracy' as variations of the same basic Enlightenment model which

> by defining all conflicts in economic terms, has successfully occluded a more pervasive logic of domination beyond labor/capital conflicts and predicated on the political power and obtaining between the

rulers and the ruled, the experts and the masses, the administrators and the administrated.

The main implication of this theory about a newly emerging new class of politicians, intellectuals, and bureaucrats, for Piccone, is

> the displacement of *economic* conflicts between labor and capital as the *deus ex machina* of social dynamics, in favor of *political* conflicts between those possessing a 'cultural capital' redeemable as social and political power and those with mere 'cultural liabilities'.

The inspiration for this political analysis of cultural class is quarried both from left-wing theorists such as Gouldner and Konrad and Szelenyi, and from the critique of (left-wing) intellectuals such as advanced by the New Right (1993–4: 8–11).

Laclau and Mouffe's writings offer another singular illustration of the internal groundswell which has swept Gramscian Marxism towards a Schmittian invocation of the primordiality of the political. While some commentators already saw Laclau's early *Politics and Ideology in Marxist Theory* (1977) as drifting towards a 'power conception of class' (Wolff and Resnick 1986: 108), Laclau and Mouffe's 'post-Marxist' work *Hegemony and Socialist Strategy* (1985) more emphatically distanced itself from the orthodox reductionist and essentialist economic paradigm in order to affirm 'the new articulatory and recomposing logic of hegemony' as an autonomous *political* logic which itself structured the space of the economic (1985: 4, 75ff.). Crossing the Marxist threshold in an even more decisive manner, Mouffe's appropriately entitled *The Return of the Political* (1993) further extends their collaborative project by entering upon a close engagement with the legacy of Schmitt, with a view to articulating a radical project of 'agonistic' pluralism which is set squarely against the 'anti-political' rationalism of Rawlsian political philosophy. Adopting Schmitt's conviction that 'the political cannot be restricted to a certain type of institution, or envisaged as constituting a specific sphere or level of society', she chooses to understand it 'as a dimension that is inherent to every human society and that determines our very ontological condition'. In doing so, she closely follows Lefort's call for a new political philosophy, as well as his expansive understanding of politics as 'a specific mode of institution of the social', as the 'disciplinary matrix' of social life (1993: 3, 11, 18ff., 51–2).

Perhaps it is Lefort's political theory of democracy which provides the closest and most comprehensive approximation to Schmittian concerns, even while it is likewise formulated in the strictest opposition to all totalitarian presumptions of identity (cf. De Wit 1992: 479ff.). The 'great swerve' from sophisticated Marxist economism towards political philosophy repeats itself in the history of Castoriadis's and Lefort's *Socialisme ou Barbarie* group, which gradually emancipated itself from a Trotskyite critique of 'bureaucratic collectivism' towards a recognition of new politically based forms of exploitation and domination, carrying the questioning step by step 'to the heart of Marxist certainty' (Lefort 1986: 297). Socialist thought, Lefort estimated, had insufficiently liberated itself from the liberal problematic, which proclaimed that reality 'was to be disclosed at the level of the economy' and thus repressed the question of the political. Marxism's rejection of the political, its 'refusal to think in political terms', resulted not simply in a deficient theory of the state, but more profoundly, in a complete lack of a conception of political society, including the nature of totalitarian regimes instituted under the aegis of Marxism itself. Hence the need for a new political philosophy that could rehabilitate the political beyond its 'positivist' delineation as sector or domain in the social structure towards a broader recognition of it as a generative, originary principle of society, after the model of the Platonic *politeia* (1988: 2–3).

'Politics' (*la politique*), as specific domanial activity, should be differentiated from 'the political' (*le politique*), which defined the primal dimensionality of the social, configuring society's overall schema, and governing the articulation of its various levels or dimensions. It was precisely the focus upon narrower 'politics', Lefort argued, that obscured the broader acting of 'the political' as the primal giving-form of society, taken in the double sense of giving meaning (*mise en sens*) and staging (*mise en scène*) (1988: 11, 219).[21] In democratic societies, this political configuration of the social crucially implied a disentangling of state and society, a separation of the autonomous spheres of power, law, and knowledge. Henceforth, the locus of power no longer constituted a substance but an 'empty space'; it could not be occupied or appropriated, and no individual or group could be consubstantial with it. This strictly opposed the democratic political configuration to the identitarian logic of totalitarianism, which strove to recover power as a substantial reality, with the purpose of reunifying society as a homogeneous social body governed by a supreme, sovereign power (Lefort 1988: 233). In this fashion, a totalizing conception of the political closely resembling that of Schmitt was paradoxically deflected against the Schmittian politics of homogeneity, subverting its totalitarian temptation by means of a 'divisive' vision of democratic difference.

Fifty years after the fascist defeat, this left-wing reinvention of the political is also seconded by parallel reactivating efforts issuing from the New Right. The repressed has also returned under its own flag, aided by the natural obliviousness that belongs to a new generational experience. The fact remains that social criticism directed at the universal 'marketing' or 'economization' of modern life and the triumphant proclamation of the liberal 'end of history' is no longer solely operated from the left, but is also nurtured by a new radicalism of the right which is increasingly implicated in a process of intellectual rationalization. This new intellectualization of the right promotes, among other things, an intense rereading of the neglected legacy of the Conservative Revolution, including its prominent theme of the 'primacy of the political'.

Aschheim has observed that, while the resuscitation of Nietzsche into something like a 'European vogue figure' required that he emigrate to France in order to 'catch' the poststructuralist revolution of the 1970s, there are signs that he is presently emigrating back in order to be reappropriated by a new German intellectual right (1992: 305–6). In France itself, however, De Benoist has from an early date incorporated Nietzsche's legacy, as well as that of Schmitt, Niekisch, and other conservative revolutionaries, in his synthetic project of a *Nouvelle Droite*; his 'Aristotelian' and communitarian conceptions of democracy and citizenship run largely parallel to conservative-revolutionary vindications of the primordial nature of the political (De Benoist 1983: 7ff.; 1984: 7ff.; 1993: 65ff.; Taguieff 1993–4). Among the leftist ideas also appropriated in the mid-1970s was Gramsci's converging theory of cultural and political hegemony (Piccone 1993–4: 9; Wegierski 1993–4: 63), thus compounding the spectacle of a right-inspired leftism with the reverse one of a left-inspired paradigm of the right.

In this fashion, the radical-conservative version of the 'primacy of the political' may be celebrating an unexpected return. Intellectuals such as Jünger, Heidegger, Freyer, and Schmitt once again figure as house gods of right-wing intellectual journals such as the German *Junge Freiheit* or *Etappe* or the Russian *Elementy*, which not only communicate with De Benoist but also negotiate with the thought of Foucault and other representatives of French poststructuralism (cf. Dahl 1996). Significantly, the new conservatism has also joined forces with radical political ecology and its apocalyptic sense of a civilization in disarray, boosting its penchant for totalizing and authoritarian solutions. 'Eco-fascism' (or what is sometimes referred to as *Blut-und-Boden* ecology) calls for a strong state in order to protect the ecological 'commonwealth' and its 'natural order' from destruction both through natural disasters and through overpopulation and *Überfremdung*, which collectively threaten the identity and integrity of the people and the natural habitat. Calls for a 'Patriotische Umweltschutz', as phrased in the 1990 programme of the Republikaner Party, are not far from more radical proposals such as entertained by former *Grünen* ideologist Herbert Gruhl, who activates familiar Schmittian themes in emphasizing the ecological 'state of exception' which is necessarily governed by 'martial law', the imperative need for an authoritarian state to plot a strategy of survival and implement it with force, and the concomitant need for abolishing democratic procedure in favour of a dictatorship – in the present context, of an elite of the ecologically enlightened (Jahn and Wehling 1991).

5

SOCIAL SCIENCE AS POWER THEORY

What is really important in sociology is nothing but political science.

Gramsci

THE ELUSIVE OBJECT OF SOCIOLOGY

According to a widely held idol of the tribe, sociology started its career with the discovery of 'society' as an entity distinct from and independent of the state (Collins and Makowsky 1972; Goudsblom 1977; Bottomore and Nisbet 1979; Heilbron 1995). Sociology, Aron has argued, marks a moment in human reflection on historical reality 'when the concept of the social, of society, becomes the centre of interest, replacing the concept of politics or of the régime or of the state' (1965 I: 15). Early sociology, Gouldner agreed, rejected the dominance of society by the state, and more generally, defocalized the importance of politics in order to concentrate upon 'civil society' as its principal scientific object (1980: 363–4). Most significant in the sociological experience, Elias has written, is the conceptualization of 'society' as a self-regulating nexus of events, and as something which was not determined in its course and its functioning by governments (1984: 38).

The idea appears to add the virtues of simplicity to those of self-evidence, and offers a classical justification for the existence of sociology as an autonomous intellectual enterprise. It is the existence of this autonomous order of social events intermediary between private individuals and the strictly political sphere which is held to justify the territorial and theoretical claims of sociology *vis-à-vis* the other human sciences, and especially, to mark a clear boundary with older-style political philosophy. Looking back gratefully to Durkheim, sociologists routinely affirm the presence of something like the social realm (*règne social*) as a reality *sui generis*, which has its own structure and regularities and generates its own quasi-natural patterns of development. To an important degree, it is this postulated autonomy of the sociological *object* which is taken to legitimize the relative autonomy of the sociological *project*.[1]

Despite its textbook popularity and its evident common-sense appeal, however, many social theorists and historians of the discipline have agonized over the irritating vagueness of the blanket term 'society', and searched for more specific delimitations through a study of the political and intellectual context of its discovery. In doing so, they have come up with widely divergent answers. Nisbet, for instance, found it 'neither sufficient nor accurate to say, as many historians have, that the most distinctive feature of the rise of sociology in the nineteenth century is the idea of "society". This says too much and too little.' It was 'community' rather than 'society' which had to be viewed as sociology's most fundamental and characteristic unit-idea (1966: 48). In Therborn's neo-Marxist perspective, on the other hand, society was defined as those 'social arrangements determined in the last instance by a specific combination of forces and relations of production'. While reclaiming 'society' or 'civil society' as the scientific object of historical materialism, the prime contribution of sociology was said to lie in its discovery of the 'ideological community', i.e. the community of values, norms, and beliefs — which edged rather close to Nisbet's conception (1976: 73). And somewhere in between Nisbet's communitarianism and Therborn's economism stands Gouldner's attempt to retrieve 'civil society' as the legitimate object and 'historical mission' of sociology, now stripped of its materialist connotation and embracing the diffuse entirety of 'social organization' or 'group life' (1980: 363ff.).

Without doubt, much of the vagueness of the undifferentiated concept of 'society' is ascribable to its historically defined negative or demarcative intent.[2] The concept was born as part of a polemic and a struggle for intellectual independence, and this circumstance has probably made it less pressing for (proto)sociologists to know what the social *was* than to agree upon what it *was not*. This polemic was conducted on several fronts simultaneously, since 'society' was generally taken as ontologically broader and more fundamental than the political state, while it also referred to a spontaneously evolving reality that was relatively independent from conscious individual designs — whether in terms of the actions of freely contracting individual citizens, or in the form of conscious interventions by princes, legislators, or founders of states. This double demarcation left much interpretative room, since the vast space 'in between' the discrete individuals or households and political institutions could be filled in quite different ways. In broad outline, Marx's classical injunction to seek the anatomy of civil society in a critically revised political economy stood opposed to the French positivists' equally classical attempt to demarcate their object against *both* the political *and* the economic, while mainstream German sociology tended towards a concept of civil society which retained a much closer continuity with the older *staatswissenschaftliche* conception of the state.

While it is generally acknowledged that the concept of society arose within a political and evaluative ambience, it is also thought that this has somehow worn off with the passage of time and the growing maturity of the discipline (cf. Elias 1984; Heilbron 1995). However, it takes only a cursory glance at the above-cited definitions in order to realize that there is no question of a definitive transcendence of such normative and political commitments. Nisbet's idea of community is manifestly designed as a normative counterpart to what he describes as the 'Enlightenment' conception of society; Therborn's definition is unthinkable if divorced from the opposition between bourgeois sociology and historical materialism; while Gouldner's notion of civil society represents nothing less than an attempt to cheat Marxism out of one of its master concepts. As we shall notice, even the traditional Comtean–Durkheimian notion of the relative autonomy of the social turns out to be heavily laden with polemics, although it is normally advertised as an escape from it. It is a move in the game which denies the existence of the same game in which it is a move.[3]

Apart from such – perhaps ineradicable – polemics, the common-sense notion of the social also labours under a peculiar ambiguity of parts and wholes. 'Society' can be either conceived as a *residual* category and refer to the nexus of relations and functions in between government and individual, or state and market, or polity and economy, but it may also describe the *totality* of social relations under which both individual actions and political relations are subsumed. Historically, the notion of *société civile*, as it emerged in the writings of the *philosophes*, typically oscillated between partial and holist definitions, designating rising sectors such as the economy or culture, but simultaneously expanding its scope towards all social sectors and units (Heilbron 1995: 87, 91). As Gouldner has expressed it, sociology, especially in its early phase, hesitated between a view of itself as a 'n + 1 science' which took up the leftovers of disciplines such as political philosophy and political economy, and a less humble conception of itself as queen of the social sciences, 'concerning itself with all that the others do, and more; possessing a distinctive concern with the *totality* of sectors, with their incorporation into a new and higher level of integration, and with the unique laws of this higher whole' (1970: 92–4). In *The Two Marxisms*, he reiterated the view that sociology's object was largely residual, 'including at the largest remove all groups and institutions not directly part of the state'; but his suggestion was not simply that civil society was intermediary between the political and the economic but also somehow transcended them, since both political and economic spheres were differentiations of a more basic *social* material (1980: 364, 356; cf. 1985: 240ff.). This 'sphere of human connectedness' was hence not unequivocally coextensive with what thinkers such as Montesquieu, Proudhon, Tocqueville, and Durkheim identified as the *corps intermédiaires*, but potentially encompassed the totality of social relationships and institutions.

It is disconcerting that this almost studied and deliberate ambiguity, which recurs in virtually all attempts to establish the distinctive nature of the sociological object/project, is so little reflected upon and so much taken for granted. Even if distance is taken from 'domanial' legitimations and distinctiveness is sought in sociology's peculiar analytic perspective, one is tempted to premise the existence of a social element in all human relationships to which sociology provides privileged access. In Aron's view, for example, the specifically social may be located either on the level of the part, the element, or the level of the whole, the entity; sociology, as the study of 'the social as such', is then characterized by a 'fluctuation between element and entity'. It is not at all clear what is meant by this, not even when Aron adds that the social is 'either the element present in all social relations or the larger and vaguer entity embracing and uniting the various sectors of collective life' (1965: 15–16). The 'partial' concern with interpersonal relations and the 'totalist' concern with the global society do not quite combine into an acceptable and transparent view of what sociology is about.

A NEW THEORY OF POLITICS?

Taken in its simplest form, therefore, the idea of the 'discovery of society' stands as a truism which, at best, is too true to be good, and at worst, may be seriously misleading. Society, in this undifferentiated sense, does not exist, and cannot by itself legitimate the specific difference of the sociological enterprise (cf. Frisby and Sayer 1986: 121–2). The consensus which it commands has a superficial ring, because it tends to rule out and define away deeper-lying disagreements about what 'society' or the 'social' are like, and thus easily overstates both the intellectual uniformity and the historical originality of what is termed 'the' sociological tradition. More precisely, I shall argue, the presumption of a uniform and autonomous tradition tends to paper over significant discrepancies, tensions, and displacements between at least three major currents of thought, which have offered three divergent interpretations of 'the social' as the privileged object/project of sociology, and which are all much more closely aligned with contemporary political ideologies than is normally acknowledged in academic histories of the discipline.

In conformity with my earlier perspective of a rivalry-oriented 'geography of knowledge', and of the permeable boundaries between social science and politically committed ideology, the discursive field of emerging sociology might be viewed as a tripartite space embracing a centre, occupied by the French positivist tradition, and two peripheries or 'wings', Western and Eastern/Southern, which accommodate the Anglo-Saxon liberal–utilitarian and the mid- and south-European etatist traditions. While the Anglo-Saxon wing, as represented most conspicuously by Spencerian utilitarian and anti-statist sociology, steers close to the Lockean and Smithian conception of civil society as market-based *Gesellschaft*, the other two currents are more nearly deployed around the Nisbetian 'unit-idea' of community or *Gemeinschaft* – that is, if we take immediate care to differentiate between the 'French' emphasis upon *intermediary* communal structures between individual and state and the 'German' and 'Italian' tendency to subsume the social more directly under the *statal* community.[4] In this scheme of things, Marxism occupies an intriguingly dual place, since it straddles the two peripheral paradigms, in continuing the ontological priorities of classical political economy while remaining subversively loyal to 'Germanic' etatist and centralizing sentiments. In this more differentiated tableau, the constitutive splitting of society from the state (and of social science from classical political philosophy) takes rather different routes and issues in incongruous conceptions of the social, some of which are polemically demarcated against the political, while others resist any clear-cut delineation in such terms.

In some of its variants, the historical object/project of sociology is actually closer to that of political philosophy (and farther removed from that of liberal and Marxist political economy) than is brought out by the traditional idea of a state–society split. This demarcation, in other words, tends to obscure the extent to which major currents of early sociology represented not a rupture but a *continuation* or *renovation* of classical political philosophy, dissimulating that their conception of society-as-community was still heavily marked by this Aristotelian genealogy. If this perspective is adopted, sociology is deprived of part of its taken-for-granted domanial legitimation (it loses some of the 'property' of its traditional object) because it is revealed as a critical successor to the older tradition of Aristotelian political theory, while the schism between academic sociology and Marxism, which is often emphasized as constitutive by both academic and Marxist historians of the discipline (cf. Nisbet 1966: viii; Zeitlin 1968: vii–viii; Szacki 1982: 368), does not so much result from a binary fission developing from Saint-Simon onwards (Gouldner 1970: 111–13), but in some respects may be seen as another instalment of the much older rivalry between the master sciences of political philosophy and political economy.

Göran Therborn has offered the suggestive idea that sociology began as a theory of postrevolutionary politics, focusing primarily on the relationship between politics and society at large: 'sociology emerged as a discourse on politics after the bourgeois revolution'. In his estimate, the pioneer sociologists saw themselves first and foremost as critical heirs to the tradition of political philosophy, so that 'political theory . . . seems to be the real intellectual background against which sociology's claim to represent a new science of society should be analysed' (1976: 416–17, 127). Both Saint-Simon's *physico-politique* and Comte's *physique sociale* were above all intended as new comprehensive sciences of politics, and did not distinguish sharply between social and political science (Comte 1970: 467–71, 477; Ionescu 1976: 6–8). Comte entitled his major sociological treatise *Système de politique positive*, and confidently rated his work as the crowning completion of the long tradition of political theory initiated by Aristotle ('l'incomparable Aristote', as he repeatedly chants) and continued by Hobbes (Comte 1852: 299, 351; 1975a: 433). Fletcher has likewise observed that Comte's view of politics remained close to that of Aristotle; it was broader than conventional 'politics' and implied the study of political order as (part of) a social system (1974: 27–8). In *Système de politique positive*, Comte indeed proposed that 'the admirable conception of Aristotle respecting the distribution of functions and the combination of efforts happily correlates the two necessary elements of every political idea: society and government' (1852: 295; 1975a: 430).[5]

The suggestion that sociology began as a social theory of politics is inspiring, but Therborn drops this promising lead almost as quickly as he introduces it, in order to narrate the 'remarkable transformation' which soon changed sociology, in its classical period, into a discourse about the 'ideological community'. But, as I shall argue, there is little evidence for such a remarkable caesura. The classical themes of community and value integration are not particularly distinct from the political concerns of the early positivists, and neither are the works of sociology's classical age innocent of political theory in the above-cited sense. It is hardly fortuitous that Nisbet names 'authority' as runner-up in his hierarchy of sociology's unit-ideas, encountering it dominantly even in Durkheim, the archetypal sociologist of moral community and moral discipline (1966: 47, 150).[6] The stronger suggestion, for that matter, was offered by Richter, who anticipated the extensive reappraisal of the Durkheimian legacy which has been consolidated in the writings of Gouldner (1958), Lukes (1973; 1982), Giddens (1972b; 1977; 1982), Filloux (1977; 1993), Lacroix (1981), and Pearce (1989).[7] Durkheim's political sociology, Richter proposed, could in fact be seen as the 'parricidal offspring' of Aristotelian political science (1960: 170). Filloux and Lacroix concurred that the object of Durkheimian sociology was 'political in a broad sense of this term' (cf. Filloux 1977: 9).

Hence there is ample reason to pursue the idea that some branches of early sociology directly descended from the tradition which we have named the Aristotelian one (cf. Frisby and Sayer 1986: 14–17), or that early sociology was identical in reach with a broadly conceived *political* sociology. Theorists such as Saint-Simon, Comte, Mosca, Pareto, and Michels shared the central project of a positive politics, and tended to use terms such as sociology, social science, and political science interchangeably. Their agreement did therefore not exhaust itself in the search for a new scientific *foundation* of political action, since they additionally shared the idea of an *extension* or *generalization* of the analysis of political institutions and processes towards the broader field of the social. Forms of government, it was argued, could not be properly analysed if they were divorced from the determining laws of social organization in general (cf. Therborn 1976: 145; Wagner 1990: 491).[8]

The positivist emphasis upon moral community and the elitist emphasis upon hierarchy and domination were in this respect closer than is often realized. The axiom that organization necessarily implied authority and hierarchy was shared by both traditions; Saint-Simon's sociocratic elitism likewise provided inspiration for both. Literally repeating Montesquieu (1969: 54),

Comte laid down as the fundamental axiom of all healthy politics that 'society cannot exist without government and government cannot exist without society' (1852: 267, 281, 295). As in De Bonald and De Maistre, the necessity of government was derived from the ubiquitous fact of social organization and division of labour, the 'separation of offices' requiring a 'concourse of efforts' which was not spontaneous but resulted from 'the force of social cohesion which is everywhere known under the name of government' (Comte 1974: 227).[9] While it remains open to speculation whether Saint-Simon thought that government would die off in the industrial age (cf. Durkheim 1958: 186ff.), it was less doubtful that his pupil rejected this idea from an early date. In a first outline of the *Système de politique positive* dating from 1822–4, Comte wrote about

> the government which in a regular state of affairs stands at the head of society as the guide and agent of general activity . . . the head of society destined to bind together the component units and to direct their activity to a common end

anticipating large elements of Durkheim's notion of the state as social organizer and social brain (Comte 1974: 115). Durkheim himself agreed that an 'essential element of any political group is the opposition between governing and governed, between authority and those subject to it', stipulating that 'the State is nothing if it is not an organ distinct from the rest of society' (1992: 42, 82, 91–2).

This set of concerns does not differ radically from the early elitists' preoccupation with a new science of politics, again if taken in the twofold sense of a 'positive' *grounding* of political intervention and of an *extension* of the scope of analysis from state sovereignty towards a more inclusive theory of the generation and distribution of social power. Mosca's major work, of course, was entitled *Elementi di Scienza Politica*, and as a political scientist he took a considered distance to the Comtean neologism of 'sociology'. Despite its economic origins, Pareto's work has been justifiably characterized as 'essentially a political sociology' (Therborn 1976: 122). Such a description also fits Michels' surprising itinerary from Sorelian anarcho-syndicalism *via* elitist sociology towards fascist political philosophy (Beetham 1977). The early elitist tradition, indeed, consistently opted for a more conflictual or 'Machiavellian' interpretation of the same quintessential phenomena of power, authority, and domination (and of the correlative distinction between rulers and ruled) which the French positivists gave a softer, more consensualist reading.[10] Gumplowicz' social theory, for example, which deeply influenced both Italian and German thinkers, was entirely focused around such a 'hard' conception of the *ewige Kampf um Herrschaft*. He immediately joined the Aristotelian lineage by maintaining that *Eigentum* was essentially a means of *Herrschaft*, that society was not something different from the state, but the 'same thing under another aspect', and that sociology, as the positive science of *Herrschaft*, acted as evident foundation for all the other sciences of man (Gumplowicz 1926 [1885]: 39–42, 89–90, 97–9, 107). While he also routinely formulated the elitist credo in somewhat neutral fashion ('It is of the nature of all domination that it can only be practised by a minority. The domination of a minority by a majority is unthinkable, since it is a contradiction' (cit. Therborn 1976: 193; cf. Szacki 1979: 280–6), neither Gumplowicz, nor Mosca, Pareto, or Michels after him took much trouble to hide the polemical intent which inspired the much stronger presumption in the background.[11]

Sociology as a critical continuation of classical political philosophy is also a guiding thread in Aron's 'Weberian' history of the sociological tradition. Although Aron is less explicit about it than Therborn, the idea is much more consistently patterned into his thought. One major effect of his interpretation as compared with more orthodox communitarian ones is the relative displacement of intellectual weight from the Comte–Durkheim lineage towards the axis which links Tocqueville backward to Montesquieu and forward to Weber. This also involves a calendar change, since the beginnings of sociology are fixed earlier in historical time. In this perspective, Montesquieu is not so much a precursor of sociology but rather 'one of its great theorists' (as incidentally Durkheim also thought), whose work forged a *trait d'union* between classical political theory and early sociology (Aron 1965 I: 62; Durkheim 1966). The first books of *The Spirit of the Laws* were no doubt directly inspired by Aristotle's *Politics*; allusions to and comments upon it appear 'on almost every page'. Montesquieu's distinctively sociological contribution should rather be sought in his study of the relationship between types of political superstructure and the organization of society as infrastructure of the political realm: his decisive contribution was precisely to have combined the analysis of forms of government with the study of social organizations in such a way that each regime is also seen as a certain type of society (Aron 1965 I: 25). Hence the beginnings of sociology are not found in a sharp discontinuity between society and state ('There is in *The Spirit of the Laws* neither the primacy of economic nor the primacy of society in relation to the state') but rather in the *generalization* of the analytic emphasis upon the 'political' towards the wider context of the 'social'.[12]

Heilbron has recently shown that early French social theory emerged to a large degree as a new branch of the already firmly entrenched 'moralistic' tradition, as it had evolved from Montaigne and La Rouchefoucauld to the *philosophes* and Montesquieu (1995: 20–1, 69–77). Its naturalistic descriptions of *morale* and forms of sociability departed from the core notion that social order represented a reality *sui generis*, occurring spontaneously and in relative detachment from the actions and decisions of legislative bodies. This view, however, easily overstates the 'stateless' character of what after all continued to be called the *sciences morales et politiques*, and erroneously extends this view to early Comtean and Durkheimian sociology, in which the state 'plays a similarly negligible role' (ibid.: 22–3; cf. Wagner 1990: 163). Heilbron's subsequent account, to be sure, suggests that the state–society distinction was never drawn very sharply; indeed, both Montesquieu and Rousseau are explicitly introduced as representing a *synthesis* of moral philosophy and the politico-legal tradition, so that social theory effectively emerged not so much from an effort to *sever* moral from political theory but rather from an effort to *integrate* them (1985: 80–1, 270).

Broadly, this set of intellectual concerns is also characteristic of Hegel, who after Hobbes and Montesquieu counts as the third great negotiator between classical political theory and modern social science. Although Hegel adopted the socio-economic definition of 'civil society' which was current since Locke, he was also careful to subordinate it to the higher and more universal essence of the state. However, as Szacki observes,

> it is not easy to say what is Hegel's conception of the state. The current idea of the state as the political and legal framework within which the society or the nation lives turns out to be most misleading in his case. The state in his conception does not reduce to that frame-work and brings to mind, rather, the idea of Aristotle's *polis* or Montesquieu's state, which can more readily be associated with our idea of society than with our idea of the state as an organisation.

Szacki even suggests that the most suitable translation of Hegel's term 'state' would be *community*, if taken in a normatively benign sense, i.e. assuming a high level of consciousness, individual autonomy, and freedom. In this defini-tion, the state constitutes an 'infinitely finer link between human beings than which results from the struggle for the satisfaction of material needs – that is, finer than civil society' (Szacki 1979: 136–9). In the early decades of the twen-tieth century, this communitarian and holistic view would be radicalized by right-wing thinkers such as Gentile, Michels, and Spirito in fascist Italy, and Sombart, Freyer, and Schmitt in Weimar Germany, who sharpened the Hegelian identification of state, community, and civil society into an uncom-promisingly totalitarian view of socio-political life.

THREE WINGS OF SOCIAL THEORY

My present effort to add plausibility to early sociology's Aristotelian creden-tials is also an attempt to counteract the tendency to homogenize its past from what can be called an overly 'Anglo-Saxon' or 'liberal' image of its early history. The fixation on the state–society split and on the demarcation from traditional political philosophy has resulted in an exaggeratedly 'anti-statist' or *laissez-faire* view of the sociological object-and-project, which has critically foreshortened our perception of the differentiated historical canvas on which the early gestation of social theory was played out. If, admittedly, all three currents of emerging sociology tended to distance themselves in some way from the strictly governmental, top-down concerns of Aristotelian political philosophy, looking for structural realities 'below' the state in order to sociologize the political, the break was not everywhere as clean as often suggested, and reference points for disciplinary boundary work were rather unevenly spread across the differentiated cognitive field. Indeed, for rising social theory, boundary-drawing efforts against classical political economy were equally significant as those directed against political philosophy (cf. Wagner 1990: 496), while the weights and measures of the various demarcative exercises (and their net balance) also differed markedly across various socio-geographical contexts.

As suggested above, both the unity and the diversity of the sociological project can be fruitfully respecified by introducing a triadic historical tableau, which distinguishes between a central building and two wings, or a central zone and two peripheral ones, which simultaneously delineate geographical regions, political and economic contexts, and intellectual fields. In mapping a graded space of disciplinary rivalries, this political geography of knowledge attempts to do justice to the ambiguous position of emerging social theory as simultaneously caught up and weighed down by the old antagonism between 'power theory' and 'property theory', and as occupying a precariously delimited third or 'in between' position which claims to supersede it. Where, as in Germany, the sociological imagination arose in the filiation of a historical economics which remained securely attached to the sciences of the state, the demarcation from 'Manchesterian' political economy was much more sharply drawn than that from the political philosophy of which it formed a virtual extension, whilst in France the distance measured by budding social science from economics was more or less equal to that taken from traditional politics. In the British context, by contrast, the rupture with traditional political philosophy tended to be more dramatic, while the cognitive continuities with utilitarian and liberal political economy were more diligently preserved.[13]

If France can truly claim to be the heartland of predisciplinary social theory (cf. Heilbron 1995: 271), the 'central' tradition of French positivism, through its dual rupture from politics and economics, also demonstrated the largest measure of independence from the historical rivalry between the two master sciences and their entrenched binary oppositions. While in France the new object of 'the social' was typically positioned in between political state and economic market, it was metaphorically drawn towards either the former or the latter in the German and British experience, without being completely absorbed by either of them. Both in the English and German intellectual zones, the state–society split accordingly tended to be conceived in binary terms ('civil society' being closely identified with 'market' or 'sphere of production'), even though the weight of causal determination 'in the last instance' was placed at opposite ends of the societal spectrum. In France, by contrast, civil society was more nearly considered a 'third' option, since social relations were taken to fall outside political and legal frameworks without being reducible to a zone of merely private or economic affairs. Such a differential topography of state–society conceptions also defines the crucial importance of Marxism as a 'travelling theory', bridging at least two national contexts and intellectual traditions with its explosive mixture of economism and politicization. Marxism, indeed, doubly preserved and fortified the state–society binary and, in so doing, emerged as an inevitable adversary of those sociological currents that sought to mediate and circumvent such acute ontological polarization. In this context, Gouldner has justifiably contrasted Marxism's neglect and 'surrender' of civil society (now taken in the 'third' or intermediary sense) with early sociology's ambition to claim it as its principal object (1980: 346, 363).[14]

A cautionary note may be inserted here, which further details my provisional topography of the three wings of rising social theory. The tripartite division, of course, repeats itself within the three knowledge-political spaces themselves, whose internal structure of competition refracts the demarcative struggles which also divide the larger intellectual field. The triangular division between moral sciences, political sciences, and economic sciences which Heilbron has usefully delineated in the case of France (1995: 23) is also encountered in other national contexts, albeit in less symmetrical proportions, since the 'field weights' are everywhere placed differently. In this fashion, 'English' liberal individualists and 'German' etatists may equally be encountered in France as elsewhere, and national disputes are invariably codetermined by international ones. The familiar debate between Durkheim and Tarde, for example, may illustrate a conflict between a 'French' communitarian and an 'Anglo-Saxon' individualist on French soil, while Weber may be characterized as an 'etatist liberal' in the different context of dispute which ranged the younger against the older generation in the German *Verein für Sozialpolitik*. On the English scene, one might highlight differences between Spencer's individualism, Hobhouse's interventionist 'liberal socialism', and the etatism of the Fabian Society or, alternatively, some of the frictions which developed in the mid-1920s between Ginsberg and Mannheim. From a cross-national perspective, one might accentuate crucial similarities between the liberal–socialist 'third positions' of, for example, Hobhouse, Durkheim, and Schäffle. All of these examples sensitize towards the close interpenetration and mutual reinforcement of internal and external intellectual affairs.

A strategic illustration of such entanglements is offered by the different national inflections of the organicist analogy which was broadly diffused in early social science, and by correspondent differences in the way in which one pictured the relationship between individual, society, and the state. Spencer's influential essay 'The Social Organism' (1860) fed the sociological mainstream in so far as it purported to analyse social development on its own terms, as determined neither by legislators nor by the collective wisdom of individuals, but as evolving slowly, silently, and spontaneously (Spencer 1969: 196). Political organization could only be adequately understood as part of a larger social structure, since the social organism performed as an integrated functional whole through a close mutual interdependence of parts. As was evident from his early *The Proper Sphere of Government* (1843) up to his mature *The Man versus the State* (1884), Spencer's organicism was immediately bent in an anti-statist direction, and closely approximated to the model of *economic* organization, which was identified as the 'all-essential' one. The grand evolutionary shift from 'militant' towards 'industrial' society was primarily described as a development from 'hierarchical' towards 'contractual' or from 'political' towards 'economic' principles of organization, which substituted a coercive, omnipotent state for a minimal state of peaceful competition. The normative blueprint of 'industrial' society was modelled in all its major features after the Smithian perception of free market transactions as a system of spontaneous economic coordination.

Spencer's text was remarkable for its careful specification of the points of similarity and difference between biological and societal organisms (1969: 201ff.). Society might be thinglike and objective, but it was totally unlike any other object. The original factor was the character of the individuals, from which the character of society was derived. The social community as a whole could not possess a corporate consciousness; this was the 'everlasting reason' why the welfare of citizens could not be sacrificed to some supposed benefit of the state, and why the state was to be maintained solely for the benefit of citizens. Corporate life was subservient to the life of the parts, not the other way around. Hobbes was criticized precisely for drawing too tight an analogy in his artificial construction of the Leviathan as a unified body politic (1969: 200–5). Spencer rejected a similar complicity between organicism and etatism in his 'Reasons for Dissenting from the Philosophy of M. Comte' (1864). Repeating J. S. Mill's dismissal of Comte's authoritarian politics, he stipulated that Comte's ideal of society was 'one in which *government* is developed to the greatest extent', whereas 'that form of society towards we are progressing, I hold to be one in which government will be reduced to the smallest amount possible' (cit. Gordon 1991: 431).

It might be argued in somewhat formulaic fashion that, whereas Spencer adamantly resisted all forms of reification of the social organism, and embraced methodological and moral individualism in close conjugation, Durkheim severed this connection by defending moral individualism while emphatically rejecting its methodological counterpart. The French positivists, in describing social facts as ontologically *sui generis*, explicitly prioritized the whole over the part, stipulating the thinglike existence of a collective consciousness and of collective bonds of solidarity as preceding and determining individual actions and beliefs. Simultaneously, the progress of moral individualism was viewed as eminently compatible with, if not constitutionally dependent upon, a managing and expansionary role of the state, which was positioned at the upper end of a graded organizational continuum as the 'reflexive organ' of social life. Unlike Spencer, Comte and Durkheim also held a rather low opinion of economics, and consistently subordinated it to the new master science of sociology. Anti-economism, however, was balanced by anti-statism, in so far as symmetrical distance was taken from the 'German' claim of primacy of the sovereign ethical state. More precisely, if Saint-Simon was still attracted to a more liberal view of the state, and Comte veered in the opposite etatist direction, it was Durkheim who struck the classical balance by outlining a reformist sociology which was demarcated at once against Spencerian individualism and against the etatism of the *Kathedersozialisten*. Durkheimian sociology thus negotiated successfully between the reductionary alternatives presented by Hobbes (society is constituted by the sovereign) and Smith (society is constituted by market relationships), suggesting a social ontology which located the fundamental cementing forces of society some-where 'in the middle', in shared conventions, morals, and beliefs, and in the secondary groups which mediated between individual and state. By executing soft, continuous demarcations on both flanks, this third position eschewed all strict dichotomizing between state and society.

While the French positivists thus tended to divorce methodological and moral individualism, German statist thinkers characteristically united them in order to reject them in tandem and claim a double priority of the 'ethical' state over both individual and economic action. If the whole was likewise taken to precede the parts, its true ontological weight and cementing force were not so much found in the intermediary structures but placed in closer vicinity to the state itself, while individuals were more emphatically viewed as constituted by and subordinated to the statal community. As elsewhere, political questions were increasingly addressed from a 'societal' perspective; nevertheless, in German social science the analytical and normative centrality of the state was never seriously contested (Wagner 1990: 79). From its eighteenth-century inception, German *Staatswissenschaft* absorbed the study of both society and economy, liberally drawing upon classical Aristotelian conceptions of *oikos* and *polis*, and offering 'state' as a generic term for socio-political organization in general – as was reflected in the first German translation of Aristotle's *Politics*, which virtually synonymized 'state' and 'society' (Tribe 1988: 8ff., 153). This state–society symbiosis remained a self-evident point of departure through-out the entire tradition which linked eighteenth-century Cameralism to its nineteenth-century successor, *Nationalökonomie*, dominating even Weber's 1895 inaugural lecture as Professor of the *Staatswissenschaften* at Freiburg University (Weber 1971: 1ff.; Hennis 1987). Early Cameralist writers interpreted economics as household economy in the Aristotelian sense, in which patriarchal authority defined and dominated property relations, and subordinated it to what was called *Polizeiwissenschaft*, i.e. the general science of social regulation, discipline, security, and welfare. Such close linkages between the science of 'good householding' and the 'science of police' turned Cameralistics into a truly *political* economy.

Owing to the spreading influence of Smithian conceptions from 1790 onwards, however, German economic discourse shifted towards a more serious appreciation of market rationality and the novel independence of civil society, where the impersonal rule of social and economic laws replaced the regulative force of the ruler (Tribe 1988: 149–50). The successor science of *Nationalökonomie* no longer considered economic action (or *Verkehr*) as synonymous with state regulation, but rather as creating a relatively independent social sphere which spontaneously proceeded from needs- and interest-oriented individual action. Nevertheless, for Von Mohl and other founders, 'national economy' clearly remained an auxiliary of political science. The school of historical economics subsequently initiated by Roscher, Hildebrand, List, and Knies likewise continued to describe this national economy in terms of *Staatswirtschaft* (Tribe 1988: 204–5; Hennis 1987: 33–4). Although pleading the necessity of a separate *Gesellschaftswissenschaft* that would address matters of production and distribution, division of labour, property, and family, Lorenz von Stein also sought to enlarge the concept of society with that of 'community', with the express purpose of reconnecting the discourse of the social with the political discourse of the *Staatswissenschaften* (von Stein 1971: 21, 32–3). Influenced, as were the national economists, by the Hegelian conception of the state as the personified communal will, *Gemeinschaft* for von Stein encompassed both state and society as 'the two life elements of all human community' (Riedel 1975: 843–4; Weiss 1963: 79).

A vigorous indication for the persistence of this etatist legacy is found in Treitschke's *Die Gesellschaftswissenschaft* (1859), which elaborated a sweeping critique of sociology as pretended science of society, and mobilized the old Aristotelian postulate of identity against its 'chimerical' separation of state and society. Sociology, Treitschke charged, lacked an object of its own, since the *Staatswissenschaften* already included both state and society in their classical conception of the political. Because the state in fact constituted 'die Gesellschaft in ihrer eigentlichen Organisation', political science was legitimated to act as an 'oppositional science' against emerging sociology (Riedel 1975: 793–8; cf. Freyer 1930: 159–60). While Treitschke's broadside clearly manifested how much of a threat advancing social science had meanwhile become for conservative etatists, the second generation of historical economists, which was dominated by Wagner, Brentano, Bücher, and especially Schmoller, was much more sympathetically disposed towards it, although it did not relinquish its fundamental indebtedness to the Hegelian tradition. From 1873 onwards, the *Verein für Sozialpolitik* united scholars in search of a third way between Manchesterian liberal capitalism and fully fledged state socialism, who pleaded a reformist interventionism which nonetheless remained firmly wedded to the notion of the ethical mission of the state (cf. Lindenlaub 1967). Schmoller's view of the state harked back to Fichte and Hegel in identifying it as the pivotal social institution, the supreme ethical power which dominated individual existence and embodied the highest form of morality (ibid.: 94; Wagner 1990: 89–90). It is hardly fortuitous that Durkheim, in his attempt to secure independence for sociology as an 'intermediary' discipline, early on preferred the organicism of Schäffle, who remained critical of the etatist leanings of the *Verein* and pleaded a more communitarian solution to the social question (Therborn 1976: 245–6), over against the mixture of moral science and authoritarianism served up by *Kathedersozialisten* such as Wagner and Schmoller (Durkheim 1975: 282ff., 379).

KNOWLEDGEABLE ORGANIZATION

As claimed, this political topography of the three wings of social theory fruitfully exhibits the idea that early sociology, while striving for a 'third' object-and-project, also remained significantly constrained by the old rivalry between the master sciences of political economy and political philosophy, and at least in two of its three wings might be seen as theorizing a *continuity* rather than a *dichotomy* between state and society. It should be added at this point that, even in the central wing, where early sociology was negotiating an intermediate position and hence maximally retreated from the reductionary dilemma of economism vs. etatism, it did not drop the imperialistic claims that were originally raised by the rivalling master sciences of the economy and the state, but installed a *third imperialism* which was grounded in an equally expansive conception of the social. If the economy was still the modelling organization for Spencer, and the state remained the essential organization for Treitschke and Schmoller, Durkheim claimed a similar 'essentialism' and grounding position for his encompassing science of social solidarity. The oscillatory dialectic of parts and wholes, as previously encountered in the Aristotelian view of the political and the Smithian view of the economic, was not forced to a halt but transposed to the intermediate level of 'social facts'. The tradition of moralistics had already stretched the concept of *morale* into a general synonym for human reality; the *philosophes*, in turn, typically took 'civil society' to refer both to the social part and the social whole (Heilbron 1995: 78–9, 91). In Saint-Simon, Comte, and Durkheim, the claim about the *autonomy* of social facts likewise continually shifted into a claim of ultimate constitutive *dominance*; the double demarcation from political and economic facts, far from simply destroying the alleged autonomy of politics and economics, actually prepared their annexation in a new scientific hierarchy administered by the master discipline of moral sociology.

Another feature of the tripartite model is its useful tendency to blur the strict boundaries that are believed to run between social science and political ideology. In all three intellectual spaces, emerging social theory remained enmeshed in 'discourse coalitions' which stretched across the traditional divide separating science from politics, and retained close affinities with various political configurations (Wagner 1990). Across the entire breadth of the sociological spectrum, the 'scientific' problematic of the relationship between individual and society was constitutively interwoven with the 'ideological' opposition between individualism and collectivism (of both the socialist and the nationalist variety). In England, the first usages of both 'social science' and 'socialism' occurred together in the late 1820s in Owenite and Ricardian socialist criticisms of the 'individual science' of political economy (Claeys 1986).[15] Hobhouse's 'new sociology' and his 'new liberalism' were clearly mutually supportive, and attempted to steer a middle course in the pervasive political opposition between *laissez-faire* individualism and state collectivism, e.g. of the Fabian variety (Collini 1979). Durkheim's original formulation of the project which would eventually result in *De la division du travail social* was 'Rapports entre l'individualisme et le socialisme', to be changed somewhat later into the apparently more neutral 'Rapports de l'individu et de la société'; but as Filloux has argued, the first formulation remained the key to and the point of convergence of the entire Durkheimian project (1977: 3, 15).[16] The search for compatibility, if not unity, of the opposite ideologies of individualism and socialism also defined the politics of solidarism, which for some time offered something like the official social philosophy of the French Third Republic (Hayward 1961). It was similarly constitutive of the reformist socialism of Jaurès who, like Durkheim, tended to view socialism not so much as a counterforce to but as the logical completion of individualism (Lukes 1973: 326). These currents to some extent converged in the 'societal' corporatism preached by Durkheim, Duguit, Bourgeois, Fouillée, and other solidarists, and was also embraced by social catholics such as La Tour du Pin and De Mun, social nationalists such as Maurras, and social economists such as Gide (Hayward 1960; Elbow 1953).

In Germany, rising social science demonstrated a similar affinity with political discourse, as was especially manifest in attempts by the *Verein für Sozialpolitik* to trace another third way between liberalism and (especially Marxist) socialism. In the early decades of the twentieth century, this legacy of the *Verein* was subjected to something like a binary fission, marked by a (second) *Methodenstreit* in which a new generation of national economists, represented by Tönnies, Sombart, and Weber, moved to oppose the generation of Schmoller and Wagner.[17] This primarily epistemological debate on the supposed value-freedom of the social sciences was partly infused with the knowledge-political ambition of the younger generation to break with the mystification of the state as carried over by the older *Kathedersozialisten* from idealist philosophy, and hence to achieve a greater distanciation between state and social science (Proctor 1991: 86–7; cf. Weber 1968: 309). If Weber's work, as compared with the 'etatist liberalism' of his 1895 inaugural lecture, progressively developed in a more modernist and individualist direction, Sombart's thinking gradually gravitated towards the opposite illiberal standpoint, ultimately linking up with the 'conservative revolutionary' and state corporatist ideas of Freyer, Spann, and Schmitt (cf. Lenger 1994). Since sociology, Freyer wrote in 1934, had originated in the separation of civil society from the state, the end of this separation would eventually result in the absorption of sociology by the *Staatswissenschaften* (Muller 1987: 271). Freyer's fusion of the Hegelian and Weberian legacies in an explicitly normative sociology of *Herrschaft* and state-directed *Planung* was paralleled by like-minded efforts of Sombart and Spann to move the state to centre stage, and plead the supersession of the liberal differentiation of state and society (Wagner 1990: 344).[18]

Among the benefits incurred by mapping such discursive coalitions across the traditional science–ideology divide is a new openness to continuities between rising social science and what may be called the tradition of radical 'anti-modernism'. If various conjunctions can be traced between social science and classical liberalism, conservative etatism, reformist socialism, and Marxism, there also exist important linkages with radical varieties of right-wing thought which develop into a coherent ideology of 'national socialism' in the course of the 1920s and 1930s. König's familiar thesis that the development of sociology in Germany was 'brutally arrested' in 1933 tends to overlook the 'binary fission' which distributed the legacy of the *Verein* between a liberal and an anti-liberal current, and accordingly underestimates both their common origins and the intellectual seriousness of the anti-liberal tradition itself (cf. Lepenies 1985: 405–6; Klingemann 1996: *passim*). In the same vein, one might thematize the close affinity which coupled Italian sociology to national syndicalist and fascist political philosophy after the demise of a more positivistic and liberal social science in the closing decades of the nineteenth century (Wagner 1990: 238ff.), or the important filiation through which, in France, Durkheimian reformist sociology and liberal socialism were 'etatized' and 'politicized' in Déat's *néo-socialisme* of the late 1930s.

Rather than exploring such conjunctions and interfaces of the triangular model, I will presently single out the theme of 'knowledgeable organization', which may introduce a more specific delineation of the elusive object-and-project of sociology than is provided by freely stretchable and tendentially objectivist notions such as 'society', 'the social', or 'social facts', while it may also lend greater clarity to its original 'projective' or political commitments. It conveniently straddles the science–ideology divide, and connects to the wider intellectual tableau without extinguishing the singularity of mainstream sociology as centring primarily in the French positivist tradition. It offers a natural bridgehead between the reformist sociologies of the mainstream and the more radical sociologies of the left and the right, and also permits of further specification which narrows down its scope in order to elucidate the core sociological project as a 'third' one. In this respect, it usefully approaches both the Nisbetian topos of 'community' and the Gouldnerian one of 'civil society', if these are similarly taken to circumscribe a third project set at equal remove from etatist and economistic programmes (cf. Cohen and Arato

1992: 30). Finally, it illustrates the important extent to which the sociological tradition converges upon a generalized theory of the political or of social power, and thereby helps to accentuate its demarcative interface with the Smithian (and Marxian) tradition of political economy.

'Knowledgeable organization' seems an apposite term if we wish to do justice both to sociology's historical affinity with the tradition of political theory and to its enduring polemical relationship with political economy – which is difficult if we stick with the conventional meaning of society or the social as demarcated first of all against the state. Indeed, the idea of 'knowledgeable organization' or that of 'scientific social management' would not fare badly as a modern rendering of 'politics' in the comprehensive Aristotelian sense. Even Nisbet, who otherwise championed the unit-idea of 'community', was tempted to cast the long-term development of sociology as a gradual extension of Tocquevillean political theory towards the general theory of rational organization and domination which was perfected by Weber. Weber was introduced as the prime sociologist of the 'organizational revolution', which was also the revolution 'which Marx failed to sense, as he had to fail, given his single-minded emphasis upon the dominance of private property' (Nisbet 1966: 147). This view is close to that espoused by Aron, who emphasized the organizational and managerial imprint of Saint-Simonian and Comtean sociology, and extrapolates this to the writers of the classical age. Durkheim, he argued, developed a socialist sociology which might be summarized in the key terms of 'organization' and 'moralization', while the core of Weber's sociology was found to lie in the closely federated themes of rationalization, organization, and domination (Aron 1965 I: 74–5; II: 86, 188, 218, 239). Filloux has recently abridged Durkheim's central project as that of 'intelligent organization' (1993: 221).

'Knowledgeable organization', in this sense, defines at once the classical promise and the classical *hubris* of the sociological tradition, which has always been tempted to replace the chaotic spontaneity of society-as-market, and its unconscious strivings and uncontrollable effects, by a consciously planned and scientifically based project of social reconstruction. The organizers were to be knowledgeable, and positive social science promised to lay an objective groundwork for this knowledge, which would offer trustworthy analyses of social facts and regularities from which reformers could safely operate. Organization and scientific knowledge were recognized as new, autonomous productive forces which had gradually risen alongside and increasingly came to dominate established forces such as land, labour, and capital. As a corollary of this prediction of the 'knowledge society', many early sociologists also envisaged the rise of a 'new class' of sociologically capable intellectuals which would theoretically spearhead this movement, who would collaborate with more practical people in the scientific reconstitution and management of society. This new elite would be seated immediately in the state institutions themselves, as was the usual tendency in the Hegelian neo-idealist tradition, or be placed at some remove from the administrative and executive system, as was the case in French positivist social philosophy. Even where such philosophers did not immediately aspire to be kings, however, and allowed for some division of labour between politicians and intellectuals, the sociological project of 'knowledgeable organization' introduced a pronounced claim to social and political power of the *savants*.

SAINT-SIMON AND COMTE REVISITED

In this perspective, the focus of our historical interest is naturally attracted by the axial figure of Saint-Simon, who was the *auctor intellectualis* of the organizational project of sociology and has been recruited with equal fervour by both left-wing and right-wing social theorists as a founding father. Saint-Simon's first public profession of the necessity of a new kind of political science might well be his unsuccessful entry into a discussion held in 1802 at the Lycée républicain, where he proposed the gathering should collaborate in the creation of a new 'science of sciences' (Dautry 1951). In his *Lettre d'un habitant de Genève* of the following year, his *Introduction aux travaux scientifiques* of 1807, and his scattered sketches for a 'New Encyclopedia', this projected *résumé* of the human sciences was laid out in the form of a positively grounded politics. *The Reorganization of the European Community* (1814), written in collaboration with Augustin Thierry, enquired in the Aristotelian manner after the best possible constitution, pleading a reconstitution of the body politic in conformity with the present state of enlightenment, since 'the troubles of the social order arise from obscurities in political theory' (Saint-Simon 1964: 66, 40).

Paradoxically, however, while exalting positive politics as the queen of sciences, Saint-Simon seemed to contemplate a similar elevation of political economy. His *l'Industrie* of 1818 approvingly quoted Say's influential declaration of (economic) independence:

> For a long time politics in the proper sense of this term, i.e. the science of the organization of societies, has been confounded with political economy, which teaches how the riches which satisfy the needs of society are formed, distributed, and consumed . . . riches are essentially independent of political organization.
>
> (Saint-Simon 1966 I: 185)

Saint-Simon, for his part, rightly suspected that this demarcative claim concealed a much more imperious gesture: the author, he suggested, 'vaguely and as it were involuntarily sensed that political economy is the veritable and unique foundation of politics'. Politics should indeed become the 'science of production', and by that very fact would finally turn into a positive science (Saint-Simon 1966 I: 188–9; Ionescu 1976: 106–8). However, this contradiction was more apparent than real. Durkheim, for one, clearly saw that Saint-Simon precisely *distinguished* himself here from the classical economists, for whom economic life remained entirely outside of politics, while for Saint-Simon it was the very substance of politics itself (1958: 179). Saint-Simon himself specified this contrast in the following manner. After Smith had explained the principles which guided the development of industry, the problem remained of 'discovering legal means for transferring "le grand *pouvoir politique*" into the hands of industry' (1966 II: 159; Ionescu 1976: 124). The main problem thus was organizational (the expression *l'organisation du travail* is not yet encountered in Saint-Simon, but was first employed by his pupil Bazard, before being spread by Louis Blanc's 1839 book of the same title), and therefore of a political nature.[19] The rather ill-defined class of *indus-triels* or *producteurs*, as whose mouthpiece Saint-Simon presented himself, though formally embracing all those who laboured with the head or the hand, turned out to be primarily staffed with organizers, managers, and politically minded savants.[20]

A major contrast between Saint-Simon and Smith, therefore, was a more radical application of the standard of social utility, which implied the precedence of the organizational project over that of 'laissez faire le propriétaire'. Saint-Simon's opposition between producers and idlers was a far more powerful one than Smith's more tranquil distinction between productive and unproductive labourers. Unlike Smith, Saint-Simon did not halt before the sanctified principles of possessive individualism, pioneering both the functional theory of property and the critique of the right of inheritance which would be continued by Bazard, Comte, Durkheim, Duguit, and numerous others. The very first proposition of Saint-Simon's 'science of production' already contained the germs of this conflict between the principle of production and that of property; it asserted

> that the production of useful things is the sole reasonable and positive aim which political societies can propose to set themselves; and consequently, that the principle of *respect towards production and producers* is infinitely more fruitful than this one: *respect towards property and proprietors*.
>
> (1966 I: 186)[21]

The 'superior law' which overruled the right of individual property was that of the progress of the human spirit, which presently dictated that the claims of private property were subordinate to those of merit and talent.[22] In a somewhat peculiar defence of the property-owners, Saint-Simon alleged that the haves should govern the have-nots, but not because they owned property; they owned property and governed because, collectively, they were superior in enlightenment than the have-nots, and the general interest dictated that 'domination should be proportionate to enlightenment'. Science was useful because it possessed the means of prediction, which made scientists superior to all other people. The opening lines of Saint-Simon's famous 'Parabole' accordingly listed scientists, artists, writers, and engineers before bankers, businessmen, and farmers as most eminently useful to the nation (1964: 4–8, 72).

In his pupil Comte, the focus upon social reorganization directed by positive science (most clearly announced in the title of his programmatic *Plan des travaux scientifiques nécessaires pour réorganiser la société* from 1822)[23] was likewise combined with a functionalist conception of property. Comte's 'positive theory of property', however, acquired a stronger elitist and etatist coloration. True philosophers, he taught, would not hesitate to underwrite the instinctive reclamations of proletarians against the 'vicious definition' adopted by the majority of modern jurists, who attributed to property an 'absolute individuality' and defined it as a right to use and abuse. This 'anti-social theory' was equally devoid of justice as of reality. Since no species of property could be created or even transmitted by its sole possessor without the indispensable contribution of public cooperation, its exercise could never be a purely individual act. At all times and places, the community intervened to a greater or lesser degree in order to subordinate it to social needs. In every normal state of humanity, each citizen was in fact a public functionary, whose attributions determined both the citizen's rights and obligations. This universal principle, Comte held, had to be extended to the institution of property, 'which positivism considers above all to be an indispensable social function', designated to create and administer the capital by means of which each generation prepared the labour of the next.[24]

In his essay 'Considerations on the Spiritual Power', Comte outlined the tensionful relationship between political economy and social science in the following terms:

> The essential vice of political economy, regarded as a social theory, consists in this. Having proved, as to certain matters, far from being the most important, the spontaneous and permanent tendency of human societies towards a certain necessary order, it infers that this tendency does not require to be regulated by positive institutions. On the contrary this great political truth, apprehended in its ensemble, only proves *the possibility of an organisation*, and leads us to a correct appreciation of its vast importance.
>
> (1974: 240; italics mine)

Comtean positivism was accordingly not adverse to state intervention of an entrepreneurial or welfare nature, and remained largely indifferent to the distinction between private and public ownership. Comte denied that the substitution of one regime of ownership for another would materially change the structure of the social order, since the main cleavage in the stratificational pyramid was not found in the opposition between proprietors and propertyless, but in the inevitable distinction between those who had power and those who lacked it.

Comte's sociology, in addition, was straightforwardly elitist, advocating a sociocracy in which the able were to be the powerful, and the powerful the wealthy – in this order of accretion (Comte 1974: 129ff., 209ff.; Aron 1965 I: 76, 96). Whereas the general public could only indicate the ends of government, the consideration of measures for effecting it exclusively belonged to 'scientific politicians' (*savants en politique*). The business of the public was to form aspirations, that of 'publicists' to propose measures, and that of rulers to realize them. Spiritual power would accordingly be confided to the *savants*, while the temporal power would befall to the heads of industrial enterprises, but the spiritual function ought to be treated first and the temporal one was to follow. The *savants* possessed the two fundamental elements of spiritual government, capacity and authority in matters of theory, to the exclusion of all other classes; hence the necessity 'for confiding to the cultivators of Positive Science the theoretical labour of reorganizing society'. A new class of *savants* should be formed, that of social physicists or sociologists, that would synthesize the *ensemble* of specialist knowledges in a positive philosophy and establish its spiritual power (1974: 131–3, 210–13).

DURKHEIM'S THIRD PROJECT

It is almost inevitable, given the drift of the present argument, to delve somewhat deeper into the intriguing case of Durkheim, and review some recent reappraisals of his work. At first sight Durkheim's writings present the most formidable obstacle to the interpretation which I am developing, since conventional 'territorial' conceptions of the sociological object lean heavily upon his epoch-making formula about the *sui generis* character of social facts, and because his work has long been interpreted as a theory of consensual order (or 'community' or 'solidarity') which has laid the groundwork of much of modern functionalist sociology and anthropology. In the disputes which ravaged 'crisis-ridden' sociology in the 1970s and 1980s, the ancestral figure of Durkheim was thus very much at stake: both partisans and detractors of mainstream functionalism sought to articulate and legitimize their different programmatic statements through an interested appropriation of his work. In the course of these polemics, the long-standing 'conservative' (mis)interpretation by theorists such as Parsons, Nisbet, Coser, and Zeitlin (which was fully shared by Marxists such as Nizan, Hahn, and Therborn) progressively evaporated. According to this view, Durkheim was centrally concerned with the problem of order as logically prior to the problem of change, and neglected to analyse issues of power, violence, and social class. In addition, he subordinated the individual to the claims of society, and strongly repudiated socialism. As a result, his work expressed an abiding conservatism which inserted it into the broader context of the revolt against Enlightenment thought (cf. Parsons 1968; Coser 1960; Nisbet 1966; Zeitlin 1974).

Giddens, among others, has countered that, far from having been his central problem from an early stage, the problem of order was not a problem for Durkheim at all, since his central issue was how to conceptualize the change from traditional society to the emergent modern or industrial type, and to theorize the forms of authority appropriate to the latter – a problematic which stood rather close to that of Weber (Giddens 1977: 250, 238; 1982). The Parsonian view was untrue to the intellectual influences which Durkheim sought to process, because it exclusively concentrated on his polemic with utilitarianism and neglected his (largely sympathetic) discussion of *Katheder-sozialismus*, solidarism, and neo-Kantianism. It also misconceived the political grounding of Durkheim's sociology, which was not derived from a call to order *tout court*, but from the problem of how to order a liberal and democratic republic by means of far-reaching reorganizations in the political system and class structure. But if theorists such as Giddens, Lukes (1973), and Gouldner (1958) successfully reversed the systematic neglect in which Durkheim's political sociology had fallen, French commentators such as Filloux (1977) and Lacroix (1981) appeared to go one step further. Misled by Durkheim's own demarcation of sociology from political philosophy, Lacroix contended, mainstream sociology missed the evident fact that his social science represented a critical continuation or improvement of 'les sciences politiques'. Durkheim's early object was 'nothing other than the political object' and his so-called sociology, in its own time, was only a different way of practising the moral and political sciences (Lacroix 1981: 20, 304).

It is essential not to overdraw this radical Foucaldian interpretation, in order to appreciate the true scope and direction of this 'political' object-and-project. It is intriguing, in this context, to watch Durkheim enter, in his early articles and reviews, upon simultaneous negotiations on the 'left' and the 'right' (or on the 'Eastern' and 'Western' perimeters) of the intellectual field, and carefully edge forward in order to clear a third intellectual position intermediary between individualism and etatism. His long review of the 'positive science of morality in Germany' (1887), as its title notified, significantly (mis)interpreted Wagner's and Schmoller's state-oriented, *political* economy as a *moral* science,[25] and defended it as such against the orthodox Smithian school (represented in France by Levasseur, Leroy-Beaulieu, and others grouped around the *Journal des économistes*) which, from its *laissez-faire* point of view, could only dismiss it for its 'superstitious respect for the authority of the State'. Its prime focus and major inspiration, to Durkheim, was rather the idea of social realism, i.e. of the existence of a *sui generis* order of social facts which followed autonomous laws of development and preceded both the intentions of legislators and the acts of the individuals which were so dear to the economic utilitarians. Clearly implying that political economy, in its classical guise, had to subordinate itself to a more encompassing *science des mœurs*,

Durkheim also objected to the exaggerated confidence which the *Kathedersozialisten* placed in authoritarian legislative action. This betrayed a similar (and unsound) view of society as a *Kunstprodukt*, which was freely malleable by conscious (statal) intervention, whereas the laws of morality were natural laws, products of a long evolution, whose course could not be arbitrarily changed (1975: 268, 281–2, 369).

It was Schäffle, Durkheim claimed, who uniquely escaped this grave error in refusing to admit the 'excessive plasticity' that Wagner and other *Kathedersozialisten* attributed to moral facts. Whereas the latter tended to describe society as a machine steered from the outside, Schäffle instead considered it a living being which steered itself from the inside (Durkheim 1975: 283–4). Moral force was not a result of exterior and mechanic pressure; not the state exercised it but society as a whole; it was not concentrated in a few hands, but was disseminated across the entire nation. An earlier review of Schäffle (1885) – Durkheim's first printed publication – had already indicated that the study of moral facts was coextensive both with the study of social organization and that of moral authority:

> Every social mass gravitates around a central point, and submits to the action of a directive force, which regulates and combines the elementary movements and which Schäffle calls 'authority'. The various authorities, in their turn, subordinate themselves to one another and this is how a new life results out of the individual activities, which is simultaneously unified and complex. Authority might be represented by one man, or by a class, or by a formula. But in one or another form, it is indispensable.
>
> (Durkheim 1975: 366)[26]

The true import of this view about the ubiquity and the balanced articulation of authority is appreciated only if it is interpreted as anti-collectivist and anti-centralist. Durkheim, at least, repeatedly defended Schäffle against such charges, which were variously raised by economists such as Leroy-Beaulieu, socialists such as Benoit-Malon, and solidarists such as Fouillée. In this particular sense, Durkheim explained, Schäffle's 'authoritarian socialism' manifestly opposed itself to the centralizing tendencies of 'social democracy' as advocated by Rodbertus or Marx. 'Authoritarian socialism' was simply *organized* socialism, in which the industrial forces were grouped around centres of action which regulated their course; each of these mutually coordinating and subordinate centres constituted an 'authority'. Egalitarian democracy à la Marx failed to admit the existence of such a plurality of 'nervous centres' in the social organism (1975: 378–9).

In this fashion, Durkheim's double demarcation, by locating the organizational impulse in the middle regions of society, repeated the 'centring' movement of the French positivist school as a whole, which spiralled from

Saint-Simon's 'productionist' organizational project through Comte's more etatist one towards the 'third-way', corporatist variant which Durkheim initially derived from Schäffle and Montesquieu. The true weight of the political was similarly placed in the intermediate zone, defining both the continuity and the rupture from traditional political philosophy. Durkheim's Latin thesis on Montesquieu (1892) once again bore witness to this dual concern.[27] Montesquieu was the first to have established the fundamental principles of social science, even though he had erred in assuming that social forms resulted from types of sovereignty and were exhaustively defined by them (Durkheim 1966: 110–11). Despite its 'political' phrasing, Montesquieu's classification of types of regime actually referred to underlying types of society. Radicalizing Montesquieu's criticism of the 'Legislator myth' and his incipient sensitivity to autonomously functioning laws of morality, Durkheim pleaded a more serious recognition of the fact that (political) laws were actually derivative of *mœurs*, not the other way around, and constituted nothing other than 'des mœurs mieux définis'. Social life was best organized through a corporatist division of public functions and powers, which would balance each other through competition and hold each other in check. This arrangement was set in clear contrast to the despotic state, which abolished all 'orders' and all division of labour; this was a 'monstrous being in which only the head lived', because it had drawn towards itself all the forces of the social organism (1966: 85, 64, 67).

Notwithstanding his explicit demarcations from traditional political philosophy (cf. 1975: 225; 1958: 187), Durkheim's 'moral science' therefore admitted close continuities between the political and the social, including an 'organizational' and 'knowledgeable' conception of the state which identified it as the intelligent command centre of a complex hierarchy of social institutions. Once again, this conception of the state was carefully designed to mediate between individualistic and economistic 'nightwatchman' conceptions, as advanced by, for example, Kant, Spencer, and the classical economists, and what Durkheim referred to as the 'mystical' or transcendent view, which was attributed to the Hegelians (and in an important degree also to Comte) (1992: 51–4, 72; 1975: 198–9). While being continuous with other societal organs (as the 'institution of institutions' or the 'organization of organizations', as solidarists phrased it), the state also fulfilled a specific function as the reflective 'social brain'. Although it enjoyed relative autonomy as 'the embodiment of the collectivity', it was still merely a derivation from the power immanent in the collective consciousness.[28] Arguing directly against Comte, who had claimed that the dispersive effects of the division of labour could only be checked by government regulation, Durkheim countered that, normally, the unity of organized societies resulted from the spontaneous consensus of the parts, and that therefore 'it was not the brain that creates the unity of the organism, but it expresses it, setting its seal upon it' (1984: 42–3, 295–7; cf. Gouldner 1958: 18). Although the state was above all 'an organ of reflection', whose principal function was to think, it did not itself create the psychic life of society, but concentrated and organized it (Durkheim 1986: 46–7; 1992: 50–1). Since collective representations were spontaneous, unstructured, and obscure, state consciousness had to acquire a higher degree of reflective clarity, in order to ensure the vital interplay between diffuse sentiments, ideas, and beliefs and the clear-headed decisions made by the state. Statal reflection was essentially *organized* thought (Durkheim 1992: 79–80). Even though Durkheim explicitly remarked that the work of the sociologist was not that of the statesman (1984: 1), this intellectualist view of the state minimally suggested that sociological enlightenment was indispensable to it. His view of the calling of intellectuals was never very distant from that of Saint-Simon's *industriels théoriques* or Comte's *savants en politique* (cf. Hearn 1985: 163–4).

By characterizing it as the supreme organ of social reflection and moral discipline, Durkheim still seemed dangerously attracted to the Hegelian view of the ethical–reasonable state. This impression is enhanced by his further claim that the field which opened itself to the state's moral activity was 'immeasurable', and its advance was bound to go on indefinitely in the future (1992: 68). However, Durkheim's view of the state remained consistently opposed to radical (neo-)Hegelian views about the 'total state' and the prodigious identity of state and individual as advocated by state socialists or nationalists such as Treitschke – who in all respects anticipated the subsequent fascist and 'conservative revolutionary' etatism of, for example, Gentile, Rocco, Freyer, and Schmitt. Treitschke, we should recall, had written a scathing critique of sociology from the imperialistic perspective of the *Staatswis-senschaften*, decrying its 'chimerical' distinction between state and society, and defending the contrary claim that the state 'represented society in its true organization' (cf. Freyer 1930: 159–60). The more interesting was Durkheim's wartime criticism of Treitschke, which focused upon the latter's *Politik* as representative of German etatist thinking in its entirety (Durkheim 1986: 224ff.). The 'German' idea of the state, by celebrating its unlimited sovereignty and proud self-sufficiency, was essentially warlike, because it was propelled by a morbid inflation of the will-to-power. Wishing to organize all individuals into a concentrated whole, it acted as a collective 'superman' that was superior to all private wills. This 'morbid enormity' represented a clear-cut case of social pathology, confirming France and her allies in their legitimate confidence, 'for there is no greater strength than to have on one's side what is the very nature of things' (ibid.: 231–2).

Durkheim's conception of state and individual remained diametrically opposed to this postulate of identity and 'total mobilization'. Rather than being in essential conflict, moral individualism and state intervention were mutually constitutive and progressed together. Far from tyrannizing over the individual, it was precisely the state that redeemed the individual from society. Moral individuality was not antagonistic to the state, but was instead set free by it; its tendency was to ensure the most complete individuation that the state of society would allow (Durkheim 1992: 57, 68–9). This 'social' (as opposed to 'egocentric') individualism (cf. Durkheim 1970: 262ff.; 1986: 262ff.) was crucially dependent upon the institutionalized checks and balances installed by the corporatist reorganization of civil society. The formation of secondary groups as politically recognized organs of public life, especially associations of a functional or professional nature, established a cluster of collective forces intercalated between individual and state, which simultaneously connected and separated them. In contrast to the state, these secondary groups stood close enough to the individuals to be able to adapt to individual diversity and morally act upon them. However, in order to prevent such secondary authorities from swallowing up their members and exerting a repressive monopoly over them, they had to be capped by a higher authority that would neutralize their tendency to 'collective particularism' and represent the whole against the parts. By thus holding its constituent societies in check, the state would liberate individual personalities, while the despotic tendencies of the state itself would in turn be neutralized by the counterforce of the secondary groups. It was out of this conflict of social forces that individual liberties were born (1992: 62–3; 1986: 144–5).

It has been insufficiently appreciated how intimately and constitutively sociology's classical demarcation of its *object* ('society', 'the social') was linked to its *project* of a 'societal' (as opposed to a 'state') corporatism.[29] Its 'third object' simultaneously represented a 'third project', because the resolution of the scientific problem of solidarity and moral order was in all respects the same as that of the political problem of balancing and mediating between individualism and collectivism. Taking his initial cue from Montesquieu and Schäffle, but also 'centring' between Saint-Simon's technocratic–industrial corporatism and Comte's more etatist version, Durkheim once again placed his knowledge-political cards on the secondary groups. Corporatism, by requiring a double transfer of political jurisdictions and economic competences towards the intermediate zone, installed both a 'mixed' or socialized economy and a 'mixed' or decentralized state which were simultaneously connected and separated through the buffer zone of the secondary associations.[30] The organizational or organic view of the state was accordingly supplemented by an equally organizational and organic view of the economy. Adopting Schäffle's outline of a liberal socialism (cf. Schäffle 1894: 20, 55ff., 61),[31] Durkheim also supported the latter's diagnosis that, at present, the economy constituted an ensemble of reflexes, which had to be reconnected to the conscious centres of the social organism. His own defence of socialism likewise focused upon the 'absence of organization' of the economic functions as defining the true morbidity and abnormalcy of the present crisis-ridden social (dis)order (Durkheim 1958: 379–84; 1984: xxxi–xxxiii).

Socialism, to Durkheim as well as to Schäffle and Saint-Simon, was 'essentially a movement to organize . . . a process of economic concentration and centralization'. It had to bring economic functions from the diffuse or dispersed state to the organized or moral state, where they would be connected to the 'knowing and managing organs of society' (1958: 58, 89). In his lectures on Saint-Simon, Durkheim clearly defined as socialist every doctrine 'demanding the connection of all economic functions, or of certain among them, to the directing and conscious centres of society', stipulating at once that 'connection' was not equal to centralist subordination: 'socialists do not demand that the economic life be put into the hands of the state, but into contact with it'. While the corporations were to take over important political functions from the central state, they would simultaneously become the focus of important economic competences and rights. In his earliest writings, Durkheim had already sympathized with Wagner's and Ihering's social conception of ownership, and had defended Fouillée's solidarist view of personal ownership against varieties of state collectivism. His mature socialism likewise defined ownership as a social function and service, and criticized the principles of absolute property and inheritance as archaic survivals contrary to the spirit of individualism, and as generative of a 'negative solidarity' (1984: lvi–lvii, 72–5; 1992: 174–5, 214–17). The true problem of reform was not where things were located or who enjoyed ownership of them, but that the activity which they occasioned remained unregulated (1984: lvi). The assertion of the eminent right of the collectivity, however, did not imply state inheritance but inheritance by the professional groups which, different from the state, satisfied all the conditions for becoming the heirs of the family in the economic sphere (ibid.: xlv–lvi; 1992: 218).

SOCIOLOGICAL DIALECTICS

Durkheimian socialism, like that of Saint-Simon, hence practically exhausted itself in the project of 'knowledgeable organization', as specifically narrowed down to the blueprint of a 'societal' corporatism. Both the theme of organization and that of corporatism also extended 'sideways' (or 'Eastward'), linking up with the strong organizational impulses of the neo-Hegelian tradition and its more statal version of the corporatist project. However, if the sociological enterprise thus bordered on and shaded into types of etatist ideology, it still demonstrated larger elective affinities with the 'third' project of *mediating* between polity and economy and of *mixing* etatism with individualism. My argument in the following will be that the classical positivistic delineation of the sociological *objet* ('society', 'the social', 'social facts') served to conceal, but in this concealment simultaneously to legitimize, the ideological or political *project* of sociology as previously outlined.[32] The objectivistic demarcation of the sociological object, to be more precise, was loaded with projective intentions on at least two levels, aiming to justify both the immediately political project of a societal corporatism, and the mediate, knowledge-political project of establishing sociology as a new master science in a doubly contested field. Squeezed in between the old imperialisms of political philosophy and political economy, the third imperialism of incipient sociology similarly expressed itself through a characteristic dialectic of part and whole. This section will chart some aspects of this double clash and of the imperial dialectic of positivist sociology.

Durkheim's proposed *science des mœurs*, it is claimed, meant to encompass the various social sciences in roughly the same manner as both political philosophy and political economy had set out to do from their opposite vantage points of political idealism and economic materialism. His initial intellectual double play, we recall, was to 'socialize' and 'moralize' both political sovereignty and economic property by connecting them through the institutional staircase of the professional corporations. Throughout Durkheim's early writings, his stated objective was to remove the unfortunate 'isolation' in which both the state (and political science) and the economy (and economics) dwelt, so as to bring them back into the fold of the truly social sciences. However, his more hidden and imperious ambition was to pull both the *Staatswissenschaften* and political economy from their elevated seats in order to establish sociology as the only viable scientific alternative. We have already highlighted the tendency of the *staatswissenschaftliche* tradition, as represented by von Stein and Treitschke but also by the *Kathedersozialisten*, to absorb the social into an encompassing conception of the state and hence to deny any specific autonomy to the sociological object.[33] The following throws additional light upon the conflictuous interface which separated emerging sociology from the well-entrenched science of political economy.

In 1908, Durkheim confronted members of the ultra-individualistic 'groupe de Paris' such as Limousin, Villey, and Leroy-Beaulieu, which he had already censured two decades before for misreading Schäffle and the *Kathedersozialisten*, and for unwarrantedly claiming the disciplinary primacy of political economy. Limousin now again faced Durkheim with the characteristic claim that political economy served 'as a focus (*foyer*) and to some extent as the mother of the other sociological sciences'. Dismissing Comte as a metaphysician and a utopian 'sociocrat', Limousin charged that the latter did not understand a thing about political economy, and, aiming more directly at Comte's professed pupil, sharply concluded that sociology did 'not yet exist'. Durkheim countered with confident reserve, limiting himself to a rejection of the idea that economic life constituted the substructure of all social life, and implying that political economy thereby lost its preponderance and should instead become 'a social science like the others, linked to them in a close bond of solidarity, without however pretending to direct them' (1982: 232). Villey and Leroy-Beaulieu, however, dogmatically restated the acquired rights of their own master discipline. The latter went so far as to conclude that political economy was currently the only truly positive social science and hence legitimately occupied pride of place; it alone rested upon a basis that was indestructible and positive, because its laws were immutable, whatever the variations of opinion (1982: 235).

Already in his earliest works, however, Durkheim's revindication of an autonomous science of morality and an independent *être social* had bordered upon similar totalizing claims. If economic facts were indeed functions of the solidary organism, political economy could not but lose its alleged autonomy; it had to become – as Sismondi had phrased it against Say – 'a branch of the art of governing' (Lacroix and Landerer 1972: 161, 168). Or as Durkheim wrote: it could 'not do without a science of the State' (1970: 208). He went on to enumerate three particular sciences falling within the scope of general sociology, one of which studied the state, another the three great 'regulative' functions (law, morality, religion), while a third studied the economic functions; these were to be capped by a general or 'synthetic' sociology which alone was capable of restoring the idea of the organic unity of society (1970: 213–14). Other writings, however, omitted a separate subscience of the state, although they likewise inserted both the study of religious and that of economic phenomena in the sociological framework (e.g. 1975: 347; 1970: 146–7). Apparently, this was not because political sociology ceased to occupy Durkheim (virtually the reverse would be arguable), but rather because he no longer distinguished it from the sociology of the regulative functions more generally. In any event, sociology was offered as the natural corpus organizing the particular sciences into a consistent whole, on the basis of a *unité du genre* which was defined by the 'social fact in abstracto', the organic unity of the social realm itself (1970: 152; 1975: 158–9).

Reflecting the logic of Gouldner's dialectic of recovery and wholeness (1985: 240ff.), morality, authority, and the social – terms which Durkheim used more or less coextensively – loosely referred at once to a residual or 'intermediate' reality and to an all-pervasive and all-embracing one. In their Foucaldian idiom, both Filloux and Lacroix have likewise taken notice of this dialectical peculiarity. According to Filloux, the *champ politique*, as identified by Durkheim, did not coincide with the state, but encompassed all social phenomena which concerned 'the *direction of collective conduct in communal historical action*'. Durkheim's political sociology was therefore a general science of power which viewed the special organ of the political state as a modality of the *pouvoir du groupe* that formed the totality or global structure; as the *Division* phrased it, political power was only a 'derivation' of the force which was immanent in the communal conscience. The very term 'derivation' occurred because Durkheim acknowledged the difficulty of assigning to political sociology a field which was freed from all equivocation: it was not simply the state, nor the relationship between rulers and ruled, nor simply 'power', but all of these at one and the same time. Durkheim's originality resided precisely in the fact that he situated his questions 'in the centre of this equivocation', between politics as a partial system and politics as an *aspect englobant* of the collectivity as a whole (Filloux 1977: 220–3). Likewise, for Lacroix, Durkheimian politics was not so much incarnated by a specific institution, practice, or form of belief; it was not an instance that was analytically isolable from the social whole, but an aspect or an effect of its synthetic functioning. Power, for Durkheim, was not a quality or a substance belonging to an individual, or issuing from the unequal effect of a dual relation. It overflowed all institutions and all groups; it was disseminated across the entire breadth of society as a necessary modality of its constitution (Lacroix 1981: 306–11).

Both Filloux and Lacroix hence appear to congratulate Durkheim for his ambiguous delineation of the *champ politique* as the object of sociology, and take his dialectical mixture of partial and totalist definitions largely for granted. The *ventilation du pouvoir* about which Filloux speaks and his idiom of derivation and articulation suggest a formal conceptual structure which closely resembles the Marxian dialectic of the last instance or the Althusserian theory of overdetermination. But here it is power and politics rather than property and production which constitute the 'categories of origin'. Durkheim's dialectic of the *règne social*, which is interpreted by Filloux and Lacroix as a dialectic of *pouvoir/croyance*, simultaneously 'inverts' the materialist dialectic of political economy and, on the opposite flank, the Hegelian dialectic of state sovereignty, but its own peculiar equivocation of part and whole nurses a similar conquistadorial intention. The Durkheimian dialectic of *pouvoir/croyance* does not therefore 'open up our way', as Lacroix wishfully supposes; rather, it must be explained as a product of intellectual rivalry, and as symbiotically chained to the counter-dialectics of sovereignty and property.

This complicitous inversionism was also evident in Durkheim's double-flanked dismissal of Marxism, which was criticized both as economic reductionism and as collectivist etatism (which in his view expressed another, *political* reductionism). By resisting both its Smithian and its Hegelian inclinations, the sociological critique of Marxism once again emphasized the latter's intriguing bi-zonal position straddling the British economist and the German etatist traditions – which posed an obvious double challenge for any intellectual sparring partner who decided to rise 'through the centre'. In this perspective, Marxism's *ontological* prioritizing of the *economy* as causally determinant in the *last* instance both concealed and sanctioned the *practical first* instance determination of the *political* (including the claim to dominance of political intellectuals cognizant of historical materialism). From his early defences of Schäffle to his later adoption of the industrial socialism of Saint-Simon, Durkheim did not cease to oppose the despotic tendencies lurking in what he regularly called 'authoritarian communism', while he also had no difficulty in extrapolating his earlier critique of individualist political economy to its radical collectivist successors. Durkheim's lectures on socialism precisely identified the tendency towards economic materialism as a *feeble* element in Saint-Simon's thought, and repeatedly praised Comte for having rectified this error; his reviews of books on socialism by Labriola, Merlino, and Richard extended this critique more explicitly to classical Marxism (1975: 236ff.; 1986: 121ff.). Durkheim's review of Labriola (1897) became notorious for his substitution of religion for economics as dialectical category of origin, from which in his view all other manifestations of collective activity (such as law, morality, art, science, and politics) had successively emerged. In a perfect mirror image of the Marxian multicausal-yet-last-instance model of economic determination, Durkheim suggested that such secondary structures, far from being epiphenomenal, enjoyed a relative autonomy and an independent effectivity in reacting back upon the religious substratum, which all the while remained determinant in the last instance (1975: 253–4; 1986: 135–6).[34]

WEBERIAN DIALECTICS OF *HERRSCHAFT*

At this point, let me briefly turn to Weber, in order to add substance to my thesis about the relative unity of the sociological project as converging, across its various knowledge-geographical divisions, upon the theme of 'knowledge-able organization' and a generalized theory of social power. Far more than the Durkheimian consensualist view of moral authority, it has been Weber's darker view about the inexorable advance of rational domination which has provided the essential grounding of the modern sociological theory of power and organization, as well as the most formidable alternative to the Marxian theory of production and property. Like that of Durkheim, Weber's sociology to some extent eludes the binary dimensions of our dilemma of reduction and occupies a third outpost which is demarcated both ways. In comparison, however, Weber stays closer to a more traditional state–economy problematic, while rising more seriously to the challenge posed by the contemporary spread of Marxist theory and politics. His primary emphasis upon the analysis of *Herrschaft* can therefore be plausibly interpreted as 'counter-intelligence' against the 'property bias' of historical materialism, while his view of the sequence of modern history is typically cast in terms of 'organizational stages' and 'structures of domination' rather than 'modes of production'. Giddens has summarized this reversal as follows:

> Rather than generalising from the economic to the political, Weber generalises from the political to the economic: bureaucratic speciali-sation of tasks (which is, first and foremost, the characteristic of the legal-rational state) is treated as the most integral feature of capi-talism.
> (Giddens 1972a: 35; cf. Szacki 1979: 366; Mommsen 1989: 60)

Throughout his prolific writings Weber was concerned, at the very least, to elicit the autonomy of the political dimension (and especially the role of rational domination) against both liberal and Marxist economism, as he also demanded a relative autonomy for the role of ideas over against all types of sociological reductionism. It has been argued, in this context, that Weberian sociology suffered from a contrary 'spiritualist bias', since it ended up by assigning ultimate primacy to the logic of *religious* rationalization and its subsequent secularization, which allegedly subordinates all other societal domains to the commanding impulse of worldviews and ideas (cf. Breuer 1991: 21–2). Other commentators, however, have vindicated Weber's own methodological resolve not to exchange one-sided materialist causal interpretations for equally one-sided idealist ones, and to lend equal weight, at least provisionally, to various types and flows of causal determination (cf. Mommsen 1989: 57; cf. Weber 1963: 10–12, 83; 1968: 294–6). In a sense, Weber exactly mediates between the two contrasting positions by saying that human conduct is directly governed not by ideas, but by *interests* (which can be both material and ideal), significantly adding that 'very frequently the "world images" that have been created by "ideas" have, like signallers, determined the tracks along which action has been pushed by the dynamic of interest' (Weber 1970b: 280).

Weber's *Freiburger Antrittsrede*, as we noted, was still heavily marked by the etatist inclination of 'National Economy' in its celebration of the supremacy of the power interests of the German nation above all other considerations (cf. Mommsen 1974: 37ff.; Giddens 1972a: 16–17; Hennis 1987). Even though, as a member of the younger generation in the *Verein*, Weber adopted a more liberal and value-free stance than precursors such as Schmoller and Wagner, his core problematic continued to be political rather than economic, encircling the problem of the advance of rational bureaucracy and the erosion of political leadership in post-Bismarckian Germany. Simultaneously, the problem of bureaucratic management and leadership was set out in much broader terms than on the level of the state proper, since Weber tracked the progress of rational discipline in all the major social organizations and institutions, betting everywhere on the force of charismatic authority to avert the threat of complete imprisonment in the 'iron cage' of bureaucratic rule. This question also dominated his economic sociology, which in large part centred upon an analysis of the consequences of the 'managerial revolution' and the bureaucratization of private enterprise. It was not the Marxian 'paradox of property' (those who work lack property, while the propertied do not work) which acted as the explosive mainspring of capitalist society; on the contrary, the logic of managerial control which was implicit in the modern division of labour demanded an ever sharper separation between the worker or functionary and the tools of his or her trade.

In Weber's judgement, the socialist slogan about the separation of the producer from the means of production functioned precisely to *conceal* the crucial fact that this 'expropriation' was an essential characteristic of rational domination, defining all complex institutions and organizations in modern society. Factories, armies, universities, political parties, and states were all indelibly stamped by the progress of rational discipline, and could be analysed more fruitfully as *Herrschaftsverbände* or *Herrschaftsbetriebe* than as proprietary institutions (Weber 1968: 475ff.). The trend towards disciplinary expropriation would only be extended by rationally organized socialism, since it 'would retain the expropriation of all workers and merely bring it to completion by the expropriation of the private owners' (Weber 1970a: 199, 201; 1978: 218–19). In his 1918 lecture on socialism, the pressure of factory *discipline* was identified as the actual and original ferment of the socialist movement, and the rise of rational bureaucracy was defined as the most fatal of socialism's unintended consequences, precisely because socialists had been trained to subordinate power questions to questions of property. The elimination of private capitalism was certainly conceivable, but it would fail to destroy the steel frame of discipline in which modern industrial work was encased. Abolition of private capitalism and private property would simply mean that the top management of the nationalized or socialized enterprises would become bureaucratic as well: 'State bureaucracy would rule *alone* if private capitalism were eliminated' (1978: 1401–2).

Weber's fascination with the interface of power and organization was clearly reflected in the conceptual framework which was prefixed to *Wirtschaft und Gesellschaft*. His account of the various types of social action was immediately succeeded by a discussion of 'legitimate order', which prepared the way for a first conceptualization of the closely interlinked phenomena of organization, power, and domination. In between, he entered upon a seminal discussion of open and closed relationships, which departed from a general conception of 'advantages' (including material benefits and resources as well as workers' jobs, managerial functions, or educational qualifications), which could be appropriated or enclosed with different degrees of permanency. However, domination and leadership were quickly identified as central phenomena of all social life, which were responsible for the very constitution of rational association (1978: 941, 948ff.).[35] *Herrschaft*, or power to command within an institutional setting (also referred to as *Befehlsgewalt* or *Autorität*), was seen as a specific instance of the exercise of power (*Macht*), which in Weber's celebrated definition, was 'the chance of a man or a number of men to realize their own will in a social action even against the resistance of others who are participating in the action'. As Weber himself realized, this definition was so broad as to be sociologically amorphous, embracing 'all conceivable qualities of a person and all conceivable combinations of circumstances'. The concept of *Herrschaft*, however, though ostensibly placed on a lesser plane of abstraction, was hardly less comprehensive and not shorn of ambiguities of its own. In this manner, ambivalences of a dialectical kind appeared to be structurally latent in Weber's political sociology, as they also were in Durkheim's. They were clearly recognizable in his typology of domination, but equally in his definition of the scope of politics and his three-dimensional view of social stratification.

In an important passage, Weber distinguished two diametrically contrasting types of domination, namely domination by virtue of a *constellation of interests* and domination by virtue of *authority*, i.e. power to command and duty to obey. If it is seen that the purest type of the former was monopolistic domination in the market and the purest type of the latter was patriarchal, magisterial, or princely power, we are not very far from a distinction between economic property and authority as special cases of *Herrschaft* (Weber 1978: 943). However, Weber also narrowed down the concept of *Herrschaft* to exclude market opportunities and to identify it with 'authoritarian power of command' (*autoritärer Befehlsgewalt*); *Herrschaft* then referred to the situation 'in which the manifested will (command) of the ruler or rulers is meant to influence the conduct of one or more others (the ruled)' (1978: 946). *Herrschaft* accordingly figured both as the generic category which embraced market monopoly and as the narrower category which excluded it. This ambivalence resurged in Weber's ambiguous demarcation of the scope of politics. In *Politics as a Vocation*, he defended an extremely broad conception of it as 'any kind of independent leadership in action', but simultaneously alluded to a more restricted view of politics as 'striving to influence the distribution of power either among states or among groups within a state' (Weber 1970b: 77–8; 1978: 54–5). Here politics was *both* the generic term which included all forms of economic, political, or cultural leadership *and* the specific term which was tied to the more restricted statal domain.

Similar vacillations occurred in Weber's discussion of the master concepts of social stratification. Class position, for Weber as for Marx, was determined by the volume and kind of disposition (*Verfügungsgewalt*) over goods and services, which implied that property and lack of property constituted the basic categories of all class situations (1978: 927).[36] But the main thrust of Weber's theory of stratification, of course, was to underscore that class (or economically conditioned) power was not coextensive with power as such, and to distinguish between an *economic* order, the seat of economically conditioned classes, a *social* order which gave rise to stratification by status, and a *political* order where 'parties' were seen to operate. The three orders were not unidirectionally dependent, but conditioned each other in multilinear fashion, whereas the Marxian view of class not only ranged these dimensions in a hierarchy of ultimate determination, but also introduced a broader conception of class which explained inequalities in the two other spheres as well. However, the Weberian dialectic of power reversed the Marxian dialectic of property in a much more immediate sense than is suggested by this multidimensional view. It is interesting to note that older interpretations of Weber's model, such as those offered by Runciman, Lipset and Bendix, and Mills tended to discriminate 'power' as a third dimension adjacent to 'class' and 'status'. Modern authors such as Parkin and Giddens have been critical of this, pointing to the obvious fact that the third dimension was referred to as 'party' and that, as Weber clearly stated, classes, status groups, and parties were 'phenomena of the distribution of power within a community'. In this conception, the distribution of power was not a separate dimension of stratification at all, but rather its constitutive principle in all three dimensions.[37] But Weber once again complicates things, so that the older interpretation is perhaps less misguided than Parkin and Giddens have realized. When discussing his notion of 'party', Weber indeed positioned classes within the economic order and status groups within the social order, but went on to locate parties in the sphere of 'power' (1978: 938). Once again, Weber appeared to shuttle between a restrictive and an inclusive view of power, as he did in the case of domination and politics. Both interpretations therefore appear textually legitimate, even if neither of them really faces the complication that Weber's political sociology is structurally undecided about the scope of its own master concepts.

POWER AND DISCIPLINE

This chapter has presented a rough and partial sketch of the early history and the intellectual specificity of the sociological project which differs in significant respects from what was termed the traditional or 'Durkheimian' view of its object. Our picture of the sociological enterprise, it was claimed, becomes more comprehensive and careful if we discard the tribal myth about the discovery of 'society', and recognize the varied historical ties which attached it to the venerable legacy of political philosophy. In the process, we have come closer to what might be called a 'Foucaldian' image of its historical project, in which the concern with the social is not particularly distinct from a concern with the political, and in which authority, power, and discipline are centripetal concepts. Given this original vocation, sociology does not enjoy the disciplinary uniqueness or independence which many present-day practitioners are still ready to ascribe to it. Rather, it appears to have been the sociologists' prior search for social space and intellectual distinction within the then-existing field of the social sciences which has at least coproduced the discovery of 'society' – which was as much, and inseparably, a theoretical acknowledgement of a developing 'objective' reality as a transmission belt for the interests of specific social experts in the demarcation and justification of their own discipline. Thus, the sequence of cause and effect is also reversed: the object is to a large extent also configured by the project (Tenbruck 1981; Lacroix 1981; Pels 1983).

In redrawing these lines of intellectual descent, I have also submitted that the original project of sociology could best be characterized as the theory and practice of 'knowledgeable organization' – which could be taken as a contemporary translation of the broad scope of Aristotelian 'politics'. This designation once more brings out the crucial impact of the competitional network in which sociology is locked together with political economy, both in its liberal and Marxist–socialist variety. Master disciplines such as political economy and political philosophy are not content to divide their intellectual labours, but channel their demarcative will and their imperial claims through the medium of rivalling 'last instances'. Despite the sociological quest for a mediating 'third' position, the old reductionary dilemma therefore still to

161

some extent survives in modern social analysis, and mortgages the definition of a whole series of basic concepts. 'Power' is perhaps the most important of these on the sociological side. Its sheer, almost totemic centrality, its logical primacy, the reduction of 'property' to a special case of it, the dialectical vagaries which surround its definition, which in its simplest versions invariably borders on the tautological, can perhaps be set in clearer perspective if we conceive of them in part as products or signatures of intellectual rivalry. Power cannot be 'realistically' taken for granted as the 'stuff' of social relations or as the stratificational spine of the social order, if only because it plays an additional and subliminal role as an engine of intellectual competition and demarcation.

Let me, by way of conclusion, illustrate this proposition by listing some remarkable continuities between classical sociology's 'third project' and the reinvention of 'the social' as the ensemble of disciplinary technologies in the recent writings of Foucault, Deleuze, and Donzelot. In their various conceptions, emerging social theory is clearly seen as complicitous with the rise of a general science of policing (*la police*, *Polizei*), or a general science of social regulation, which is intimately bound to the state but not identical with it (cf. Donzelot 1979; 1984; Foucault 1977: 213, 305). Foucault has been among the first to have interpreted the Durkheimian sociological object as the 'system of discipline' and Durkheim's 'social realm' as synonymous with 'the disciplinary' (Foucault 1977: 23). His studies of the disciplinary society have also been read as complementing Weber's formal analysis of the modern bureaucratic state and economy, and as extending the latter's concept of rational–legal discipline (Weber 1978: 1148ff.; O'Neill 1986; Gordon 1987; Warren 1992). In this light, it is arguable that Foucault's conception of disciplinary power to some extent synthesizes the 'productive' or consensualist strand in the theory of power as represented by Durkheim and the 'repressive' or conflictual view which has been primarily diffused through Weber. In addition, Foucault's grounding ontology has been widely criticized for offering a highly overdrawn, demiurgical, and elusive conception of power which, while ostensibly focusing upon the disciplinary mechanisms and institutions in between state and economy, may also be taken as synonymous with the social whole itself (cf. Habermas 1987; Fraser 1989; Cohen and Arato 1992; Pels 1995b).

Like Durkheimian sociology, Foucaldian genealogy is doubly demarcated against classical metaphors of sovereignty and classical 'proprietary' models of power and action. Rather than deriving from a single macro-institution such as the state, disciplinary power is considered to be coextensive with the social body. The state can only operate on the basis of a vast underlying system of micro-powers of surveillance, normalization, and control; it is 'superstructural in relation to a whole series of power networks that invest the body, sexuality, the family, kinship, knowledge, technology, and so forth'. This 'swarming' of disciplinary mechanisms and technologies, which appear indefinitely generalizable (Foucault 1977: 211), forms the privileged target of genealogical description. It is not the 'uniform edifice of sovereignty' that should retain us, but 'the multiple forms of subjugation that have a place and function within the social organism'; we must not study power at its extremities, in its ultimate destinations, but in its local, capillary forms (Foucault 1980: 96). Hence the need for a political philosophy that discards the problem of sovereignty and the prohibitive and 'possessive' conception of power which is derived from it. We must eschew the model of the *Leviathan* in the study of power; in political theory, we still need to cut off the king's head (ibid.: 102, 97–98, 104ff., 121–2).

Simultaneously, Foucault entered strong reservations with regard to the economistic bias common to both the liberal and Marxist views of power, which conceptualized it respectively as a possessory right or commodity, or emphasized the economic functionality of power relations (1980: 88–9). To counter it, he pleaded an autonomous conceptualization of power which transcended economic metaphors and economic causal determinism. New power techniques geared towards 'the accumulation of men', for example, have always been inseparable from and indispensable to the economic system that promoted the accumulation of capital (ibid.: 125; 1977: 220–1).[38] Hence the need for a 'non-economic' analysis of power which clearly acknowledged

> that the power exercised on the body is conceived not as a property, but as a strategy, that its effects of domination are attributed not to 'appropriation', but to dispositions, manoeuvres, tactics, techniques, functionings; that one should decipher in it a network of relations, constantly in tension, in activity, rather than a privilege that one might possess.
>
> (1977: 26)

Power relations are not localized in the relations between state and citizens or on the frontier between classes, but go right down into the depths of society. Although it is true that its pyramidal organization gives this power machinery a 'head', it is the apparatus as a whole that produces power and distributes individuals across a permanent and continuous field. Like Durkheim, therefore, Foucault thematized not only the productive nature of discipline, and its infrastructural location with regard to the power of the 'social brain', but also the parallel progression of discipline and individualization, and the moralizing techniques for constituting individuals as correlates of power and knowledge (cf. 1977: 193–4). But like Weber, he has also remained acutely aware of the sombre underside of rational domination as a disciplining 'iron cage' which normalizes subjects in houses of *Herrschaft*, and leaves precious little room for authenticity and resistance (cf. Turner 1987: 231–3).

6

POWER, PROPERTY, AND
MANAGERIALISM

We have begun, in a word, to encounter the vocabulary of power while
thinking in terms of a property frame.

Adolf Berle

FROM PROPERTY TO POWER?

Presumably, I need not further insist that the power theme is written all over
the face of contemporary sociology; many sociologists take it for granted as the
stuff out of which all things social are made. It has been central to the conflict
paradigm of, for example, Mills, Rex, and Dahrendorf, that long-standing
alternative to normative functionalism which, in the course of the 1960s and
early 1970s, managed to reshuttle the basic themes of domination theory back
into the sociological mainstream. It has been equally constitutive for the
exchange theory of Emerson and Blau, for Bell's, Aron's, and Touraine's
proposals about the 'post-industrial' society, for the actionism of Giddens and
Lukes, for the neo-Weberian 'closure' paradigm of Parkin and Murphy, for
Luhmann's systems theory, for the historical sociology of Elias and Mann, for
Foucault's and Donzelot's analyses of the 'disciplinary' society, and more
recently, for the Beck/Giddens paradigm of 'reflexive modernization' in late
modern 'risk societies'. Without putting too fine a point upon it, Foucault's
catholic conception of disciplinary power may well represent something like a
journey's end for sociology; it in a sense completes the secular process of generalization which has slowly transfigured the political sociology pioneered by
Mosca, Pareto, Comte, and Tocqueville into the general theory of societal
power advanced by their modern descendants. To some extent, Foucault also
reconciles the Durkheimian or consensualist and the Weberian or conflictual
strands in the theory of power.[1]

It is often assumed, in this context, that the 'crisis' which ravaged sociology
during the 1960s and early 1970s resulted in a broad pendulum swing from a
'Durkheimian' emphasis on value consensus and integration towards a supposedly more realistic 'Weberian' analytic of conflict and power. But the truth in

this is only partial, and remains so if the broader historical backdrop of the power–property dualism is ignored. As Giddens has demonstrated, one of the pervasive myths of the sociological trade was precisely this 'myth of the schism' between consensus and conflict theory, which in his view was sterile and artificial, and did little to clarify the issues separating academic sociology (and its theory of industrial society) from Marxism (and its theory of capitalist society) (1977: 208ff.). Parsons' well-known polemic with Mills, for example, departed from a functionalist theory of power-as-authority which closely approached the Durkheimian one; by redefining power as 'a facility for the achievement of collective goals', Parsons did not so much *avoid* issues of power but instead *resolved* them in a particular direction (Parsons 1967; 1968; Giddens 1977: 333ff.). The intra-sociological dispute, from this aspect, did not so much concern the relative theoretical weight of consensus vs. power, but was rather conducted in terms of consensualist vs. conflictual theories of 'knowledgeable organization'. While in the former, legitimacy entered into the very definition of power ('power-to'), and social organization was immediately specified as 'value community', the latter chose to identify normative conflict, forced consensus, and domination ('power-over') as the main structuring principles of the social order. Much of the apparent landslide of the 1970s therefore involved an intra-sociological resettlement of these two major strands.

To adopt the larger perspective of a cross-cutting fault line between the sociological tradition (both consensualist and conflictual) and the tradition of Marxist theorizing is was once again to mark the unique positional centrality and the curious dialectical mirror-play of their two key concepts of power and property. In both traditions, centrality was paired to paucity of definition, so that both concepts gravitated towards something like the 'raw material' of social life, the 'stuff' of social inequality, or the 'vertical axis' of social structure. In addition, both concepts tended to include and subordinate one another, following a pattern of ontological prioritizing which implied contrary and competing definitional expansions and contractions. Pioneer sociologists such as Saint-Simon, Comte, Durkheim, and Weber considered power or social authority as larger in scope and causally 'deeper' than property, while the concept of property itself was often whittled down to become equal to 'income' or 'wealth'. Thus transformed into a residual category, it bore but little resemblance to 'heavy' property in the Marxist sense, which was normally taken to include decisional or control rights over the major means of production.[2]

In the modern sociology of stratification, the gradual turn away from the logic of property towards the logic of power marked a virtually uncontested theoretical baseline. Many theorists followed the path broken by Weber, Mannheim, and Geiger, who all observed a long-term shift *from* property *to* power as the dominant axis of social stratification in Western societies (cf. Geiger 1949). C. Wright Mills, in his seminal analysis of the rising new middle class, similarly proposed that negatively, the transformation of the middle class is a shift from property to no-property; positively, it is a shift from property to a new axis of stratification, occupation. . . . In modern society, occupations are specific functions within a social division of labour, as well as skills sold for income on a labour market.

This new occupational hierarchy, in his view, simultaneously constituted an unequal division of power or effective control over the means of production (Mills 1951: 65). The social structure of capitalism, he argued, had changed to such an extent as to require a new statement of the causal weight of economic institutions and of their causal relationships with other institutions; it was politics or 'political forms' more especially, which increasingly proved decisive (1969: 121–3).

Although the prevailing view in the modern sociology of stratification thus stressed a secular shift away from the property axis towards a function/ skill/power axis, important differences of emphasis remained. Whereas the functionalist wing tended to place its main emphasis upon occupation and functional authority, its critical or 'agonistic' counterpart restored the idea of power *inequality* to a position of prominence. For Parsons and others, traditional property-based class inequality was being replaced by a hierarchy of roles defined by their functional importance for collective social goals; status groups were pictured as accessible and fluid and as being filled through individual achievement rather than ascription (cf. Parsons 1954). Critics such as Dahrendorf, Lenski or Parkin thought differently. Social stratification, Dahrendorf argued, was 'only a secondary consequence of the social structure of power' (1969: 38). Lenski emphasized that it was *not* system needs nor objective functions that determined social distribution, but that *power* should be seen as the key variable: 'class' was then redefinable as the aggregate of those who stood in a similar position with respect to some form of power, privilege, or prestige. He added a fundamental distinction between the 'power of position' and the 'power of property', whose linkage was neither necessary nor inevitable since property was frequently dissociated from occupancy of a particular office or role (1966: 58, 74–5). For Parkin, likewise, the occupational order constituted the backbone of the class structure and of the entire reward system of Western society, a notion which was immediately extended towards a Weberian interpretation of class, status, and party as phenomena of the distribution of power (1972: 46).

Notwithstanding such differences, it was agreed upon by both schools that, generally speaking, property inequalities, since the turn of the century, had greatly diminished in stratificational significance, and had ceded before inequalities due to either functional authority or conflictual power. In this respect, they together confronted another tradition of thought which took the erosion of property by no means for granted, but affirmed its continuing impact as an ultimately decisive stratificational variable. This tradition, of course, included the many strands of palaeo- and neo-Marxism. In the 1950s, for example, Mills' *The Power Elite* became the subject of a wide controversy which once again lined up the protagonists of the power idiom over against the advocates of property theory. Many of the latter worried about the 'disarming simplicity' and the circular nature of Mills' definition of the power elite as those who occupied the command posts of the major economic, military, and political institutions (Sweezy 1968: 115ff.; Lynd 1968: 103ff.; Bottomore 1966: 33ff.). Mills' tautological conception of power, his critics charged, was wedded to unduly restricted conceptions of economics, property, and class.[3] Since when, one of them queried, was the concept of class only 'an economic term' that no longer referred to social aggregates (Lynd 1968: 112)?

Mills only fully explicated his definition of property in *The Marxists*, a book of final reckoning which postdated the power elite debate. In his exposé of Marx's doctrine, he translated the variable 'relations of men to the means of production' into 'property as a source of income'. He went on to affirm the indispensability of this property criterion to the understanding of the stratification of capitalist society, not as the ultimate dimension, but as one dimension among others, such as occupation, status, and of course, power (Mills 1969: 84, 105–6; cf. 1963: 305ff.; 1951: 71). Such stratificational pluralism proved to be anathema to his Marxist critics, who univocally supported the theory of the ruling class and the ultimate significance of economic property. Herbert Aptheker could do no better than repeat Noah Webster's conjuration: 'In what, then, does *real* power consist? The answer is short, plain – in *property*.' Mills, in Lynd's accusation, reserved property as a basis of power only for one discrete set within the elite, and made no solid effort 'to appraise the relative weight and the diffused spread of the power of property throughout all institutions under capitalism'. 'What we have in the United States', Sweezy proclaimed, 'is a ruling class with its roots deeply sunk in the apparatus of appropriation which is the corporate system' (Domhoff and Ballard 1968: 160, 111, 127–9).

Mills' argument may be briefly compared with Dahrendorf's near-contemporary view, which likewise originated in a studied rejection of Marxist class theory and elicited a similar critical response. Unlike Mills, however, Dahrendorf accepted the Marxian position that class conflicts did not spring from differences of income or income sources, but in property as an effective force of production, or 'ownership of means of production and its denial to others'. However, the role of property in Marx's theory of class posed a problem of interpretation: did Marx employ a broad definition in terms of 'factual control and subordination' in the enterprises of industrial production, or did he mean authority relations in so far as these were based on the legal title of property? Was there still class and class conflict after the separation of legal title and factual control? Was property for Marx a special case of authority – or vice versa, authority a special case of property? (1959: 20–2) Dahrendorf decided that Marx's analyses were indeed based upon the narrow, legal concept. In his own view, however, it was evident that power and authority were not tied to the legal title, and that a class theory which was based upon the criterion of possession of, or exclusion from, effective private property lost its analytical value as soon as legal ownership and factual control were separated. The more basic criterion of class was the exercise of, or exclusion from authority:

> Power and authority are irreducible factors from which the social relations associated with legal private property as well as those associated with communal property can be derived. . . . But property is by no means the only form of authority; it is but one of its numerous types. Whoever tries, therefore, to define authority by property defines the general by the particular – an obvious logical fallacy.
>
> (Dahrendorf 1959: 136)

'Class' could then be newly defined as referring to social conflict groups which were primarily determined by participation in or exclusion from authority, exercised within what Dahrendorf called 'imperatively coordinated associations'. Economic classes now only constituted a special case of the larger phenomenon of class itself (1959: 136–9). It had been the failure of the Soviet experiment to eliminate conflict by abolishing property, which had led many to abandon the 'century-old obsession with property' as the basic social force:

> Instead of the legal and economic implications of ownership, the political and social ones of power came to the fore. Relations of property may indeed give rise to conflict, but if they do, they do so because they are a special case of relations of power. There is conflict, and class, after property.
>
> (Dahrendorf 1967: 5; cf. 1988: 141ff.)

The Marxist riposte to this stuck to familiar terms. While being disfigured by a 'misleading' and 'erroneous' evaluation of Marx's work, Dahrendorf's analysis was also said to be tainted by a 'liberal ideological bias' which diverted attention away from the actual sources of power and conflict in capitalist society, in which the principal structural cleavage derived from the private ownership of productive property. Dahrendorf's account clearly depended upon a 'transparently metaphysical reification of authority as the key determinant'. At no point did he systematically approach power as a problem to be examined by scientific methods, or attempt to explicate theoretically the source of power itself. In circular and tautologous fashion, it was assumed to lie in the ubiquitous authority relations which were a defining characteristic of social institutions as 'imperatively coordinated associations' (Binns 1977: 78–9, 88–9, 98).[4]

SMALL SHOES, BIG FEET

Such polemics illustrate a logic of conceptual expansion and contraction which is characteristic of the entire history of the dispute between Marxism and sociology, from its beginnings in the criticism of economic determinism by Durkheim, Weber, and the Italian elitists up to these middle and late twentieth-century disputes. On one side, one witnesses a gradual enlargement of the vocabulary of power or authority, which is balanced by narrow conceptions of property as legal private ownership or as source of wealth or income. On the other side, one encounters an enlargement of the alternative vocabulary of property and possession, which now emphatically includes rights to control productive assets as well as income rights, and hence tendentially coincides with generalized conceptions of domination or control. In this fashion, the long-standing tension between a 'property' and a 'power' theory of social class, while showing a continual repetition of reductionist reversals of the argument, also exemplifies a long drift (explicit or implicit) in the direction of the vocabulary of power or domination (cf. Wolff and Resnick 1986: 107–8). Parkin has footnoted this trend with the ironic comment that 'inside every neo-Marxist there seems to be a Weberian struggling to get out' (1979: 25).

In a more politically charged ambiance, the double reductionist pattern is also evident in the reaction by New Left critics to the argument about the 'demise of ownership', as it was forwarded both by sociologists and by postwar revisionist social democratic writers. Conceptually restricting ownership to legal form, Crosland for example concluded that it was no longer of overtowering relevance to the constitution of social class since, as a result of the 'technological fact' of growing complexity and scale of factory organization, capitalist ownership was increasingly being divorced from effective control (Crosland 1963: 36–7, 42). This argument was already a well-rehearsed one within the socialist movement, reaching back to the debates about the significance of the new middle class of *Angestellten*, entered upon by orthodox Marxists such as Kautsky, revisionists such as Bernstein and De Man, and 'academic socialists' such as Schmoller and Wagner (cf. Burris 1986). As noted in Chapter 4, De Man's influential conception of *planisme* articulated a shift from property to power or authority, as did Déat's *néo-socialisme* in contemporary France. Right-wing political thought, as represented by Spengler, Sombart, Freyer, and the intellectuals around *Die Tat*, had also emphasized this 'political' turn in ownership relations. In Crosland's postwar analysis, power similarly figured as the dominant stratifying factor in industry, in the politico-administrative sphere and in the professions. It was a basic variable in industry

> where a clear hierarchy exists in respect of power to sack, demote or promote, pay higher or lower incomes, move people from one place to another, organise work in a particular way, and generally influence, if

not determine, the income, nature of employment, and occupational status of employees. This hierarchy is not, as the Marxists suppose, related to an index of ownership, but simply to location in the organisational structure.

(Crosland 1963: 112)

New Left writers such as Sweezy, Poulantzas, Carchedi, and Wright typically chose to counter this argument by introducing a fundamental distinction between 'formal' legal ownership and the more strategically decisive variable of 'factual', 'effective', or 'economic' property – which was largely coincident with the exercise of decisional power or discretionary control in the (economic) division of labour, and hence was no longer definitionally tied to *individual* legal property. The same long-term institutional development, i.e. the gradual disaggregation of the full liberal package of ownership rights into various component parts (cf. Grey 1980), which sociologists and revisionists saw as a 'separation of ownership from control', could be alternatively interpreted in terms of a *strengthening* of the constitutional bond between them. Since ownership-as-control or as management still identified the strategic core of the 'global function of capital', in practice the 'capitalist' or 'bourgeois' class label was conferred according to a criterion of differential power (cf. Johnson 1977: 211, 222; Parkin 1979: 23–5). For Carchedi, to mention but one example, the 'function of capital' was so completely separable from private ownership that it left 'position in a hierarchy of control and surveillance' as the only tangible criterion of class membership. 'Real ownership', on the other hand, identified the top range of a positional hierarchy of control and supervision, so that the 'global function of capital' was definitionally exercised by a hierarchy of controllers and a bureaucracy of command (Carchedi 1977).

The presumed ideological shift 'from property to power' can hence only be treated as an object of general consensus if one remains confined within a narrow sociological (or revisionist) perspective. The Marxist 'property theory' of social class could successfully adapt to the embarrassment posed by the rise of new, formally 'propertyless' economic elites, by diluting the concept of ownership itself from strictly private to collective forms. The method was already latently active in Marx's own analyses of management and bureaucracy, and took advantage of the structural ambiguity in the master concept of property itself. Marx's own account of the growing positional separation in large-scale capitalist firms between the 'functioning' or 'productive' capitalist (the *Anwender*) and the passive owner or speculator (the *Eigentümer*) even anticipated a full separation between 'pure' functionaries and 'pure' proprietors, which would bring all real economic functions into the hands of the former and hasten the disappearance of the latter from the process of production. However, this apparent demise of private ownership (and the private capitalist) did not imply the disappearance of capitalism as a profit-based competitive economic system. At this point, Marx typically vacillated

170

between the narrow criterion of private capital ownership and a broader view which identified the 'function of capital' with 'command over alien labour' and hence edged closer to a power theory of capitalism and the managerial class (Marx 1894: 400–1; 452–6).

More recently, this conceptual elasticity has condoned various enlargements of the classical class vocabulary by a vocal group of 'analytical' Marxists, who have variously attempted to stretch the scope of concepts such as 'exploitation' and 'property' in order to encompass managerial control of production, access to organizational or bureaucratic positions, command of 'skill assets', 'job property', and even citizenship (Roemer 1982a, b; 1986; Wright 1985a, b; Van Parijs 1993) (see also Chapter 3). A veritable proliferation of productive assets, correspondent forms of ownership, and dimensions of inequality has ensued, which is once again suggestive of the large measure of arbitrariness and verbalism which often inhabits these reductionary disputes across the property–power binary. Roemer's initial rephrasing of the concept of exploitation in terms of property relations, conceived as unequal access to alienable means of production, was quickly enlarged towards a more general taxonomy which also accommodated 'feudal' ownership of people and 'socialist' or 'status' exploitation resulting from the unequal distribution of skills. To this list, Wright has added 'organizational' assets and 'organizational' exploitation, while the 'ownership problem' with regard to these organizational forces of production was resolved by means of the well-tried extension towards 'effective' (and collectively exercisable) economic control (1985b: 80–1). In an even more radical generalization, Van Parijs has included 'job property' and 'job exploitation' as defining the structural axis of a new class struggle under welfare-state capitalism. He has also broadened the Roemerian category of 'status exploitation' by subsuming inequalities resulting from race, gender, and citizenship, effectively postulating as many potential class divides as there are factors which systematically effect the distribution of material advantages (1993: 119).

One recent example of a contrary set of generalizations along the power axis is the neo-Weberian 'closure paradigm' advocated by Parkin and Murphy. As originally employed by Weber, the concept of closure referred to processes of subordination whereby one group monopolized advantages by closing off opportunities to another group of outsiders which it defined as inferior and ineligible. Any convenient, visible characteristic, such as race, language, social origin, religion, or lack of a particular school diploma, could in principle be used to label competitors as outsiders (Murphy 1988: 8). Enlarging the focus of the concept of exploitation from its restricted Marxist application, this Weberian view of monopolization is taken to provide an overarching model for the analysis of all forms of domination, e.g. by replacing Marx's labour theory of value with a power theory of profits and prices (ibid.: 83ff.). Even though Roemer's new departure is praised for a certain convergence with this Weberian analysis, it is also criticized for not extending far enough, and for its resultant inability to account for gender, racial, ethnic, and religious exclusion (ibid.: 103, 104n.). To Murphy, a rigorous conception of exploitation can only be developed as a subcategory of social closure-as-power. Rather than stretching the concept of property to fit positional, credential, cultural, and other species of exclusion, it is far more advisable to begin with more general concepts: 'Why stretch small shoes to big feet when big shoes are available?' (ibid.: 175).

In this context, Parkin has likewise discouraged any further expansion of the original definition of property to include cultural assets. It is unlikely, he has argued, that Marxists would welcome such additional tampering, 'given the exegetical difficulties already encountered in reconciling the notion of managerial control with the classical formula of pure ownership'. Other than property which, even in the revised neo-Marxist sense, still refers to the productive sphere, cultural capital and credentialism are notions that do not easily fit into the vocabulary of modes of production, other than as mere epiphenomena. Indeed, they have the suspicious appearance of concepts relating to the distributive system, with all that this implies in the way of 'Weberian contamination' (1979: 59). But Parkin's argument has a somewhat arbitrary ring, not only because he simultaneously favours an expansion of the Marxian notion of exploitation, but also because he ignores that similar objections may well be raised against his own theory of closure-as-power. In presuming the impossibility of a generalized theory of property and capital, Parkin also implicitly respects some of the restrictions imposed by a traditional materialist theory of productivity. This 'Marxian contamination' of closure theory includes a taken-for-granted dichotomy between a productive base and a cultural 'service sector', and contrasts property, as providing access to productive capital, to credentials, as providing access to key positions in the division of labour (ibid.: 45–8, 54–8). But there is no *a priori* reason why knowledge, skills, or educational credentials cannot themselves count as forces of production either in the sense of functionalist 'human capital' theory or in that of conflict-oriented theories of 'cultural capital', while it is also obvious that property is as much a 'controlling device for key positions in the division of labour' (and was so conceived by Marx) as a means of access to physical stock.

It is peculiar, in this context, that Murphy recruits both Collins and Bourdieu to the colours of his closure paradigm, even though neither employs the closure vocabulary itself, and both lean over towards generalized metaphors of property and capital. In addition, their writings manifest a rather advanced state of *mixture* of the two rivalling repertoires (e.g. Collins 1986: 6–16). Collins' 'political economy of culture' defines the two major classes in contemporary capitalism as a working class that performs 'productive' labour, and a dominant class that performs 'political' labour, which includes the forging of alliances and the shaping of others' views within organizational settings (1979: 50ff.). This is indeed close to Bourdieu's notions of social, cultural, and political capital, as well as to the Roemer–Wright conception of organizational and skill exploitation. Collins also pleads an enlargement of the concept of property beyond traditional notions of material and financial possessions towards 'positional property' (cf. Van Parijs's 'job property'), which also crucially includes definitional struggles about how positions are shaped.[5] In this perspective, theorists such as Bourdieu and Collins become more interesting as idiomatic 'mixers' than as defenders of one or another reductionist position. The theoretical quarrel about who has the bigger feet (or the bigger shoes) had better be brought to a stop. Indeed, the concept of social closure gains in attractiveness the more it is loosened from the Parkin–Murphy identification with power theory, and made to bridge the old divide between a power theory of social stratification and a property theory of social class.

POWER WITHOUT PROPERTY

Map-making and boundary-drawing problems such as the above reappear in prismatic form in the celebrated and wide-ranging debate over the 'managerial revolution' – one crucial facet of the many-faceted 'class debate' which I will concentrate upon in the remainder of this chapter. The dispute on managerialism usefully refocuses my concern with the sociological object-and-project of 'knowledgeable organization', while it also identifies at least one (upper) echelon in the larger 'new middle class' that might be described as a positional bearer of this new productive force. In academic sociology, the first systematic exposition of the managerial idea is found in Berle and Means' seminal *The Modern Corporation and Private Property* (1932), which described the modern corporate revolution as resulting in the rise of 'control' through the dissolution of the old atom of property. As can be gathered from the title of Berle's postwar *Power Without Property* (1959), the basic contention was similar to that of the more comprehensive power theories of stratification referred to above. Power, for Berle as for other managerialists, constituted the 'thread of their narrative'. Modern corporations were unified and concentrated systems of organization and command, and therefore 'essentially political constructs'; their study should be undertaken first of all from 'the staging area of political science' (Berle 1959: 57; Berle and Means 1968: xxvi; Berle 1954: 21, 32).[6] It is also not difficult to recognize both a functionalist or solidarist and a conflictual or agonistic school of managerial theory. The former expected the rise of a 'soulful' corporation to attenuate the alienation of a soulless capitalism, the development of a new corporate conscience of responsible managers who were increasingly subservient to the 'public consensus', and the advent of a largely beneficial system of people's capitalism or collectivism. The conflict tradition expected a fearful concentration of economic power in the hands of a new self-interested elite, which administered capitalism – or what came after it – as a new breed of absolutist princes. As I will illustrate, this core issue remained largely undecided in Berle and Means' pioneer work and Berle's postwar writings. In comparison, Crosland's *The Future of Socialism* (1963) or Bell's *The Coming of Post-Industrial Society* (1976a) nursed a variant of managerial theory which was more rigorously optimistic and functionalist. The darker, conflictual version found classical expression in Burnham's *The Managerial Revolution* (1945), which popularized the thesis, and thus paradoxically also prompted the diffusion of more optimistic interpretations. Nevertheless, it is important to separate the dispute *among* the managerialists from that between managerialists and non-managerialists (or Marxists, which is virtually the same thing) which arguably remained the fundamental division of opinion (cf. Nichols 1969: 38).[7]

In setting out to review the much-reviewed dispute over the managerial revolution, I had better clarify at once where my attention is focused. I will not embark on a meticulous examination of the facts under discussion – if these are at all worthy of that honorific name, since the various modes of establishing them are themselves hotly disputed – nor will I endeavour to study the history of the dispute in any great detail (cf. Zeitlin 1974; Scott 1979; Chandler 1977; Grint 1995). Instead, and predictably, what I will seek to show is to what extent the intellectual competition between class/property analysis and power/elite analysis has slanted the debate towards dogmatic choices between supposedly foreordained alternatives. The dispute has both a real and an unreal quality: its 'unreal' competitive drive obscures both the real communion which underlies apparent conflict and the substantive conflicts which of course remain. Much of the non-issue again appears to derive from the false dilemma of wishing to reduce the property to the power logic, or the other way around. While managerialists emphasize the growing irrelevance of ownership and the rise of a new managerial elite (whether neutral or self-interested) which is placing the old moneyed class on the historical shelf, (neo-)Marxists typically go no further than to concede something like a 'managerial reorganization of the propertied class'. Between them, they largely agree on the secular trend and much of the substance of the issue, if only their political and intellectual commitments would let them.

Since Berle and Means' work has been such an enduring model for emulation and target of criticism, it is fair to summarize its argument briefly. Its main thesis, as already reported, was that the package of rights and privileges comprising the old bundle of property had been split, resulting in a divorce between the attribute of 'risking collective wealth in profit-seeking enterprise' and the attribute of 'ultimate management of responsibility for that enterprise'. Although, numerically speaking, most corporations were still 'close' corporations in which stockholders were also directors or exercised a dominating influence, there existed already in 1929 124 large corporations whose stockholder lists ran from 5,000 to 500,000. Such a dispersion of ownership tended to play the controlling power into the hands of management; although stockholders retained nominal voting rights as well as rights to initiate actions

against the board of directors, these rights vanished to the extent that ownership was more fragmented and the corporation itself larger in scale. Formerly
assumed to be merely a function of ownership, 'control' now appeared as a
separate, separable factor:

> Power over industrial property has been cut off from the beneficial
> ownership of this property – or, in less technical language, from the
> legal right to enjoy its fruits. Control of physical assets has passed
> from the individual owner to those who direct the quasi-public insti-
> tutions, while the owner retains an interest in their product and
> increase. We see, in fact, the surrender and regrouping of the inci-
> dence of ownership which formerly bracketed full power of manual
> disposition with complete right to enjoy the use, the fruits, and the
> proceeds of physical assets. There has resulted the dissolution of the
> old atom of ownership into its component parts, control and benefi-
> cial ownership.
>
> (Berle and Means 1968: 111)[8]

Berle and Means presented the following typology of control situations, which
they described as phases in the emancipation of managers from stockholders:
private ownership, majority ownership, minority control, control by legal
device (e.g. pyramiding of firms through holding companies; issuing non-
voting and preferential stock; organizing a voting trust, which might
guarantee control for a nominal ownership less than 1 per cent of total assets),
and management control. In the final type or phase, ownership was sufficiently subdivided to preclude minority control, so that management became
a self-perpetuating body even though its share in the ownership was negligible. Applying their historical typology to the 200 largest non-financial
American corporations in 1929 – and setting the basic criterion separating
minority from management control at a minimum of 20 per cent of controlling stock ownership – Berle and Means found that 65 per cent was either
management controlled or controlled by a legal device involving a small
proportion of ownership. A study by Larner which duplicated the Berle and
Means study for 1963 already classified 84 per cent of the top 200 and 70 per
cent of the next 300 largest non-financial corporations as management
controlled. It should be noted that Larner considered control by legal device a
form of *ownership* control, and also fixed the minority ownership criterion at
10 per cent instead of 20 per cent of voting stock, leaving Berle and Means
with 'only' 44 per cent management-controlled corporations in 1929. On this
basis, he proclaimed the corporate revolution 'close to complete' in 1966. In
his introduction to the 1968 edition of *The Modern Corporation* Berle somewhat
moderated his previous optimism in considering that this silent revolution
was no longer just a possibility, but was 'at least half-way along'; in historical
terms, it was 'moving rapidly' (Berle and Means 1968: xxv).

175

Unsurprisingly, empirical criticism of Berle and Means and other managerialists has usually taken the form of a meticulous subtraction game. Referring
to a reanalysis of the 1929 data by Burch, and an independent study by
Goldsmith and Parmelee for 1937, Scott for example found that management
control of large corporations during the 1930s was not as extensive as Berle
and Means had suggested and that majority ownership and family control
'were still persistent features of the economy'. Citing other studies which were
critical of Larner's results, he concluded that the magnitude of the shift had
been systematically overrated, even though all of Larner's critics agreed to a
secular trend towards managerial control of big business (Scott 1979: 51–9).
Zeitlin more emphatically dismissed the separation of ownership from control
as a 'pseudofact' which gave rise to a series of 'pseudoproblems', and claimed
that a specific minority percentage of ownership could in itself tell little about
the potential for control represented by it. Following Larner's reduction of
Berle and Means' percentage of management-controlled firms, he further
scaled down their 44 per cent to 22 per cent, since – as Berle and Means had
themselves conceded – reasonably definite and reliable information was available on only two-thirds of the companies investigated (Zeitlin 1974: 1090,
1081). An examination by Villarejo of the 250 largest companies on the 1960
Fortune list similarly contradicted the Larner study, arguing that 54 per cent or
perhaps 61 per cent were still controlled by ownership interests. A *Fortune*
study for 1967, reported by Sheehan, found 147 of the top 500 companies to
be subject to ownership control – over half as many as Larner's original figure
of ninety-five for 1963. The Patman Committee's report, in turn, showed a
total of 170 firms or 34 per cent of the 500 largest to be ownership controlled
in 1968; by adding another twenty-six companies controlled by legal device
and two 'likely' candidates for ownership control, one would arrive at 198
firms or 39.6 per cent of the total – which would more than double Larner's
original 19 per cent. Following the Committee's conjecture that effective
control could be assured with less than a 5 per cent holding (the *Fortune*
studies had operated with the 10 per cent criterion) one could well add
another fourteen firms and reach a total of 211 or 42.2 per cent for 1968
(Zeitlin 1974: 1084–7).[9]

Much of the dispute, we may begin to see, is triggered by something
resembling the problem of the half-full/half-empty bottle. In the empirical no
man's land in between the battling theories, the 'probables' and 'possibles'
work both ways: fortifying either the calculations of those who wish to establish the continuing impact of private property and family control, or the
estimates of those who wish to chart the pending transformation of the capitalist into the managerial class.[10] As transpires from Berle's own account, their
pioneering study should have been read as a trend report rather than as the
proclamation of an accomplished historical fact (cf. Scott 1979: 49; Allen
1976: 885). If it is now seen that they, and Larner more especially, consistently
overstated their case, it is also widely recognized that, indeed, they *had* one. In

a comment on Zeitlin, Allen recalls that not only Larner but also his critics still showed a majority of the 500 largest companies as being under the control of their managements, which confirmed the theory of the split between ownership and control 'inasmuch as management control is positively associated with the *size* of corporations' (ibid.: 886–7). For Miliband, who was otherwise critical of the thesis, the separation had become one of the most important features in the internal organization of capitalist enterprise, although it would be entirely incorrect to imply that this process was 'all but complete'. The trend itself was uneven but also 'very strong and quite irreversible' (1973: 29). Giddens similarly realized that a number of objections raised against managerial theory should be read as qualifications, and that the crucial question was *how far* there was a distinguishable trend in the direction presumed (1973: 172). Discounting Zeitlin's argument as 'essentially a rearguard action', Gouldner (1979: 13) likewise suggested that the important consideration was the trend line: 'Is management control becoming more or less, growing or declining over the long duration?'

WHO CONTROLS THE CONTROLLERS?

If we reconsider this question, two issues immediately present themselves which cannot be treated as distinct: the issue of the dispersion of stock ownership and that of the relationship of inside to outside control. Here we encounter a characteristic displacement of the debate over the social significance of the managerial revolution, which has tendentially drawn back from the individual corporation as the primary level of analysis in order to substitute the question 'who manages the managers?' for the initial question: 'who *de facto* manages?' However, it also appears that, on this proximate level of analysis, the earlier arguments are rehearsed rather than reconciled, and that both the managerial thesis and 'property theory' permit themselves a new lease of life and inject new vitality into the dispute. With regard to the dispersion of ownership, managerialists dropped much of their original contention, acknowledging not only the fundamental and persistent *inequality* of shareholding in Western societies, but also the basically ambiguous nature of the centrifugal movement itself – which may equally increase the power of those who possess large holdings. As was shown by the various attempts to shuttle down the critical percentage of minority control (20 per cent to 10 per cent to 5 per cent) or control by legal device (1 per cent or less of total assets), the anti-managerialists have largely won this part of their case; it is now widely recognized that formal criteria provide insufficient information on the actual control situation.

In addition, as Max Weber already realized, bureaucratic management is not necessarily identical with bureaucratic control. If the immediate appropriation of managerial functions is no longer in the hands of owners, it does not entail that control is separated from ownership, but rather that ownership is separated from managerial *function*: 'By virtue of their ownership, control over managerial positions may rest in the hands of property interests outside the organization as such' (cit. Zeitlin 1974: 1077–8). 'Outside control', indeed, has been a subject on which managerialist theory was consistently weak; Berle and Means set the example by focusing their analysis upon the largest *non-financial* corporations. It is here that non-managerialists have raised another set of weighty objections, in order to prove the enduring significance of capital markets, outside financing, and the control by commercial banks and fiduciary institutions.

Lundberg (1968), who analysed the same corporations as Berle and Means, argued already in the 1930s that 'a very small group of families, through their ownership interests and control of the major banks, were still in control of the industrial system'. In a study of the fifty largest banks, Sweezy (1953) discovered a set of interest groups which encompassed half of the top 200 and sixteen of the banks, which were controlled by wealthy families and/or their financial associates and investment bankers. The 1968 Patman report concluded that

> the trend of the last 30 or 40 years towards a separation of ownership from control because of the fragmentation of stock ownership has been radically changed towards a concentration of voting power in the hands of a relatively few financial institutions, while the fragmentation in the distribution of cash payments has been continued.
>
> (cit. Scott 1979, 77)

If supporters of the theory of 'finance capitalism' therefore believed that management control had not happened at all, some of their opponents described it as a *transitional* phase which linked a 'capitalism of the investment banker' to a 'capitalism of the financial institutions'. Around the turn of the century, Daniel Bell argued, a form of finance capitalism emerged, typified by the rise of the commercial banker, which effected a radical separation of property and family by installing propertyless professional managers in the enterprise. During the 1930s, however, the power of the banking establishment declined as managers detached themselves from financial controls and won independent power. Economic growth, especially after the Second World War, enabled them to finance their expansion from corporate profits rather than by borrowing on the money market (Bell 1961; Scott 1979: 83ff.).[11]

The main contention of managerial theory had so far been that management control constituted the 'next' or contemporary phase of industrial control. This was clearly implied by Berle and Means, whose five-stage theory somehow bypassed the era of banking power entirely. In *Power Without Property*, however, Berle qualified his earlier views by recognizing the diffusion of stockholding on the company level as a transitional stage:

The rise of the corporate system, with attendant separation of owner-ship from management due to the concentration of industry in the corporate form, was the first great 20th century change. In three decades it led to the rise of autonomous corporation management. The second tendency, pooling of savings, voluntary or forced, in fiduciary institutions now is steadily separating the owner (if the stockholder can properly be called an 'owner') from his residual ultimate power – that of voting for management. In effect this is gradually removing power of selecting boards of directors and managements from these managements themselves as self-perpetuating oligarchies, to a diff-erent and rising group of interest-pension trustees, mutual fund managers and (less importantly) insurance company managements.

(1959: 59)

Two points of interest stand out from this. First, the commercial banks were once again conspicuously absent from Berle's story – the 'new' outside control being primarily imputed to the mutual companies. This was peculiar because, as non-managerialists argued, finance capital constituted the continuously dominant controlling force *throughout* these three phases, although they recog-nized that the relationship between external and internal funding was also subject to historical variation. Second, the countertrend was *not* regarded by Berle as an invalidation of managerial theory itself since, on the analytical level of concentrated financial control, the fiduciary institution represented an even more dramatic diffusion of beneficial interests and a still more effective separation of control from ownership than was accomplished by the manage-rial company. The ultimate power to determine who managed a corporation and, within certain limits, how this was done, now passed into the hands of a new breed of 'managers of managers' who were not owners but officials. For Berle, this next stage in the '*chassé* of property and power' only completed the divorce between 'men' and 'industrial things' which was long ago set in motion, a development which, if it was to be compared with anything, perhaps came closest to a communist revolution (ibid.: 75–6).

Once again, therefore, managerial theory conceded much without really conceding anything. If managerialists were now prepared to see the justice of the Marxian objection that, all along, internal management control was prob-ably less important than outside financial control, and that self-financing through the ploughing-back of investments varied with the business cycle, they maintained that this still begged the question of the separation of owner-ship from control. In Berle's second-line defence, the new institutional concentration of ownership presupposed both a wide dispersion of ownership of company shares and a 'second-order' fragmentation of ownership of income-bearing participations in large financial institutions. At this point, the managerialists re-entered the race, in successfully insisting upon the second-order dominance of managerial control of the large banks and other financial institutions. Was finance capitalism a capitalism of owners or a capitalism of managers?

Unfortunately, although both contestants had grown somewhat closer, they carried their subtraction game over from the first round into the second. Here Vernon's conclusions about the extent of management control of commercial banks formed the main bone of contention. Applying the 10 per cent minimum for family or minority control, Vernon classified a large majority (74.5 per cent) of the 200 largest commercial banks as subject to management control, and discovered a decisive correlation between management control and institutional size (Vernon 1970; cf. Scott, 78ff.; Allen 1979: 890). Zeitlin, however, quickly mobilized the contrary finding that 'only' twenty-four of the fifty largest banks were 'probably' management controlled and that 30 per cent was 'probably', 22 per cent 'possibly' under family control, adding the hopeful conjecture that 'studies with appropriate data would reveal that the other largest banks, behind the managerial veil protecting their proprietary modesty, are also controlled by principal owners of capital' (Zeitlin 1974: 1105; 1976: 899). Even if, once again, the 10 per cent minimum could be disputed as an arbitrary standard, possibly revealing that banking families continued in strength, this could hardly do more than qualify the solid case about the secular trend.

CLASSWIDE PROPERTY?

At this point, 'property theory' reimported the basic ambiguity which was already latent in its first-line critique of managerial theory, enabling it to win a verbal victory while suffering a substantive defeat. This ambiguity has accompanied the theory of finance capitalism from its inception by Hilferding and Lenin up to the more recent criticisms by Zeitlin and Scott. It entails a silent identification of bank control – and outside control more generally – with *proprietary* control in the narrow sense and a parallel aggregation of private owners and managers into an amorphous class of 'finance capitalists'. Marxists have accordingly been able to explain the decline of private ownership and the rise of managerial power in terms of a 'managerial reorganization of the capitalist class', without abandoning the basic idea of a ruling class of capitalist owners. In the process, however, they have imperceptibly shifted their argumentative ground from the narrow conception of ownership as private and subject to familial inheritance to the wider conception of ownership as institutional, impersonal, and formally non-heritable (cf. Poulantzas 1974a: 194; Baran and Sweezy 1968: 46; Fennema 1982; Wright 1978; 1985b; McDermott 1991).[12]

This definitional shift has also been executed, with some elegance, by Maurice Zeitlin. Although he admitted that managers were replacing capitalists as the new ruling class, he dismissed the notion of a 'capitalism without capitalists' in order to affirm that the large corporations were still 'units in a class-controlled apparatus of appropriation', and that 'the whole gamut of functionaries and owners of capital participate in varying degrees, and as members of the same social class, in its direction'. This view of the continuing presence of the bourgeois class remained undergirded by a kinship-oriented notion of class appropriation and ownership interests. Upon closer examination, however, Zeitlin's conception of the property–family linkage proved remarkably fluid. If, contrary to his own expectation, the banks would not be controlled by principal owners of capital but by managers, this would not dramatically alter the fact of hegemony of the capitalist class:

> Although the largest banks and corporations might conceivably develop a relative autonomy from *particular* proprietary interests, it would be limited by the *general* proprietary interests of the principal owners of capital. To the extent that the largest banks and corporations constitute a new form of class property – of *social ownership of the means of production by a single social class* – the 'inner group' . . . of interlocking officers and directors and particularly the finance capitalists, become the leading organizers of this system of classwide property.
> (Zeitlin 1976: 900–1; cf. Zeitlin *et al.* 1974: 108)

This conceptual innovation of 'classwide property' conveniently blurred the distinction between private and institutional ownership, as did the closely related concept of the 'kinecon group', which described the continuing interlinkage between such classwide economic interests and kinship bonds, and identified a new type of extended family which developed coextensively with the new types of intercorporate control. While moving beyond Bell's notion of 'family capitalism', Zeitlin's conception did not clarify how far these extended families extended, and what, in this case, was to be understood by the familial inheritance of property.

Similar difficulties were attendant upon John Scott's interesting idea of 'control through a constellation of interests'. This mode of control, which was becoming predominant in modern capitalism, stood somewhere in between minority and management control, since the major shareholders remained in a position of effective possession without forming a compact group. No single coalition of shareholders was considered strong enough to achieve minority control, but neither did the board achieve full autonomy from stockholder interests. The period of the 1930s, in which minority and management control were dominant, should hence be seen as a phase of transition from personal possession by particular families and interests to impersonal possession through an interweaving of ownership interests and control through a constellation of interests. But one may well enquire why, if property and possession were depersonalized or socialized – a tendency which was seen as equally characteristic of financial companies as of industrials – it was still fruitful to speak of a managerial reorganization of the *propertied* class. If the internal structure of the propertied class was being transformed 'from a system of family compacts to a unified national class' (1979: 123), why still speak in terms of kinship systems?[13]

Naturally, what made partisanships so stubborn and loyalties so definitive in this dispute was its close proximity to the 'Is This Still Capitalism?' issue – with which it was often made to coincide. Dahrendorf, for example, thought it advisable 'to insist upon the union of private ownership and factual control of the instruments of production as the distinguishing feature of a capitalist form of society', so that in his view capitalism was tendentially superseded as soon as ownership was separated from control (1959: 40). Burnham's definition of capitalism likewise depended upon the criterion of private property rights vested in individuals 'as individuals', so that state ownership of production brought capitalism to a close and ushered in the managerial society: 'You cannot call an economy of state ownership capitalist, because in it there are no capitalists' (1945: 18, 23, 99). For Crosland, ownership was increasingly irrelevant in modern postcapitalism, where political authority was emerging as the 'final arbiter of economic life' (1963: 29–30). If managerialists thus proclaimed the approaching demise of capitalism owing to the retreat of the capitalist class, their antipodes fell prey to the inverse seduction of conceptually prolonging the capitalist class because of the continued survival of the capitalist world system. Blackburn, for example, in mobilizing the idea of a 'new capitalism' against the theories of Crosland, Strachey, Burnham, and Dahrendorf, included the survival-in-strength of the propertied class as a mainstay of his argument (1965: 115). Zeitlin's rejection of the notion of a separation of ownership and control was prompted by the dual fear that capitalism shared the fate of the capitalist, and that class theory and property theory stood or fell together (1976: 897–8, 901). Miliband remained on the safe side in defining the ruling class as that class which owned and controlled the means of production (1973: 23). As noted earlier, Parisian Marxists such as Poulantzas set the modern *imprimatur* to this by including all higher incumbents of the 'place of capital' into the pliant category of the 'bourgeoisie'.

In this regard, both sides failed to separate two separable issues: the fate of private property and the capitalist class, and the survival of capitalism as an economic system, an international division of labour, and a world market. Instead, one might have followed Hendrik De Man's long-standing suggestion to treat as distinct the economic category of 'capitalism' and the sociological category of 'bourgeoisie', and entertain the idea of a 'capitalism without capitalists' (De Man 1926: 162, 144). Berle put it concisely: 'The capital is there; and so is capitalism. The waning factor is the capitalist' (1954: 39). If, originally, individual or familial property and the capitalist market had presupposed one another, and the supersession of individual property rights was eventuated by changes in production scale and market structure, this coincidence is not altogether linear. To some extent, and ideal-typically, the variable of *openness/closure towards the (world) market* appears autonomous from the variable of *subject of dispositional rights*, so that corporate, institutional, or state ownership may correlate with different degrees of system closure. If private capitalism correlates with low closure (geographical incongruence of economic and political structures) and centralism (state socialism) with high closure (geographical congruence, autarky), intermediate systems may combine both factors in a more variable manner, as shown in Figure 6.

Organized or corporate capitalism combines institutional ownership and relatively low closure whereas, for example, market socialism adds a significant statal element. Corporatist socialism remains comparatively more closed to the outside and combines elements of institutional and state ownership. In 'state capitalism', state ownership of major productive resources predominates, without the full closure which characterizes the war economy of state socialism (both of the left and the right).[14]

On the double premise that, first, managerial theory is interpreted as a trend report, and second, that some distanciation is allowed between the property variable and the variable of system closure, the idea of a 'capitalism without capitalists' appears to offer something like a theoretical middle ground, where some aspects of the rivalry lose their meaning, but where other discords may be fruitfully replayed.[15] If we think of 'organized capitalism' (Hilferding's phrase) as being staffed by a class of *organizers* rather than a class of capitalists, old partisanships may attenuate and new questions may arise to direct new research. In terms of this perspectival shift, I will select two further issues for brief examination: that of the nature of the profit motive and its alleged replacement by alternative managerial incentives; and the more general

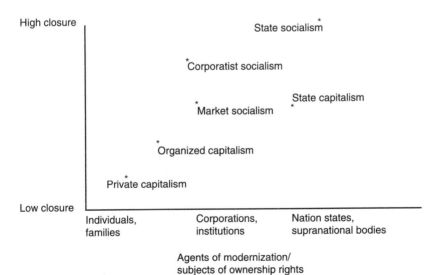

Figure 6 System closure and property regimes

query whether managers must be seen as a socially responsible or at least techno-cratically 'neutral' elite, or conversely, as a self-interested new dominant class.

Once again it would be well to take our distance from the mirror-like exaggerations of both contending repertoires. One exaggeration says that managerial motives are not really different from the traditional capitalist motive of profit maximization, since both continue to be dictated by market discipline. Marxist critics such as Zeitlin readily concur that profit maximiza-tion is an objective requirement 'since profits constitute both the only unambiguous criterion of successful managerial performance and an irre-ducible necessity for corporate survival' (Zeitlin 1974: 1097). The mirror-image theory, here represented by Dahrendorf, asserts instead that the separation of ownership from control is producing

> two sets of roles the incumbents of which increasingly move apart in their outlook on and attitudes toward society in general and toward the enterprise in particular. Their reference groups differ and different reference groups make for different values. . . . Never has the imputation of a profit motive been further from the real motives of men than it is for modern bureaucratic managers. Economically, managers are interested in such things as rentability, efficiency, and productivity.
>
> (Dahrendorf 1959: 46)

But, as many commentators agreed, goals such as these cannot verily be opposed to capital accumulation and profit making as long as corporations continue to operate within the constraints of competitive capitalist markets. It is also widely agreed, on the other hand, that the logic of managerial action is qualitatively different from that which is generated by dispersed atomistic competition. If the framework of competition may be ultimately constraining, it is also a framework of imperfect oligopolistic or monopolistic competition which orients corporate strategy towards the long-term stabilization of profits, and tends to displace competition to non-price areas such as cutting production costs, promoting sales through advertising, product variation, and planned obsolescence. The corporation is a long-term profit seeker, but its ultimate goal includes market policies which are aimed at size, strength, and growth; big corporations therefore generate a 'political' logic of large size, complex organization, and extensive planning which is relatively independent from outside market constraints. Hence, corporate strategy is determined by a complex structural environment in which the pressures of competition are superimposed upon a bureaucratic logic of scale. Ultimately, the relative weight of both market and non-market factors (*to what extent* the market still rules) is a matter for empirical assessment.

A mandarin of managerialism such as Adolf Berle, to be sure, never denied the continuing impact of market constraints and the profit motive. In *Power*

Without Property, he viewed the modern corporate system as being subject to four important limitations: oligopolistic competition, the 'obvious' need for profits, public consensus as it translated into corporate conscience, and political intervention by the state and organized labour (1959: 90). For Crosland, similarly, the profit motive remained an essential personal and corporate incentive although, in his view, business leaders did not primarily seek profit in order to maximize shareholders' rewards, but because in the long run their own remuneration, status, power, and prestige depended upon the company's level of profits, which remained 'both the conventional test of business performance and the source of business power'. Simultaneously, he judged the managerial pursuit of profit to be less aggressive and immediate, while managers also tended to display more sociable attitudes and motives (1963: 7ff.; cf. Bell 1976a: 283, 296). But the growing divorce between executives and shareholders was not in itself sufficient to induce a greater amount of social responsibility in the former. On the contrary, the decrease in shareholding power, instead of creating something like a 'soulful' corporate elite, could also remove the final impediments to managerial indiscretion. Were managers 'involuntary rulers' or self-interested 'new princes'?

Different from what Nichols, Miliband, or Zeitlin may lead us to believe, this moral issue was not clearly settled by Berle and Means; nor was it clearly decided upon in Berle's subsequent writings. If, in 1932, they described the control of the great corporations as a 'purely neutral technocracy' which balanced various community claims on the basis of public policy rather than private cupidity, many of their statements also suggested the opposite. The concentration of economic power separate from ownership had created economic empires and delivered these into the hands of 'a new form of absolutism', relegating owners to the position of suppliers of the means through which such 'new princes' exercised their power (Berle and Means 1968: 4, 46, 124). In *The Twentieth-Century Capitalist Revolution*, Berle underlined the virtually absolute character of managerial power:

> In practice, institutional corporations are guided by tiny self-perpetuating oligarchies. These in turn are drawn from and judged by the group opinion of a small fragment of America – its business and financial community. Change of management by contesting for stockholders' votes is extremely rare, and increasingly difficult and expensive to the point of impossibility. The legal presumption in favour of management, and the natural unwillingness of courts to control or reverse management action save in case of the more elementary types of dishonesty and fraud, leaves management with substantially absolute power. Thus the only real control which guides or limits their economic and social action is the real, though undefined and tacit philosophy of the men who compose them.
>
> (Berle 1954: 180; 1959: 59)

In passages such as these, it was clear that managerial capitalism was still far removed from the benign people's capitalism or collectivism with which Berle is otherwise so readily identified.

MANAGERS AS INTELLECTUALS

Writing in 1926, and anticipating both the theory of managerialism and that of the 'rise of intellectuals' to class power, Hendrik De Man identified the *Intelligenzler* as the actual ruling class in present-day society, and described the 'will to power of the intellectuals as a class' as preparatory of a non-bourgeois and, eventually, non-capitalist form of class domination. Marxism, he argued, actively negated this latent class identity of the intelligentsia, cutting it in two or three slices in order to subdivide it among the capitalist class, the proletariat, and the middle class. Blinding itself to obvious similarities of labour function and labour ethic, it denied itself the possibility of accounting for the ponderous fact that 'there exists a social stratum which neither coincides with entrepreneurdom nor with labour, but which exercises all the directive functions in political and economic life'. If the rise of the intellectuals remained unacknowledged, De Man argued, it would also remain impossible to do justice to the sociological *sui generis* character of the state, which he went on to define in Durkheimian (and Hegelian) fashion as a *Machinerie der Intelligenz* (De Man 1926: 144–8, 153–4, 162–8).

One might object that, on the strength of De Man's broad definition of intellectuals, even the 'labour of superintendence' as circumscribed by Marx could be seen as a species of intellectual work; as early as Gramsci, Marxists indeed sometimes identified the capitalist entrepreneur as a 'technician' or an 'organizing intellectual'. However, intellectual functions were always subordinated to the predominant 'function of capital', which implied that professional intellectuals were normally characterized as organically subservient to either one of the great class contenders. But even when Marxists confronted the rise of intellectual classes in a more straightforward manner, they did not as a rule emigrate from the kingdom of materialism or attempt to think beyond the conventional grammar of property. This observation applies with some force to James Burnham, whose dramatic vision of a worldwide drive for social dominance by the class of the managers never took leave of the most crucial of Marxian assumptions. For Burnham, effective class domination did not require individual private property rights, but could also be secured through corporate control rights vested in institutions. The core concept of control remained curiously indefinite. As a synonym for ownership in general, it simultaneously focused the most important of its two 'crucial phases' or 'chief factors' (the other being the right of preferential treatment in income distribution) (1945: 39, 42, 58, 81ff.). The ownership criterion itself was enlarged towards non-individual, non-heritable rights, which predicated the idea of a ruling class and class exploitation upon *any* form of closure of access to the means of production. The crux of such ownership rights were *power* rights, i.e. rights to prevent access by others to the object controlled (owned), such as rights to nominate or dismiss or to hire and fire. In addition, the means of production themselves were tacitly thought of as material or physical – which tended to marginalize symbolic skill and organizational ability as forces of production (ibid.: 106, 109, 53–4).

Burnham's loyalty to the property repertoire and his penchant for productive materialism set the theoretical conditions for the familiar 'two-step model' of class which became common currency to many neo-Marxist critics (and which is not far removed from Zeitlin's model of 'classwide property'). The economic framework for the social dominance of the rising managerial class was based upon institutional, especially state, ownership of the major instruments of production:

> The managers will exercise their control over the instruments of production and gain preference in the distribution of the products, not directly, through property rights vested in them as individuals, but indirectly, through their control of the state which in turn will own and control the instruments of production. The state – that is, the institutions which comprise the state – will, if we wish to put it that way, be the 'property' of the managers. And that will be quite enough to place them in the position of the ruling class.
>
> (Burnham 1945: 64–5)

This two-step model of 'indirect property', which identified the managerial class in terms of its *functional* relation to the *material* instruments of production, tends to neglect a triad of issues. First, it cannot anticipate the possibility that the managerial class may *itself* be the most significant force of production in presence, and control some of its productive assets in a more direct fashion. Second, it does not sufficiently account for the heterogeneous and stratified nature of these assets, which are both thinglike and relational, both privately and collectively held, both material and immaterial. Arguably, this new configuration is no longer describable in classical property or power terms, because neither the individual's command of symbolic and technical skills nor the individual's tenure of institutional positions can be meaningfully equated with traditional ownership, while that individual also 'has' something which is more varied and solid than 'power over people'. Third, it does not suspect that, given the centrality of symbolic expertise as a productive force, assessments of functional importance can never be objective or performatively innocent, but are 'essentially contested and contestable'. Managers do not emerge as a ruling group because they simply *are* functionally or economically indispensable, but because their actions are widely *accredited* as such, since their economic leadership is routinely *legitimized* on the grounds of superior knowledge and organizational skills.[16] Managers not simply *are* new forces of production, but skilfully and dramatically *represent themselves as such* with greater or lesser success. Their ability to manipulate things (plant, material inputs and outputs, money) depends in large fashion upon their skill in manipulating symbols and people, while symbolic proficiency in turn opens avenues towards organizational mobilization. If managers are to be called 'capitalists', it is because they are bearers of this *cultural* and *organizational* capital – which needs uninterrupted 'certification work' and symbolic maintenance in order to be recognized as such and be socially effective.

'Postindustrial' sociologists such as Bell, Touraine, and Galbraith, who recognized the increasing productive magnitude of the knowledge variable and the rise to power of educated specialists, typically underrated this essentially negotiable character of the 'axial' knowledge resource itself, and often treated science and technology as a black box (cf. Stehr 1994a). Galbraith's analysis of the emerging 'technostructure' (which includes all who bring specialized knowledge, talent, or experience to collective decision making within the enterprise) begins by distinguishing it from management proper, but this distinction remains inconclusive, and begs the question of the relationship between specialized technical expertise and the general, more diffuse, and therefore more contestable leadership competences which are usually attributed to managers (Galbraith 1972: 17, 66, 72–4, 86; cf. Stabile 1984: 237ff.). If it can be demonstrated that the generalists are still in power, the shift *from* capital *to* 'organized intelligence' is less dramatic and complete than Galbraith has made it out to be. The generalist's competence, moreover, is less easily fixed or (ac)credited than that of the specialist. If 'technicians' can be more readily thought of as functionally indispensable to modern production, the utility of 'leadership competence' is more elusive, and more narrowly depends upon skilful 'legitimacy work' by both leaders and followers (cf. Grint 1995: 124ff.).

Collins, who has extensively criticized the 'technocratic myth' upheld by theorists such as Bell and Galbraith, has correctly sensed that the linkage between technology and domination is a much more intimate one. Both managers and specialists are heavily implicated in organizational politics, and struggle with the incidents and spoils of 'positional property' which, as we saw before, includes not only the control of entry to the organization and of career sequences within it but also the shaping of the positions themselves. Occupations and skills are structured and defined in the course of organizational conflicts, and are always functional to some and not to others; the way in which they are constituted at any one time may in turn arouse new reshaping attempts. Positions are thus continually being redefined, redivided, and regrouped; what *counts* as 'work', 'skill', or 'competence' over against bureaucratic 'hot air' is continually at stake and open to negotiation. Managers, says Collins, are interested in formulating entry requirements, career patterns, and positions not only with an eye to efficiency and costs, but also in order to exercise control over their subordinates. Even professional and technical specialists who lack explicit line authority have considerable influence by their ability to define expertly what technical problems exist or will be encountered, and hence what numbers of specialists with what qualifications are needed (Collins 1979: 23, 50).[17] The shaping of the division of labour is always a major issue in the political life of any organization, and definitions of what constitutes 'labour' and what constitutes 'competence' are themselves heavily implicated in this.

However this may be, technical expertise and education are undeniably advancing both as factors of production and as legitimation bases in processes of social closure around managerial positions (cf. Useem and Karabel 1986). For Dahrendorf, writing in 1959, managers were either recruited from the ranks, or acquired their jobs on the strength of specialized education or university degrees (Dahrendorf 1959: 46; cf. Scott 1979, 129). Increasingly, educational certificates were replacing stock ownership, wealth, or family connections as tickets of admission to the inside of the great corporations and as vehicles for selection and promotion – even though such criteria still often worked in the same direction. Eligibility for managerial positions increasingly depended on cultural competence which was inheritable through propertied families but could also be acquired through peer group socialization in educational establishments. The property/family component and the credential component of the admission ticket were evidently changing place, potentially channelling 'new men' into the jobs where alone the real inside knowledge and power was to be gained.[18]

But once again we should be circumspect and interpret this as a trend report rather than as solid historical fact. Baran and Sweezy, for example, still took it for granted that wealth and family were 'normally decisive' in the recruitment and promotion of managerial personnel, although they agreed that these assets no longer provided control over corporations from the outside (Baran and Sweezy 1968: 29; Mills 1956: 116). Nichols, in his study of Northern City, discovered only a low level of professionalization and little formal training among managers, although younger managers were better educated than older ones and educational competence also corresponded with size of firm (1969: 80–1). In a broader perspective, however, Nichols' British case might well be the exception proving the rule (or the trend), since on the whole British management lags behind as compared with the USA, Germany, or France, where professionalization is much further advanced and educational levels are higher (Bourdieu and De Saint-Martin 1978; Marceau et al. 1978; Chandler 1977: 464ff.; Pross and Boetticher 1971; Dronkers 1983). In all 'postindustrial' states one may observe a significant, often dramatic, upward trend, and a corresponding erosion of traditional intuitive criteria of managerial ability in favour of formal certification. In all countries also, there is a close linkage between the level and impact of educational qualifications and formal criteria of recruitment, the property regime (private and familial vs. managerial and institutional), the size of the firms which managers direct, and the centrality of the firms in the economic network.[19]

It is impossible, in the present context, to report on the full extent of ongoing research into educational backgrounds and professionalization of managers in advanced Western countries. For my own purpose, it is sufficient to note the secular trend line, as well as the probability that the extent of 'intellectual-ization' of managerial activity is both overstated by managerialists such as Dahrendorf, Crosland, or Chandler and understated by non-managerialists such as Nichols, Zeitlin, or Scott. In general, the division of opinion occurs between those who emphasize the 'additive' or *legitimating* character of educa-tion, by which the familial inheritance of economic positions is supplemented with possession of educational diplomas, and those who emphasize the opening of new public channels of recruitment and a new mode of 'scholarly' reproduction of the managerial class (cf. Bourdieu 1989). The basic question, therefore, is whether the educational system primarily functions to transform 'heirs' into 'professionals', or whether it serves the production of a 'new class' of professional leaders of business and legitimates a new principle of indirect transmission of class privilege which is based upon the 'life peerage' conferred by non-hereditary educational titles (cf. Marceau *et al.* 1978: 140, 146–7).

Another line of research which could further clarify the process of 'intellec-tualization' of managerial activity concerns the phenomenon of interlocking directorates (cf. Fennema and Schijf 1978–9). Already thematized by Hilferding in his early theory of finance capitalism, networks of shared direc-torships are now recognized as a central feature of modern organized capitalism, where the 'visible hand' of managerial coordination has partly replaced the invisible hand of the market (Chandler 1977: 1, 11).[20] Once again, diverging theoretical positions are distributed around a trend line and the shared recognition of a stable correlation between the size and the economic centrality of the firms concerned, the type of control they are subjected to (familial or managerial), and the number and spread of interlocks. Whereas managerialists usually characterize such networks in terms of power elite theory, non-managerialists tend to regard interlocking directorates as a kind of superstructure of new 'classwide' property relations and the persons who inhabit them as the advance guard of a (transfigured) propertied class.

As we saw before, some theorists suggest that the separation of rights of disposal and rights of revenue at the level of the individual company is progressively annulled on the higher level of intercorporate control, so that the two incidents of ownership are effectively recombined in the network of interlocks (Fennema 1982: 17). Although it is acknowledged that interlocks are significant as channels of communication and have important 'scanning' functions, the control of information is usually seen as something which 'over-lays' the more fundamental network of strategic control through property. For Scott, information flow is a possible basis of power 'over and above the power involved in capital flows', and interlocking directorates represent switchboards of communication as much as control channels for the exercise of property rights, but ultimately his emphasis is upon interlocking directors as the core group of the propertied class (1979: 99–100, 125). The same applies to Fennema's 'network specialists', who are described as politicians, coordinators, and opinion leaders of big business, but whose specifically intellectual qualities remain submerged in his primary characterization of them as 'finance capitalists' (Fennema 1982). Useem's 'inner circle' of political organizers of the corporate class, who are the articulators and carriers of a new 'classwide rationality', is more convincingly described as a new type of intelligentsia – although the network of shared directorships is once again seen as supplementary to an underlying economic foundation of intercorporate ownership (Useem 1982; 1984; 1985; 1990).

The degree of autonomy which is conceded to 'cultural' *vis-à-vis* 'economic' capital as productive resource and legitimation base is therefore rather variable. Nevertheless, I think we follow a promising lead if we redescribe managers as 'knowledgeable organizers' or even as 'intellectuals', and go on to enquire into the closure patterns and legitimation strategies which are typical of such a 'knowledge class' (cf. Eyal *et al*. 1997).[21] It is precisely the *dual* nature of knowledge, technology, and organizational competence as forces of production *and* as indexes which justify closure practices which now presents itself as a new and central problematic. But this means that we are already at some remove from the terms in which debates about the 'managerial revolution' are traditionally conducted. The Marxist theory of property and its mirror image, the managerialist theory of power, must be left to confirm and reconfirm each other's prejudices. Managers, indeed, should not so much be seen as a (part of the) propertied class or as a class of power-holders or controllers, but as members of a 'knowledge class' whose dispositional chances extend from indirect, collectively exercised control over material assets and types of combined labour, through tenure of non-heritable positions and the more directly appropriable privileges which issue from it, to quasi-ownership of educational titles, work experiences, and leadership competences. It is the control of such forms of cultural capital (which includes knowledge of the formal and informal rules of the game, standards of civilized behaviour, organizing skills, linguistic competences, and theoretical knowledge) which increasingly determines what positions are acquired, held, and forfeited, and how managerial strata are able to practise closure successfully and perpetuate themselves over time.

7

INTELLECTUAL CLOSURE
AND THE NEW CLASS

Knowledge is the most solid form of wealth.

Karl Marx

Les *Intellectuels* ne sont pas, comme on le dit souvent, les hommes qui pensent: ce sont les gens qui *font profession de penser* et qui prélèvent un *salaire aristocratique* en raison de la noblesse de cette profession.

Georges Sorel

BUREAUCRATIC INTELLIGENCE

In previous chapters, I have argued that the problem of 'knowledgeable organization' was historically posed and elaborated within the limiting conditions of a tenacious rivalry, conducted between two traditions issuing from Aristotelian political theory and Smithian political economy. In the theoretical systems deriving from the latter, the problem could only be introduced in ambiguous fashion, because the productive status of mental or immaterial labour *vis-à-vis* material labour was never adequately clarified. It was apparent from the works of Smith through those of the Ricardian socialists up to Marx that, in so far as mental labour was studied at all, emphasis was normally laid upon the organizational or managerial element (the so-called 'labour of inspection and direction'); only with Gramsci did the generic term 'intellectual labour' begin to be used – and sparingly at that – in order to circumscribe the broader category of managers, bureaucrats, professionals, and intellectuals.[1] In the Aristotelian tradition of political theory, which was never constrained by the materialist prejudices of its rival, the problem of knowledgeable organization could be more squarely faced, but here as well there was a tendency to conflate it with the problem of management in the broad connotation of Aristotelian 'politics'. Sociology, which inherited the intellectual perspective of this latter tradition, began its career as a new science of politics or of the orderly, science-based reorganization of society, which was routinely taken to imply that henceforth the problem of power took precedence over that of property. In whichever way it was handled – residually and ambiguously in an economic framework, or principally and focally in a political one – the analysis of knowledgeable organization was poised towards the organizational dimension, and was to a lesser extent occupied with an independent appreciation of knowledge or skill as forces of production or species of capital in their own right. This remains true despite the fact that most writers followed Saint-Simon in presuming a close linkage between symbolic proficiency and the expert handling of people.

Such differential emphases are illustratively encountered in Marx's passing intuitions and Weber's more articulated conceptualizations of *bureaucracy* as an apparatus of rational, knowledge-based power. Although Marx did not countenance the structural independence of managers or bureaucrats as emerging knowledge classes, and his early comments on Hegel's notion of bureaucracy were not followed by systematic discussions in his mature writings, they nevertheless offer acutely suggestive premonitions of the logic of intellectual closure that Weber would subsequently theorize more directly and less burdened with materialist restrictions. Indeed, in his early critique of Hegel, his scattered remarks on the functional bureaucracies of the Asiatic mode of production, and his account of the imperial bureaucracy of Louis Napoleon, Marx did not directly impute the relative independence of state and bureaucracy to their powers of knowledgeable organization, but belaboured himself to search out an underlying class base – even if in the case of Bonapartism it could only be found in the peasantry, the petty bourgeoisie, or the lumpenproletariat (cf. 1852: 142, 160–1, 198–9). There might be exceptional periods in which the warring classes balanced each other so nearly that the state power, as ostensible mediator, momentarily acquired a certain degree of independence from both, but this state of affairs was necessarily ephemeral, and was likewise reduced to an underlying class configuration.[2] That the quest was directed to an exogenous class base was confirmed in terms of a broader view of class, also endorsed by Marx, which departed from the 'primordial division of labour' between mental and material activity. Although many Marxist critics of 'really existing socialism' acknowledged the structural independence of the communist bureaucracy, and explained its relative autonomization as a return to this 'primordial' division, they tended to locate the axial principle of bureaucratic disposition in some form of *institutional* property of the *material* means of production, following the characteristic 'two-step reduction' which was discussed in the previous chapter (the state bureaucracy 'owns' the means of production, while the state elite in turn 'owns' the bureaucratic apparatus).

That the productive forces of technical expertise and organizational skill were 'seen but unnoticed' was evident, among other things, from Marx's own early description of bureaucracy as both a hierarchy of control and supervision and a *Hierarchie des Wissens* (1981: 106–8).[3] This hierarchy of knowledge was intrinsically a hierarchy of *secrecy*:

the universal spirit of bureaucracy is secrecy, it is mystery which is inwardly preserved by hierarchy, outwardly by the closed character of the corporation. . . . Authority, therefore, is its principle of knowledge, and deification of authority its mentality. . . . The bureaucracy is *la république prêtre*.

Bureaucratic monopolies were established by recruitment through education and exams. On the one hand, the threshold raised by educational closure implied a relative accessibility of bureaucratic offices, since birth and/or wealth were discounted as immediate criteria of social placement, and entrances were opened up to competent members of all social classes. On the other hand, the exam was 'nothing but a masonic formula, the legal recognition of civic knowledge as a privilege'. It was, in Marx's famous epigram, the 'bureaucratic baptism of knowledge', the official recognition of the transsubstantiation of profane into sacred knowledge. There existed an immediate relationship between the bureaucratic secret and the passive submission to bureaucratic authority, which transformed the 'spiritual essence of society' into the private property of the bureaucrats. Hence there existed an immediate linkage between secrecy, obedience, and the inner dynamic of bureaucracy, which wished 'to do everything' and only viewed the world as a mere object of its own activity (1981: 108–9).

It is curious to see how close Marx came to a recognition of the productive dynamic and the typical closure pattern of 'knowledgeable organization', without being able to negotiate the conceptual barrier, or to conceive his own socialist project in terms of it. Bureaucracy remained a 'formal' system, the content of which resided not within but outside: it constituted the mind or 'brain' of the corporations. The unmasking of Hegel's bureaucracy as a pseudo-universal class turned upon the dialectical antithesis of civil society and the state, the alleged self-sufficiency of civil society, and the idea of the state as the 'alienated community' of the citizens' warring interests. That is to say, it did *not* derive from the idea, still present in Hegel, that the 'universal class' could perhaps assume 'the isolated position of an aristocracy' and use its education and skill 'as means to an arbitrary tyranny' (cit. Marx 1981: 104).

But if we think of bureaucracy as having its own sociological substance, and of the triad of mind–will–action as a force of production in its own right, the Marxian model may yield prismatic insights. The bureaucracy, indeed, is a hierarchy of power/knowledge, and its knowledge is empowered precisely because it is enclosed and kept secret. Although it opens itself to all classes, since intellectual competence is the only relevant criterion of membership selection, each novice must be trained and initiated in the sacred knowledge of the apparatus, and be personally baptized as a 'knowledgeable' apparatus person. The bureaucratic examination marks the threshold of a new class of knowledgeable organizers whose 'spiritualism' is 'active' because it is self-certain, and whose spiritual certainty derives from the authoritarian imprint of its knowledge. Knowledge is power, not because it is representationally true, but because it is rarefied and made inaccessible; because bureaucratic truth is taken for granted and affirmed in an authoritarian manner. Knowledge is private property, not simply because individuals 'have' it, but because they define their 'classwide' ownership of particular knowledge as exclusive.[4]

Marx, to be sure, never permitted himself to see his own socialist project in these or similar terms. Because his own revolutionary programme was so much geared to the creation of a dynamic apparatus of knowledgeable organization, the theoretical gap between (the enemy's) bureaucracy and those very similar practices of the organized proletariat could never be theoretically closed. As Michael Bakunin well foresaw, the Marxist movement, if successful, would establish its own 'priestly republic' and staff it with tenant-farmers of truth; 'scientific socialism' fatally worshipped the same idols of certainty and authority (God and the state) as its enemies. Since the Marxist movements tended to externalize the unintended consequences of their internally generated power (imputing them to the Other, the Enemy, the Bourgeoisie), they were blinded to the logic of their own interventions in history: as the mobilizing productive force of 'knowledgeable organization', personified by a new class of intellectual organizers, who sought to hide their voluntarism behind constructs such as the historic mission of the proletariat and the objective dialectic of the forces and relations of production. But the historic mission was first of all their own, and the crucial and perhaps decisive force of production was constituted by no one else but themselves.

Shorn of materialist misrecognitions, many of Marx's suggestive premonitions recurred in Weber's perception of bureaucracy as epitomizing the modern rational–legal organization – an analysis which was of course in large part polemically articulated against Marxism itself. Perhaps one may distinguish two rivalling interpretations of Weber's classical analysis of rationalization in terms of the inexorable rise of bureaucratic domination. One of these claims that Weber's main emphasis was placed upon the rational exercise of authority over human beings or the control over others' behaviour, i.e. on disciplined and calculable organization rather than on knowledgeability or rationality in its own right. Bureaucratic organization, in this interpretation, is singled out by its rule-committed nature, its division of competences and authorities, and its separation between administrators and means of administration (or between ownership and control). Put more critically, this view implies that knowledge and expertise are to a certain extent 'blackboxed', although to a lesser extent than is the case in Marx' self-negating materialist conception of management and bureaucracy. To some commentators at any rate, Weber's analysis of bureaucratization clearly understates the informational dimension of the rise of organized society (cf. Webster 1995: 54). On a more charitable interpretation, however, Weber's theory of bureaucracy might be seen as precisely addressing the mutual articulation of power and knowledge, and hence as offering 'one of the most famous and consequential analyses of the authority of knowledge and experts' made available by social science (Stehr 1994a: 172; cf. Bell 1976a: 67–8). This alternative view highlights Weber's conviction that the superiority of bureaucratic administration is primarily found in the role of technical knowledge, that bureaucracy essentially means 'domination through knowledge' (*Herrschaft kraft Wissen*), and that it is precisely this feature which turns it into a specifically rational enterprise (Weber 1978: 223–5).

It is not an easy matter to decide which is the more plausible view. Does Weber consider bureaucracy primarily as a 'power house', a house of *Herrschaft*, or does he prophetically anticipate the 'new' institutional logic of knowledge closure? Somewhat like Marx, although more systematically, Weber digresses on the intrinsically dual nature of bureaucratic knowledge as conjugating technical knowledge, acquired through specialized training, with knowledge growing out of experience acquired in the conduct of office. He also perceptively remarks, as Marx had done before him, on the bureaucracy's inherent tendency towards informational closure, as exemplified by the phenomenon of the 'official secret': information which is exclusively available through administrative channels, and which is transformed into classified material by means of the notorious concept of the *Dienstgeheimnis* (1978: 225, 958, 992, 1417–18). The dimensions of power and knowledge are immediately collated in the following striking passage:

> An inanimate machine is mind objectified (*geronnener Geist*). . . . Objectified intelligence is also that animated machine, the bureaucratic organization, with its specialization of trained skills, its division of jurisdiction, its rules and hierarchical relations of authority. Together with the inanimate machine it is busy fabricating the shell of bondage (*Gehäuse jener Hörigkeit der Zukunft*) which men will perhaps be forced to inhabit some day, as powerless as the fellahs of ancient Egypt.
>
> (Weber 1978: 1402)

Nevertheless, I think it is fair to say that Weber expended far more energy on the analysis of ideal-typical forms of authority, management, and organization (both economic and political) than on an independent investigation of cultural skills and professionalized science as productive forces in their own right, and did not (nor could he be expected to) anticipate the stratificational significance which the cultural variable gradually assumed in late twentieth-century 'knowledge societies'. As in Marx, modern rational organization was primarily identified as separating physical ownership from management or bureaucratic control, rather than as instituting new forms of credential ownership of intellectual resources. More ponderously, perhaps, the Weberian thematic of rationalization continued to be predicated upon a universalistic and foundationalist conception of scientific knowledge, which separated means and ends, facts and values, science and politics as a matter of principle; his *verstehende* sociology was more focally concerned with dissecting various forms of legitimacy of organizational domination than with understanding the construction of legitimacy of scientific knowledge itself. In this manner, Weber's neo-Kantian *Wissenschaftsgläubigkeit*, and his partial blackboxing of science, technology, and instrumental rationality more generally, went far towards defining the intellectual parameters of subsequent theorizing about the 'intellectualization' of Western society, up to and including many of the 'postindustrial' studies of the 1960s and 1970s.[5]

INTO THE KNOWLEDGE SOCIETY

Hence the demand for a more focal consideration of the new accelerative spurt in the ongoing process of rationalization that was first charted by Weber at the beginning of this century, and which, towards its close, lays out the contours of an emerging 'knowledge society' or 'technological civilization' (Bell 1976a; Böhme and Stehr 1986; Stehr and Ericson 1992; Böhme 1992; Stehr 1994a, b). Amidst an extraordinary divergence of opinion on this issue, all theorists minimally agree that there is 'something special' about information in the modern world: there is simply more of it around than ever before, and it plays a central and strategic role in virtually everything we do (Webster 1995: 2, 215). Modern societies are increasingly organized around knowledge-intensive production and knowledgeable consumption, and knowledge-based occupations have emerged at the centre of the modern labour force. As measured by GNP and percentage of the working population, the weight of advanced societies is gradually shifting towards the knowledge field (Bell 1976a). Economic and social developments are increasingly driven by science and technology, inaugurating a new phase in the secular transition from material towards monetary towards *symbolic* economies, or 'economies of sign' which operate new regimes of 'reflexive' accumulation (Stehr 1994a; Lash and Urry 1994). This penetration of all social domains by scientific knowledge and technology also tends to promote a de-differentiation of formerly separate and autonomous spheres such as science and politics or culture and economics: a 'culturalization' or 'intellectualization' of society in which relations of production, organization, and consumption become increasingly discursive, information saturated, and communication based (Castells 1989; Lash 1990; Lash and Urry 1994). From 'superstructural' phenomena, knowledge and information have accordingly turned into immediate productive forces and new principles of social hierarchy; command of information has become a new stratifying principle, a focal variable of social inequality around which new types of social and political struggle develop (Beck 1992: 214).

Beyond such (not so) minimal agreements about broad empirical tendencies, the vast field of disputation with regard to the rising 'knowledge society' might be provisionally differentiated by cross-tabulating two antinomies or sets of controversies which were already transversally deployed in the previous chapter: that of functionalist vs. agonistic perspectives, and that of power theory vs. property theory (see Figure 7). As suggested before, current controversies surrounding culture, knowledge, and technology as autonomous productive and stratifying forces typically display an advanced state of generalization and hence of *convergence* or even *osmosis* of the traditional property and power vocabularies, even though they remain in various degrees conceptually indebted to their different languages of origin. From Lane's vision of the 'knowledgeable' society towards the 'postindustrial' paradigm of Touraine, Bell, Galbraith, and others, sociological theorizing about the knowledge society initially stuck to a rather traditional 'from property to power' framework, while extensions of economic categories were for example undertaken in the contemporary 'economics of information' pioneered by Machlup, Drucker, and Porat (cf. Webster 1995: 10–13), the neo-classical Chicago paradigm of human capital theory (cf. Becker 1964), and the Marxist conception of the 'scientific-technological revolution' as elaborated in the influential Richta report (cf. Stehr 1994a: 5ff.).

More recent conceptualizations, apart from being almost unanimously critical of the functionalist and scientistic presumptions that linger in these earlier theories, are also manifestly oriented towards further closure of the traditional property–power binary and further mixture of economic and political metaphors, even though ultimate preferences often remain divided, and the hegemonic metaphors residually tend to absorb and subordinate one another. Schiller's 'political economy of information', Castells' view of the 'informational mode of development', 'cultural capital' theory as advanced by Gouldner, Bourdieu, and Collins, 'analytical Marxism' in the mode of Roemer, Wright, and Van Parijs, or Lash and Urry's culturalist political economy 'of sign and space', all liberally extend economic metaphors to the analysis of

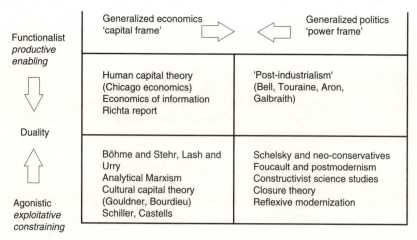

Figure 7 Theories of the knowledge society

cultural variables. From the other end of the intellectual spectrum, the socio-political frame of analysis has been similarly exploited by, for example, Schelsky, Kristol, De Benoist, and other neo-conservatives, by Foucault in his vision of the 'disciplinary society', by postmodernists such as Lyotard, Baudrillard, and Poster, by Parkin and other theorists of 'social closure', by constructivist studies of science and technology (Latour, Knorr, Woolgar), and by theorists of 'reflexive modernization' such as Giddens and Beck. However, such classifications on the property–power axis already carry a distinctly arbi-trary ring, in view of the substantial vicinity and the widening areas of overlap between many of the listed theoretical contributions. While 'analytical' and 'cultural' Marxists are completing the subliminal drift towards the power repertoire which is evident in the Marxist tradition as a whole, post-Marxist sociologists such as Gouldner, Bourdieu, Collins, Stehr, Lash, or Urry circulate rather unconcernedly in and out of the capital and power frames. From across the (sinking) fence, closure theorists, Foucaldians, and constructivist students of science likewise fuse the analytical frames and push the old ritual dichotomy towards the realm of indifference.

Further evidence of closure of the idiomatic gap is provided by some recent approaches which conceptualize knowledge as a set or bundle of *competences* that provide a generalized 'capacity for social action' (cf. Stehr 1994b: 194ff.). Because in such definitions competences are as much 'powers' as they are 'properties', the idea of knowledge-as-competence once again reflects the new intimate mixture which is progressively erasing all inherited distinctions between the two hegemonic metaphors. In Barnes' approach, for example, society is analysable in terms of a persisting distribution of knowledge, and social power is a prime aspect or characteristic of this distribution. Any specific distribution of knowledge confers 'a generalized capacity for action upon those individuals who carry it and constitute it, and that capacity for action is their social power' (1988: 57). Despite this 'deep equivalence' of knowledge and power (Barnes 1993: 213), the 'residential' and 'distributive' connotations of the property metaphor are not far away when Barnes talks about power in terms of an 'ability', 'capacity', or 'potentiality' to do some-thing or to produce effects, and asserts that 'social power is possessed by those with discretion in the direction of social action' (1993: 197; 1988: 58).

But this same relationship can also be characterized in terms of the property idiom, as is demonstrated by Sharrock's view of 'owning knowledge' and Böhme and Stehr's conception of knowledge as a form of 'appropriation' of the cultural resources of society.[6] Sharrock presumes an immediate relationship between the activities of society's members and their social corpus of know-ledge, as is evidenced by the universal practice of naming (Azande witchcraft, Aboriginal kinship rules, Marxist political economy, Western physics). This naming of knowledge is never merely descriptive, but specifies something like an ownership relation between a corpus of knowledge and its social constituency (Sharrock 1974: 49). Böhme and Stehr similarly describe the state of knowing things, facts, rules, or programmes as 'appropriating' them in some manner, although they respect Simmel's long-standing suggestion that the intellect, owing to its apparently unrestricted availability and capacity for effortless travel, remains peculiarly resistant to *private* appropriation (Simmel 1990: 438; Böhme 1992: 98; Stehr 1994a: 13, 93–5, 111). Defining knowledge (like Barnes) as a 'capacity for social action', Stehr indicates that such a conception also usefully resonates with von Mises' definition of property as 'capacity to determine the use of economic goods' (1994a: 95n.), which is indeed close to conventional relationist definitions of property as a right of action upon things and towards persons.[7]

The transversal division or axis of contestation highlighted in the above table shows a similar osmotic drift, although the integration of functionalist and conflictual perspectives is more irregular and not as far advanced as the more systematic erasures of the property–power binary. Foucault's dual view of the productive/repressive functionality of power, Gouldner's neo-dialectical conception of the New Class, and Parkin's notion of 'credential closure' would offer cases in point. Even though I have pleaded analytical distanciation between both divisions and have initially placed them at right angles, there are some interesting elective affinities and 'diagonal' oppositions in which a switch of 'horizontal' preferences also induces a 'vertical' vocabulary switch. One example is offered by Daniel Bell, whose vision of the 'postindustrial society' is primarily set in a power frame, but who also irregularly treats knowledge as an intellectual property or saleable commodity, and identifies the new postindustrial elite as a new knowledge class (e.g. 1976a: 176, 213ff.). Critics such as Stehr remark that Bell and other 'postindustrial' writers share in a tacit rationalist or scientist consensus, and easily treat knowledge as a blackbox in their analysis of the knowledgeable restructuring of society (Stehr 1994a: 49, 65–70). Characteristically, the 'capital' idiom intrudes as soon as the darker side of the 'intellectualization' of society comes into purview: while Bell is criticized for optimistically privileging its *enabling* consequences, he is also censured for the fact that an elaborated notion of symbolic *capital* is effectively absent in his work (ibid.: 50, 66, 109–12). Stehr, for one, remains interested in a formula of 'duality' which is capable of simultaneously accommodating the enabling and constraining features of the knowledge society and the performance of its new knowledgeable elites (ibid.: 13, 106, 176).

NEW CLASS?

As many theorists have repeated after Bell, the emerging knowledge society also entails the rise to pre-eminence of a technical–professional 'knowledge class' which is increasingly powerful owing to its discretionary command of cultural and intellectual resources (Bell 1976a: 14–15, 43, 213ff.). How can this class of 'knowledgeable organizers' be profiled sociologically, given the swiftly diminishing tension between the entrenched power and property approaches to social stratification? Let me first briefly discuss the possible candidacy of appelations such as 'managerial class' or 'bureaucratic class', which loosely derive from generalized political economy and socio-political theory. Both the vocabulary of management and that of bureaucracy admit of considerable extension beyond their respective home grounds, and have become increasingly interchangeable in various conceptualizations of the growing structural convergence of administrative regimes in advanced Western societies. Weber already traced them as virtual synonyms when pointing towards the rational concentration of the means of management and the attendant separation of ownership from administrative office and discretionary control, which was even more decisively accomplished in political bureaucracies than in managerial enterprises (1978: 980, 218–19). In his perception, the logic of bureaucratic rule was largely indifferent to the distinction between private and public legal regimes, profit and non-profit sectors, market and state, or capitalism and socialism. Abolition of private capitalism would simply mean that private and public bureaucracies would merge into a single hierarchy; socialism would inevitably enhance the degree of formal bureaucratization already featured by advanced capitalism (ibid.: 225, 1401–2).

The analysis of management and bureaucracy became similarly entwined in neo-Marxist, especially dissident Trotskyite, criticisms of Soviet-type societies, which concentrated upon the emergence of a 'bureaucratic collectivism' or a 'polit-bureaucracy' (cf. Bell 1976a: 86ff; Bellis 1979).[8] Among these, Burnham's *The Managerial Revolution* (1945) was most emphatic in stating that, in consolidated managerial states with a state monopoly of productive enterprise, managers and bureaucrats would merge into a single class with a united interest. Even in the absence of state economic ownership, the locus of sovereignty was perceptibly shifting towards the administrative bureaux, the active heads of which were the managers-in-government, who were nearly the same in training, functions, skills, and habits of thought as the managers-in-industry. Like Weber, Burnham professed relative indifference towards the legal or financial form (individual, corporate, governmental) which the process of management itself adopted, given the inexorable interfusion to which the political and economic realms were subject (1945: 71, 126–9, 135, 232ff.).

Although, in view of the above, one might conceivably adopt broad definitions of management or bureaucracy in order to characterize the class of 'knowledgeable organizers' in its entirety, I will here opt for 'knowledge class' or 'intellectuals' as the generic term.[9] In doing so, I distance myself equally from Burnhamite predictions concerning the universal rise of the managers as from parallel attempts to stretch the theory of bureaucratic domination, in order sympathetically to resume what is known (but not much loved) as 'New Class' theory (Bazelon 1967; 1979; Gouldner 1979; Konrad and Szelényi

1979; Stabile 1984; Berger 1986; Disco 1987; Szelényi and Martin 1988; Kriesi 1989; Kellner and Heuberger 1992). My choice of 'intellectuals' as *pars pro toto* category is therefore not inspired by a wish to exclude managers and bureaucrats, but instead proposes to include them in a more generic description of the new class of information professionals which more definitely neutralizes the cognitive constraints of the two rivalling repertoires, and focuses more intently upon recent accelerations in the process of reflexive modernization. In this option, it is not so much the *dual* interfusion of economics and politics which commands analytic attention, but the *triangular* osmosis between the economic, political, and cultural spheres which is engineered by the progressive intrusion of an 'intellectual' or 'cultural' production logic in corporate management, government bureaucracies, and other large organizational establishments, all of which increasingly recognize the processing of information as pivotal to their productive activity.

In this class categorization of 'intellectuals', I follow an early lead by anarchists such as Bakunin, Machajski, and Nomad and revisionist socialists such as Hendrik de Man, whose comprehensive definitions of the knowledge class have resurfaced in the writings of many late twentieth-century New Class theorists. Although, for example, Gouldner's 'cultural bourgeoisie' of intellectuals and intelligentsia incorporated educated managers and particular species of bureaucrats, and Konrad and Szelényi's category of the 'rational redistributors' similarly fused the three categories, they evidently shifted the weight of their analysis from the managerial towards the mental or cultural dimension. Bazelon's New Class was pictured as consisting of

> *working intellectuals* . . . non-property-holding individuals whose life conditions are determined by their position within, or relation to, the corporate order . . . people gaining status and income through organizational position. They achieve their positions . . . mostly by virtue of educational status. . . . Education, like capital in the past, is now a manipulable and alienable property.
> (cit. Bruce-Briggs 1979: 7; Bazelon 1967: 307ff.)

Adoption of such a broad definition also implies an option for a 'leftist' view of the new knowledge class – as opposed to a neo-conservative one which includes academia, journalism, and the mass media, and usually adds specific sectors of the government bureaucracy, but pointedly excludes managers and technicians in the profit sector. Although the analyses by American, German, and French neo-conservative publicists such as Kristol, Bruce-Briggs, Schelsky, and De Benoist are important, I take their demarcation of intellectuals as New Class pretenders to be overly restrictive. In Schelsky's *Die Arbeit tun die Anderen* (1975), for example, they are primarily identified as *Sinnproduzenten*, i.e. those who perform the social functions of socialization and information – although the author frequently slips towards a broader view which includes functions of caring (*Betreuung*) and planning (*Beplanung*) besides those of 'indoctrination' (*Belehrung*). Bruce-Briggs (1979) supposes that New Class values and attitudes are penetrating business schools and the public relations, planning, and education departments of business corporations, but he does not nearly go as far as Bazelon or Gouldner, who are less reticent to affix the New Class label to the bulk of corporate managers themselves.

An array of sceptical reactions to the idea of a putative new knowledge class has cultivated the suspicion that it may be neither new nor very much class-like (Bell 1979; Wrong 1983; Brint 1984; 1994; Freidson 1986; Stehr and Ericson 1992; Stehr 1994a; Rootes 1995). It is important to recall that the New Class idea, as it was reinvented by left-wing and right-wing publicists during the 1970s, functioned to add sociological clout to quite discrepant political hopes and fears; both the intellectuals of the left and the right were busily 'shopping for a historical agent' (to employ Gouldner's felicitous expression against its author) and exploited the gravity of the conventional class vocabulary in order to identify either history's 'best card' for a radical politics (Gouldner's own vanguard of humanistic intellectuals and technical intelligentsia) or the historic class enemy (Schelsky's 'new priests' or Kristol's and Podhoretz's status-envious class of the university educated).[10] Over against such attempts to 'solidify' the political ally or adversary by sociological means, critics repeatedly insisted that the New Class was too fragmented intellectually and occupationally, and too diverse in its cultural and political allegiances to be able to perform successfully as a 'classical' class. Shifting his allegiance from the class to the elite vocabulary, Bell soon dismissed the New Class idea as a linguistic and sociological 'muddle', because it conflated the idea of an emerging knowledge stratum with that of an adversary cultural attitude, which were not necessarily related. Moreover, the rising knowledge elite demonstrated insufficient community of interest and commonness of ideology to be able to act as a coherent class; its vertically organized locations or 'situses' (such as economic enterprises, government agencies, universities, and hospitals) importantly cut across its rather loose horizontal corporative organization in terms of professional 'estates'. Not a class, the New Class at most represented a spreading hedonistic and anti-bourgeois *mentality*, which seriously pressurized economic efficiency and exacerbated what Bell called the 'cultural contradiction' of capitalism (Bell 1979; 1976b).

Subsequent theorizing and research have done much to dissipate this widely shared hypothesis about the anti-capitalist animus of the intelligentsia, which defined both the hopes of the left and the fears of the right, who commonly saw the new class of knowledge workers as engaged in a historic struggle for status and power with an old dominant class of business owners and executives. Surprisingly, however, while the old propertied bourgeoisie was tendentially replaced by a cultural capital-based new class, it did not bode an end to capitalism, but initiated a remarkable renovation of its structure, which absorbed many of the previous elements and bearers of the 'adversary culture' in what has been justifiably called a 'historic compromise' between the old and the new class projects. While New Class theory was correct in perceiving the basic cultural clash and its political manifestations, it incorrectly visualized as a classical, Marxian class struggle what was instead a 'mutual cultural exchange', in the course of which the new professionals, while modifying the old industrial order, were simultaneously modified and coopted by it (Kellner and Berger 1992: 18–19; Martin 1992: 122ff.). In this perspective, the New Class was not so much a distinct class opposed to capitalism, but a sector of the economy that became part and parcel of the evolution of American capitalism itself (Hunter and Fessenden 1992: 159). Such analyses chime in with guarded conceptions about the emerging knowledge society as representing not so much a 'system break' which inaugurates a new postcapitalist order, but as exemplifying important continuities with its immediate past. According to such conceptions, the 'information revolution' sustains and refines capitalism, even while radically recasting its logic of accumulation and the sociological identity of its leading personnel (cf. Stehr 1994a; Lash and Urry 1994; Webster 1995).

In view of this historic compromise between capitalism and the counter-culture, it may be fruitful to pursue the idea of a knowledge-intensive or 'reflexive' capitalism, which is no longer private property – but organization – based, and which is increasingly run by a new class of 'knowledgeable organizers'.[11] At this point, let me profess some indifference towards the oppositional labelling of this category in terms of traditional conceptions of 'class' or 'elite', which I advise may be used interchangeably, although both appear to miss important aspects of the variegated complex of the new class's holdings and doings. Nonetheless, the 'class' label may be retained, not in order to feed a specific commitment in the ritual property–power contest, but in order to sensitize to the relative homogeneity of the newly dominant group and the relative fluidity of its capabilities of social engineering, which easily cross the boundaries separating economic from political and cultural institutions, or private from public legal regimes (cf. Kellner and Berger 1992: 4–5). Instead of a historic rift between the business class and the intellectual class, we appear to witness a process of *intellectualization* or *culturalization* of the economy (and polity) which involves the penetration of a cultural logic (Bell's 'intellectual technology') in all major organizational settings. This spread of New Class cultural values and patterns of behaviour results in a kind of 'cognitive contamination' of the business world, spawning corporate executives who not only dress and behave in ways resembling New Class academics, but who also appear to have internalized important elements of New Class ideology, and are thus very different from the old 'Protestant' type of the sober, conformist, and hierarchy-conscious business person (Kellner and Berger 1992: 21).

This universal process of 'acculturation', and its concomitant blurring of private/public distinctions, to some extent entails a *de*-differentiation of Bell's various 'situses', reversing his prediction about the aggravating tensions and contradictions between the economic, political, and cultural spheres. This partial reversal of direction of the 'classical' modernization process, which has been remarked upon by various students of the knowledge society (Lash 1990; Lash and Urry 1994; Beck 1993; Stehr 1994a), is concomitant with the rise of new sociological actors: the generalist power-broker and universal manager whose abstract competences enable them to circulate ever more freely among the top structures of the large corporate, political, and cultural institutions. Expert manipulators of images and identities, these 'organizers of organizations' act as indispensable change agents which monitor the permanent revolution to which present-day large institutions are chronically subjected. As Bevers and Zijderveld for example suggest for the Netherlands, there is an increasing similarity of attitudes and behaviour among the New Class employees of government, industry, and the world of art, especially on the highest organizational levels, which is stimulated by a type of standardized professionalism which they all share by virtue of their training and organizational position (1992: 108–9). Given the presence of such standardized, generalizable competences, there is some support for calling such agents of knowledgeable organization by the name of 'intellectuals', precisely because they operate as *generalists* of system maintenance and system change, and in this regard subordinate the specialists who remain localized in their various domains of expertise.[12]

If such a broad idea of the New Class is provisionally allowed, our next query must concern the specificity of its holdings or assets, i.e. the nature of its dispositional chances and the specific mechanisms of social closure which are a corollary to them. For my present purpose, to specify what such 'intellectuals' have and do is important, not just because we stumble upon a traditional vacuum in the theory of class structuration, but also because there is no other approach to a workable theory of intellectual *rivalry*, i.e. a theory which is capable of discriminating the specific stakes and interests about which intellectuals find themselves in competition. We may only begin to see why individuals are incorporated in stable, seemingly supra-individual traditions of thought which inherit transfixed antagonisms, if we are able to clarify to some extent what specific investments intellectuals make, profit from, and defend, and through this to discover which are the specific laws of inheritance and strategies of competition which govern intellectual fields.

Of course, I am far from suggesting that there no longer obtain significant differences in the way economic, political, and cultural fields are developing; such fields guard a relative autonomy that lends to each a specific axial logic and defines for each a distinctive actorial habitus. What I do propose, however, is that the traditional 'property' and 'power' logics have to some extent interfused, but perhaps more importantly, that the *modus operandi* of the cultural field has infiltrated the two other domains to such an extent as to force both economic and political actors partially to 'take on' its specific mechanisms of accumulation and competition. Hence it is not the intellectuals in any narrow 'domanial' sense who are 'on the road to class power' (academic intellectuals normally cherish their professional autonomy, and gladly leave the chores of power mongering and profit making to others), but the 'knowledgeable organizers' of large economic, political, and cultural establishments who to some extent adopt a behavioural logic which is most visibly and autonomously operative within the intellectual field.[13] In all organizational 'situses', they embark upon reputational and image-making tasks (and hence upon reputational rivalries), in so far as production, marketing, and personnel management increasingly presuppose the management of research, public relations, and the cultivation of a distinctive corporate culture or 'mission'. Hence the question: what is at stake here? What is the specific structural configuration of intellectual property-and-power?

TOWARDS A MODEL OF INTELLECTUAL CLOSURE

In answering this question, we must first countenance a (possibly vicious) circularity, which derives from the residual hold which the competing theoretical alternatives exercise over New Class theory itself – hence the importance of screening it for remnants of the property–power dilemma, without relinquishing the advantages which accrue from the simultaneous exploitation of *both* metaphors. In an important sense, a class theory of intellectuals must make the most of *both* the property and power repertoires, and should freely mix the connotations of 'symbolic power' and 'cultural capital' wherever possible. Much of the fuzziness and uncertainty of the New Class vocabulary arises from the fact that it constitutes a meeting point of two generalizing tendencies which are inadequately synthesized. But the two metaphors simultaneously appear to run against their limits, in so far as a full description of the patrimony of the new 'knowledge classes' will identify a complex of dispositional chances, the core of which constitutes both something *less* than free property of tangible things, but also something *more* than power-over-people. Since it represents a fusion of both types of dispositional right which is not equal to the sum of its parts, we require broader conceptions which are capable of pooling the elements that go into the traditional property and power bundles, in order to facilitate new factor decompositions and more flexible aggregations of constituent rights. As intermittently suggested, concepts such as 'disposition' and 'closure' may offer such a focus of fusion and decomposition, if only we remain aware of the fact that, in helping us to evade some of the historical prejudices of the traditional repertoires, their first service is of a negative kind.

The resources which constitute objects of New Class disposition may be classified under three major headings: 'external' or material resources (land, buildings, installations, machines, money), human or organizational resources (access to institutions, command over divisions of labour, control over mobilizable social networks), and 'internal' or cultural resources (incorporated knowledge, skills, etc.). Broadly, this classification is in accord with Bourdieu's tripartite division of economic capital, social capital, and cultural capital, although I propose to expand the second category (social capital) by adding the crucial element of access to institutional and organizational positions and hence to divisions of labour (Collins' 'positional property'; Wright's organizational assets; Van Parijs's 'job property'). In Bourdieu, managerial disposition is ranged with economic capital, but also disappears somewhat in between the first and the second category. Social capital indicates the profitable effect of social relations or of belonging to a group (familial or other social networks), the volume of which depends upon the width and depth of the relational networks which one can effectively mobilize, including the capitals attached to each of the points in the network (Bourdieu 1986; cf. J. S. Coleman 1988). But if one envisages family networks which control enterprises or networks of interlocking directorates, it is clear that this type of social capital shades off into the managerial control of large institutions (economic, political, educational, and otherwise) and the organized labour power which is collected in them. It is advisable, then, to place greater emphasis upon the 'vertical' aspect of social capital and lend it separate analytical status.

The axial stature of this type of institutional or positional control is affirmed consecutively by Bazelon, Gouldner, and by Konrad and Szelényi, and agrees with an already time-honoured sociological conviction that occupations constitute the backbone of the modern stratificational order (cf. Parkin 1972: 18). Here, I will only add two illustrative converging statements from the power and the property side. The first of these is taken from Mills, who observed that the powerful are only so because of their positions in the great institutions which are the necessary bases of power:

> No one . . . can be truly powerful unless he has access to the command of major institutions, for it is over these institutional means of power that the truly powerful are, in the first instance, powerful.
>
> (Mills 1956: 9)

A similar conviction underpins Collins' notions about 'political labour' and 'positional property'. As previously noted, Collins extends the property metaphor to the domain of organizational politics, where Mills would talk about access to the means of power and Parkin would prefer the vocabulary of closure. In so far as it is a matter of forming social alliances within and across organizations, and of influencing others' views of the realities of work, 'political labour' overlaps with but also appears broader than Bourdieu's notion of social capital – both the organizational and cultural dimensions are more prominently on display. Political labour consists of efforts to structure and restructure the positional distribution within organizations in three main respects: the control of gatekeeping, the structuration of career channels, and the shaping of the positions themselves and, through this, of the organization as a whole. The struggle about gatekeeping, career formation, and position shaping results in specific configurations of positional property which, in Collins' perception, offer the real stakes of the modern class struggle:

> It is *property in positions* that is crucial in determining most of class organization and class struggle in everyday life. . . . People without jobs (or with a succession of marginal positions) are without power over the main property resources of our society (and usually without political influence as well), and that is the reason they are poor.
>
> (Collins 1979: 54–5)

If we incorporate the general idea formulated by both Mills and Collins, one major feature of our model of New Class disposition is that access to material resources is channelled through positional property or institutional control, and is collectively rather than privately held. It is only in this sense that one may say that power relations dominate or 'precede' property relations, although it could be maintained with equal force that property rights now effectively reside in large institutions, transforming 'property' in institutional positions into the dominant axis of contemporary class structuration. As a corollary, disposition of materially productive resources and of positions of command is no longer transmitted through family networks and enclosed by the legal device of private property, but through quasi-political succession mechanisms such as appointment, sponsorship, and election.[14]

However, the specificity of New Class holdings is not that big property is now held through big institutions, but that access to the institutional exercise of *amalgamated* property and power resources is increasingly dominated by the closure mechanisms of cultural capital. It is the intimate linkage between typically personal and incorporated cultural holdings and access to institutional positions which constitutes the real sinew of this new matrix of social closure. In Bazelon's brief formula, it is 'education translated into organizational position' (1979: 444). It is this 'second-order' domination through cultural disposition which introduces mechanisms of discretion and transmission which are simultaneously different from private inheritance of external material resources and from transmission of organizational resources through political processes. The law of inheritance which obtains for cultural disposition concerns 'private properties' which are less easily heritable through channels of kinship and which in this respect are like 'powers', but they are also partly inalienable, since they are not acquired and accumulated through nomination or election to social positions but through personal investment in schooling and education.

In order to complete our model, it is therefore necessary to concentrate more closely upon the phenomenon of cultural capital, without losing from view the all-important dimension of access to large-scale institutions. It is unfortunate, in this respect, that Collins' theory of political labour leans over so heavily towards the politico-organizational dimension, but this can easily be compensated for by drawing once again upon Bourdieu.[15] In the latter's conception, cultural capital may exist in three main states: the *incorporated* state, the *objectivated* state, and the *institutionalized* state (Bourdieu 1986).[16] The incorporated state is most fundamental because it involves cultural 'havings' or 'goods' which have taken the form of durable dispositions of the organism, instilled through the cultural heritage of families and processes of formal education. Although cultural backgrounds and inheritances differ, the accumulation and upkeep of cultural capital invariably presuppose personal investment and individual acquisition. It is intrinsically tied to the person in his or her biological singularity, and cannot be instantaneously transmitted by either gift or bequest, sale or exchange. In the *objectivated* state, cultural capital takes the form of 'external' cultural goods (writings, paintings, maps, dictionaries, instruments, buildings) which are appropriable and transmissible in their materiality, but the conditions of appropriation of these goods (cultural consumption) are such that they are in fact dominated by the laws of transmission of incorporated capital. A third form of objectivation is the *institutionalized* state, where cultural capital takes the form of titles of cultural competence which furnish their bearers with a continuous, juridically sustained social value, which is relatively autonomous *vis-à-vis* the effective cultural capital which exists at any given moment. Educational titles institutionalize the capital, and consecrate it socially through the mobilization and fixation of the public power of *recognition*.

The core of cultural capital is accordingly made up of disposition of immaterial goods, which is rather like the 'property of one's own self' which John Locke postulated as an innate generative source of rights to the fruits of one's own and other people's labour. Since it is not divorceable from the person, cultural disposition is *less* than traditional private property but also *more* than what is traditionally understood by 'power' as controlling other people's behaviour: it is first of all *controlling oneself*. If relatively autonomous, as in the case of credentials, it is still attached to a personal creditor and cannot be inherited or sold. If materialized in books, journals, pictures, cameras, TV screens, data banks, or computer software, the appropriation of such external goods is still dictated by the laws of appropriation, reproduction, and inheritance of the internal or embodied part of the dispositional bundle. But if the production and reproduction of cultural competences are so much a matter of the production and reproduction of competent actors, it is evident once again that cultural capital is doomed to wither if it is structurally disengaged from social institutions. The social conditions of the capitalization and reproduction of culture are nowadays to a very large extent determined by big institutions of the schooling system and of the economic and political systems, which not only monopolize the material supports of intellectual production (the means of information) but simultaneously regulate credential entry to those positions and networks where 'real' competences and skills can be acquired (work experiences, training on the job, inside information about bureaucratic secrets and the rules of the institutional game). Tenure of positions and cultural property therefore mutually determine and augment each other; they form a configuration of disposition, both elements of which are individually held, while simultaneously presupposing collective or institutional supports as well as public recognition.

In this perspective, symbolic expertise is given more weight as an autonomously productive force than is feasible within the framework of Collins' residually materialist model. Credentials are not simply understood as artificial goods or relatively arbitrary entry tickets to large organizations, but also as social consecrations of real 'properties' which do have independent social effects, even though their capitalization normally presupposes the advantages of an institutional setting. On the other hand, there remains a lack of clarity and an incompleteness in Bourdieu's theory with regard to the various forms of objectivation of cultural capital, which include credentials and material carriers of culture but do not extend to the social apparatuses themselves – and thus to the structuration efforts (position shaping, institution building) which are so central to Collins' notion of political labour. However, culture is perhaps most massively objectified in social institutions, and the juridical recognition of expertise through credentials is always closely allied to the juridical maintenance of positional rights of tenure.[17] Once again, both approaches display a considerable overlap but also leave an intermediate space which it is necessary to bridge from both sides.

DIALECTICS OF CULTURE

By taking New Class theory as a base for further operations, I have also undertaken to liberate it from contaminations which result from the double heritage of property and power theory. First, New Class theory shows no reserve in acknowledging the *sui generis* character of cultural capital and of the knowledge class's structural position, which is difficult or downright impossible in classical political economy and socio-political theory. Second, it has the virtue of replacing one-dimensional and optimist theories about culture as a stratifying variable by more complex conflictual or dialectical perspectives which do not hesitate to wield the vocabulary of self-interest, domination, and exploitation. In spite of such advantages, New Class theory is still tainted by two imperfections which originate in the Marxist tradition, but which are retained in many Weberian amendations of it. One of these has already been commented upon in passing, and concerns the survival of a taken-for-granted *productive materialism* in the theory of social class; the second flaw is the survival of an objectivistic conception of the *dialectic*. In the following, I will therefore voice some reservations with regard to such traces of productive materialism as still remain in New Class theory, but perhaps more importantly, I will venture a critical examination of the dialectical frame in which the most advanced contributions to this field are still set. In some conceptualizations, such as those of Parkin and Collins, dialectical concerns do not yet arise, because their materialist distinction between a productive base and a cultural superstructure is allied to a rather straightforward conflict theory of knowledgeable organization. Other theorists, however, advance towards a notion of the ambiguity or duality of the New Class's position and holdings in which productive and exploitative dimensions are more fully integrated. However, as is exemplified by Konrad and Szelényi's conception of the generic and genetic functions of intellectuals or by Gouldner's idea of intellectuals as a 'flawed universal class', this duality tends to be conceptualized along the lines of a Hegelian (and Marxian) grammar of objective dialectics.

Productive materialism has cast a long shadow forward in social theory, and goes on to contaminate present-day thinking about the stratificational position of 'intellectual labour' or 'knowledgeable organization'. Konrad and Szelényi, for example, have visualized the social structure of early state socialism in terms of a basic dichotomy between 'redistributive power' and 'productive labour', in which the evolving class of intellectuals or 'teleological redistributors' disposed of and redistributed the human and physical resources of society, while the working class produced the social surplus (1979: 220ff.). As his title *Die Arbeit tun die Anderen* made evident, Schelsky's theory of the evolving class rule of the 'producers and mediators of meaning' similarly departed from such a crude 'syndicalist' distinction between producers and intellectuals. Despite his indebtedness to the Weberian theory of domination, Schelsky therefore retained important ingredients of the Marxian theory of class, namely the idea of a dichotomous opposition between the producers of 'material goods which reproduced and improved life' (which now also included organizational and political services) and the producers of 'meaning' who did not participate in the production of wealth either directly or indirectly (university and high-school teachers, students, journalists, artists, etc.). However, Schelsky quickly admitted that this distinction begged the question of the concept of 'material goods' itself as well as that of the variable distance from 'real' productive labour, and retreated towards a softer theory which acknowledged the functional indispensability of the *Sinn-Vermittler*, and perceived their potential class rule as a consequence of successful monopolization of a necessary social function (Schelsky 1975: 167, 179–80).

In Collins' conception, the distinction between political labour and productive labour likewise separates the two major social classes, both of which 'expend energy', although the dominant class which runs the 'sinecure sector' distributes the wealth which is produced by the working class.[18] But Collins appears lost in his own logic when abruptly condemning the entire spectrum of political labour (government, the educational system, and the tertiary sector more generally) as a 'sinecure sector', while also defining as a primary element of political labour the ability to impress others with definitions of what *counts as* 'work' or 'productive labour'. If political labour and positional property include the capacity to impress others with a given definition of reality, the assessment of productivity is an essentially contestable issue, the solution of which cannot be short-circuited by means of a materialist criterion of wealth. In this interpretation, productive materialism encourages a pre-emptive 'naturalization' of judgements of social utility, since it offers an apparently self-evident and solid grounding for productivity ratings which turn out to be vastly more arbitrary and controversial if examined at closer range.

Murphy provides a discussion of alternative readings of 'credential closure' which is relevant to the issue at hand (1988: 168ff.). For Collins, credentials are primarily devices for controlling occupations and for appropriating their rewards; they represent essentially arbitrary and unfounded honorific titles that support predatory claims to the fruits of the productive labour of others. For Parkin, on the other hand, credentials monopolize 'real' skills, knowledge, and techniques which are marketable owing to their functional scarcity in the occupational order. By focusing upon the successful self-selling of credentialled groups to a believing (and paying) public, Collins tends to lose sight of this aspect, even though it is true that the presence of real skills cannot be taken for granted, and their marketability may indeed result from successful salesmanship. Hence the need for a theory that recognizes the intimate coherence of both aspects; rather than focusing upon status–cultural requirements and neglecting technical–functional requirements as criteria for exclusion (or committing the reverse sin), it would be better to develop a conception that captures both simultaneously. This conception would allow both technical and status–cultural requirements to function within particular power contexts, while both would remain 'arbitrary in an absolute sense' (Murphy 1988: 184).

Such an approach to the 'duality' of credential closure has the virtue of suggesting that the process of 'accreditation' or legitimation, of gaining and sustaining credibility, is much more intrinsic to the productive status of cultural skills and the mechanism of intellectual closure than is usually acknowledged by New Class theorists. In this sense, Collins' presumption about the fundamental arbitrariness and 'irreality' of credential claims, and Parkin's opposite view of the 'reality' of functional skills which are preferentially marketed, both understate the inherent controversiality or contestability of all judgements of productive contribution. Parkin and Collins are actually closer on this point than Murphy makes out, since they both retain a dichotomy between a productive base and a 'cultural service sector', and tend to interpret credentialism and professionalism in terms of exploitative closure (cf. Parkin 1979: 54ff.). In both, the analytic focus is not so much upon what specific knowledgeable individuals 'have' (competences which are certified by educational titles), but upon what they are able to 'do'; namely, to wield power over others and exclude them from rewards. Together they stand opposed to the more traditional functionalist paradigm of professionalism in which the productivity or 'social necessity' of professional knowledge and skills is more thoroughly blackboxed and questions of power and monopolistic closure cannot even arise. A more principled view of 'duality' would need to circumvent such functionalist theories but also the conflictual theories which invert them, and encourage a more serious integration of their rivalling perspectives about the productive/enabling vs. the exploitative/constraining character of credentials and credentialled groups.

Via this route, we may attain a dual conception of the role of the New Class which, despite some obvious differences, still resembles Marx's dialectical conception of the 'twofold' character of mental labour, as it is revived in neo-Marxist elaborations of the 'contradictory' location of the new middle classes.[19] On this premise of 'duality', the intellectuals (the professional knowledge workers) perform a socially necessary function, but subject it to social closure in order to restrict access to the privileges (property, power, prestige) which are consequent upon its exercise. The new class's performance is grounded in the fact that it is *both* socially indispensable *and* potentially anti-social; in terms of social function, the intellectuals are equally necessary as they are dangerous (Schelsky 1975: 106, 117–18). More precisely, they pose a threat as a result of the very same competences which make them socially useful (Pels 1995a: 98). The theme of duality therefore arises as soon as one negates the self-sufficiency of *both* a one-dimensional functional *and* a one-dimensional conflict theory of culture, and attempts to reconcile both the productive and the exploitative dimensions in a single theoretical framework (cf. Stehr 1994a: 13, 106, 176).

This has also been attempted by Gouldner, whose theory of intellectuals as a 'flawed universal class' was designed precisely in order to negotiate the terms of this traditional dilemma. When discussing the theme of professionalism, for example, Gouldner contrasted Parsons' flattering and optimistic conception of the professions (and that of the Harvard–Columbia school more generally) with the Chicago school's efforts to secularize it – citing Eliot Freidson's work as epitomizing the latter tradition (Gouldner 1979: 19, 37, 107–8; 1970: 115ff.; cf. Freidson 1986). The Chicago approach minimized the relevance of skill, craftsmanship, and knowledge and focused upon the self-seeking, 'guild-political' behaviour of the professions; it saw professionalism not so much as an expression of legitimate skills and moral dedication, but rather as an *ideology* which harboured a tacit claim to professional monopoly and dominance. In the related matter of educational credentialism, Gouldner drew a parallel contrast between functionalist theories of human capital, which assumed an immediate causal relationship between education and the rise of productivity, and conflict theories (such as that of Collins) which questioned the empirical significance of skill, technique, and knowledge, and viewed educational requirements as mere *legitimations* of privilege and as techniques for job and income allocation which reflected the interests of those groups which had the power to set them (Gouldner 1979: 108).

It is informative to assess how far Gouldner travelled along with what he saw as a 'refreshingly realistic' approach, but it is no less illuminating to see where (and for what reasons) he halted and veered towards his own dialectical conception of the 'flawed universal class'. Collins' conflict theory was taken to task for being 'radically relativistic' and 'nihilist' because, as Gouldner argued, all status groups were seen as 'equally selfish', while none was regarded 'as actually contributing any more than others to the collective interest; the claim to do so would be seen as an *ideology* furthering that group's struggle for special privilege'. In other words, Gouldner wished to salvage not only the capability of rating differential contributions to the collective interest but also to rescue and reaffirm the partial truth which was apparently contained in the benign self-image of the modern *Bildungsklasse*. Accordingly, Collins' 'nihilism' was rejected in favour of a view of the New Class as a 'morally ambiguous, historically transient, but still "universal class"' (1979: 109). The paradoxical formulation captured the contradiction of a class that was self-seeking and might develop into 'the nucleus of a new hierarchy and the elite of a new form of cultural capital', but which also transiently embodied the collective interest as 'the most progressive force in modern society . . . the center of whatever human emancipation is possible in the foreseeable future'. Although its universalism was 'badly flawed', it was nonetheless real. The New Class might simply be 'the best card that history has presently given us to play' (Gouldner 1979: 83, 7).

That such dialectical phrasing answered to a crucial theoretical dilemma is suggested by a number of parallel formulations, of which I only cite that of Konrad and Szelényi here. Their version of the New Class similarly identified it as 'schizoid' and 'dual', because it embodied a living contradiction between its 'generic' and 'genetic' roles. Intellectuals were not simply identifiable through their traditional 'generic' function, i.e. the tendency towards transcendence which was implicit in intellectual activity and the creation of culture, but simultaneously through their 'genetic' or historically determined being. This conflict became especially acute as soon as the social group which undertook to create, preserve, and transmit both culture and social goals came to function as a class, and subordinated its cognitive activity to its own class interests. One should therefore not identify the empirical intelligentsia with 'its own transcendence', since this implied a genuflection for its self-image as the bearer of universalistic, transcendent knowledge, while

in every age the intellectuals define as such whatever knowledge best serves the particular interests connected with their social role – and that is whatever portion of the knowledge of the age serves to maintain their monopoly of their role.

(Konrad and Szelényi 1979: 10, 14)

214

FROM DIALECTICS TO DUALITY

In this fashion, the dialectic not simply claims to supersede the antinomy of universal and particular interests, but simultaneously reintegrates normative and empirical concerns; indeed, it secures an objective grounding for both in the law of motion which supposedly energizes the contradictory reality of which it is a theoretical reflection. The Hegelian postulate that 'all things are contradictory in themselves' invites the idea of a structurally immanent tension between essence and existence, i.e. of an objective contradiction between a potential, 'true' state and a negative or 'finite' present state. Since the contradiction of the intellectual class is depicted as objectively inherent, one expects a peculiar 'restlessness' of motion, since the empirical or historical class is chronically contradicted by 'its own' underlying universalist essence and thus forced to transcend its given historical limits.

That this dialectical teleology also dominated Gouldner's theory can be demonstrated by critically reflecting upon his views about the distinctive language behaviour or 'culture of critical discourse' which supposedly unified the New Class and the specific nature of its cultural capital. In utilizing the notion of the 'culture of critical discourse' (CCD) as definitional base of the New Class, Gouldner projected a specific ideal of rationality into the generic definition of intellectuals as a community of 'careful speakers'. His conception therefore intermittently celebrated and identified with an ideal of impersonal and self-grounded speech which found its ultimate matrix in the Enlightenment conception of critique. A closer examination of this residual idealization of critical reason advances us towards a more realistic and practical conception which erases such vestiges of intellectualism. But this is only practicable if we radically extirpate the notion of a 'universal class' and cross the boundary towards some form of relativism – which was precisely the step which Gouldner was not prepared to take. The CCD, in his conception,

> is an historically evolved set of rules, a grammar of discourse, which (1) is concerned to *justify* its assertions, but (2) whose *mode* of justification does not proceed by invoking authorities, and (3) prefers to elicit the *voluntary* consent of those addressed solely on the basis of arguments adduced. CCD is centered on a specific speech act: justification. It is a culture of discourse in which there is nothing that speakers will on principle permanently refuse to discuss or make problematic. . . . This grammar is the deep structure of the common ideology shared by the New Class.
>
> (1979: 28)

Basic to the culture of critical speech was a concern with its own argumentative grounding, and a style of discursive justification which forbade contextual reliance upon the speaker's person, authority, or social position but attended solely to the logical and persuasive qualities of speech itself. The CCD disestablished and de-authorized all speech grounded in tradition, and made all authority-referring claims to rationality and legitimacy potentially problematic. It was relatively more situation-free or decontextualized than everyday languages or specific technical idioms, and harboured a greater potential for reflexivity; hence it was poised towards continual self-transcendence, towards a revolution in permanence which tendentially subverted all establishments, social limits, and privileges, including its own (1979: 60). It was this anti-authoritarian, historically emancipatory grammar of rationality which constituted the dominant generic feature of the New Class and defined the radicalizing, cosmopolitan, and universalistic dimension of its dual character.

Notably, Gouldner also referred to the CCD as deep structure of the common *ideology* of the New Class, although it was not particularly clear how this fugitive term should be understood (*collective* or *false* consciousness?)[20] New Class rationality had an inherent dark side and invited specific historical costs, so that at least some of the flaws of the universal class were accountable to its use of the CCD itself. However, Gouldner's enumeration of such negative traits read like a hasty anthology of afterthoughts: they showed little coherence among themselves and were not seriously integrated into the wider theory (1979: 84). In so far as the New Class inaugurated new hierarchies and new inequalities, it was rather imputed to its ambitions as a cultural bourgeoisie, i.e. its use of cultural capital as a vehicle of generating incomes and other social privileges. Despite some remnants of dualism in both CCD and cultural capital theory, the two notions were ultimately set to organize a polar distribution of positive and negative traits, which were then 'added up' to the structural duplicity of the 'flawed universal class'. But this meant that CCD theory and cultural capital theory were not adequately integrated: they were rather 'joined at the back' like the two faces of a Janus head. The dualism of enablement and constraint was not resolved, but dialectically 'contained' by redistributing its contrary terms over two different levels of an objective 'unity of opposites'.

In order to substantiate this claim, let me further concentrate upon the ambiguities of the CCD itself. If it claimed the right 'to sit in judgment over the actions and claims of any social class and all power elites', and overhauled traditional hierarchies by means of a deeper distinction between 'those who speak and understand truly and those who do not' (1979: 59), the CCD inevitably reinstated a specific authority claim through the exclusive legitimation of its rules of speech and its certified, rule-bound speakers. While the CCD sometimes entailed that *all* authority-referring claims came under critical scrutiny, including its own, in other passages it only undermined *traditional* authority claims – that is, all except one: that of the CCD speakers themselves. Situation-freeness and argumentative justification were identified as 'essential' CCD impulses which were 'essentially' opposed to traditional forms of rationality, but also conceived as relative conditions which produced only gradual differences. Although the CCD was presented as the apex of critical rationality, it was simultaneously pictured as the outward polish of an interested class ideology, as in the following darkly toned formulation:

> The New Class begins by monopolizing truth and by making itself its guardian. . . . The New Class sets itself above others, holding that its speech is better than theirs. . . . Even as it subverts old inequities, the New Class silently inaugurates a new hierarchy of the knowing, the knowledgeable, the reflexive and the insightful.
>
> (Gouldner 1979: 85)

But how are we to reconcile the idea that the New Class is 'a center of opposition to almost all forms of censorship' to the facts of its historical record, which reveals it to be the main progenitor and practitioner of censorship in both East and West? How is it sayable in a single breath that the New Class is the most international and cosmopolitan of all elites, but also stands 'at the center of nationalist movements throughout the world'? Why did Gouldner appraise professionalism as a New Class *ideology*, whereas its axial value was that very same autonomy which was presupposed by the CCD? Curiously, the New Class's fountain of critical rationality remained unpolluted, even though all the historical 'sociolects' which derived from it, and which alone were empirically graspable, were spoilt by context-bound, rationality-limiting interests. The partisanship which energized its historical struggle for class autonomy was not unequivocally seen as limiting its rationality, but somehow also coincided with the universal interests of humankind.

But in my conception, a class *cannot* be universal and flawed at one and the same time; universalism represents an interested, partisan claim in *all* contexts. The CCD is only another title of substitution which intellectuals may adopt in order to universalize their mundane interests and sublimate these into a self-propelling historical force. It presents a specific 'disinterested' conception of critical rationality as an inherent feature of rational discourse, which dogmatizes it and silently erases other types of rationality from the roster of acceptable forms of intellectual speech. In this perspective, New Class vices and virtues are closer partners than in Gouldner's theory, which first separated CCD and cultural capital and subsequently brought them together in an uneasy state of conciliation and contrariety. But if the CCD and cultural capital were theoretically merged in a more satisfactory manner, it would not only extradite lingering romantic delusions about the universalism of the New Class but also take care of a number of difficulties arising from the specifics of Gouldnerian capital theory itself. The intellectuals were identified as a rising cultural bourgeoisie precisely because their special privileges and powers were grounded in their control of valuable cultures, i.e. because they were led to capitalize upon their knowledgeability and cultural competence. But Gouldner remained enigmatic about what the 'individual control' or the 'private appropriation' of culture entailed, how the original accumulation and valorization of cultural capital took place, and in what sense this capital stock might be withheld and serve as a basis of enforceable claims to class incomes.

This relative neglect of the 'control' dimension has also been spotted by Szelényi, who has critically observed that Gouldner placed the main weight of his generic definition of capital upon the acquisition of *incomes* (and secondarily, of political powers). But this idea of capital as income-earning capacity was in his view only of limited use in defining class relations (Szelényi 1982; cf. Martin and Szelényi 1987; Disco 1987). Gouldner's emphasis was not upon how culture itself might become private property, but upon how it could generate streams of income which were privately appropriable; not upon the control of the capital stock itself but rather upon the appropriation of the external goods which it produced (cf. Gouldner 1979: 22–5). A second and related problem was that, even though cultural capital was intermittently described as a dual structure (its public goal was increased economic productivity, while its latent function was increased income), all attention was drawn towards its dark side. Capital, Gouldner claimed, typically sought something for nothing; its first concern was with its incomes, its 'partisan perquisites' rather than its contribution to society. The strategy of moral segregation which was already characteristic of CCD theory was here repeated in inverse form – so much so that the generalized metaphor of capital often appeared to function as a simple synonym of self-interestedness or partiality.

A third disadvantage of this income-oriented conception of capital, one might add, is that the specific differences with other types of capital tend to be underplayed. While it is already risky to equate physical capital with *money* capital, it is likewise disadvantageous to identify the latter too closely with *cultural* or *symbolic* capital. This may have the effect of missing the specificity of both 'old' and 'new' capital, because one is systematically led to overemphasize the fiduciary character of the former, while simultaneously understating the 'confidential' or 'credential' nature of the latter. While financial capital is already less material and fiduciary than land or physical stock, cultural capital is even less tangible and real (although not necessarily more mobile). In the familiar triadic sequence of land–money–information as historically dominant forces of production, there is decreasing fixity and security of possession, and increasing pressure for discursive public justification. Unlike land and material stock, or even financial capital, which are both naturally and socially scarce, cultural capital is more nearly scarce in a 'social–epistemological' sense. With Gouldner, however, culture is still too much seen as a tool or object over which one has control (e.g. educational assets or linguistic techniques), so that one may privately appropriate the benefits which it helps to produce. But the reifying drift of the property and capital metaphors may easily mislead us here: these 'objects' are also 'subjects', because stocks of culture are typically incorporated or personalized. This means that the capitalization of culture requires a continual upkeep of its credibility, i.e. of the belief in its social productivity – a work of maintenance which is much more intrinsically necessary to its survival and market value than is the case for money capital or material stock.

'Cultural closure' is therefore different from the control over money flows, not merely because the coinage is invisible and often inseparable from individuals, but also because it is much more closely dependent upon processes of cultural definition, identity maintenance, and legitimation work. For some considerable part, of course, cultural capital means 'possessing' symbolic proficiency or 'having (acquired)' an education, so that cultural closure may be operationalized as providing unequal access to the establishments where symbolic skills and cultural competences are produced, and as resulting in an unequal command of the arts of reading, speaking, and writing well. But cultural capital has also an important epistemological side, because the production of cultural legitimacy is a confidence game which requires the uninterrupted monitoring, negotiation, and validation of claims to cultural competence. That is why a theory of cultural productivity moves in the near vicinity of a theory of rationality, and why cultural closure may adopt the specific form of a monopoly of *truth* which functions to certificate 'true speakers' and thus to separate the knowledgeable (the haves) from the ignorant or innocent (the have-nots).

In this way, we advance towards a more relativistic theory of cultural disposition which distances itself from the essentialist framework of the CCD dialectic, without removing the basic structural feature of *duality* which the dialectic inadequately theorizes. CCD theory does have the virtue of rephrasing the problem of the productive force of culture and knowledge as a problem of the legitimation of rationality claims, but it also tends to substitute the traditional materialist (or 'labour') criterion of productivity for a dogmatically asserted idealist one. But criteria of productive contribution, cultural or otherwise, are inescapably context dependent and cannot be justified or grounded outside of such contexts. Utility ratings or rationality claims have an ineradicably interested or opportunistic side; since they are at stake in quasi-political struggles between interested groups (of intellectuals), they are always advanced in contaminated situations. What 'duality' means, therefore, is that rationality and self-interest are not easily separable, and are normally encountered only in a state of mixture. Konrad and Szelényi provide a useful 'Foucaldian' phrasing of this idea:

> 'Knowledge is power' implies a dual process. Knowledge creates its own kind of power, but at the same time power also brings into being its own knowledge. . . . The essence of the intelligentsia's social function does not lie in the fact that knowledge of a certain complexity guarantees power and reward in certain positions; rather, the intelligentsia seeks to obtain power and reward for itself by exploiting its relative monopoly of complex knowledge as a means of achieving

those goals. The heart of the matter, then, is not to be found in a knowledge that is functionally necessary, but rather in the desire to legitimize aspirations to power.

(1979: 26)

But if we add precision, the heart of the matter is not so much the predominance of the power-interested or 'exploitative' side over the functional or 'productive' side, but the *duality* of functional necessity and dispositional interests, i.e. the intrinsic entanglement or inseparability of 'good' and 'bad' dimensions (cf. Pels 1995b). Judgements of differential rationality are both possible and necessary, but cannot and need not be emancipated from underlying existential interests, and can do without the reassuring aura of determinacy which exudes from the idea of universalistic justification. In the absence of such criteria, what may and may not *count as* 'knowledge' or 'expertise' is ineluctably at stake in social struggles and negotiations.

HAVINGS AND DOINGS

Once again, we realize that the alternative idioms of a generalized political economy and a generalized political theory are virtually interchangeable, because the radicalized notions of cultural capital or cultural property and that of *pouvoir/savoir* come together to express an identical idea. But let us also note that, in this generalized state, both idioms do little more than sensitize us to the ever-present dimension of 'interestedness', and only vaguely declare that culture is a productive force which is routinely monopolized or enclosed in order to usurp social privileges. On this level, preferences for the metaphor of property or that of power are arbitrary and may be mixed without theoretical risk. Another reason for mixture derives from the fact that, while property is still residually connotated with objective, material 'havings', and power residually refers to subjective, interpersonal 'doings', the singularity of New Class disposition precisely resides in its intricate *composition* of thing-directed, other-directed, and self-directed actions. Like a new *noblesse de robe* (although bare of familial rights of hereditary transmission), the 'property' of the knowledge class first of all consists of its tenure of institutionally based positions, which lend it indirect access to material and monetary means of production which are likewise institutionally held. Although such positional rights provide it with a variable measure of control over other people's intellect and labour, this is hardly distinguishable from its immediate disposition of its own intellectual, as well as its mediate disposition of the material, intellectual, and human resources which reside in the institutions controlled by it. New Class closure accordingly recombines elements of the traditional bundles of property and power in a new type of composite holding, the axis of which is formed by individual tenure of institutional positions and individual command of cultural competences, which precondition each other and accelerate each other's increase (or decrease) as in a magic circle. Both skills and positions are subject to a dispositional regime which is simultaneously private and social, because individuals possess these resources partly as 'property of their own self', but are only able to preserve them through continuous efforts of structuration, negotiation, and legitimation, which are themselves inevitably framed in situations of unequal property-and-power.

Hence the knowledge class also 'owns' means of production in a more immediate, indeed virtually inalienable, sense. Although the realities of large-scale corporate and bureaucratic organization demand that physical means of production and administration are 'separated' from the producer, other kinds of means are inseparable from him or her. Producers control some means of production directly, but not in the manner in which physical assets can be owned. Their property is transferable, but not in the way physical assets are transmitted. It does not permit – or demand – something like full closure, since spending it may mean increasing it, while transferring it does not necessarily mean forfeiting it. However, it is one peculiarity of knowledge capital or the capital of expertise that it can come to fruition only at the intersection of the personal and the institutional. Without institutional position, the manager, bureaucrat, or intellectual remains a disconnected petty proprietor; with institutional tenure such a person is 'plugged in'. The brain, as Konrad and Szelényi assert, is not enough: brains must be joined to the material and technical tools of intellectual labour, which only capitalist or technocratic organizations can afford, and without which intellectual knowledge cannot realize its potential (1979: 77–8). Knowledge societies favour a new type of social integration which is crucially sustained by technical and informational infrastructures; individuals increasingly partake of society as a 'terminal' or a 'connection' (Böhme 1992: 87). This means that command of informational capital is increasingly dependent upon competent access to institutionalized data banks, and upon the new skills of information retrieval and information processing which are typically mastered in such institutional settings.

An inclusive account of the heterogeneity and complexity of cultural closure hence requires a close meshing of the property and power lexicons and their lingering connotations of 'having' vs. 'doing', possession vs. performance, things vs. people, or 'substance' vs. 'relation'. As I explained in the first chapter, the rivalry constellation of property and power is governed by a complex indeterminacy, since they are either conceived as 'domanial' media, which most primitively refer to actions upon things and actions upon people, and finding their 'home grounds' in the economic and political realms, while they simultaneously represent more abstract types of tenure which cut across such spheres of action. Otherwise put, *both* property (as command over tangible objects) *and* power (as command over people's actions) admit of a more 'thinglike' (property-like, distributive) interpretation or a more 'relational' (power-like, performative) one, which is contingent upon the comparative fullness of command and discretion which are historically associated with their exercise. The classical concept of political sovereignty, for example, could easily be taken for a form of property on account of its point-like, concentrated, and heritable nature, a 'possessory' view which is still recognizable in early twentieth-century elitist and late twentieth-century economistic theories of power (cf. Schmitt 1922; Barry 1991; Moriss 1987). Economic property, on the other hand, in progressively losing the sovereign and thinglike character which was impressed upon it by classical liberalism, was increasingly interpreted as dynamic, relational, and conditional, and as reinstating a 'power-like' stewardship of physical and other assets.

Notwithstanding such metaphoric cross-modulations, modern social thinking has retained a dualistic contrast between what I shall call 'residential' or 'substantial' vs. 'relational' or 'performative' conceptions of *both* property *and* power. It has also developed a marked preference for the latter over the former, riding the long conceptual wave which has progressively erased all vestiges of 'substantialist' thinking in favour of 'relationist' social-scientific methodologies (Cassirer 1910; Simmel 1990; Elias 1978; Foucault 1980; Bourdieu and Wacquant 1992). In a previous chapter, I have already briefly indicated how various modern conceptions of power marshalled the contrasting idioms of 'having' and 'doing', of possession and action, in the service of a general critique of reification (cf. Elias 1978; Foucault 1980; Latour 1986; Young 1990). Young has for instance objected to a 'distributive' conception of power, which views it as 'a kind of stuff possessed by individual agents in greater or lesser amounts' and consequently obscures the fact that it 'is a relation rather than a thing' (1990: 27, 31). For Latour, similarly, power is not something that one can own, have, capitalize, collect, or hold in storage (*in potentia*); it is something that has continually to be made and remade by others (*in actu*). It is meaningless to appeal to an initial source of energy, be it 'capital' or 'power', to explain the obedient behaviour of the multitudes. There is no initial impetus or inner force that causes diffusion of power; its displacement is rather a consequence of the energy given to the powerful by every single actor down the chain of command (Latour 1986).

Contrary to such views, my present point is that we stand in need of *both* metaphoric connotations, both the 'residential' and the 'performative' one, if we wish to make sense of the modern 'heterogeneous engineering' of things, humans, and symbols (cf. Law 1989) which is characteristically undertaken by members of the new knowledge class. In a slight variation on Simmel, our task is to follow the 'chain from doing to having and from having to doing' (1990: 307). As our discussion of Bourdieu's distributive (but non-reificatory) approach to cultural capital has shown, its 'spinal cord' is located in the disposition over non-material incorporated goods, which strongly governs the conditions of appropriation of other relevant resources, both material and immaterial. This durable bodily disposition, which is formed by cultural inheritances and maintained by permanent education, pertinently suggests a 'residential' conception of competence-as-property, whereas simultaneously a 'performative' or 'relational' conception is required in order to acknowledge that such durable capacities and skills remain crucially dependent upon the recursive attribution of trust and confidence by others. Authors such as Barnes (1988) and Law (1991b) similarly favour a combination of the 'storage' approach and a more nominalist or performative one. The latter insists that the 'storage' conception is quite compatible with a radical relationism, and that in fact relations and capacities are indissolubly linked, since power storage characteristically occurs at the points of high density, the stable nodes of relational networks (1991b: 166–8, 174). In this fashion, the idiom of possession and accumulation has the virtue of restoring the crucial aspect of the stabilization of social 'doings' into differential 'havings' which is tendentially lost in radical actionist and relational accounts of knowledge/power.

It is this strategically mediating function of *internalized* or *embodied* culture and knowledge which is insufficiently captured by the lingering 'externalist' connotations of both the traditional vocabularies of property and power. If we attempt to draw the whole spectrum of resources and strategies (see Figure 8), we may face the eventuality that the full tissue of cultural disposition cannot be adequately characterized by a mere mixing of the two metaphors. This dispositional spectrum runs all the way from access to 'external' material goods (buildings, offices, laboratories, sophisticated communication technologies), tenure of professional positions and incomes, club connections and boardroom affiliations, educational titles, 'technical' capacities and skills (practical dexterities, linguistic competences), towards 'goods' the utility of which is more resolutely dependent upon the 'confidence game' (and confidence tricks) of the recursive attribution of legitimacy (e.g. analytic and leadership capabilities, reputational identities of institutions, individuals, ideas, and theories).

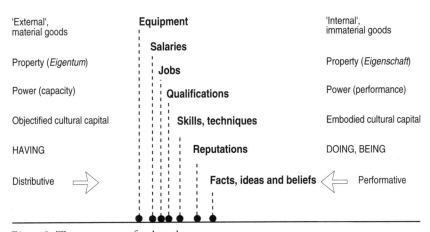

Figure 8 The spectrum of cultural resources

This wide spectrum of havings and doings not only accommodates the relative 'hardness' or material stability of cultural appropriations, but simultaneously (and perhaps paradoxically) their essential 'softness' or precariousness, which results from the fact that they must ceaselessly be instantiated through the performative power of definition and recognition. While recognizing the relational, institutional, and socially constructed nature of virtually all material goods (which, for one thing, must be perpetually reconstituted as goods rather than bads), it also accommodates the distributive quality of attributes or properties which are indissolubly linked to natural persons (skills, stocks of knowledge, identities, reputations). In pressing home the twin economic and political analogies, it emphasizes both the performative magic of instituting objects and subjects, and the distributive quality of even the most ethereal and definition-sensitive forms of cultural capital. In this respect, all resources along the continuum are simultaneously external and internal, hard and soft, thinglike and credibility dependent, although they are so in different proportions. Indeed, if cultural havings and doings derive their true specificity from their being inscribed in human bodies, they exemplify the peculiar mix of hardness and softness which identifies the *habitus* as Bourdieu has defined it. It may be here, also, that the mixed metaphors of capital and power, of having and doing, run up against their limits and ultimately fail to grasp the thing in the middle.

8

TOWARDS A THEORY OF
INTELLECTUAL RIVALRY

> Theory-work is not done just by 'adding another brick to the wall of science' but often involves throwing bricks as well; it not only involves paying one's intellectual debts but also (and rather differently) 'settling accounts'.
>
> Alvin Gouldner

MIXING THE METAPHORS: KARL MANNHEIM

The notion that intellectual rivalry is a basic energetic force in the development of knowledge and science is one of the few ideas which modern philosophers and sociologists of science agree upon without reserve. In this context, the economic metaphor of the 'market-place of ideas' is as much favoured as the political model of contained 'parliamentary' dialogue, and in either case descriptive purposes are intimately wedded to normative ones. Free competition is traditionally associated with liberty, tolerance, and progress, while its absence is interpreted as a definite cause of intellectual vegetation, dogmatism, and arrogance. However, such consensus as may exist is only a thin film which scarcely subdues the differences of opinion which lie underneath. These disagreements not only concern the specific balance of competition and cooperation which obtains in scientific work, and hence how far their psychological and structural impact should extend, but they also touch the question to what degree scientific developments are steered by local, position-, or group-bound interests, and what this signifies for the alleged 'truth' or global rationality of the scientific enterprise.

If we attempt to impose some order upon such disputes, it appears that they can be deployed along a continuum which is limited by two extreme positions. One of these says that intellectual competition is a struggle between *true and false ideas*, and that truth radiates with such irresistible force that it ultimately prevails against all superstition and ideology. Although this model acknowledges the presence of competition, its effect is neutralized by a primordial consensus about the rules of the scientific game, which are in turn

225

derived from a privileged and peremptory logic of scientific discovery. In so far as interests play a role, they are normally reduced to the abstract 'truth interest' which acts as the normative backdrop of, for example, Max Weber's principle of value-freedom. As we travel towards the opposite pole, the balance of rivalry and consensus gradually alters. The weight of the agonistic factor increases while the volume of prior agreement dwindles, and the practice of competition spells more danger to the principle of scientific rationality itself, because the production of knowledge is made to depend to a larger extent upon 'opportunistic' struggles between mundane, position-bound interests. It is more decisively acknowledged that, in Derek Phillips's words, 'it is not only theories that are in competition, but human beings as well', and that scientists engage in a never-ending struggle to establish as legitimate the ideas of specific individuals or groups against others. One is increasingly prepared to tolerate structural dissent about how the game of science is to be played; it is recognized that the rules, and hence also the limits of the playing field itself (object boundaries, disciplinary fences, research methodologies, legitimate players), are routinely and perhaps essentially contested (Phillips 1977: 161, 168; Gallie 1955–6; Bourdieu 1981).

Both political and economic metaphors lose their virginity here, and shed a good deal of their metaphoric character. They increasingly operate as alternative (although converging) expressions of a radical mutual implication of cognitive and social dimensions in knowledge and science (*pouvoir/savoir*; cultural capital), and of the situated, contextual, and contingent nature of their professional production. They offer two ways of saying that science (and intellectual practices more generally) are social through-and-through, that they constitute 'nothing special', and do not present a privileged exception to the rule of mundanely interested social practices. The two vocabularies disenchant and deconstruct because they register something analogous to the search for profit or the will-to-power as intrinsic features of the professional quest for knowledge; they twice emphasize the inseparable duality of scientific and social interest and the resulting agonistic structure of scientific endeavour. In this fashion, the two metaphors are equally useful in hastening the desecration of what Nietzsche dubbed the 'ascetic' ideal of philosophical truth, and in robbing science of its conventional epistemological privileges.

The sociology of knowledge has not been slow to discover this constitutive significance of intellectual competition. It is remarkable that Mannheim's first essays on the subject, written in the course of the 1920s, already breathe a quite radical spirit – in ascribing a decisive causal weight to the factor of rivalry itself, in unreservedly allying the production of knowledge to strategic group interests, and in adopting a sceptical attitude with regard to the utility of universally compelling, context-free standards of scientific rationality. In this regard, Mannheim is certainly identifiable as the *Urheber* of the agonistic model of scientific development in either of its currently popular quasi-economic or quasi-political formulations (Pels 1997). Indeed, in his early work, Mannheim liberally *mixes* the metaphors of 'competition' and 'power struggle' as more or less equivalent specifications of his grounding intuition about the existential determination of thought and the 'essential perspectivity' of all social and political knowledge. It is striking that subsequently influential contributions to the sociology of knowledge, such as Merton's normative–functionalist paradigm, to some extent back down from this radical perspective in order to present a more serene and disinterested image of the scientific struggle and its major stake: the acquisition of reputational prestige. It is only during the 1970s, in the wake of the newly emerging philosophy and historiography of science after the Kuhnian turn, that the agonistic model of science is reinvented through the largely disparate efforts of French theorists such as Foucault, Lyotard, and Bourdieu, of constructivist science studies issuing from the Strong Programme in Britain, and feminist standpoint epistemologies developing mainly in the USA. All of these currents almost 'naturally' revert to the disenchanting metaphors of economics and politics as critical tools for assessing the workings of interests in scientific change.

Mannheim's early views are advanced most expressly in 'Die Bedeutung der Konkurrenz im Gebiete des Geistigen', a lecture first given at the Sixth German Convention of Sociologists in Zürich in 1928. Although competition is considered a universal feature of social life, Mannheim finds too little acknowledgement of its effects on processes of idea formation and the production of culture more generally. Instead of constituting only a marginal or sporadic cause of intellectual production, competition 'enters as a constituent element into the form and content (*Gestalt und Gehalt*) of every cultural product or movement' (1952: 191). Phenomena traditionally diagnosed as resulting from immanent laws of spiritual life, such as the 'dialectical' patterning of cognitive development, may now be explained in terms of social patterns and structures, such as the impact of intellectual competition and the rise and fall of (intellectual) generations. This strong dismissal of cognitive internalism and affirmation of the constitutive role of the social, however, is immediately set off against an 'unbridled sociologism' which tends to view cultural creations as 'nothing but a by-product of the social process of competition'. Social factors such as competition, Mannheim insists, are neither peripheral nor all-determinant but *co-determinant* of the content of intellectual products (1952: 192–3).

This anti-reductionism is further articulated when Mannheim parries the criticism of 'projecting specifically economic categories into the mental sphere'. Anticipating Bourdieu's notion of an anti-economistic economy of practices, he points out that actually the reverse is the case. When early political economists demonstrated the important role of competition, they were only discovering a general social relationship in the particular context of the economic system. While the existence of the social, the 'interplay of vital forces between the individuals of a group', became first visible in the economic sphere, the ultimate aim of sociology must nevertheless be 'to strip our categorial apparatus of anything specifically economic in order to grasp the social fact sui generis'. Theoretical conflict ('*das theoretische Gegeneinander*') constitutes a self-contained sphere of experience, and cannot be reduced to an immediate reflection of current social competition. It is sociology's task not only to account for the distinction between the various planes of experience, but also to explore their interpenetration and togetherness as manifestations of the 'general social'. The question then becomes: what is the specific nature of competition as it manifests itself in the sphere of thought?

In answering this question, Mannheim loosely interweaves the idioms of appropriation and domination. Intellectual competition is basically about 'the possession of the correct social diagnosis (*Besitz der richtigen {sozialen} Sicht*)', or at least about the prestige which it lends its proprietors, while furthermore

all historical, ideological, and sociological knowledge (even should it prove to be Absolute Truth itself) is clearly rooted in and carried by the desire for power and recognition (*Macht- und Geltungstrieb*) of particular social groups who want to make their interpretation of the world the universal (*öffentlichen*) one.

(Mannheim 1952: 196–7)

Sociology and the cultural sciences offer no exception to this sociological rule; the old battle for universal acceptance of a particular interpretation of reality is here carried on with modern scientific weapons. The 'public interpretation of reality' is a 'stake for which men fight'; a struggle which is not directed by motives of 'pure contemplative thirst for knowledge' but by the interested positions which various groups occupy in their struggle for power (ibid.: 197–8).

Somewhat later in the text, Mannheim more frankly adopts this knowledge-political vernacular, and provides additional evidence of his anti-reductionist intentions. Politics is initially conceived in extremely broad fashion, as coincident with the activist, pragmatic, or 'impulsive' basis of knowledge which is also suggested by the closely related notion of a 'style of thought' (1952: 209–10). Politics is simply the natural telos of all activity which is directed at changing the world (e.g. ibid.: 214; cf. Mannheim 1953: 84). Hence one runs far less risk of going astray, Mannheim believes,

if one proposes to explain intellectual movements in political terms than if one takes the opposite course and from a purely theoretical attitude projects a merely contemplative internal, theoretical thought pattern on to the concrete, actual life process itself. In actual life, it is always some volitional centre which sets thought going; competition, victory, and the selection based upon it, largely determine the movement of thought.

(Mannheim 1952: 212)

Once again, the languages of politics and economics appear virtually inter-changeable as indicators of the interested infrastructure of thought, and as critical counterstatements against the 'merely contemplative' conception. In close parallel to the economics case, however, Mannheim immediately quali-fies his vaguely extended conception of politics. The use of political terms must not give the impression 'that mental life as a whole is a purely political matter, any more than earlier we wished to make of it a mere segment of economic life'. The aim is once again to direct attention to the vital and voli-tional (*voluntaristische*) element in existentially determined thought, 'which is easiest to grasp in the political sphere' (1952: 212).

POLITICS AND AUTONOMY OF SCIENCE:
SCHMITT TO MERTON

It has been insufficiently appreciated that Mannheim's potentially radical theorem about the existential rootedness of thought was in fact widely shared among his Weimar contemporaries, across a broad spectrum extending from Lukàcs' left-proletarian standpoint epistemology (which long held Mannheim's critical fascination) towards the right-wing political existentialism embraced by writers such as Freyer, Jünger, and Schmitt. If our purpose is to trace early conceptions of intellectual rivalry, we are invited to some remarkable cross-borrowings and reactive positionings among these various advocates of sociological or political existentialism, all of whom in a sense viewed science and ideology as a vehicle of 'continuing politics by other means'. However, while the reception of Mannheim's sociology of knowledge on the left and centre of the professional and political spectrum has been given systematic attention (cf. Meja and Stehr 1982), his relationship to the Weimar 'conservative-revolutionary' right has been equally systematically neglected (Pels 1993c). In the present context, I can only trace a few connecting strands with the early writings of Schmitt and Freyer, in order to acknowledge the former's anticipa-tion of the idea of a 'politics of theory' in his trenchant criticism of liberal parliamentary dialogue, and to demonstrate, if only briefly, that much of Mannheim's own retreat from the idea of the 'existential relativity' of thought after 1930 was triggered by anxieties about the more categorical politicization of this grounding idea by right-wing social and political theorists.

In his lecture on intellectual competition (1928) and his book *Ideologie und Utopie* of the following year, Mannheim sympathetically paraphrased Schmitt's scathing attack upon the 'intellectualism' of liberal political ideology, which mistakenly believed that 'rational tensions grounded in exist-ential differences' could be reduced to differences in thinking, and that these could in turn be ironed out by virtue of 'the uniformity of reason'. Since liberal theory held that evaluation could be separated from theorizing as a matter of principle, it refused to recognize the phenomenon of existentially determined thought, of a thought 'containing by definition, and inseparably, irrational elements woven into its very texture'. This self-deception deprived it from seeing that behind every theory stood collective forces that were expressive of group purposes, group power, and group interests (1952: 216–17; 1968: 133). Carl Schmitt's early writings on political sovereignty and parliamentary democracy had indeed dismissed the same rationalistic 'belief in discussion' and 'truth-finding' – and in parliamentary representatives as impersonating the 'particles of Reason' – as fatally dependent upon the liberal dogma of free competition within a pre-established harmony of interests. The utopia of 'government by discussion', according to Schmitt, divorced the *Kampf der Meinungen* from the *Kampf der Interessen*, separated argumentative discussion from negotiation, and ignored the need for 'decision' as striking ontologically deeper than any set of communal norms. It would be perhaps advisable, he had therefore concluded, to 'put up for discussion discussion itself' (1926: 9–11, 43–5, 89–90).

Liberalism, in seeking to eliminate the primordial quality of the political, tended to neutralize it either through economic-organizational technique or the 'eternal conversation' of democratic dispute. The 'Western' concept of truth, in translating this liberal obsession for peaceful consensus to the theoretical plane, was likewise a product of liberal neutralization. For Schmitt, by contrast, theorizing and concept-formation constituted an arena of struggle, a field of force in which concepts, propositions, and distinctions functioned as weaponry, and where one had to be on continual alert in order to ward off the tactical manoeuvres of one's intellectual adversaries. The method of science itself was intensely polemical, and one should be constantly aware of tensions within and between theories, of objective moments of negation and 'enmity' between concepts (cf. Mannheim's contemporary notion of 'counter-concepts' (1952: 208; 1968: 197, 207, 244).[1] This struggle for words, names, and concepts was constitutive of the knowledge process itself, and represented an immediate extrapolation of the struggle between social groups, classes, and peoples (cf. De Wit 1992: 15–16, 456–9). All political concepts, images, and terms, Schmitt proclaimed in a striking passage of his *Der Begriff der Politischen*,

> have a polemical meaning. They are focused on a specific conflict and are bound to a concrete situation; the result (which manifests itself in war or revolution) is a friend-enemy grouping, and they turn into empty and ghost-like abstractions when this situation disappears. Words such as state, republic, society, class, as well as sovereignty, constitutional state, absolutism, dictatorship, economic planning, neutral or total state, and so on [might we not add property and power to this list?] are incomprehensible if one does not know exactly who is to be affected, combated, refuted, or negated by such a term.
>
> (Schmitt 1996: 30–1)

Terminological disputes consequently turned into matters of high political import; a word or expression might simultaneously be 'reflex, signal, password, and weapon in a hostile confrontation'. This polemical character naturally also dominated the usage of the term 'political' itself; the struggle over the concept of the political was a political struggle like any other (ibid.: 31–2).[2]

Like Carl Schmitt, Hans Freyer attentively read Mannheim's *Ideologie und Utopie* on publication, and lost no time in marshalling its basic insights in the service of his own conception of a radically activist and politicized sociology. In *Soziologie als Wirklichkeitswissenschaft* (1930), Mannheim's still hesitant criticism of liberal Weberian conceptions of value-freedom was extended into a defence of a politically committed *Ethoswissenschaft*, in the course of which the idea of the volitional or existential grounding of social and political knowledge acquired a strong decisionist twist ('Wahres Wollen fundiert wahre Erkenntnis') (Freyer 1964: 307). In reverse, Mannheim's initial sympathies for Freyer's line of argument soon faded, especially after the latter had scored a major success with his 'national socialist' pamphlet *Revolution von Rechts* in the following year, which proclaimed that 'true knowledge' of history was grounded in and guaranteed by the 'true will' of the German nation (Freyer 1931).[3] Gradually, in the years leading up to the Nazi coup and his exile in 1933, Mannheim adopted a more defensive stance, taking greater distance from the relativistic implications of his earlier formulations, and approaching a more distinctly academic conception of scientific rationality – without, however, fully endorsing a Weberian principle of value-freedom or resolving his enduring ambivalence between political involvement and scientific detachment (Kettler *et al.* 1984: 70–6; Pels 1993c: 61–2; 1996a: 43). A textual comparison of the original German and subsequent English editions of *Ideologie und Utopie* not only evidences this 'positivistic' drift but also demonstrates that Mannheim's sociology of knowledge reached a broader audience primarily in this second, more academically polished, version.[4]

A major force in the diffusion of this deradicalized conception was Merton's influential reading of Mannheim's work (Merton 1941). Dominated by Merton's *Science, Technology and Society* (1938), early American historiography of science developed from the start a much stronger sense about the constitutive autonomy of science, its essential detachment from the political, and the attendant need to discriminate more pertinently between 'internal' cognitive and 'external' social factors of scientific change. In major part, this emphasis upon the autonomy of the 'community of scholars' *vis-à-vis* external pressures was polemically levelled against the same particularist politics of theory which had induced Mannheim to shift his allegiances towards more positivistic and universalistic views. Both in his early account of the normative structure of science (1942) and his subsequent critique of 'positional' thinking (1972) – as in various other writings – Merton was explicitly concerned to rescue the dignity of the intellectual enterprise from 'anti-intellectualist' attempts to continue politics by scientific means, of which right-wing scholars collaborating with the Nazi regime provided an obvious first example (e.g. 1973: 136, 267–8, 278).[5] Merton's stricter delineation of scientific autonomy in normative-functional terms was accompanied by a significant readjustment of the balance between competition and cooperation in science, which neutralized the agonistic risk of the former by the overriding imperatives of the normative structure, and ensured that the shared discipline of the 'pursuit of truth' transcended all particularistic loyalties of a political or social kind. This model also included a view of intellectual property which emphasized 'communism' over private interest, distinguishing it sharply from other types of property, and limiting its scope to a mere interest in 'recognition' or 'esteem'.

Science as a social institution, Merton maintained, was governed by a distinctive body of authoritative norms, which paradigmatically included those of universalism, intellectual communism, disinterestedness, and organized scepticism (1973: 270ff.). Property rights in science were whittled down to a bare minimum, since the products of the 'competitive cooperation' between scientists became part of the public domain of science, while the individual scientist was rewarded with recognition for his contribution to the communal stock. Recognition was therefore the true 'coin of the scientific realm'. The interest in it was generated by an institutional premium on originality, which in turn fuelled an intense concern with intellectual priority. Hence the 'rigorous policing' to which intellectual experts subjected their fellows, and the remarkable frequency of priority battles in which scientists pressed each other for recognition and pursued reputed violations of the property norm (1973: 286ff.). Nevertheless, this social pressure for competition was 'dampened' and rendered institutionally innocuous by the functional ethos of communism and disinterestedness. More generally, the relevance of positionally conditioned thought, as for example reflected in the influence of polarized ideological commitments, was lessened by the unique discipline which was imposed by scientific method. The 'margin of autonomy in the culture and institution of science' evidently meant that

> the intellectual criteria, as distinct from the social ones, for judging the validity and worth of that work transcend extraneous group allegiances. The acceptance of criteria of craftsmanship and integrity in science and learning cuts across differences in the social affiliations and loyalties of scientists and scholars. Commitment to the intellectual values dampens group-induced pressures to advance the interests of groups at the expense of these values and of the intellectual product.
>
> (Merton 1973: 136)

In science, as elsewhere, conflict easily turned into the 'gadfly' of truth: in social conflict, cognitive issues became warped and distorted as they were pressed into the service of 'scoring off the other fellow'. When the conflict was regulated by the community of peers, however, it could have its uses for the advancement of the discipline (1973: 58).

As compared with the Mannheimian paradigm, the Mertonian one thus insisted upon a much stricter demarcation of the scientific subsystem, and drew a much sharper dichotomy between internal and external generators of scientific change. In identifying the former with cognitively rational factors and the latter with socially contextual ones, it also decisively constrained the explanatory scope of the external–social dimension itself. Although Mannheim, as we saw, tended to resist explanations in terms of unmediated 'reflection', and did not take existential determination in a politically or economically reductionist sense, he had been none too precise on the explanatory status and scope of intellectual interests themselves. Surely, concepts such as *Weltanschauung* and *Denkstil* offered intermediary terms which grasped indirect connections between intellectual contents and social class interests (1952: 184; 1953: 74–84). Mannheim also distinguished between 'immediate' social interest and 'indirect committedness' to styles of thought, precisely in order to emphasize the complex variety of forms of social determination (1982: 273–6; 1952: 183–7). But on balance, he still seemed more interested in how forms of competition between extraneous classes or political groups infiltrated in the intellectual sphere, tending to neglect the internal politics of theory which were conducted by the intellectual stratum itself or competing factions within it.

In comparison, the Mertonian approach (which during the Cold War period increasingly profiled itself against left-wing 'economic' rather than right-wing 'political' externalism) not only accentuated the protective boundaries between science and 'outside' society, but simultaneously 'detonated' and depoliticized the idea of internal strife by putting a large trust in the neutralizing force of the scientific ethos. Although intellectual competition could be fierce and ugly, as was demonstrated by the endemic contests for priority of discovery, the normative structure of science guaranteed that such ugliness was institutionally contained, turning science into an essentially cooperative enterprise. Barber's *Science and the Social Order* (1952), which codified the distinction between internal and external explanatory factors, was complemented by exchange models such as those of Hagström (*The Scientific Community*, 1965) or Storer (*The Social System of Science*, 1966), which described scientific interaction as gift-giving in a normatively integrated community, rather than as maximizing profit in an agonistic market (Shapin 1992: 340; Knorr-Cetina 1981a: 70). Analysing conflicts between various sociological currents and styles, Merton himself had suggested that often such polemics were not so much about cognitive oppositions as about contrasting evaluations of the worth of various kinds of sociological work, or 'bids for support by the social system of sociologists', thereby clearly separating 'intellectual criticism' from 'social conflict' and 'status battles' from the 'search for truth' (1973: 54–8).

STRONGER PROGRAMMES

It was the 'Kuhnian turn' in the philosophy and historiography of science which cleared the decks for the introduction of stronger programmes in science studies which worked towards closure of the gap between cognitive internalism and social contextualism. Invariably, these new approaches exploded the double equation between the external and the social and the internal and the cognitive, and pleaded a more sophisticated conception of social determination according to which 'intrascientific' social factors should be clearly distinguished from 'extrascientific' ones. The novel recognition of the close conjuncture, if not coincidence, of the cognitive and the social within the domain of science itself did not therefore backslide into a reductionist theory of 'reflection', which even Merton occasionally embraced (cf. 1973: 110–11), but gradually detailed a perspective of 'refraction' of external by internal determinants which retained the idea of the structural autonomy of science, even if changing considerably the view of how its internal logic was acted out. Kuhn's *The Structure of Scientific Revolutions* (1962) already broke the communalist and cooperative image of science more or less 'in half' by discovering an alternating logic of 'normal' and 'revolutionary' phases in the development of science, and by suggesting that paradigm conflicts in the revolutionary phase knew moments of 'incommensurability' which ultimately prevented their being resolved by fully or exclusively cognitive–rational means. This turn towards naturalism, and this tendency to shift the balance between cooperation and rivalry in favour of the latter, was considerably 'aggravated' both by the Strong Programme initiated by Bloor, Barnes, and Mulkay in Britain in the early 1970s and by the nascent 'field theory' of science and culture which simultaneously emerged from Bourdieu's intellectual workshop in France.

Before discussing these trends in any detail, let me briefly allude to a parallel filiation for a stronger conception of intellectual rivalry which is encountered in political theory, especially where it took its cue from Gallie's germinal account of 'essentially contested concepts' (Gallie 1955–6). As intimated before, the very idea was vaguely anticipated by Mannheim and, in rather more martial and insistent terms, also by Schmitt, to be subsequently taken up in much softer terms (and without reference to either predecessor) by Lukes (1974) and Connolly (1974). For Gallie, concepts, such as 'art', 'democracy', 'social justice', or 'Christianity' were concepts, the proper use of which inevitably involved 'endless disputes about their proper uses on the part of their users'. Although sustained by perfectly respectable arguments and evidence, such disputes were not considered resolvable by rational argument, since core aesthetic, political, or religious terms were invariably both descriptive and appraisive, internally complex, and as a result very much 'open-ended'. To use an essentially contested concept meant using it against other uses, and recognizing that one's own use of it had to be maintained against these; it was 'to use it both aggressively and defensively' (1955–6: 172). The radical impact of this inherent controversiality (i.e. scepticism about the capacity to command rational assent) was still somewhat contained by Gallie's retention of a firm distinction between 'appraisive' and 'scientific' concepts, and his manifest separation between science on the one hand and politics, morality, and aesthetics on the other (1955–6: 196–8). Lukes and Connolly, for their part, partially effaced this latter boundary by transferring the idea of essential contestability to (the philosophy of) social and political science, and applying its relativizing logic to concepts such as 'power', 'politics', 'interest', 'freedom', and 'responsibility'. Predictably, this extension was greeted both by critical rejoinders (e.g. Gray 1983; Wartenberg 1990: 12–17) and by spirited defences, one of which directly compared the contest about 'essential contestability' with the debate on Kuhnian incommensurability and with Rorty's postmodernist concern to 'keep the conversation going' (Garver 1990: 254, 268n.).[6]

Taking their inspiration from Kuhn's new historiography and from the later Wittgenstein's pragmatics of language, British writers such as Bloor, Barnes, Mulkay, MacKenzie, Shapin, and Collins dispensed with dominant normative epistemologies and their functionalist sociological counterparts, in order to approach a naturalistic and agnosticist methodology which revealed science as 'just another' interested social practice (cf. Bloor [1976] 1991; Barnes 1974; Mulkay 1977; Barnes and MacKenzie 1979). In this respect, the Strong Programme's emergent theme of the 'natural' (e.g. intrinsically social) rationality of science rekindled Mannheim's early sociological radicalism, even though the Mannheimian programme itself was routinely dismissed for its supposed 'failure of nerve' in refusing to carry its demystifying sociological toolkit into the walled sanctum of mathematics, logic, and natural science (cf. Pels 1996a). By accentuating the relative independence of intrascientific from extrascientific social interests (cf. Lynch 1993: 67–8, 72), the new sociology of scientific knowledge shifted its analytic focus towards the inner practices and workings of 'hard-core' science, and undertook to dissect this 'internal social' by way of fine-grained empirical studies of scientific controversies and ethnographies of laboratory work. Through its principled dissolution of the cognitive/social dichotomy in the domain of science itself, and its concentration upon the inner politics of scientific fact construction and cognitive conflict, it gradually revealed the decisional, tinkering, locally contingent, and idiosyncratic character of scientific practices, as exemplified by skills of fact construction and literary persuasion, techniques of mobilizing allies and negotiating resources, and strategies of investment in scientific subjects and careers (e.g. Knorr-Cetina 1977; Knorr-Cetina and Mulkay 1983).

This fresh concentration upon the agonistic logic and the inextricable alliance between cognitive and political manoeuvring within the scientific domain also had the effect of tendentially bracketing much of the outside political and social world from analytic sight. This was to a lesser extent the case in Bourdieu's emerging conception of the 'intellectual field', which was set in the broader framework of a general 'political economy of practices' and a generalized vocabulary of profit, capital, credit, and investment. As early as 1966 (first printed in English in 1969), Bourdieu's 'Intellectual Field and Creative Project' emphasized the structural autonomy of the intellectual field as giving rise to a specific logic of competition for cultural legitimacy, according to which intellectual and artistic stances were significantly determined by a field of structurally unequal and agonistically related positions, so that all forms of constraint by outside authorities or interests were necessarily 'refracted' by the competitional structure of the intellectual field itself. Capping his article with a Proustean motto about theories and schools 'which devour each other like microbes and globules', and by their very struggle 'ensure the continuing of life', Bourdieu went on to suggest that conflicts which divided the intellectual field found their ultimate cause at least as much in objective positional factors as in the reasons which the participants gave, to others as well as to themselves, for engaging in them. Open conflicts between tendencies and doctrines often tended to occlude an underlying complicity which constituted the objective unity of the intellectual field of a given period, even though this 'consensus within the dissensus' could only become visible to an outside observer (Bourdieu 1971: 161, 179–80, 183).

A few years later, Bourdieu's classical study of the 'specificity of the scientific field' (1975) sketched a similar picture of the agonistic logic of intellectual rivalry, which was now more frontally contrasted with the 'irenic' and 'hagiographic' image of scientific communitarianism as projected by the Mertonian paradigm. To Bourdieu, the scientific field functioned as a market of scientific goods which was subject to immanent laws which had 'nothing to do with ethics'; indeed, scientists typically euphemized their forcible submission to these laws as an elective obedience to norms of disinterested truth-seeking (1981: 266; cf. 1990: 298). The specific issue and interest at stake in this competition were the monopoly of scientific authority or scientific competence, which identified an indistinguishable mixture of technical capacity and social power. In analysing scientific controversies it was fruitless, Bourdieu maintained, to isolate a purely political dimension from a purely intellectual one, or to distinguish between the strictly scientific and the strictly social; the Mertonian demarcation itself constituted an inseparably social *and* intellectual strategy for imposing a particular delimitation of the object of legitimate argument. A veritable science of science would radically challenge the abstract opposition between the 'internal' analysis of truth conditions and the 'external' analysis of social conditions, since epistemological conflicts were always and inseparably political conflicts. It was the scientific field which, as the locus of a political struggle for scientific domination, assigned to each researcher his or her indissociably political and scientific problems and methods – scientific strategies which were at the same time political investment strategies directed towards maximization of strictly scientific profit, i.e. of potential recognition of researchers by their competitors–peers (Bourdieu 1981: 257–62).

Although Mannheim's work was never cited, it was evident that Bourdieu, leaning backwards across Merton, reinstated much of the former's radical approach to cultural competition, including his liberal mixture of the demystifying metaphors of politics and economics, his view of intellectual conflict as 'refracting' rather than 'reflecting' extraneous group interests, and his crucial appreciation of the emergence of 'truth' from the criss-crossing censure induced by divergent positional interests (cf. Pels 1995a).[7] Obviously, Bourdieu was also far more Mannheimian than Mertonian in his characterization of the constitutive link between the autonomization of the scientific field and its internal 'rivalry constitution'. While, for Merton, scientific autonomy is legislated by the dominant normative structure, which also guarantees the ultimate predominance of cooperation over conflict, for Bourdieu such autonomy is instituted and sustained by means of a corporative politics of interest. It is the uninhibited expansion of the logic of competitional censure within science itself which induces antagonists willy-nilly to cooperate and realize whatever 'truth' there is currently to be gained. In this Smithian rather than Durkheimian image of science, 'organized scepticism' is not organized by norm-abiding sceptics, but rather 'disorganized' by calculating strategists in their interest-driven scramble for recognition. In Bourdieu's market model, producers cannot expect to receive recognition of the value of their products from anyone except other producers, who are simultaneously their competitors, and hence 'least inclined to grant recognition without discussion and scrutiny'. Competitors must not simply distinguish themselves from already recognized (read: powerful, established, authoritative) predecessors, but must also 'integrate their predecessors' and rivals' work into the distinct and distinctive construction which transcends it'. For every competitor, what is at stake is the power to impose the definition of science best suited to their specific interests:

> The definition of what is at stake in the scientific struggle is thus one of the issues at stake in the scientific struggle, and the dominant are those who manage to impose the definition of science which says that the most accomplished realization of science consists in having, being, and doing what they have, are, or do.
>
> (1981: 262–3)[8]

Bourdieu's radical interest theory of science proved foundational for another naturalistic approach which emerged as an influential school of constructivist ethnography of laboratory work during the late 1970s and early 1980s. Freely mixing the generalized metaphors of economics and politics, both Knorr-Cetina's early statements of constructivism (1977; 1981a) and Latour and Woolgar's exemplary study *Laboratory Life* (1979) leaned heavily upon

Bourdieu, although they already sought to modify aspects of his market model of science in a more micro-oriented direction. Knorr-Cetina linked the dynamics of scientific production to a competitive struggle for scientific capital, which was characterized as a struggle for the accumulation of 'say' or of 'holdings' in the scientific 'scriptures' (1977: 687). Latour and Woolgar offered an 'integrated economic model of the production of facts' in which the concept of symbolic capital functioned as central lever of a constructivist analysis of the accumulation and maintenance of scientific credibility. Bourdieu and Foucault were mentioned in a single breath as having together outlined a general framework for a political economy of truth-as-credit. The concept of credibility itself synthesized economics and epistemology by suggesting that cognitive interests and quasi-economic calculations were simultaneous and inseparable. Switching metaphors in free association, Latour and Woolgar assumed that scientists were simultaneously occupied with the rational production of 'hard' knowledge and with the 'political calculation of their assets and investments'. Their political competence stood at the heart of their scientific work: 'the better politicians and strategists they are, the better the science they produce'. There was hence little to be gained from maintaining a distinction between the 'politics' of science and its 'truth': the same political qualities were required both to make a point and to outmanoeuvre a competitor (1979: 197–8, 213, 237–9, 258–9n.).

Soon, however, Knorr-Cetina, Latour, and others waxed more critical of economistic models and metaphors, and began to profile their agonistic conception of science more exclusively in quasi-political terms. It is therefore striking that the modern sociology of science once again exemplifies a growing polarization with regard to the priority of the vocabulary of 'capital' or that of 'power' – a repertoire switch which to a large extent is also a switch of intellectual loyalties from Marx to Nietzsche, or more proximately, from Bourdieu to Foucault.[9] Some of this may be accountable to the effect of scholarly distinction, which induces opponents to sharpen their differences of concept and vocabulary, but another impulse for this displacement may be found in the increasingly articulate dismissal by the younger sociologists of science of the lingering structuralist emphasis of Bourdieu's sociology, and their increasingly self-conscious affirmation of a micro- or actor-oriented methodology. Defending a microsocial and 'situationalist' ethnography of knowledge, Knorr-Cetina soon exchanged a Bourdieu-inspired macro-oriented economics for a more Foucaldian 'microphysics' of power/knowledge:

> As the study of science has shown, to construe a certain representation
> of the world is in principle always at the same time a matter of truth
> (correspondence, equivalence) *and* a matter of political strategy, that
> is of imposing one's say and of instituting certain consequences with
> or against others.
>
> (Knorr-Cetina 1981b: 36–7)

Influenced by Callon's 'actor-network theory', Latour has likewise channelled his elaboration of a radical actionism towards a more exclusively Nietzschean or Foucaldian theory of power. The new vocabulary switch, so it is thought, more easily accommodates the symmetrical extension of the actorial frame from human towards non-human 'actants', and the consecutive broadening of the vocabulary of political representation to include the scientific representation of things (cf. Callon 1986; Latour 1993).[10] Latour's intriguing study of the way in which Pasteur turned into a successful macro-actor by enrolling masses of both human and non-human 'actants' drops economic nomenclature altogether, closely identifies reason and force, and (notoriously) describes science as a 'form of politics continued by other means' (Latour 1984). It is nonsensical, Latour argues, to divorce Pasteur the scientist from Pasteur the politician; by adding the new force of the microbe to the overall balance of forces in society, and by posing as its only legitimate spokespersons, Pasteur and his laboratory turn into a workshop for new assemblies of humans and non-humans which generate unprecedented networks of socio-technical power. In subsequent works, Latour, Callon, and others have only further tightened this associative link between actor-network theory and the extended vocabulary of political representation (Callon 1986; Callon *et al.* 1986; Latour 1986; 1993).

THE POLITICS OF RECOGNITION

At this point I enquire in what sense the model of intellectual disposition, as so far developed, may enlighten the (still rather shapeless) notion of intellectual interest, and circumscribe with greater precision what is the nature of the stakes about which scientists – and intellectuals more generally – find themselves in competition. What are they existentially interested in? What is the specificity of their holdings and doings? How are ideas empowered or capitalized? In what sense are intellectual interests simultaneously describable as material and ideal, external and internal, residential and performative? In order to elucidate such questions I will first recall Mannheim's early views on reputational prestige, and then trace the subsequent handling of this strategically important concept (and related ones such as recognition, credibility, and distinction) in Merton, Bourdieu, and others. There is a twofold purpose to this discussion. First, if the search for recognition or credibility is identified as the primary stake of the intellectual struggle, it will be seen that metaphors of capital and power intrude almost naturally if this idea is put into a more radical key. Second, it will transpire once again that we cannot treat these repertoires as competing alternatives, as is still residually the case in some recent schools in the sociology of science, but should mix their discursive connotations in order to grasp what scientific 'holdings' and 'doings' are specifically about.

In his 1928 essay, as we saw, Mannheim provided an intriguing *aperçu* of the stakes of intellectual competition when intimating that social groups rival with regard to the possession of the 'correct social diagnosis', or at least the *prestige* which its 'proprietors' might derive from it. The undecided, lapidary nature of this formulation alerts to the basic difficulty involved: does the 'correct' social diagnosis resemble a thinglike resource which can be taken into possessive custody, or do 'truth', property, and prestige interact much more closely and critically? The difficulty is similar in Mannheim's adjacent proposition that all knowledge is rooted in the desire for power and recognition of particular social groups, 'even should it prove to be absolute Truth itself'. Perhaps there is some irony in this manner of speaking, but not enough to wave the impression that the relationship between reputational value and the validity which is normally ascribed to truth claims is judiciously left in the dark. Mannheim's linkage between the metaphors of property or power and concepts such as prestige and recognition remains a distinctly 'external' one. He still lacks the radical constructivist insight according to which scientific authority arises from an immediate *fusion* of technical competence and symbolic power, which renders the accumulation of scientific capital (the stabilization of powerful networks) virtually synonymous with the accumulation of credibility itself. Instead, he remains committed to a more traditional Mertonian conception, which sees credit or recognition as a social incentive for the selective reinforcement of truth-seeking behaviour. Recognition, in this view, functions as an external reward for valued role performance, rather than as the 'stuff' of scientific capital itself (cf. Knorr-Cetina 1977: 690n.; 1981a: 70–1).

For Merton, indeed, appropriation of intellectual products is foreclosed by the communal structure of science, leaving only the enjoyment of prestige. Since contributions that are valued as original and true enter into common ownership, recognition is basically divorced from intellectual property. The dispersive effect of the institutional emphasis on originality and priority is sufficiently balanced by the norm of communism, which induces scientists to recognize one another's distinctive contributions. Hence the 'deep and agitated ambivalence towards priority' which is typically manifested in scientific rivalries (1973: 307). While Merton thus accentuates the differences between individual property in science and other forms of property, Bourdieu precisely reintroduces the idiom of scientific capital (as Latour and others reinstate the idiom of power/knowledge) in order to identify a darker logic in which competitional interests play a far more directive role. If recognition, as Merton and Bourdieu would agree, is the true 'coin of the scientific realm', the latter places it in a much harsher analytic light. In his perception, the stakes of the scientific struggle are intrinsically dual, since there is no way to divorce cognitive strategies from strategies for domination, and 'truth' and 'originality' are bound to remain essentially contested honorific terms.

In Bourdieu's analysis, the capital of recognition is unequally shared out between established and newcomers, who permanently struggle about its distribution within the basic parameters of the scientific field. While the dominant (or the haves) are committed to the conservation of the established scientific order, new entrants (the have-nots) struggle for the right of access, and either embark upon a relatively risk-free strategy of succession or upon a much more costly strategy of subversion. Established and newcomers thus cultivate opposite interests which are dictated by their different social positions, but they also share interests which are generic to the field itself, in which they all place a greater or smaller investment. But apart from investing in the game as such and in the strengthening of their own positions, rivalling scientists also, and most significantly, invest *in themselves* as human capital. A socially consecrated reputation, typically condensed in a distinctive 'name', is a form of capital which confers power over the constitutive mechanisms of the field, and is variably convertible into other forms of capital (1981: 266, 269–72). Such 'recognition capital' is simultaneously dependent upon social processes of accrediting (in the broad sense of 'giving credence' or 'extending belief') and incorporated in the individual scientist, who makes a name for him- or herself and through this asserts his or her distinctive value as a legitimate producer.[11]

Intriguingly, a well-reputed name is something which *synthesizes* some of the conventional connotations of property and power, while also appearing to fall in between categorical stools. The competences which it 'names' are both residential and relational, both intimately private and eminently public, both intransitive because incorporated in the person and freely transferable and convertible into alternative sources of power. Such competences transgress the conventional boundaries between the internal and the external in a quite literal sense, since they constitute a form of property (*Eigentum*) which has also become a bodily property (*Eigenschaft*) of a person, or a habitus; it is a form of 'having' which is simultaneously a form of 'being' (cf. Bourdieu 1986: 244–5).[12] Because the original accumulation of intellectual capital is the making of a name, and all producers are obliged to force recognition of their productivity, intellectuals are typically committed to strategies of *distinction* which further the social acknowledgement of their originality. A name is only made by making a difference, by standing out from the crowd: to be is *to be different* in the intellectual field. This profit may be redoubled when the underlying strategic interest – the profit motive itself – is hidden from sight:

> The profit of distinction is the profit that flows from the *difference*, the gap, that separates one from what is common. And this direct profit is accompanied by an additional profit, that is both subjective and objective, the profit that comes from seeing oneself – and being seen – as totally disinterested.
>
> (Bourdieu 1993b: 1)

In Knorr-Cetina's similar view, an intense concern with names routinely pervades all practical work in the scientific laboratory. The name of a famous co-author, a prestigious journal, or a well-received publishing company weighs heavily in scientific calculations of value, as does the name of a respected university or department head. In fact, the question of who a scientist *is* seems literally answered by the string of names which the scientist is able to attach to his or her own in a curriculum vitae: universities attended, institutional positions held, association memberships, fellowships awarded, etc. The value at stake here is not the value of some product, but that of the scientists themselves; unlike the businessman, the scientist who invests his capital invests 'himself' (Knorr-Cetina 1977: 671):

> The string of institutions and positions we find in curricula vitae provides an updated balance sheet for a scientist, not for a product. The quality at issue in choosing an experiment, a piece of apparatus or a journal is the quality of the scientist. And the success to which scientists most often refer is their own. If we want to use the economic metaphor, we can say that scientists' concern with their investments and returns, with the risks and productivity of a line of research, with opportunities, or the interest of results, does indeed refer us to a market. But it is a market of positions where the commodity is scientists, and not a market for the products of free – or semi-free – entrepreneurs.
>
> (Knorr-Cetina 1982: 112)

Similarly drawing on Bourdieu, Latour and Woolgar initially developed an extended notion of credibility which likewise amalgamated cognitive options and quasi-economic calculations, in order to reveal the sheer heterogeneity of interests which were invested in scientists' efforts to enter and speed up their 'cycles of credibility'. Persons accumulate stocks of credentials and receive credit from credit-worthy institutions; their essential ambition is to gain sufficient credibility so as to be able to reinvest it and accumulate various further gains. In this process, no apparent distinction is made between the person (the name) and the 'thing' (the claim), or between the credibility of the proposal and the proposer. Scientific claims are invariably related to who advance them, against the background of reputations, authority positions, and controversies in the agonistic field. The evaluation of problems as 'interesting', of research fields as 'promising', of data, methods, and theories as 'robust', of colleagues and audiences as 'serious' and 'trustworthy', typically merge with calculations which bear upon career strategies, the raising of funds, or the forging of powerful alliances; such considerations all constitute part of a single circle through which one form of credit is converted into another. The curriculum vitae represents a true balance sheet of all previous investments, including the names of persons, positions, institutions, journals, and publishing houses, which all add to the total credit a particular person can effectively mobilize. 'Position' simultaneously indicates academic rank, location in a particular problem field, and socio-geographical location (university, laboratory); it is a highly complex notion which points to the intersection of individual strategy and field configuration, in which neither the field nor the individual are independent variables, and the nature of the positions is constantly the focus of negotation (1979: 197ff.).[13]

Examining such radical conceptions of recognition and credibility, we may reiterate that neither the power nor the property metaphor are fully apposite here, even though each of them does capture part of what there is to say. Intellectual capacity or competence, as expressed in a reputation or recognized name, somehow mediates between 'havings' and 'doings' and between things and actions; it refers to assets which, though immaterial, can be immediately held as incorporated acquisitions which are tied to the individual person. Despite this inalienable core, they can still be externalized, i.e. marketed or used as levers for social mobilization. Closure around the productive force of knowledge immediately entails enclosure of the producers and holders themselves, i.e. their formation into a restricted professional corporation. In the previous chapter, I have laid especial emphasis upon the necessary interaction between the tenure of institutional positions and the incorporated disposition of certified symbolic and organizational skills, and suggested that cultural property is near-to-valueless when not fused with positional and institutional resources.[14]

The preceding discussion likewise underscores that this interaction between personally held and institutionally anchored resources is also crucial to the acceleration (and slowing down) of cycles of credibility in science. Because producers and productive forces partly coincide, the 'force' of such forces significantly depends upon processes of attribution of legitimacy. Personal command of cultural competences is therefore both private and social property, not simply because personal and institutional competences are mutually supportive, but also because they are almost viscerally tied to the production of faith in their 'competential' character. The capitalization of culture, in both its personal and positional dimension, requires a continual upkeep of credibility, of maintenance of belief in its very legitimacy which, as we have seen, is much more intrinsically necessary for cultural creations and intellectual skills than is the case for money capital or material stock (cf. Bourdieu 1991: 192–3). This is another way of saying that social closure around the productive forces of culture and knowledge is intimately linked to the production of belief in their own productivity. A theory of cultural productivity hence necessarily moves in the direction of a theory of rationality and the justification of truth claims, so that cultural closure may adopt the specific form of a monopoly of truth which certifies 'true speakers' and separates the knowledgeable 'haves' from those who 'have not'.

THE DIAMOND PATTERN REVISITED

It is this radical rivalry perspective, inaugurated by Mannheim and Schmitt in the late 1920s, and resuscitated by Bourdieu and constructivist science studies in the 1970s and 1980s, which has offered both the point of departure and the point of return for my present study. Its first objective, of course, has been to shift the account of the origin and meaning of particular social and political concepts tendentially away from purely cognitive explanations towards the analysis of the intrinsic co-production of the cognitive and the social, and thus to advance another step along the high road pointed out by the early sociology of knowledge. Many phenomena that were originally diagnosed as manifestations of immanent laws of the mind, Mannheim declared, could be explained in terms of social-structural patterns. Shifting the analysis away from the manifest content and structure of ideas towards their 'vital' or 'volitional' source could inject new meaning into the old question of 'what intellectual currents really are, what factors determine their inner rhythm'. What from the perspective of traditional intellectual history appeared as an inner dialectic of the development of ideas, the sociology of knowledge revealed as a rhythmic movement which was primarily affected by the twin factors of intellectual competition and generational succession. While competition furnished the motor impulse behind diverse interpretations of the world which expressed the interests of conflicting groups struggling for power, differently situated generations in many cases influenced the principles of selection, organization, and polarization of theories and points of view (1952: 192–3; 1968: 241–2).

In the present study, my aim has been to add precision to Mannheim's argument but also to go beyond it, by sensitizing towards the multilayered nature of the existential determination of thought itself – which is by no means a simple or immediately transparent notion (cf. Merton 1941; Knorr-Cetina and Mulkay 1983: 6). I have insisted more clearly upon the complex filtering of outside interests by inside ones, and upon the impact which such intellectual brokerage has exercised upon the articulated content of social and political concepts. Mannheim's own emphasis on cultural competition already demonstrated that existential determination was not taken in a reductionist sense, and that privileged attention was given to the strategic intermediary position of the professional articulators of ideas, whose interested 'interference' made for a crucial addition of ideological effect to the finished product. However, even though he saw theoretical conflict as a relatively self-contained sphere, Mannheim's enquiry was still slanted towards assessing the way in which economic classes or political elites 'intellectualized' their struggle for power, rather than towards analysing the intimate meshing of theoretical and social conflict in positional struggles inside the intellectual arena itself. If, as Mannheim wrote, it was primarily the conflict of intellectuals which transformed the conflict of interests into a conflict of ideas (1968: 142), he did not clearly acknowledge that intellectual conflicts generate powerful interests of their own, which not only influence the way in which the ideas and interests of external social groups are represented within the intellectual field, but also determine how intellectuals themselves are strategically positioned as spokespersons for competing theoretical standpoints, methods, styles, or schools of thought.[15]

For Mannheim, recognition of the intrinsically social character of knowing implies, crucially, that individuals find themselves in an 'inherited situation' with preformed patterns of thought, which are further elaborated or modified in response to new situational challenges. The fundamentally collective character of knowing impels us to recognize the 'force of the collective unconscious' (1968: 3, 28). Bourdieu has similarly described intellectual choices in terms of 'field assignments': rather than selecting their problems, methods, and strategies of explanation on rational methodological grounds, actors 'inherit' these, or are allocated to specific tasks by the strategic interests which are attached to their different field positions (1981: 262). One dominant purpose of the present study has indeed been to reveal the extraordinary historical stability and 'hardness' of the traditions of property theory and power theory, not just in terms of their diamond-shaped matrix of fission and fusion, but also in terms of the dilemma of primacy and reduction, which in the course of time has adopted a great variety of forms but always conformed to the same basic pattern. The compulsory law-like succession which is inscribed in the diamond pattern of property and power, and the oscillating rhythm which is dictated by their objective constellation of rivalry, constitute regularities which have survived across century-long chains of intellectual inheritance, and exhibit linear changes which can only be registered over extended periods of time.

There is a sublime enigma in this extraordinary power of ideas, which appear to master those who wish to master them, and weigh down so heavily upon human minds that they hardly ever escape from the basic parameters which are set for them. Evidently, intellectuals are appropriated by the same traditions which they set out to appropriate; they enter predefined worlds which are structured by stable divisions, where rejection of one particular option normally enforces the adoption of its traditional alternative. The old procreative metaphor of 'ideas begetting ideas' is therefore not so much out of place as is often suggested by critics of an exclusively 'immanent' history of ideas. Stable intellectual traditions offer the optical illusion of a self-perpetuation of ideas over extended periods of time, in the course of which they appear to invest their human users instead of being invested in and brought to life by them. This is not accountable to a metaphysical property of truthful ideas to persuade and spread, but to the fact that ideas are routinely but unconsciously invested with power, and include power effects in their very formulation. Their performative, mobilizing force is intrinsic in a very special sense, because it lies hidden in definitions and locutions which are designed so as to conceal their empowered nature. Symbols appear forceful and compelling of their own accord, but only because they are suffused with symbolic force as part of their very articulation, and because the motives with which they are charged resonate with the strategic interests of new intellectual recruits who recognize them and are intuitively willing ('called upon') to invest in them.

Whether expressed in the idiom of power/knowledge or in that of cultural capitalization, this is the same idea of the ineradicably interest-committed and agonistic nature of knowledge which has previously been referred to as the principle of 'duality'. In this view, the quest for valid knowledge (for a truthful or adequate representation of reality) is inescapably tied to reputational interests and strategies of intellectual warfare. This means that the logic of intellectual discovery is dominated by a will to mastery which is directed *both* towards reality *and* against intellectual rivals, and that it answers as much to a postulate of adequacy as to the dictates of a configuration of intellectual enmity and friendship. If this duality is indeed irreducible, the concepts which one uses simultaneously describe and mobilize, so that another venerated distinction in social science, that between fact and value, tends to become blurred. If many core concepts of social science are not only tools of cognition and representation but also tools of counter-intelligence, it is useless to prolong Weber's venerated distinction between words that are like swords which are brandished against the enemy, and words that are rather like ploughshares which 'loosen the soil of contemplative thought' (Weber 1970b: 145); the very prospect of being able to melt swords into ploughshares might be no more than a pious idyll.

Mannheim, Merton, and Bourdieu have variously thematized this antinomian logic and the way in which competitional factors affect the dynamic of intellectual polarization and intellectual synthesis. To Mannheim, for example, the very function of rivalling doctrinal currents is to 'gather up' and concentrate fragmented local controversies, which polarize around a few dominant poles or thought styles in the transition from 'atomistic' towards 'monopolistic' intellectual competition. Such competition also produces a drive towards synthesis, since the logic of statement and counterstatement forces each party to 'catch up' with its opponent, and to incorporate the latter's achievements in its own distinctive conceptualizations (1952: 207–8, 212, 221–2).[16] For Merton, cognitive controversy easily leads polarized groups to respond to stereotyped and selective versions of what is being done by the other. This hostile stereotyping induces a 'reciprocity of contempt' between the positions involved and leaves little room for the third, uncommitted party 'who might convert social conflict into intellectual criticism' (1973: 57). For Bourdieu (who of course refuses to separate social and intellectual conflict in this manner), intellectuals simultaneously invest in their distinctive theories or scholarly affiliations and in the intellectual field which envelops and structures their competition, so that opponents in an entrenched theoretical binary usually act as 'objective accomplices' who, while opting for one or the other of the opposing camps, are unable to see that their very antagonism demarcates and encloses the field of legitimate argument (Bourdieu 1981: 282). The concepts which constitute such a binary form *couples ennemis* or antagonistic pairs, which structure the dominant view of social reality by their adversarial relationship, and as such tend to exclude or frustrate alternative options (Bourdieu 1988).[17]

Incorporating elements from these various conceptualizations, the present study has focused upon the field of contestation of a single magnetic antinomy, and ventured to trace in considerable detail how it has expanded and contracted across an extended stretch of historical time. In doing so, it has revealed a distinct triadic pattern of development which advanced from a state of amalgamation in the feudal concept of dominion towards the bipolar division which was drawn by classical absolutist, and most distinctively, by liberal political and economy theory (Figure 9). Increasingly, it set the logic of private material property at right angles to that of political sovereignty, and positioned both as pointlike, totalizing essences which went into a chronic competition for the status of 'last instances' of social ontology. The liberal dichotomy, however, did not mark a final state but once again dissolved in a symmetrically shaped de-differentiating movement, in the course of which the congealed binary gradually melted down, and inaugurated an ever-accelerating process of conceptual fusion which restored elements of the initial feudal view of a stratified and socially conditional disposition over both people and things. As the nascent antinomy opened up cognitive space between its widening poles, an oscillatory pattern of switches and reversals of 'last instances' gathered strength, and gradually fixated a repetitive dilemma of ontological supremacy and reduction. Predictably, this dilemma has once again lost much of its force in the 'postliberal' closure of the semantic space, which has seen accelerating traffic between the previously separate zones of the property–power binary.

In this fashion, the 'semiotic diamond' of property and power helps to frame a diachronic pattern of fission and fusion which may also clarify the emergence, stabilization, and eventual demise of other grand binaries in the Western tradition of thought.[18] It evokes a distinctive pattern of fragmentation and polarization, in the course of which property and power increasingly develop as counter-concepts which are locked in an exclusionary competition for pride of ontological place, a pattern which, past the point of greatest

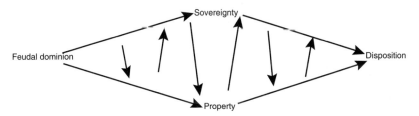

Figure 9 Rivalry within the diamond pattern

amplitude, is once again reversed in a tendential movement of synthesis or 'synonymization'. In doing so, it gradually exhibits the close historical conjunction of both concepts, which derive much of their substantive content from their continually shifting relationship of identity and difference. The diamond pattern hence also excites a strong sense of the historical fragility and variability of the property–power axis, and of the essentially contested nature of all demarcations across it. The first chapters of this study have extensively illustrated how various incidents and qualities shuttled back and forth between the sovereignty bundle and the property bundle before finally being stabilized in the great debates between the absolutist and liberal thinkers. A possessory or thinglike character was first ascribed to the concept of sovereignty, while ownership long continued to be seen as naturally limited, fragmented, and socially obligated. Unlimited and indivisible public authority presupposed limited and partible ownership, while ownership could not be strengthened against political sovereignty without enforcing the latter's partition and social limitation. Hence when the liberal philosophers counterposed an absolutist definition of property to the absolutist notion of political sovereignty, property gradually 'took over' its static, thinglike, and zero-sum connotations, adding the powers of free alienability and heritability which were by the same stroke denied to the exercise of rights of sovereignty.

In this manner, both concepts developed according to a distinct pattern of inverse variation, which simultaneously consolidated the reification of property and the de-reification of public authority. The great liberal divide stabilized the distinction between power as action towards persons and property as action upon things and, by absolutizing the right of private property, ultimately promoted the confusion between the legal interest in things and the things themselves. But the diamond pattern also affirms the absence of any ontological affinity or logically necessary association between property and things, or between power and persons; it highlights the essentially contested and negotiable character of their scope of action, and the principled instability and reversibility of their mutual demarcations. This becomes especially clear in view of the renewed traffic between the two concepts which is set in motion during the gradual meltdown of the liberal dichotomy, which once again dissolves the unitary view of ownership into a 'bundle of rights' conception, and relaxes the strict connection between property rights and material assets. Increasingly, both property and power are generalized to encompass various incidents and connotations which originally belonged to either of them exclusively, and ultimately shade into metaphors which are in principle applicable to the whole chain of assets and actions which structure social life. This double metaphorization breaks down much of the demarcative specificity which originally obtained between the liberal domanial conceptions, and diminishes the area of contest in which they can operate as alternative last instances of social ontology.

PROFITS AND LOSSES OF THE DIALECTIC

In its triadic progression from unity to divorce and back to reunion, the diamond pattern closely transcribes and resembles another venerable figure of thought, which is likewise structured in terms of polarization and synthesis: the Hegelian dialectic. If, as Mannheim also saw, social thinking is often dialectically patterned, what indeed explains its characteristically adversarial law of motion, its antinomian drive? In the above, we have already sufficiently emphasized the inseparability of cognitive and social dimensions in intellectual development in order to escape the conventional alternative of a Hegelian immanentist explanation of its inner dynamic, or a vulgar Marxian account in terms of the reflection of external material interests. The complex model of refraction and modification of extraneous by internal factors of intellectual change methodically resists both the idea of a primordial logic of antithesis and synthesis in human thought and that of a dominating *Realdialektik* (in this case, of the parallel but competitive formation of sovereign states and liberal markets in early modern Europe, and the recent realignment of political and economic institutions) which is transposed more or less faithfully into thought (in this case, the pattern of fission and fusion of property and power). In this perspective, it is less fruitful to ponder whether the 'ideational' diamond duplicates or reflects the dynamic of a 'material' diamond lying underneath, as it is to elucidate the essentially *performative* relationship between conceptual developments and 'real' historical developments, which cannot be epistemologically divorced from one another.

Concepts such as sovereignty and property, as we repeatedly found, were never simply descriptive but simultaneously 'directional' (in Mannheim's sense) or polemical (in the belligerent sense suggested by Schmitt). They invariably functioned as 'banner concepts' raised by intellectual vanguards of and spokespersons for the larger (and eventually collision-bound) political movements to *institute* or *defend* the autonomy of sovereign states and/or the autonomy of unconstrainedly operating economic markets. However, this performative logic was simultaneously enhanced and concealed by the essentialist or 'emanatist' grammar of both concepts in their early modern definitions. They both succeeded in reifying a political *project* into an ontological *object*, transcribing as an ultimately constitutive 'last instance' what was still to be constituted as such, and hence performatively securing as already existent what was still to be politically performed. When the *Politiques* or the Hobbesians described the plenitude and 'perfect singleness' of sovereign power as divine or natural fact, they were simultaneously working to concentrate it in a single institutional point. When liberals copied this model in order to exalt the monistic and absolute nature of private property, they were similarly attempting to naturalize and certify it as a single 'thing', to be reared simultaneously against the scalar structure of the feudal institutional legacy, and as an alternative 'last instance' against the concentrated primacy of established political sovereignty itself.

'Last instance' claims (professions of the ontological primacy of the political or the economic) tend to 'act upon' rather than simply to reflect the real. But precisely because the objectivist dialectic refuses to acknowledge this performative effect (or rather, actively represses it), such claims may acquire an independent causal logic, by partly bringing about what they appear only disinterestedly to describe. As noticed before, the essentializing Hegelian and Marxian dialectic could function as an efficient grammar of dissimulation because it invested its grounding concepts with a typical slippage between part and whole, a slippage which already announced itself in the early modern 'nuclear' or 'solar' theories of public office and private ownership. These theories proclaimed, as we have seen, that sovereignty or property remained substantially one and indivisible even if subordinate rights of political magistracy or material usufruct were abstracted from them. Hence they tended to be conceived as radiating, procreative wholes which somehow always remained present in their own parts as originary, energetic, and transcendent essences, permitting a structural ambiguity to settle at their very core which the dialectic preserved in a more explicit and logically more spectacular form. By conceptualizing this ambiguity in terms of a unity-in-contradiction, the objectivist dialectic also specified that the whole – which normally related to the part as classificatory genus to specific difference – could also turn against its own particular and (onto)logically 'contradict' it. (Onto)logical contradictions, it further implied, were peculiarly 'restless'; they harboured a principle of necessary motion or self-transcendence which ultimately forced them to turn themselves inside out. A logical contradiction between (or within) concepts was projected onto the structure of the real world, which was henceforth considered subject to an immanent law of dialectical self-transcendence. Effacing the constitutive presence of the theorist, this self-denying (and self-serving) transmutation was equally characteristic of the Hegelian dialectic of *Geist* and statehood as it was of the Marxian dialectic of 'civil society' and 'economic production'.

The dialectic of part and whole, as crystallized in the causality of last instances, turned sovereignty and property into concepts for mastery, and their respective sciences into 'master sciences' with a barely disguised imperial drive. By allowing a permanent drift from partial object to holistic project, their territorial and methodological demarcations went far beyond the need to establish disciplinary autonomy and distinctiveness; the very definition of their objects and their ontological primacy was clearly intended as a way of securing a primary and dominant legitimacy for each. This is also to imply that the rivalling claims for the primacy of politics or the primacy of economics never merely expressed the ambitions of rising political elites (e.g. the early modern state bureaucracy) or economic classes (e.g. the early modern bourgeoisie), but were simultaneously *intellectual* projects, and hence projects of *intellectuals* (such as the court lawyers and political jurists of the absolutist age, or the classical liberal spokesperson for a democratic capitalism). The liberal dogma of the 'propertyless' nature of public authority and the 'powerless' nature of private property, by underscoring the 'natural' self-sufficiency of civil society over against the state, profited the bourgeois class in so far as it advanced its claims to social distinction and functional necessity – so much so that 'property' and 'civil society' became honorific synonyms of the aspiring bourgeoisie itself – while it simultaneously 'naturalized' or 'externalized' them as an inherent feature of objective reality itself. A similar erasure of the interested nature of these representations was conspicuous in the adversarial tradition of political absolutism, where concepts such as 'sovereignty' and 'state', and the proclamation of their divinely or naturally ordained priority over society, likewise substituted ideologically for the interest of the political stratum which had allied itself with the centralizing crown.

However, in both cases the substitutive chain was longer and more complex, as a result of the superadded projections of 'organic' intellectual elites who offered themselves as spokespersons for either of the two political causes. If the 'last instances' of sovereignty and property were euphemized expressions for the political and economic classes themselves, they were theoretically forged by a stratum that invariably imposed its own intellectualist trademark upon the form and substance of the concepts involved. Increasingly, such master concepts also came to legitimate the needs of the legitimators themselves; 'last instances' also polemically expressed the identity of specific groups of intellectuals against rival ones: their urge for distinction, their quest for theoretical certainty, and their will-to-power in the field of ideas. A second-order projection was thus imposed upon the first-order one, since such interests were similarly 'exteriorized' in order to reappear as inherent properties of the object itself. As Bourdieu (1993b: 1) has also seen, intellectuals may cultivate an interest in 'economism', since it allows them to dissimulate their strategies of distinction and disinterestedness, and inscribe these as invisible codes in their 'last instance' conceptual schemes, thus earning for them the accolade of impartial, disinterested truth.[19] It is abundantly clear that we may duplicate this insight for 'politicism', which similarly permits intellectuals to project onto the object what is specifically due to their own (rivalry-committed) mode of producing it. If 'His Majesty the Economy' or 'His Majesty the State' are partly revealed as the character masks of wilful intellectuals, we are duty bound to reduce these concepts to more human and mundane proportions. A Last Instance is often also a 'theorist writ large'. Removing the surplus meaning produced by this 'metonymic fallacy' may provide the intellectual spokesman with a more realistic appreciation both of 'his instance' and of his own self.

In previous chapters, I have introduced a differentiated political–geographical zoning model which sought to organize a variety of paradigmatic experiences of state–society relations and the way in which these were

processed in various 'last instance' conceptualizations. This political topography of knowledge, in distinguishing a central zone of advanced capitalism, a
modernizing semiperiphery, and a retarded periphery, identified three distinct
structural settings which simultaneously constituted intellectual spaces in
which the primacy question of property and power was differently addressed. In
the Anglo-Saxon liberal conception of market-based *Gesellschaft*, civil society
was rather sharply demarcated from the state, with the purpose of emphasizing
its functional autonomy and productive priority over all 'immaterial' and
especially political relations. In the opposite German–Italian tradition of
entrepreneurial statism (and in the anarchist tradition, which repeated its logic
by putting it under a negative sign), the state continued to be seen as encompassing and energizing civil society, which was never conceived as an
independent entity, but was recurrently mobilized in nationalist and productionist revolutions initiated from above. Accordingly, the weight of causal
determination in the last instance tended to be placed at the far end of the institutional spectrum. In the intermediate zone, for which France was suggested as
exemplary, state–society relations were most typically conceived in terms of a
gradient of mediating corporations which connected rather than severed the
extremes of political state and economic market, while civil society itself was
not so much defined in opposition or subordination to the state but as coextensive with the broad range of these mediating institutions themselves. Marxism,
I also suggested, offered an especially intriguing case because it straddled the
two zones (advanced and peripheral) in which the state–society split was
pictured as a binary, although the order of primacy was reversed. Indeed, it
effectively legitimated (but also dissimulated) the political as a 'first instance'
medium under the cover of the 'last instance' determination of the economic.
Early sociology, finally, was seen to emerge in its most representative form from
the intermediate zone, defining a 'third' object/project which was most closely
aligned with corporatist ambitions to promote a mixed socialized economy
and an equally mixed or societalized state.

Against this differentiated knowledge-geographical background, the
imperial dialectic of part and whole – which was virulently active in all three
wings of emerging social theory – transcribed different efforts to universalize
and 'essentialize' historical experiences which were both socially and geographically restricted. The historical reality of the three knowledge-political spaces
exhibited a gradient of institutional differences which to some extent ordained
different positionings in terms of politics vs. economics, or power vs. property.
But in all three intellectual traditions – liberal, corporatist, and etatist – the
formulation of basic causal axioms tended to 'overflow' the limited historical
context in order to define a universal ontological condition. The *pars pro toto*
logic of the dialectic invariably suggested that the range of institutions (the
capitalist market, the modernizing state, the professional corporations) which
were identified as effective modernizing agents in these various settings, were
called upon by necessitarian laws of history to perform the work of moderniza-

252

tion in *all* conceivable contexts. This ontological exaggeration considerably sharpened the 'binary urge' or dichotomizing drive of conceptualizations along the property–power axis, and the dilemmas of reductionary inversion which were repetitively deployed around it.

In this way, we can also focus the autonomous contribution of the dynamic of intellectual rivalry which, by taking the grand binary and its dilemma of reduction as given, was germane in structuring various definitions and arguments in terms of a reificatory ontology of 'last instances'. The dialectic of power which was detected in theoretical anarchism and radical conservatism – and which, with a different emphasis, was also discernible in the revisionist socialist and the sociological traditions – turned out to be symbiotically chained to the counter-dialectic of production and property, as it was most representatively encountered in classical liberalism and Marxism. Part of the very definition of such 'last instances' was seen to derive from the sociological fact that they were very much at stake in games of inversion, and of inversion of inversion, which aimed at subordinating the opponent's last instance to one's own. The sheer 'emanative' centrality of master concepts such as power/politics or property/production, the ambiguous demarcation of their domanial scope, and the reduction of the opposite category to a special case or functional derivative of the one which was accorded primacy, can all be put in clearer perspective if they are viewed as signatures of a stable and objectified constellation of intellectual conflict.

The adversarial law of motion, which the dialectic ascribes to the immanent force of cognition itself, is hence to some extent induced by the urge for distinction felt by theorists who are interested in inverting the loyalties of their intellectual opponents, and who embrace the alternative option in a ready-made and taken-for-granted conceptual polarity. If we continue in this Mannheimian and Bourdieuan vein, we may also see how the factors of competition and generation operate together, when established and newcomers to a specific field become enmeshed in conflicts of succession which either perpetuate the prevailing intellectual orthodoxy (or reform it within authorized limits), or heretically subvert it. Such a composite picture may be helpful in elucidating specific patterns of discursive continuity (e.g. the extraordinary historical stability of the diamond pattern of property and power) as well as specific reversals of vocabulary (e.g. particular switches from property theory to power theory or vice versa), while, simultaneously, rivalling theorists continue to invest in the game as such, in which the contest for primacy is largely taken for granted and ordains fixed choices of vocabulary and method

Bourdieu's logic of distinction also clarifies the 'closure effect' which is exercised by the competing but complicitous master sciences and their jointly produced dilemma of reduction. On both sides we sensed an urge to objectify the adversary, to reverse the adversary's facts and arguments, or to 'set him back upon his feet'. But this objectifying urge was not itself objectified or turned around to its point of origin. The property and power repertoires, while being able to 'speak one another's silences' in some critical areas of theory and practice, simultaneously failed to rise to an awareness of the larger constellation in which they held each other prisoner. In this respect, their historical antagonism offers a dramatic illustration of the law of 'crossed blindness and lucidity' which Bourdieu considers a ubiquitous feature of intellectual, artistic, and political fields (cf. Bourdieu 1979: 10). Both camps have sought to accentuate differences to the exclusion of much else, and have kept silent about the investments which each of them made in the game as it was also played by the adversary. The closure effect of this subterranean 'consensus within the dissensus' is still acutely felt, especially where the survival of the dilemma of reduction has prohibited an adequate comprehension of the new competences and types of disposition which have arisen at the structural intersection of civil society and state, and which characterize the new technologies and new elites which drive the emerging 'knowledge society'.

THE REFLEXIVE DIAMOND

In this final section my purpose will be to follow the dynamics of the diamond pattern in its de-differentiating or converging movement, and see where it may leave us, if we look back upon the general framework and critical results of the present study. The diamond's 'Eastern half' suggests the image of a progressive entanglement of private (or economic) and public (or political) relations and of real and personal rights, and hence documents a growing intertwinement of the previously separate rationalities of property and power. This converging trend also reflects a political–geographical concentration process, since the previous articulation of three differentiated zones in the European West (advanced Anglo-Saxon, intermediate French, and retarded East–South) is increasingly blurred and condensed by the mixed economy and polity of the postwar democratic welfare states. In this new social topography of knowledge, the gradual contraction of the legs of the diamond also reduces the cognitive space for vocabulary switches and reductionary moves, and thus tends to slow down the pendulum swing of property and power. However, the weight of the inherited rivalry constellation and its patrimony of problems and certainties is still such that germs of this 'last instance' logic remain residually active – hence the double trend towards conceptual generalization of both property theory and power theory, each of which works to expand its basic vocabulary in order to chart this osmotic movement, without laying the primacy question finally to rest. Even though both concepts are progressively de-reified and de-essentialized, and presently favour overlaps and mixtures over sharp delineations, their 'synonymic' convergence is still arrested by hereditary loyalties to either one of the previously conflicting traditions.

Once again, I presuppose the existence of a *performative* relationship between conceptual trends and 'real' developments which can now be epistemologically radicalized for the diamond graph as a whole. The commanding notion of a reversal of the liberal dichotomy and of a mutual interpenetration of economic and political rationalities marks a secular trend line (which is not necessarily linear in its development, and remains contested both in quantitative and qualitative terms) around which intellectual rivalries are deployed which are both constrained and underdetermined by it. Such conceptions 'pull and push' reality rather than simply reflect it, and are to some extent designed to further or arrest the perceived tendency around which they are grouped. The rivalry game presumes a commitment to the game as such and hence a loosely agreed-upon demarcation of the playing field, which often coincides with the field of consensus defined by such a broad empirical trend. As we have seen, the structure and evolution of fundamental concepts such as property and power in their double generalization drive are 'dictated' as much by such actual and long-documented processes of de-differentiation (cf. Kraemer 1966; Shonfield 1978; Hall 1986; Beck 1993),[20] as they are shaped by the relatively autonomous dialectic of polarization and synthesis on the level of intellectual competition itself. In this regard, theoretical terms and linkages (such as the very presumption of a growing convergence between economy and polity) are at once 'objective' and 'projective'; they act not only upon such presumably 'underlying' realities but also upon the relations of force that obtain on the independent level of the politics of knowledge.

In this fashion, some kernel concepts and propositions in social and political theory are encrusted with rivalry effects and present a decomposable mixture of 'artificial' theory and 'real' substantive content. Much of what was offered as dependable knowledge under the aegis of property and power theory in their essentialist forms has been revealed as an artificial by-product of interest-laden intellectual competition. But I have also presumed that access to the world of 'facts' is routinely mediated by such partisan interests, and that the entrance which intellectuals force to their object is generically overdetermined or 'contaminated' by their relationship with their rivals. After Mannheim, Schmitt, and Gallie, this also supports Sloterdijk's idea of a 'transcendental polemics', which likewise demythologizes the pathos of value-freedom in presuming a primordial coalition between the production of knowledge and polemical interests. Our object of study, he suggests, is most often a literal *object*, which stands against us, which stands in our way (Sloterdijk 1983: 652ff.). One might add that objects never stand out on their own but are always 'occupied' by others who have invested in them, who have 'mixed their labour with them', and are hence easily seduced to think of them in terms of ownership. The dispossession of the present occupants is a powerful and legitimate motive for intellectuals who enter particular scientific or ideological fields. The urge to disbelieve one's competitors, to reverse their arguments, to put them under hermeneutic suspicion, to decimate their facts, to embarass them with new ones, are 'opportunistic' desires and interests which appear entirely necessary to the progress of scientific work. In this respect, the logic of scientific discovery is as much a matter of how to find facts and organize them into theories as how to win friends and make (the right) enemies.

If this urge for distinction is perhaps the temptation and original sin of all 'politics of theory', it appears ideologically poisonous only if it goes unmonitored; or otherwise, if it is projected outward in order to organize the epistemological disappearance of the producer from his or her product and to crystallize as an immanent property of reality itself. It is less risky to invest oneself in one's theories or to be present in one's objects, as it is to dissimulate this and hide behind the false objectivity of one's own creations – like Marx (or Smith) hid himself behind the Economy and Bakunin (or Schmitt) hid himself behind the State. Much of what is new in intellectual work can only emerge and flourish because it is carried forward by polemical drives, which permit it to gain strength and to survive in continual confrontation with established views. Intellectual discoveries are more seriously indebted to prior institutionalized rivalries than is often acknowledged in their mature, positively stated versions; their negatory potential is sometimes more important and effective than their 'positive' content. *Determinatio negatio est*, which may also mean that affirmations are euphemized negations. The logic of intellectual rivalry and the logic of intellectual articulation are simply one of a kind. Intellectuals who deny the presence or importance of rivals deny their own interests – in their own interests.

Both the productive and the risky dimensions of intellectual competition are highlighted by a central feature of the diamond pattern which, as emphasized earlier, shows a linear accretion of stratificational weight, throughout its long march from fission to fusion, of the variable of intellectual interest itself. Even though economic class interests or the interests of political elites are effectively overdetermined by the logic of intellectual spokespersonship from the very beginning, one may trace a gradual emancipation and autonomization of these intellectuals over against the groups which they organically represent (and of the intellectual field as a whole *vis-à-vis* the domains of politics and economics). If so, the impact of intellectual rivalry and of theoretical politics is increasingly significant in 'refracting' the *Realdialektik* of state and market formation, and performs as an ever-more potent catalyst of the two-tracked evolution of the master sciences of property and power. This secular trend only accelerates in the converging sector of the diamond where, as the previous chapter has extensively shown, the 'intellectualizing' process of the emerging knowledge society is sufficiently advanced so as to penetrate and increasingly dominate the fields of politics and production themselves. To an ever larger degree, the intertwinement of economic and political domains and rationalities is prompted and 'supervised' by the emergent logic of reflexive modernization, which is carried by a rising class of 'knowledgeable organizers' or highly educated general managers, who find themselves equally at ease in political offices and cultural bureaucracies as in the boardrooms of private and public corporations.[21]

The irony of the diamond scheme is that this epochal recasting of the inter-relations between culture, politics, and economics cannot be adequately grasped in terms of the conventional adversarial logic of property vs. power, nor be sufficiently elucidated by the double metaphorization to which both concepts have been subjected in more recent times. As we have seen, even the sociological tradition, which in a sense 'rose through the middle' of the grand binary, outlined a corporatist rather than a liberal or etatist view of civil society, and more fully anticipated the problematics of 'knowledgeable organization' and the New Class, ultimately sided with the power tradition, and developed an imperial dialectic which repeated the structure of the reductionist economic and political dialectic against which it had forged its intellectual identity. This 'third' rationality of the knowledge society, which no longer equates rationalization with sectoral differentiation, but directs a process of de-differentiation of politics, economics, and culture under the sign of institutionalized reflexivity, is a slowly surfacing rock on which traditional categorizations of property and power tend to founder. The central puzzle of power/knowledge or cultural capital can no longer be addressed in terms of residual 'last instance' ontologies or mutually exclusive metaphorizations. Instead, we should freely mix both sets of connotations (the 'residential' or 'static' imagery of property and the 'active' or 'performative' imagery traditionally associated with power) in order to do full justice to the inseparably hard *and* soft, private *and* social, open *and* closed, internalized *and* externalized, substantial *and* relational, thinglike *and* definition-dependent character of cultural competences and the closure strategies which develop around them. As capacities which are firmly embodied in natural persons, institutionalized in social apparatuses, and reified into technologies, they also act as singularly volatile and transferable mobilizing forces – while remaining uniquely dependent upon the play of negotiation, the mobilization of trust, and the maintenance of credibility. That is to say, their composite heterogeneity as havings *and* doings is only grasped in its full complexity if all traces of the old binary are conclusively erased.

This latter adhortation enables us to highlight a final and crucially relevant feature of the diamond, which does not attempt to dodge its own performative rules, and hence also acts upon and advocates what it has seemingly set out merely to describe and explain. I do not wish to deny that the present reconstruction of the fission–fusion pattern files a claim to 'truth' in the sense of correspondence with or representation of historical reality as we currently know it (as best we can). It is no less clear that my bird's-eye view of the dilemma of reduction presupposes something like a 'total' view which aims at assimilating and superseding merely partial views which are innocent of the constraints and repetitions that are imposed by the larger constellation of rivalry in which they are embedded. Such a totalizing ambition is also implicit in Bourdieu's analysis of the 'law of mutual objectivation' and of forms of 'antagonistic complicity' which operate in scientific and other fields. Indeed,

257

all varieties of ideology critique logically presuppose something like a third position from which a configuration of rivalling viewpoints is comprehensively surveyed, and which promises to escape from the dilemmas which they coproduce in their game of reciprocal unmasking. The diamond scheme represents a critically transcendent perspective if only for this bird's-eye view of the grand binary and its zigzagging pattern of mutual reduction, which none of the individual theories that compose it are able fully and clearly to perceive.

But if the truth is still in the whole, as Hegel already insisted, how can this wisdom be squared with the Foucaldian conviction that there is no truth outside power? How, indeed, do we rhyme it with the fact that the Hegelian dialectic of totalization has also constituted the original sin of all ideology critique, always maintaining a fatal silence about the reflexive parameters of the totalizing standpoint itself? This can only be accomplished if we emphasize that the position of judgement adopted here is neither value neutral nor interest free, and that 'totality' in our case should never be conceived as suprapartisan and objectively transcendent, but remains another partial intellectual construct. The diamond (Figure 10) first of all offers a *retrospective* model which is only imaginable from the specific interests and prejudices of the present; it presupposes a specific position in the contemporary intellectual field and a correlative politics of theory which doubly negates the property and power traditions and their complicitous dilemma of reduction.[22] Hence it claims to be self-reflexive and self-consciously performative, for pleading the extension of the same pattern of synonymic closure which it historically describes. Its true point of origin and source of intellectual energy are therefore not to be found at the far left (or in the far west), but rather at the far right (or far east) of the scheme, at a location which is only stabilized by extrapolating the dual trend towards its point of intersection. The entire movement is now retro-constructed, in conscious circularity, departing from its end result. Its 'finalism' does not run from left to right but against the current of historical time, and projects the hermeneutic circle backwards from its place of ultimate arrival. If this preserves the formal structure of the Hegelian dialectic in its singular progression from the *Entzweiung* of its 'alienated moments' towards their *Aufhebung* in a final synthesis, it removes all traces of objectivism, teleology, and foundationalism in favour of a radical tenet of epistemological circularity, a robust mixture of facts and values, and an equally strong presumption of performative reflexivity.

This performative logic also infuses other claims and solutions which I have advanced in the course of my work. Neither the postulate of an impending osmosis between state and civil society, nor that of a New Class which rises at their point of intersection is politically innocent in the sense of simply reflecting an empirical state of affairs. They are 'interested' observations which simultaneously claim adequacy of representation and function as polemical tools against rivals in the intellectual and political field. Indeed, the very notion of the relative autonomy or *sui generis* character of knowledge, culture,

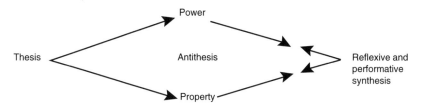

Figure 10 The reflexive diamond

and science, and the independent stratificational weight of intermediary strata such as managers, bureaucrats, or intellectuals is a value-ridden one, and logically presupposes the entire configuration of knowledge-political rivalry from which such judgements are retrojected. This 'logical proximity' of cognition and evaluation has also influenced my terminological escape from the reductionary dilemma. Alternative concepts such as 'disposition' and 'closure' are explicitly negative in neutralizing the traditional opposition between property theory and power theory and in radicalizing their synonymization, without being intended as neutral concepts in the deeper epistemological sense of value-neutrality. Disposition and closure are similarly evaluative and contestable as the concepts which they set out to replace. But if the principle of performativity and fact–value duality has something to it, this does not by itself count as a good reason *not* to replace them.

Perhaps I may end my narrative here, not by 'closing the account' but by offering another suggestion which invites work rather than assent, and is therefore likewise set in a tentative mode. I have suggested earlier that the doctrinal opposition between property theory and power theory is only one of a larger assembly of conflicts in which the contestants are simultaneously unwitting accomplices. It is hoped that the detailed analysis of this particular rivalry has erected some methodological signposts for a similar investigation of other *summae divisiones* of the social-scientific field. I venture to predict – and have sometimes implicated – that the fact–value contest, the contest between consensus and coercion theory, that of action vs. structure, or that of objectivism vs. subjectivism, display many of the traits and regularities which have been discovered in the case of property vs. power. Such grand disputes appear at least plagued by a similar politics of rivalry and similar dilemmas of reduction, and by movements of convergence and synthesis which have similarly failed to lay these dilemmas conclusively to rest. I dare not pronounce here upon the intriguing question whether (and how) such major divisions mutually enhance each other, or rather intersect at right angles, or still otherwise, simply coexist without significant area of contact. To be able to do so would require nothing less than what Proudhon would have described as a 'System of Sociological Contradictions'. Needless to say, we are still at some distance from such a formidable undertaking.

NOTES

INTRODUCTION

1 Parsons (1967: 319–20) briefly mentions property, but his treatment remains fragmentary and unimpressive. 'It is one of the most disturbing, though characteristic, aspects of Parsons' social theory', Gouldner has commented, 'that it has undertaken only the most superficial probing into the nature of property' (1970: 304ff.). Even though Parsons is benignly judged to be 'somewhat better' in this respect than other functionalists, Gouldner's only other reference is to Smelser; Wilbert Moore is excepted in a footnote, while Kingsley Davis's extensive treatment of property in *Human Society* (1970 [1948–9]) is not mentioned. It remains true that *early* American sociology was much more focally concerned with the property question than its structural–functionalist heir (cf. Veblen 1898). Cf. also Commons (1899–1900: 9ff.), in anticipation of major themes subsequently developed in his *Legal Foundations of Capitalism* (1924).

2 While they both maintain that the two dimensions are reciprocally related, Runciman and Bottomore also personify opposite preferences in this grand dilemma. In this respect, they are fully representative of the great historical contest between sociological 'power theory' and Marxist 'property theory', which is discussed extensively below. While Bottomore remains faithful to the 'last instance' primacy of the economy, Runciman adopts 'authority' or 'power' as the basic dimension of social structure, which determines a universal inequality between rulers and ruled (1963: 22–9). Elsewhere he notes that the 'chicken-and-egg debate' on the primacy of economic class or political power does not admit of a solution on its own reductionist terms, but this does not prevent him from asserting an allegedly 'empirical' principle of precedence of political power over property (Runciman 1974: 62–3).

3 Cf. Etzioni-Halévy (1993); earlier examples are found in Bottomore (1966), Olsen (1970), and Balbus (1971). Cf. also Scott (1996) for a rehabilitation of elite theory vs. class theory.

4 Proudhon anxiously dismissed all suggestions that his intellectual property might similarly be the result of theft. However, the idea (if not the literal formula) could already be found in Brissot's *Recherches sur la propriété et le vol* (1780); it was also anticipated by Saint-Simon, Morelly, and Babeuf, and can even be traced to Locke and the Fathers of the Church (cf. Proudhon 1982 II: 182n.).

260

1 THE LIBERAL DICHOTOMY AND ITS DISSOLUTION

1 'The most general use of "power" in English is as a synonym for capacity, skill, or talent. As "power to act" it merges into the physical concept of energy as the capacity to do "work"' (Wrong 1979: 1). Kahn-Freund (1949: 20) speaks about property as a *Vermögen*, the sum total of a man's assets, irrespective of their nature. Originally, Latin *proprius* is equally applicable to physical things or qualities, meaning 'own' or 'peculiar' as opposed to *communis*, 'common', or *alienus*, 'another's'. 'Even before it becomes a legal term, "property" is an abstraction of the idea of what *distinguishes* an individual or thing from a group or from another' (Donahue 1980: 31). As is illustrated below, a number of modern theories of property are effectively returning to the seventeenth-century idea which tended to conflate property–*Eigenschaft* and property–*Eigentum*. Cf. Pocock (1985: 56–7); cf. also notes 11 and 13.

2 This set of issues is extensively treated in Chapter 6.

3 Pollock and Maitland (1899: 230–1) spoke of the feudal system of law as denying the division between 'public' and 'private':

> Just in so far as the ideal of feudalism is perfectly realised, all that we can call public law is merged in private law: jurisdiction is property, office is property, the kingship itself is property; the same word *dominium* has to stand now for *ownership* and now for *lordship*.

Raymond Aron has written that 'A regime of the Soviet type, in distinction to a regime of the Western type, tends to re-establish the confusion between the concepts of society and state' (1986: 156). See also the essays collected in Keane (1988), especially Rupnik (1988).

4 'Property is essentially the distributive system in its static aspect' (Davis 1970: 452).

5 In this context, Clegg (1989) has introduced a distinction between a dominant modernist or 'foundationalist' tradition in the theory of power, which extends from Hobbes to Lukes, Giddens, and Wrong, and a more marginal 'proto-post-modernist' current which originates with Machiavelli and finds present-day advocates in Foucault, Callon, Latour, and Clegg himself. While the former tradition worked from an originary and unitary conception of power as *agency*, the latter tradition has been more sensitive towards power as a product of contingent *strategy* and context-bound *negotiation*, a contrast which Clegg also identifies with a more normative and benevolent vs. a more realist and conflictual interpretation. It is questionable, however, whether this distinction between agency and strategy really holds, and whether the contrast between a Hobbesian and a Machiavellian theory of power is relevant to the historical kinship between power and action as it is defined in this study. While modern sociologists seem far removed from notions of 'legislative' sovereignty, 'Machiavellians' such as Callon and Latour have consistently adopted a Hobbesian strategic model of agency (e.g. Callon and Latour 1981). Their actor–network model, in conceiving of the power of macro-actors as resulting from strategic 'translation' by micro-actors, does not overturn but rather preserves the historical alliance between power and agency as presently defined.

6 One example *ex contrario*, which illustrates the extent to which the imputation of powers to objects has retreated from modern Western thought, is of course found in Marx's treatment of the 'fetishism of commodities'. The commodity is precisely

called a fetish because the world of commodity production is a world upside down, in which the products of human labour have escaped the grasp of their producers, and quasi-humanly dictate their authors' social behaviour. The reversed relationship between man and object entails both a personification of the object and a reification of the person:

> the relations connecting the labour of one individual with that of the rest appear not as direct social relations between individuals at work, but as what they really are, material relations between persons and social relations between things . . . their own social action takes the form of the action of objects, which rule the producers instead of being ruled by them.
>
> (Marx 1867: 77–9)

7 Cf. Kymlicka's (1990: 103ff.) critical discussion of the liberal principle of self-ownership as advanced by Nozick (1974). Cf. Ryan (1994) for a similar critique.

8 However, there are ambiguities and inconsistencies in Blackstone's theory of property rights, which suggest that his theory of property was perhaps closer to modern functionalist notions about property as a rule-governed social artifice (Whelan 1980).

9 Iris Young has voiced similar concerns in terms of the more general concept of rights:

> Rights are not fruitfully conceived as possessions. Rights are relationships, not things; they are institutionally defined rules specifying what people can *do* in relation to one another. Rights refer to *doing* more than *having*, to social relationships that enable or constrain action.
>
> (1990: 25)

10 As Austin was to put it much later: 'an independent political society is divisible into two portions: namely, the portion of its members which is sovereign or supreme, and the portion of its members which is merely subject' (1954 [1832]: 216). On Austin's equally substantialist conception of property, see Waldron (1988: 48–9).

11 This is paralleled by a shift in the meaning of the term 'wealth' or the 'state of weal' as the subject matter of economics. The older meaning of a *state* or *condition* of human beings was lost sight of, and wealth came to be regarded as certain material possessions *of* human beings. At present, Cannan has presciently observed, we must take 'wealth' again as having reverted to its old meaning of a particular state or condition of human beings (Cannan 1917: 1, 13). Similar shifts are discernible in the meaning of property, developing from the broad meaning of 'Propriety' as that which is proper to someone or something, towards the idea of some thing being *appropriated by* someone. As already suggested, we presently witness a backtracking from property–*Eigentum* towards the older and broader connotations of property–*Eigenschaft* (cf. note 1).

12 Cf. also the sharp separation between persons and external objects which is consolidated in Austin's *Lectures on Jurisprudence* (1954 [1832]: 357–8).

13 In French, *puissance* refers to the end result, while *pouvoir* denotes process as well as condition. Both *puissance* and *pouvoir* derive from the Latin verb *posse*, or 'to be able to'. For Aron (1986), *puissance* predictably remains the more inclusive concept. The persistence of possessory connotations is also manifested by the current popularity of economic and distributive analyses of power, which are variously inspired

by exchange models and rational choice models in sociology and by analytical–normative currents in political philosophy. In Barry's view, for example, 'power, like wealth, is not an event but a possession'. In direct contradiction to Wrong's earlier-cited grammatical complaint, he finds no cause for regretting the absence of a verb form for it. Power in the economic sense should rather be understood as 'the possession of the means of securing compliance by the manipulation of rewards or punishments' (1991: 227–8, 253). Moriss likewise focuses power as an ability or capacity to do things, which is not an episodic event but a dispositional property; his prime concern is to end the confusion between disposition and contingent exercise. Power is neither a *thing* (a resource or a vehicle) nor an *event* (an exercise of power): it is a *capacity* (1987: 12–13, 19).

14 Richard Pipes has observed that, in the Russian patrimonial state, political authority was conceived as an extension of the rights of ownership, the rulers being seen both as sovereigns of the realm and as its proprietors. The existence of private property as a realm over which public authorities normally exercise no jurisdiction is the thing which distinguishes Western political experience from all the rest, whereas in more 'primitive' conditions authority over *people* and *objects* is combined (1974: xvii–xviii).

15 Kingsley Davis (1970: 453–4) considers the identifying characteristic of property rights to be their *transferability*. This, he says, 'is the difference, from a property point of view, between a husband and an automobile'. It also distinguishes property rights from the possession of skills. Teaching, for example, is not true transference because the teacher retains his or her own skill and the pupil has another one like it. On inspection, however, Davis's criterion proves to be insufficient and imprecise. The defining criterion of property is not transferability as such, but *exclusive* transferability of the *entire* object, not temporarily but *ad infinitum*. Presumably, this is what Davis has in mind when he speaks of 'true' transference.

16 Friedmann (1972: 95) calls the distinction between things and non-things 'Romantic' and 'archaic'. Honoré writes:

> it is clear that to stare at the meaning of the word 'thing' will not tell us which protected interests are conceived in terms of ownership. When the legislature or courts think that an interest should be alienable and transmissible they will reify it and say that it can be owned and is a *res* because of a prior conviction that it falls within the appropriate definition of a 'thing'. The investigation of 'things' seems to peter out in a false trail.
>
> (1961: 130)

The crux of the distinction between *ius in rem* and *ius in personam* is not that the former refer to things and the latter to persons, but that real ownership rights are good against all the world, whereas a personal right is good only against some particular person (Nicholas 1962: 99ff.).

17 On Hohfeld's theory, see Munzer (1990: 17–22), who is also critical of Grey's conception of the 'disintegration' of property (31ff.).

18 The expression 'new feudalism' occurs in Reich (1978), where the underlying philosophy of the 'public interest state' is described as the doctrine that

> the wealth that flows from government is held by its recipients conditionally, subject to confiscation in the interests of the paramount state. . . . Wealth is not 'owned' or 'vested' in the holders. Instead, it is held conditionally, the conditions being ones which seek to ensure the

fulfillment of obligations imposed by the state. Just as the feudal system linked lord and vassal through a system of mutual dependence, obligation, and loyalty, so government largess binds man to the state.

See also Renner (1949: 81–2, 196–7) on the revival of *gewere* or seisin.

19 For the *Sozialisierungsgesetz* of March 1919 and the Weimar Constitution of August of the same year, see Huber (1966: 80, 150ff.). It should be noted that there is more than one parallel with the Nazi Enabling Law (*Gesetz zur Behebung der Not von Volk und Reich*) of March 1933.

20 The idea that property is 'many and divisible' comes more naturally to common law jurists than to those raised in the Roman tradition. Whereas Roman and continental practice long regarded ownership as a single whole which could only to a limited extent be split up, the common law more easily allowed for the fragmentation of ownership, or rather the constant occurrence of the fragments in varying connections (Lawson 1958: 12). If, for example, a functional distinction develops between managerial decision making and stockholders' benefit, both the manager and the beneficiary in English law own the property in different ways: each owns a different interest, while neither owns the property in the strict Roman sense. This is different from continental legal theory, which tends to look for a single owner, and then requires conceptual auxiliaries such as a distinction between property and possession or between legal ownership and factual or 'economic' control. Cf. also Nicholas (1962: 15ff.).

21 In Djilas's definition:

> Ownership is nothing other than the right of profit and control. If one defines class benefits by this right, the communist states have seen, in the final analysis, the origin of a new form of ownership or of a new ruling and exploiting class.
>
> (1957: 35)

The ownership privileges of the new class and membership in that class are the privileges of *administration*: 'the power and the government are identical with the use, enjoyment, and disposition of all the nation's goods' (ibid.: 45–6).

22 The sheer force of this broad intellectual sweep from 'property theory' to 'power theory' is perhaps most pertinently felt in the parallel trajectories of left-leaning journals such as *Telos* (from Adorno and Gramsci to Schmitt), *Economy and Society* (from Althusser to Foucault), and *Socialisme ou Barbarie* (from Trotsky to Lefort). See Chapters 3 and 4 for further elaboration.

2 INSIDE THE DIAMOND

1 This presentation converges with and fine-tunes Pocock's view that the juxtaposition of polity and economy should not be stated as a simple antithesis but as an 'unending and unfinished debate'. The oscillatory pattern of the property–power polemic also accommodates his notion that liberal or bourgeois ideology was perhaps 'perfected less by its proponents than by its opponents, who did so with the intention of destroying it' (Pocock 1985: 70–1). Indeed, it duplicates this intuition for the political theory of sovereignty.

2 Of course, the relationship between properly intellectual and 'external' political or economic interests is not historically invariant. Even though overdetermination by intellectual interests is effectively present from the beginning, one can

postulate a linear *increase* of the stratificational weight of intellectual *vis-à-vis* external interests throughout the entire period which is covered by the diamond graph, and a concomitant tendency on the part of intellectuals to emancipate themselves from their organic subservience to other classes or elites.

3 On Chasseneuz and Du Moulin, see Church (1941: 43); on Bodin and the Politiques, *idem* (223ff.) and Gilmore (1967: 93ff.); on Le Bret and others, see Droz (1948: 29).

4 But already Baldus, Bartolus's successor, inclined once more towards Lothair's position in holding that the authority of the prince was different in character from that of the lesser magistrates. Alciato's *Paradoxes of the Civil Law* (1518), Bk II, ch. VI, was entirely devoted to the Lothair–Azo dispute and became a famous source in the course of the sixteenth century (Gilmore 1967: 47–8). On Bartolus, see Woolf (1913). On Marsiglio, see Gewirth (1951).

5 Aylmer (1980) has minutely recorded the gradual strengthening in English seventeenth-century law books, from Cowell's 1607 dictionary up to the early eighteenth-century popularizations of Locke, of the new idea of property as 'highest right'. This tendency reasserted itself throughout the different changes of political regime, although the pre-revolutionary idea that all real property was in fee and held of the king, which was de-emphasized during the Protectorate, was reaffirmed under the restored monarchy, only to lose ground once again in the tradition inspired by Locke.

6 Schlatter recalls that the question about the origins of property actually motivated Hobbes to undertake his political enquiries:

> My first enquiry was to be from whence it proceeded that any man should call anything rather his *own*, than another man's. And when I found that this proceeded not from nature, but consent (for what nature at first laid forth in common, men did afterwards distribute into several *impropriations*); I was conducted from thence to another inquiry; namely, to what end and upon what impulsives, when all was equally every man's in common, men did rather think it fitting that every man should have his inclosure.
>
> (Hobbes, *De Cive*, cit. Schlatter 1951: 138)

Rousseau likewise maintained that property rights could not antedate the political constitution (Ryan 1984: 55).

7 Carlyle and Carlyle (1928: 75) record that the original Roman idea of popular sovereignty included a specific indecision. Although all political authority was seen as representative, because the people were its original fountain, jurists remained divided on the question whether the people had wholly parted with its power at the time of the original contract, or had never really transferred it and were thus able to resume it. In this sense, a theory of rulership as *legibus solutus* is not incompatible with a notion of original popular sovereignty; the terms of this dilemma are reproduced virtually without alteration up to the age of Hobbes and Locke.

8 Pocock (1985: 103ff.) has discerned a complex interplay between a 'civic' tradition, begun by Aristotle and continued by Aquinas, and a 'juristic' tradition inaugurated by the Roman Civilians, also present in Aquinas, and carried on by jurists and natural law theorists right into the age of Locke. Whereas, in the former tradition, property primarily appeared as a prerequisite of virtuous citizenship, the juristic view tended to depict property as an original human right which was prior to social obligation. Focusing less upon political relationships between

persons than upon legally defined relations between persons and things, the juristic view was less hostile towards commercialism and accumulation than the Aristotelian tradition. Ryan has similarly emphasized that the classical 'political' conception of property saw ownership of land and arms as the condition of citizenship, and was hostile to money making, while the modern conception sees it as an *economic* resource, is friendly to money making, and regards the demands of the state as a drain on resources and a threat to a man's right to do as he will with his own (1987: 34). The historical filiation of conceptions of citizenship hence offers an intriguing case for following the grand pendulum swing from an Aristotelian political vocabulary to a Smithian economic one, as it reverts back towards a neo-Aristotelian political theory of citizenship as is once again popular today.

9 Wilsher notes that there is 'something of a textbook consensus' on the fact that Scottish natural (i.e. materialist) history was a reaction to the study of *political* history (1983: 7, 10). Cf. also Therborn (1976: 156–63) and Frisby and Sayer (1986: 22–3).

10 Another famous summary of Smith's position is provided by William Robertson:

> In every enquiry concerning the operations of men when united together in society, the first object of attention should be their mode of subsistence. According as that varies, their laws and policy must be different. Upon discovering in what state property was at any particular period, we may determine with precision what was the degree of power possessed by the King or by the nobility at that juncture.
>
> (cit. Meek 1967: 37–8)

11 Although, as Skinner argues, the economic interpretation of history was somehow in the air, the Smithian emphasis on the importance of economic forces was still remarkable, and the link which Smith forged between economic organization and social structure 'remarkably explicit' (Skinner 1975: 174–5, 155).

12 From his early writings up to *Capital* and beyond, Marx's perspective is that of the dissolution or withering away of *both* the political state *and* economic civil society in the democratic community constituted by full communism – which also entails the supersession of the contradiction within each individual between (civil) *Privatmensch* and (political) *Gemeinwesen*.

13 Actually, one may discern a transition in Smith's work from the Lockean model of a horizontal division of labour between independent artisan–owners towards the more complex vertical model. In the *Glasgow Lectures* (1776), the theory of capital profits and accumulation is still absent. Both capitalists and direct producers are classified as labourers, and capital profits are not yet separated conceptually from the natural price of labour (Meek 1973: 48–9).

14 Luhmann has similarly targeted this 'sliding from part to whole' in Marxism and various other theories of social development:

> Until now all self-thematizations of society have fallen into synecdoche, have always taken a single subsystem for the whole, and therefore have necessarily left unclarified the relations between whole and parts . . . in each case a part is necessarily hypostatized as the whole.

However, the attempt to attribute societal primacy to a single component system (first to politics, then to economics), and thereby to assign it the task of representing the whole, is today no longer convincing (Luhmann 1982: 341, 343–4).

3 MARXISM VS. ANARCHISM

1 If the property–power polarity is cross-tabulated with a distinction which focuses upon different assessments of utility and disutility, the result might be as given in Table 3.

Table 3 Positive and negative theories of property and power

	Good, benevolent, positive	Evil, critical, negative
(Private or class) property	Liberalism	Marxism
(Elite) power	Fascism	Anarchism

2 General accounts of the Marxism–anarchism dispute are also provided by Gurvitch (1965), Ansart (1969), and Miller (1984: 78ff.).
3 'The history of the social movement in all times and all nations tells us that within it there always arise two tendencies: freedom and power, or, in our language, centralism and federalism' (Maximov, cit. d'Agostino 1977: 174).
4 Heinzen's original contribution of September 1847, which repeated the gist of his earlier essay, was followed by a reply by Engels (*MEW* Bd. 4: 309), Heinzen's rejoinder, and Marx's intervention in defence of Engels (ibid.: 331ff.).
5 When Crowder locates a core argument of classical anarchism in the view that the state is destructive of freedom and ought therefore to be abolished, he characteristically employs the word state

> in the way the anarchists generally use it: to refer to that set of institutions and practices, including the Church and private property as well as government, that they identify as collectively constituting . . . the chief source of oppressive power in modern society.
>
> (1991: 4)

6 Cf. also Crowder (1991: 88, 197). An editorial note (1982: 387) to this passage in *De la Création de l'Ordre* remarks that Proudhon edges closer to Dühring than to Marx and Engels on the issue of primacy (see the next chapter for further elaboration). Notwithstanding such prioritizing of the political, Proudhon liberally expands the intellectual compass of political economy in order to include government, education, and the constitution of the family next to commerce and industry. Countering 'non-political' economists such as Say, truly 'political' economy is sacralized as the master theory of social order, the 'key to history', even as the 'final word of the Creator' (1982 V: 294, 419). A few years later, in *Système des contradictions économiques*, Proudhon similarly elevates economic science to the dignity of master science, arguing self-contradictorily that 'the invention of politics and law are exclusively due to property' (1846 II: 404).
7 Cf. typically Sebastien Faure's view that 'Authority dresses itself in two principal forms: the political form, that is the State; and the economic form, that is private property' (cit. Marshall 1992: 43).
8 Bookchin offers an ecological version of the anarchist reversal of the 'order of abolition and of withering away' when he asserts that, in sharp contrast with the Marxist reading of history, the domination of non-human nature has in fact arisen from the domination of humans by humans. If society would first be rid of all authority and hierarchy, the resolution of ecological problems would gradually follow by virtue of the generalization and extension of non-hierarchical sensibilities towards the non-human world.

9 'Marx, Bakunin and others wished to glory in various ways in the Commune . . . yet they owed more to the Commune than the Commune owed to either of them' (Thomas 1980: 250). Zeldin (1979: 371ff.) contends that the Commune was completely misunderstood by Marx, was *not* a socialist government or the result of any revolution, but rather the effect of the withdrawal of the Thiers government from Paris. Two-thirds of the ninety newly elected members of the municipal council were Jacobins who were inspired by memories of 1789, and saw the Commune as a continuation of that of 1793. State intervention was ushered in as an element of an economy of war and siege rather than as the result of an anti-capitalist animus. Zeldin largely repeats the feelings of Bakunin, who protested the Marxian appropriation of the Commune and admitted that the majority of its participants were not socialists *stricto sensu* but Jacobins. Nonetheless, Bakunin proclaimed himself an adherent of the Commune because it was 'a bold, explicit negation of the State' – which looks like another form of appropriation (Bakunin 1972: 298ff.).

10 This criticism is already voiced in strong terms by the Weimar intellectual right, e.g. by Freyer and Schmitt. In our own time, it is repeated by left-wing post-Marxists such as Lefort (cf. 1986: 240ff.). See Chapter 4 for further details.

11 For example, Bookchin (1980: 197, 200). As Crowder has recently emphasized, however, scientism or Enlightenment rationalism was not a prerogative of Marxist theory, but was widely shared by the classical anarchist thinkers themselves, an aspect of their writings which is easily overlooked in favour of their Romanticism (1991: 29–38). In spite of the traditional anarchist critique of indisputable scientific truths, and anarchists' awareness of the connection between dogmatism and organizational centralism, they usually exhibited less doubt about their own calling, about the political capacity of the masses, or the perfidity of 'statist' prejudices than would be fitting for self-proclaimed relativists. Voline, for example, tirelessly invokes the authority of 'clear and natural truths' and 'irrefutable facts', and heavily censures those who remain 'indifferent to the social whole', 'who seek to entrench themselves in their own miserable individual existence, unconscious of the enormous obstacle that they present, by their attitude, to human progress and their own *real* well-being' (1974: 193). Anarchism sometimes attempted to outdo Marxism in its appeal to a more firmly grounded science, which, as in the case of Kropotkin and Voline, meant the biological foundation laid by the former's *Mutual Aid* (d'Agostino 1977: 8, 17, 214). As Maksimov claimed, Bakuninist anarchism was 'scientific anarchism' and 'more deserving of the "scientific" appelation than Marxism' (ibid.: 157–8).

12 *The German Ideology*, Carroll notes, turned out to be such an intense and harsh polemic precisely because Stirner, for Marx, was 'the external object onto which to project an unresolved inner conflict, for exorcising the psychological man he knew that he should consider more thoroughly'. In breaking with the themes and preoccupations of Stirnerian 'anarcho-psychology', Marx and Engels consciously 'renounce questions of individual fulfilment and ethical meaning' (1974: 82, 65). Since that moment, Marxism has remained silent and evasive on the subject of individual motivation, and has condemned itself to operate from crude, because unexplicated, moral axioms. The absence of a self-reflexive 'psychology of socialism' therefore appears less excusable than was thought by a revisionist critic such as Hendrik De Man (1926): it was rooted not simply in the presumed innocence of a pre-Freudian and pre-Nietzschean age, but also in a purposeful rejection of the Stirnerian idea of individual 'ownness'.

13 Thomas (1980: 338) has emphasized the notions of hierarchy and discipline in the programme of the International Fraternity of 1866. The theoretical model of a

revolutionary dictatorship, which Bakunin already advocated at the time of the Prague uprising in 1848, returned in the period of conspirational association with the young fanatic Nechaev. The Nechaev affair demonstrated how disturbingly close anarchism stood to its opposite of authoritarian elitism. Further examples are provided by Bakunin's *Confession*, Maksimov's idea of a 'dictatorship of labour', Machno's practical centralism, and the 'Bolshevik' anarchism of Arshinov (d'Agostino 1977). D'Agostino's rich book demonstrates the growing attraction of organizational centralism as a long-term tendency in anarchist thought, and as an inevitable response to the challenge of Bolshevism. Carl Schmitt sensed such ambiguities at an early date. To him Bakunin presented the singular paradox of being 'theoretically the theologian of anti-theology, and practically the dictator of an anti-dictatorship' (1922: 84). Cf. also note 21.

14 Voline writes:

> As a general rule, an erroneous interpretation – or more often one that was deliberately inaccurate – pretended that the libertarian conception implied the absence of all organisation. Nothing is farther from the truth. It is a question, not of 'organisation or non-organisation' but of *'two different principles of organisation'*.
>
> (1974: 176)

'Natural' organisation would imply what Voline called the 'organizing spirit', i.e. 'men capable of carrying on an organization', and thus an 'elite', although its role would be to 'help' the masses rather than to direct them governmentally (ibid.: 177–8). Notice the largely verbal character of this 'diametrical' opposition. On the necessity of organization, cf. also Bookchin (1986: 236). Clark (1978) and De George (1978) similarly warn against the tendency to oversimplify the anarchist position on power, authority, and organization.

15 The politics of intellectual demarcation produced a curious battle of definitions within the First International. At first, the collectivists inspired by Bakunin admitted expressions such as the 'regenerated', 'revolutionary', or 'socialist' state as synonyms of the expression 'social collectivity'. Very soon, however, the anarchists discovered the risk of employing the same word as their authoritarian rivals while giving it a different meaning, and opted for 'federation' or 'solidarization of communes'. When the Marxists were in need of anarchist support in order to have the principle of collective property accepted, they temporarily swallowed the substitute without much enthusiasm (Guérin 1965: 73ff.).

16 Engels wrote to Lafargue (December 1871) that no form of cooperation was conceivable without an extraneous will, i.e. an authority, a 'single and directing will'. The next month, in a letter to Cuno, he likewise identified division of labour with *single* management. In a letter to Terzaghi, also from January 1872, Engels inserted a then innocent Italian word: 'Do what you like with authority etc. after the victory, but for the struggle we must unite all our forces in one *fascio* and concentrate them at one point of attack' (Marx *et al.* 1972: 58, 70, 68).

17 Thomas (1980) provides a persuasive reappraisal as well as an apt summary of the Marx–Stirner dispute, but his account remains timid as compared with Carroll's (1974) much shorter exposition, which he fails to mention.

18 Here Proudhon also reintroduced an antinomy between *propriété-vol* and *propriété-liberté*, and ended up by defending absolute property as a unique decentralizing and federative force against the despotic state, whereas 'possession' fatally tended towards unity, concentration, and universal fealty (1866: 144–5).

19 Bakunin, for example, praised Machiavelli as the first philosopher properly to understand the state: 'In Bakunin's theories can be seen the same view of the

transcendent state as that held by Machiavelli' (d'Agostino 1977: 43, 69). Bookchin has explicitly favoured Aristotelian political ontology above the Marxist ontology of production (1980: 242–3).

20 On Marxism as a product of English conditions and its non-applicability to peripheral development see Bakunin's famous letter to *La Liberté* (1972: 818, 836). Cf. also Brenan (1943: 136): 'The development of Marx's programme was impossible at that time in Russia, Italy, and Spain, as was that of Bakunin in England, Germany, and France.'

21 This proximity between anarchism and authoritarianism is also clearly evidenced in the writings of Machajski (cf. Haberkern 1987; d'Agostino 1988). Once again, Carl Schmitt was unusually perceptive in thematizing this opposition-in-similarity, more particularly that between Donoso Cortes and Proudhon (cf. Schmitt 1922: 80, 83). Somewhat later Schmitt also noted that, although Bolshevism had suppressed all expression of anarchist politics, its structure of argumentation remained remarkably dependent upon anarcho-syndicalist thought (1926: 77). The next chapter offers a more extensive treatment of this complicitous reversal of terms.

22 Cf. Miliband's present stance on the New Left reassertion of the importance of the political (1994: 8ff.).

23 Wolff and Resnick (1986: 107–10) similarly argue that many Marxist theorists, among whom they include Poulantzas, Jessop, Przeworski, Bowles and Gintis, and, ironically, also Laclau, have recently moved towards a political or power conception of social class which is not too far removed from established sociological conceptions (e.g. as presented by Dahrendorf).

24 From different perspectives, this criticism of Foucault's expansive conception of power is also developed by Giddens (1982), Habermas (1987), Dews (1987), and Fraser (1989). Cf. Pels (1995b) for a more extended consideration.

25 Rediscovering a similar 'fixation with power' in Runciman's Weber-inspired sociology of stratification, Anderson emphasizes that 'societies are not just power stuff', since at least three large domains (the production of persons, of goods, and of meanings) resist such reduction: 'demographic, economic, and cultural systems are never mere transcriptions of power relations between human actors' (1992: 151–2). With regard to the power–culture relationship, it is also instructive to note Williams' successive extensions of the concept of material production towards 'social cooperation', 'establishing a political order', 'the production of social knowledge', etc. (cf. Williams 1977: 91–7). If Anglo-Saxon 'cultural materialism' postulates culture, language, and signification as indissoluble elements of the material infrastructure, it approaches self-dissolution in the same manner as the Parisian 'politicizing' school. Such inflationary procedures invariably elicit calls to go beyond Marxism and embrace a generalized theory of domination. One such (self-directed) call has been uttered by Balbus in his comprehensive *Marxism and Domination* (1982). Other interesting cases, such as that of Lefort, and Laclau and Mouffe, will be investigated in the next chapter.

26 Carling also notes the rift between 'rational choice Marxism' with its economic and utilitarian pedigree and conceptualizations which focalize 'power', which generally draw 'on an alternative tradition of sociology and political science which has often been divorced from economic theory'. He adds that 'posing the question hints at a reconciliation between the two traditions' (1986: 43).

27 Elster, for example, defends something like the all-purpose applicability of the formal concept of economic action, and specifically denies the possibility 'to generate a conceptual counter-revolution by introducing a generalized conception of politics that might regain the ground lost' (1976: 248). But, as the present

study effusively demonstrates, such an enterprise is a perfectly legitimate one for all those who are driven by Nietzschean inspirations.

28 Cf. Wright *et al.*'s reconstruction of a 'weak' or 'restricted' historical materialism, which drops Cohen's notion of the explanatory primacy of the productive forces in favour of that of production relations, but otherwise retains the base–superstructure model (1992: 17ff., 89ff.).

29 Carter notes that Marxists and anarchists have 'a long history of bitter disagreement', and warns that any cogent green political theory should take extreme care in selecting elements drawn from such competing traditions. In the sequel, however, the anarchist primacy of the political is simply restated over against the Marxist primacy of the economy (1993: 40–5).

30 Cf. also Hartsock's criticism of Foucault's conception of power (1990).

31 Following Rubin in understanding 'the mode of production of human beings' in patriarchy primarily as a result of male control of women's labour power, Hartmann argued that patriarchy and capital existed in a mutually reinforcing structural partnership. Young's objection to this 'dual systems theory' underlined instead that patriarchal relations were internally related to production relations, and that the gender division of labour should accordingly be seen as a single system – which also suggested the need for unifying the struggle against class and gender oppressions (cf. Sargent 1986).

32 Where Young proclaims the need for a fundamental reversal of terms, analytical Marxists would see no difficulty in extending the distributive paradigm and the vocabulary of exploitation towards the distribution of immaterial goods, in order to encompass decision-making power (cf. Roemer on status exploitation), division of labour (cf. Wright on organizational assets), and culture (cf. Roemer–Wright on skills exploitation, or Van Parijs on citizenship exploitation). Cf. also Bourdieu (1986) on cultural, social, and political capital.

4 FASCISM AND THE PRIMACY OF THE POLITICAL

1 Cf. also Franz Neumann's trajectory from his rather traditionally designed *Behemoth* (1942) towards *The Democratic and the Authoritarian State*, where more room is secured for the autonomy of the political, if not for a rather categorically stated primacy of the political over the economic (1957: 257ff.).

2 Both the fascist jurist Alfredo Rocco and the 'conservative revolutionary' sociologist Hans Freyer saw Machiavelli as the founding father of both the modern sociology of power and of radical right-wing ideology. Cf. Chapter 3, note 19.

3 'Of all the folk wisdom surrounding Fascism, the conviction that it was no more than opportunistic, anti-ideological, antirational, and consequently devoid of programmatic and strategic content, is both significantly untrue and most difficult to dispel' (Gregor 1979b: 96). Umberto Eco, however, has recently re-emphasized its irrational and anti-intellectual nature (Eco 1995).

4 Representative is, for example, Ralph Miliband (1973: 81), who critically quotes Mussolini's Senate speech of 1934:

> The corporatist economy respects the principle of private property. Private property completes the human personality. It is a right. But it is also a duty. We think that property ought to be regarded as a social function; we wish therefore to encourage not passive property, but active

property, which does not confine itself to enjoying wealth, but develops it and increases it.

Mussolini here only repeats a view basic to the entire tradition of Sorelian revolutionary syndicalism. A Marxist historian such as Sternhell still fastens upon this 'lenient' stance on property as his primary criterion of critical judgement.

5 An exception is Haselbach's (1985) retrieval of Dühring as a precursor of the 'liberal socialism' of Oppenheimer and Nelson.

6 Breuer has recently voiced scepticism about the Conservative Revolution as constituting a clearly delineable community of discourse offering a minimum of common themes, aims, and methods. Given the issue at hand, however, his deconstruction appears seems to fail, in so far as the entire span of authors discussed at least tend to acknowledge this primacy of the political over the economic. Breuer judiciously demonstrates the large intellectual distance which opens between 'right-wingers' such as Spengler and Moeller van den Bruck, who insisted upon preserving private property and entrepreneurial discretion, and 'left-wingers' such as Jünger and Niekisch, who pleaded a form of state socialism. However, a case can be made (and is initially made below) that the issue of balancing politically functionalized property rights against the supreme rights of an organizing, planning state was common ground to the conservative-revolutionary left, right, and centre. As is clear from Breuer's own material, while the 'National-Bolshevik' tendency never went as far as advocating an integral 'abolition' or collectivization of private property, the 'national–liberal' tendency never disputed its political functionalization. The use of the term 'socialism' in, for example, 'German socialism' is therefore less a matter of 'conceptual confusion' than Breuer indicates (1993: 59–70). Cf. also note 9 on the 'mediating' position of *Die Tat*.

7 Spengler's *Der Untergang des Abendlandes*, part I (1918) bristles with annunciations about an apocalytic struggle between 'power' and 'money' that will end in the inevitable triumph of the former. In this battle, the leading powers of a dictatorial money economy stand against the 'purely political will toward order' of a new authoritarian state. It is politics not economics which acts as the decisive force; hence there will emerge a new primacy of politics over the economy (Herf 1984: 57–8, 62).

8 As Freyer states:

> The economy is recalcitrant and must be taken in stronger hand, both in order to subordinate it to the organized people as its collective work, and to serve as a set of instruments for its new political subject. Never has the tension between the political principle of formation and the content to be formed been stronger as in this case. That is why this tension with the forming force must be raised to the maximum (*auf stärkste angezogen werden*).

(1926: 177)

9 The crucial importance of *Die Tat* is suggested not only by the journal's unprecedented circulation in the early 1930s, far exceeding the readership of any other competitor on the intellectual right (an estimated 30,000 copies in 1932, and most probably more than one reader per copy), but also by the fact that it successfully 'centred' itself between the right-wing and the left-wing limits of the Conservative Revolution, as demarcated by Spengler's nostalgic Prussianism and Niekisch's National Bolshevism. As such, it offered an attractive platform for the

more centrist convictions of prominent intellectuals such as Sombart, Freyer, and Schmitt (cf. Lebovics 1969: 172, 210; Sontheimer 1978).

10 In *Der Begriff des Politischen* Carl Schmitt included the following typical reaction to Rathenau's statement: 'It would be more exact to say that politics continues to remain the destiny, but what has occurred is that economics has become political and thereby the destiny' (1996: 78). In 1917 Rathenau himself had already written: 'Jetzt, beim Beginn des zweiten Kriegsjahres, dämmert die Erkenntnis dass alles Wirtschaftsleben auf dem Urgrund des Staates ruht, dass Staatspolitik der Geschäftlichkeit vorangeht, dass Jeder, was er besitzt und kann, Allen schuldet' (1917: 89).

11 Jünger's *Gestalt* of the Worker–Soldier offered 'one of the most enduring of reactionary modernist symbols' (Herf, 1984: 92).

12 Cf. Schmitt's consideration of the claim by the fascist state to act as a 'dominant' or 'neutral' third, rather than as a servant of economic or social interests. Only a weak state, he argued, remained the servant of private property. Every strong state demonstrated its strength not against the weak but against the economically and socially strong. Hence the entrepreneurial class could never fully trust the fascist state, which tended to develop 'in the direction of a workers' state with a planned economy' (Schmitt 1988: 113–14). In 1931, he explicitly picked up Jünger's notion of 'total mobilization' in order to describe the turn towards the (potentially) total state and its tendency to identify state and society (1931: 79; 1988: 152). Freyer curiously wedded Jünger and Schmitt in describing Machiavelli's view of the Roman battle order as symbolizing a people which 'in die Tiefe gegliedert und im Ernstfall einer totalen Mobilmachung fähig ist', adding in conclusion that 'Die ideale Verfassung ist das Volk in Waffen' (1986: 179).

13 Sombart here adopted Spann's view that, formally, there existed private property, but in fact only communal property.

14 Although Schmitt's affinities and affiliations with the Conservative Revolution are in dispute (Bendersky 1987; Mohler 1988; Muller 1991), I find ample reason to include him in this current of thought.

15 This neutralizing drive was once again primarily accounted to the progress of *economic* rationalism. Virtually reversing the Smithian materialist 'four-stages' theory, and closely verging upon Comte's idealist three-stage theory, Schmitt pictured historical development as advancing through four stages: theological, metaphysical, moralist, and economic, each of which identified a specific central area and a specific mentality of its leading elite. The nineteenth century was characterized as 'essentially economistic', while the twentieth was described as the 'Zeitalter der Technik' which, by pushing the drift towards neutrality to its logical extreme, would (necessarily? dialectically?) reinstate the political (1993: 79ff.; Wolin 1992: 438–40).

16 On this issue, I tend to disagree with De Wit's view (1992: 168, 489, 491) that Schmitt's conception of the reconstitution of 'state-free' domains was 'surprisingly liberal in character'.

17 In 1935, during full-scale intellectual collaboration, this democratic political identity was translated as *Artgleichheit*, and definitorily excluded *artfremde* personages from the homogeneous mass of the *Volksgenosse* (Schmitt 1935: 17, 42).

18 Cf. Freyer's suggestions concerning an elite of physicians, teachers, engineers, and poets (1926: 170–80) and his explicit references to Saint-Simon (1987: 21, 26) and the 'organization of labour' (1926: 146ff.). On Zehrer's notion of a 'revolution of the intellectuals' and his borrowings from Mannheim see Pels (1993c).

19 Pleading a form of 'cultural socialism' closely influenced by De Man, the Dutch political theorist Jacques de Kadt likewise chose to call the fascist

order of evaluation *culture–politics–economics* 'the only acceptable and healthy ordering', whereas the reverse Marxist ordering of economics–politics–culture represented 'an unworthy and dishonourable sequence' (de Kadt 1939, cit. Pels 1993a: 82).

20 Cf. the special issue on 'Carl Schmitt: Enemy or Foe?', *Telos* 72, Summer 1987, e.g. the contributions by the editors and by former Althusserian Paul Hirst, as well as the section on Schmitt in the Spring issue of the same year. Since then *Telos* has regularly translated and discussed Schmitt as well as New Right polymath De Benoist. On the latter, and the New Right more generally, see extensively *Telos* 98–9, Winter 1993/Spring 1994. Cf. also the special issue on Schmitt of De Benoist's journal *Nouvelle École* 44, Spring 1987.

21 As Lefort writes:

> The political is thus revealed, not in what we call political activity, but in the double movement whereby the mode of institution of society appears and is obscured. It appears in the sense that the process whereby society is ordered and unified across its divisions becomes visible.

(1988: 11)

5 SOCIAL SCIENCE AS POWER THEORY

1 Most outspokenly perhaps in Elias: 'It was the insight into the relative autonomy of the subject matter of "sociology" which was the decisive step forward towards establishing sociology as a relatively autonomous science' (1978: 45) (italics omitted). On the inversion of project and object see more extensively Pels (1983). This constructivist wordplay also occurs in Latour (1988: 73) and Haraway ('objects are boundary projects') (1991: 201).

2 Once again, Carl Schmitt had an early inkling of this 'rivalry effect' when he described the 'polemical precision' of political and social-scientific concepts, the polemical value of the concept of 'society', and the 'oppositional' origin of sociology (1931: 73–4n). See Chapter 8 for Schmitt's anticipation of the idea of a 'politics of knowledge'.

3 Most typically, once again, in Elias (1984: 38). But Elias only reproduces the argument of Durkheim's inaugural lecture 'Cours de science sociale' (1970 [1888]: 78–85). Cf. also Heilbron (1995) and my critical review (1996b).

4 Cf. Tönnies' multiple use of this conceptual pair as summarized by Szacki (1979: 343–4).

5 Becker and Barnes (1952: 575) early on advanced that Comte did not distinguish clearly between sociology and political science, but apparently regarded sociology as 'the perfected political science of the future'. For similar views, see Gouldner (1985: 269) and Wagner (1990). For views of Comte which differ interestingly from the present one, see Vernon (1984) and Heilbron (1995).

6 For Durkheim, authority indeed constituted the dorsal spine of morality; in this respect, Nisbet's first pair of unit-ideas are mutually substitutable. Social discipline is significantly referred to as 'the vital knot of collective life' (Durkheim 1986: 145). As Durkheim typically argues, 'there are no morals without discipline and authority, and the sole rational authority is the one that a society is endowed with in relation to its members'; the state is regularly identified as the prime organ to institute and preserve this moral discipline (cf. 1992: 72–3). In a text from 1886, he already affirms that the distinction

between governors and governed is 'presque contemporaine de la vie sociale' (1970: 201).

7 Similar considerations have been expressed by Pels (1983; 1984), Wagner (1990), Turner (1992), Gane (1992), and Müller (1993). Challenger (1994) argues for a communitarian Durkheim who falls closely in line with neo-Aristotelian ethics, but curiously, he refrains from discussing professional ethics, democratic corporatism, or any other item in Durkheim's omnipresent *political* vocabulary.

8 The shift is clearly evidenced in Comte's application of his Law of Three Stages to politics. If the 'doctrine of Kings' represented the theological state of politics, and the 'doctrine of the People' expressed its metaphysical condition, the Scientific Doctrine of politics 'considers the social state in which the human race has always been found by observers as the necessary effect of its organisation' (Comte, in Fletcher, 1974: 135–6).

9 Comte makes a special point of emphasizing that the principle of the division of labour was discovered by Aristotle far earlier and formulated more suggestively than in the works of the political economists.

10 If there exists an important historical affinity between the ideas of 'community' and 'polity', we gain a view of the specificity of sociology's historical object/project which differs equally from functionalist reconstructions which emphasize normative solidarity and from conflictual ones which emphasize domination and elite rule. The analysis of power and politics is central to the sociological tradition in both these variants, and never very distant from the analysis of values, norms, and representations. Without wishing to deny that the breach between consensus and conflict theory indicates a major cleavage in the history of social thought, it is neither the only nor perhaps the most influential one. By neutralizing this old schism, we are better equipped to thematize the relative unity of the core sociological project *vis-à-vis* those theories and traditions against which it rose as a counter-science.

11 In Meisel's crisp characterization, elitism is 'at its crudest the notion that The Few should rule because they do in fact rule, and less crudely the contention that, since only a few can rule, The Many do not and never will' (1958: 3). Parry likewise notes that the elitist thesis does somewhat more than assert that a minority decides and the majority obeys, which in itself is an obvious truism with no power to explain political relationships. The elitist contention is in fact a much stronger one: 'the dominant minority cannot be controlled by the majority, whatever democratic mechanisms are used' (1969: 31).

12 It is telling that even Elias, who placed so much weight upon the institutional disjunction of society and state as major stimulus of the invention of sociology, adopted what is to all effect a Tocquevillean position when identifying the process of increasing democratization, i.e. of the diffusion of *power* as 'the basic transformation of society to which the rise of a science of society pointed'. The discovery of 'society' as the ensemble of diffused power relationships is presented as a generalization of early political economy's concern with 'civil society'; 'society' is presented as self-evidently broader than 'economy', and 'power' as self-evidently coincident with the 'social' (1984: 48–9).

13 Cf. Levine (1995) for a (re)vision of the sociological tradition which follows different fault lines, but is equally sensitive to the distinctive orientations entrenched in national traditions.

14 However, Saint-Simon and Comte also reflected the state–society dilemma in their divergent assessments of political economy and economic behaviour and their different views of the role of the state. While understating Saint-Simon's

anti-statism, Gouldner somewhat overstates Comte's commitment to 'civil society' (1980: 367). For an extended defence of the notion of civil society as a 'third project', which is also linked backwards to Tocqueville, see Cohen and Arato (1992).

15 Shapiro has located an even earlier use in a 1785 letter by John Adams, where it vaguely refers to 'political theory' (Shapiro 1984).

16 Durkheim's initial question, which continued to underlie his thinking, was: 'are individualism and socialism irreconcileable? If not, *what kind* of individualism and *what kind* of socialism are compatible?' (Filloux 1993: 212). Cf. the classically 'neutral' formulation in the preface of *Division*:

> The question that has been the starting point for our study has been that of the connection between the individual personality and social solidarity. How does it come about that the individual, whilst becoming more autonomous, depends ever more closely upon society? How can he become at the same time more of an individual and yet more linked to society? For it is indisputable that these two movements, however contradictory they appear to be, are carried on in tandem.
>
> (Durkheim 1984: xxx)

17 The first *Methodenstreit*, at the beginnings of the *Verein* in the 1870s, had ranged Schmoller against Menger in a famous criticism of the latter's individualism and non-interventionism.

18 On Sombart's 'aristocratic turn' see also Lindenlaub (1967: 314ff.). Freyer explicitly traced the emergence of German sociology both to Von Stein and to an 'anti-sociologist' such as Treitschke. On Weber in the Nazi reception, see Klingemann (1996: 171ff.); on the intellectual relationship between Freyer and Weber, see also Mommsen (1989: 176–8). In his seminal work on Weber's political thought, Mommsen extensively discussed Schmitt's radicalization of Weber's principle of plebiscitary leadership democracy (1974: 407; cf. Turner and Factor 1987). The intriguing relationship between Weber and Michels is discussed by, for example, Beetham (1977: 175–7) and Mommsen (1989: 102–5).

19 Cf. Ionescu (1976: 6–8). The titles of Saint-Simon's consecutive reviews confirm this impression: starting with *l'Industrie* (1816–18), which was designed to forge a connection between 'scientific and literary industry' and 'commercial and manufactory industry', he tried his luck again with *le Politique* (1819), edited in collaboration with Comte and Lachevardière; at the demise of the latter journal, Saint-Simon published a brochure which was expanded and enriched to form *l'Organisateur* (1819–20).

20 'The social body consists of two great families: that of intellectuals, or industrials of theory, and that of immediate producers, or scholars of application' (*Industrie* III, cit. Durkheim 1958: 176). Saint-Simon is somewhat confused about the inclusion of the savants in the 'industrial class' (which in 1803 are considered 'industriels théoriques', whereas in the *Catéchisme des industriels* of 1824 they are seen as a kind of organic intelligentsia of the actual industrials: the leaders of commerce and manufacture; throughout his writings the relative importance of both elites is variably assessed (cf. Dautry 1951: 84, 123).

21 This principle of the priority of 'production' over property is presented as the 'sommaire des faits observés de la science politique'. Although Saint-Simon considers the right of property to be 'incontestably the sole basis which it is possible to give to a political society' he refuses to conclude that it cannot be modified, 'for the *individual right of property* can only be founded upon the common

and general utility of the exercise of this right – a utility which can vary with the times' (1966 II: 89–90). Cf. Durkheim, who (sympathetically) underscored that the core of Saint-Simon's industrial politics was the reconstitution of the system of property (1958: 198–9).

22 As Saint-Simon writes:

> It is true that property makes for stable government, but it is only when property is not divorced from enlightenment that government can safely be placed on such a basis. It is right, therefore, that the government should co-opt and endow with property those who are without property but distinguished by outstanding merit, in order that talent and property should not be divided. For talent, which is the more powerful and active force, would soon seize on property if the two were not united.
>
> (1964: 47)

23 Cf. Comte's preface to his (1851 I) and his introduction to the six *opuscules* which were reprinted as an appendix to tome IV.

24 Comte's *Cours*, Leçon 47, repeated his early criticism of the 'isolation' of political economy, which was mistakenly considered to be 'entirely distinct and independent from the ensemble of political [!] science', which was not sufficiently 'observational' and hence 'metaphysical' (his prime example here was Smith's famous work), and which clung to a dogmatic notion of the 'necessary absence of all regulatory intervention' (1975b: 92ff.). Cf. also Comte's early positive appreciation of the influence of Saint-Simon on this point (1970: 475). The Saint-Simonian appraisal of political economy is of course fully restated by Durkheim (1975: 281–2; 1958). Evidence of Comte's 'third' position is provided by his symmetrical criticism of the traditional treatment of the political system as an 'isolated fact', to which are attributed 'those social forces which on the contrary produce it . . . the political order is and can only be the expression of civil order' (1974: 142–3).

25 Lorenz von Stein's *Staatswissenschaft* was interpreted in similar terms (Durkheim 1975: 336). Somewhat later, Durkheim translated *die positive Staatswirtschaft* as 'l'économie sociale positive' (id. 381). Cf. also Durkheim (1975: 148–9).

26 Reviewing Merlino's political theory, Durkheim criticized the author for failing to grasp 'the true nature and role of social discipline, that is to say what constitutes the vital centre (*nœud vital*) of collective life' (1977: 171).

27 In it, the term *scientia politica* figured as apparent equivalent for 'social science', while *civitas* could be variously rendered as 'city', 'state', or 'society' (1966: 25–6n.). Cf. Comte's similar critical appraisal of Montesquieu (1974: 157ff.).

28 In his earliest publication on Schäffle, Durkheim wrote: 'L'autorité dirige la vie sociale, mais ne la crée ni ne la remplace. Elle coordonne les mouvements, mais les suppose' (1975: 367, 369).

29 For this important distinction, see e.g. Manolescu (1934) and Schmitter (1977).

30 For various assertions of the contemporary relevance of Durkheimian democratic corporatism, cf. Hearn (1985), Pels (1988), Pearce (1989), and Hirst (1990; 1994).

31 The characteristic definition of the state as reflexive centre of society is also first found in Schäffle (1896 I: 144, 527; II: 427–8).

32 Cf. on this progression from project to object also Lacroix (1981: 62ff.). Durkheim's various demarcations of sociology against political philosophy and political economy (and against socialism) were invariably cast in terms of the positivistic distinction between 'art' and 'science', even though sociology itself was 'artful' and 'projective' from the very beginning (cf. Pels 1983; 1984). In a

suggestive article, Tenbruck has described this reverse side of the dual determination of sociology and society as 'the birth of society from the spirit of sociology', and has likewise traced it to Durkheim, the founder. 'Society' as a reality *sui generis*, he contends, is not so much 'discovered' as *derived* from the prior domanial and epistemological ambitions of Durkheimian sociology (Tenbruck 1981). On the intellectual imperialism of the Durkheimian school cf. also Karady (1979). Bourdieu has aptly characterized Durkheimian sociology as 'an ambiguous, dual, masked science; one that had to conceal and renounce its own nature as a *political* science in order to gain acceptance as an academic science' (1993b: 27–8).

33 At one point, Durkheim himself signalled the oscillatory definition of the state as both part and whole which had become this tradition's trademark (1986: 45).

34 Religion, in this context as in others, could be taken as virtually synonymous with morality or with 'collective representations'. Durkheim implicitly followed Richard, for example, in the latter's (anti-Marxist) argument that not the functions of nutrition and production are preponderant, but the 'functions of relation', i.e. the *representative* functions (1975: 240).

35 Reacting to Michels, who dedicated the first edition of *Political Parties* to him, Weber censured his pupil for having failed to recognize that all forms of social relationship, even the most personal, were in a sense power relations (*Herrschaftsbeziehungen*). Opposing Michels' residual syndicalism, Weber declared inconceivable a social order which was free from all domination (Mommsen 1989: 98). In his subsequent support of the fascist theory of power and the state, of course, Michels overtook Weber on the right flank, drawing expressly upon the latter's views about plebiscitary democracy and charismatic leadership (Beetham 1977: 175–7). More generally, Weber's notion of the irreversible advance of *Führerdemokratie* 'was by no means immune from possible reinterpretation along anti-democratic lines' (Mommsen 1989: 98; cf. also Klingemann 1996: 120ff. on Alfred Weber). Thus the Weberian sociology of *Herrschaft* developed along a dual historical track, feeding simultaneously the illiberal political theory of, for example, Schmitt and Freyer and the postwar liberal sociology of organization.

36 As Parkin has observed, Weber's argument for the ubiquitous necessity of *Verfügungsgewalt* as 'some kind of control over the necessary services of labor and of the means of production' (1979: 67–8) is not logically connected to his more central axiom about the omnipresence of domination and leadership, and also stands isolated from his discussion of social closure and property (1979: 44).

37 Parkin (1972: 44–6):

> to speak of the distribution of power could be understood as another way of describing the flow of rewards . . . it can be thought of as a concept or metaphor which is used to depict the flow of resources which constitutes this system. And as such it is not a separate dimension of stratification at all.

Cf. also Giddens (1973: 44) and Scott (1996: 38ff.).

38 Foucault has put in at least one disclaimer about not having intended to replace an explanation based upon the economy by an explanation in terms of power (1985: 75). It can be argued, however, that the net balance of his sprawling conception of power is precisely to effect such a reversal.

6 POWER, PROPERTY, AND MANAGERIALISM

1 This statement requires some qualification, in order to avoid a precipitate homo-genization of the tableau of contemporary sociological thought. In contrast to 'early modern' sociology, which is more definitely centred around a power nucleus, 'late modern' sociology once again appears divided between a generalized economic and a generalized power vocabulary. Perhaps this new situation is symp-tomatic of the relative supersession of the disciplinary contest between sociology and political economy, and more specifically, that between academic sociology and Marxism, which has long defined the outer perimeters of both. We should be aware, in other words, that sociology is no longer clearly demarcated from other forms of social enquiry, and has evolved into a transdisciplinary and pluralist enterprise. The power-oriented historical sociology of Elias and Mann, for example, is balanced by the sociological historiography which has developed from neo-Marxist impulses in the work of, for example, Moore, Wallerstein, Anderson, and Skocpol. The various 'postmodernist' currents in sociology, which are more partial to an expanded Nietzschean analytic of power, are currently balanced by the influential paradigm of rational choice (e.g. Coleman, Hechter, Opp), which is in turn close to the 'rational choice Marxism' which has been elaborated by, for example, Elster, Roemer, Wright, and Van Parijs. All of these currents in some way synthesize Marxian and Weberian problematics, as is also visible in the work of 'vocabulary mixers' such as Gouldner, Collins, and Bourdieu.

2 Particularly representative of this pattern is the 'figurational' notion of power which has been advanced by Norbert Elias. Elias's conception, somewhat like Foucault's, is intended to remove traditional suspicions about its 'unethical' nature; power is considered neither good nor bad, because it is just simply *there*, as an ever-present property of social relationships. Power balances constitute an inte-gral element of all human relationships, because they are immediately implied in the very fact of functional social interdependence (Elias 1978: 78, 100). Property or possession are largely taken for granted as special cases of power exercise (cf. Wilterdink 1984; Szirmaï 1986).

3 One of the more famous footnotes in the sociological tradition might well be Mills' note to ch. 12, in which he rejected the notion of 'ruling class' in the following terms:

> 'Ruling class' is a badly loaded phrase. 'Class' is an economic term; 'rule' is a political one. The phrase 'ruling class' thus contains the theory that an economic class rules politically. . . . Specifically, the phrase 'ruling class' does not allow enough autonomy to the political order and its agents, and it says nothing about the military as such. . . . We hold that such a simple view of 'economic determinism' must be elaborated by 'political determinism' and 'military determinism'; that the higher agents of each of these three domains now often have a noticeable degree of autonomy; and that only in the often intricate ways of *coalition* do they make up and carry through the most important decisions. Those are the major reasons we prefer 'power elite' to 'ruling class' as a characterising phrase for the higher circles when we consider them in terms of power.

> (Mills 1956: 227)

4 Dahrendorf (1979: 48ff.) concedes the formal character of his concept of power/authority (without surrendering it), and locates the substratum of social

structure and the motive force of social processes in a generalized struggle for 'life chances'.

5 This is critically signalled by Murphy, who also rejects Parkin's similar broadening of property as virtually synonymous with exploitation (1988: 68, 175).

6 Bell's and Touraine's seminal works on post-industrialism are likewise pregnant with power theory (Bell 1976a: 115, 117, 298, 361, 373–4; cf. Stehr 1994a: 19, 64; Touraine 1969: 11–13).

7 Although originally deriving his 'two-step' ownership model of the managerial class from an extension of Marxian categories, Burnham swiftly changed his allegiance to the alternative patrimony of power (elite) theory (cf. Burnham 1963 [1943]).

8 'Control', as Berle and Means defined it,

> lies in the hands of the individual or group who have the actual power to select the board of directors (or its majority), either by mobilizing the legal right to choose them – 'controlling' a majority of the votes directly or through some legal device – or by exerting pressure which influences their choice.
>
> (1968: 66–7)

Cf. Berle (1959: 70): 'Control is quite simply the capacity to make or unmake a board of directors'.

9 It is good to recall that even Berle and Means admitted the possibility of assuring effective control based upon ownership of less than 1 per cent of total assets.

10 If Bottomore (1966: 79, 82) observes that the notion of the separation of ownership from control is 'at best a half truth', one might still wish to prefer it to an undivided error.

11 Grint (1995: 42) cites research demonstrating the persistence of family control, even in large-scale enterprises such as the Japanese *zaibatsu* and the South Korean *chaebols*.

12 Fennema has spotted the existence of a 'level of analysis' problem, but mistakenly supposes that it is soluble if shifted towards a higher level of abstraction. The debate between Marxists and managerialists, he observes, 'misses the point in so far as both sides confuse the theory of *intra*corporate power (as developed by Berle and Means) with a theory of *inter*corporate power'. The managerial thesis might be true if corporations are studied in isolation, but does not need to be correct when external relations with other firms are systematically considered (1982: 63). Instead, as I have argued before, the debate is largely replayed on the analytical level of transcorporate or 'classwide' control.

13 McDermott has likewise observed that quasi-collective ownership structures in the corporation have largely replaced the property-owning family as the central institution of modern capitalist society. The most striking feature of this new property system is that social relations themselves, not merely things and their titles, appear in property form. 'Corporate form', as a dynamic relation between management, professionals, and workers, is itself a productive force, and collectively 'owned' by the top management. This situation cannot be treated as an extension of private property, as Berle and Means do: it is *classes*, not individuals or families, that now exercise property claims. Modern capitalism, in McDermott's view, ultimately rests 'on a class owning and disposing over its common property as a class' (1991: 7, 77–80).

14 The combined parameters of high/low closure and differential agency also provide a general background for the zoning model of social theory and its

historico-geographical distribution of liberal, corporatist, and etatist theoretical emphases, as outlined in previous chapters. While liberal property theory occupies the lower left corner of the scheme, etatist power theory is more nearly located towards the top right corner, with intermediate forms spread along the diagonal.

15 Recently, Eyal *et al.* (1997) have also employed the appelation 'capitalism without capitalists' to characterize the rise of a new cultural capital-based managerial class in the countries of east Central Europe.

16 Cf. Grint's constructivist and reflexive approach to management as a matter of active symbolic ascription: 'Who managers are depends upon who has the power to constitute certain forms of action as the action of managers' (1995: 47).

17 This general perspective of the contested and contestable character of expertise is shared by Pierre Bourdieu. 'Properties' or criteria of classification are always 'at stake' and are instruments in the class struggle itself; the space of 'properties' is therefore also a field of struggle for their appropriation (cf. Bourdieu and De Saint-Martin 1978: 6).

18 The role played formerly by 'proof of ancestry', as Weber already saw, was increasingly taken by the patent of education (1978: 1000).

19 Bourdieu and De Saint-Martin's important study focuses upon the 'chiasmic' structure of the dominant class, which is not only vertically divided according to general amount of capital, but also horizontally divided between those whose patrimony is dominated by economic capital and those who are primarily *cultural* capitalists. Their major horizontal distinction separates the *patrons privés* from the *patrons d'État*, and a mode of reproduction 'à dominante familiale' from a mode of reproduction 'à composante scholaire'.

20 It is Chandler's general view that the market remains the generator of demand for goods and services, but that modern business enterprise has taken over the functions of coordinating flows of goods through existing processes of production and distribution, and of allocating funds and personnel for future production and distribution. The rise of this coordinating function is also the rise of a 'new class' of middle and top managers. Cf. also Fennema's remark that 'the interlocking directorate is halfway between market and hierarchy' (1982: 43).

21 As Webster writes: 'A good case can be made for the view that management is in essence a category of information work'. Taylor's *Scientific Management* (1947) is summarized as implying that 'the *raison d'être* of management is to act as information specialists – ideally as monopolists – as close observers, analysts, and planners of capital's interests'. Taylor's major ambition was to argue that management was designated to perform the 'brainwork' of organizations and the surveillance of the production process (Webster 1995: 71; cf. Stabile 1984: 31ff.).

7 INTELLECTUAL CLOSURE AND THE NEW CLASS

1 Evidence of the repressed role of 'knowledgeable organization' in modern Marxism is, for example, found in Nicos Poulantzas's conception of the *nouvelle petite bourgeoisie*, which was explicitly designated as a 'knowledge class', but as one which neither owned its means of production nor laboured productively. Its primary service was the part it played in the ideological and political subordination of the working class to capital; its knowledge capital resulted from an intellectual expropriation of the working class (1974a: 236–8). The Ehrenreichs' conception of the 'professional–managerial class' (PMC) offers another instructive example. PMC

functionaries are non-owners who perform essentially non-productive mental functions which reproduce capitalist culture and capitalist class relations. Although it is a 'third class' which may differ in outlook and interests from the ruling class, there is an 'ultimate concordance' between bourgeoisie and PMC, which also stands in an 'objectively' antagonistic position towards the working class. The PMC is doubly derivative because, first, its function is to reproduce capitalist culture and cultural reproduction itself is 'non-productive labour', and second, because PMC functions are based upon the expropriation of once-indigenous working-class cultures and skills (Ehrenreich and Ehrenreich 1979).

2 However, these precarious moments of balance had a habit of extending across the entire spectrum of history. Leaving aside precapitalist and postcapitalist managerial states, which were exceptional by definition, the label was attributed to absolute monarchy (two long centuries, at the very least), Bonapartism (First and Second), Bismarckism, and, by contemporary Marxists, to the fascist movements and states of the Interbellum. This turned Anglo-Saxon liberal capitalism of the eighteenth and nineteenth centuries into one of those rules which could only be proven by their exceptions.

3 Marx here repeated Hegel's observation that government and state officials constituted a 'new middle estate', which was an estate of *Bildung*, 'the class in which the consciousness of right and the developed intelligence of the mass of the people is found' (1981: 104) (translation corrected). In a near-contemporary article, Marx described the censorship hierarchy as a 'Bürokratie der Intelligenz' (1843a: 20).

4 Cf. Stehr and Ericson (1992: 10) on knowledge as a relation of social actors to things and facts, but also to rules and laws and other actors. Collins, whose notion of 'positional property' includes symbolic position shaping and hence boundary work and legitimacy work, circumscribes property generically as 'a particular degree of tenure of action towards certain objects and persons' (1979: 54).

5 A possibly rich analysis of property vs. power theories of bureaucracy, which would run parallel to the treatment of management offered in the previous chapter, is not undertaken here.

6 Berger dislikes the term 'New Class' and opts in favour of 'knowledge class' as comprising the generic purveyors of symbolic knowledge. They make up a much larger group than the people conventionally called 'intellectuals', which may be defined as the *primary* producers of symbolic knowledge, and form only a kind of 'upper crust' of the broader knowledge class (1986: 66–7).

7 Bazelon has sarcastically identified the neo-conservative outcry against the New Class as 'itself a New Class maneuver', executed by intellectuals who made believe that they were not themselves part of it (1979: 445, 447).

8 See the older analyses of a 'capitalism without capitalists', as reported in the previous chapter. Cf. also Eyal *et al.* (1997).

9 Stehr insists that the 'knowledge-based occupations' (experts, counsellors, and advisers, which he sharply distinguishes from intellectuals) will not accede to mastery of the society, and are not likely to form a social class, because the scientification of social relations generates an 'essential fragility' of social structures, which dissipates and operates against formations attempting to monopolize decisions and usurp social futures. Experts, in his view, although they wield cultural power, do not control a more traditional and more consequential form of power, namely political power, which is 'the raw capacity to impose one's will against the will of others' (1994a: 168–9). However, I believe that the 'generalists of power' identified above do combine cultural, political, and economic power to such an extent as to legitimate the hypothesis of a New Class of intellectuals.

10 This intrusion of 'intellectual technologies' is typically captured by Bell and other functionalists in terms of a shift of the 'normative centre' of society towards the ethos and the method of science; cf. his assertion that 'the scientific estate – its ethos and organization – is the monad that contains within itself the imago of the future society' (1976a: 378, 386). Although Bell acknowledges that this ethos may easily turn into an ideology, he does not face the darker prospect that this progressive culturalization of non-cultural domains may also entail the universalization of an interested logic of cultural capital and intellectual rivalry: of a mandarin logic which must continually recreate belief in its own expertise as objective, and thereby routinely turns knowledge into private property (cf. Derber *et al.* 1990: 4–5, 59).

11 Parkin remarks that 'bourgeois' forms of closure such as property or credentials are less reliable than pre-bourgeois ones in preserving family privileges intact over several generations. This 'raises the crucial question of how dedicated the modern bourgeoisie actually is to its self-perpetuation through the blood line'. The bourgeois class system appears more biased in the direction of sponsorship and careful selection of successors than in that of hereditary transmission (1979: 60–3). However, Parkin's conflation of property and credentials as 'bourgeois' closure devices has the effect of underrating the kinship variable, especially in the case of material property, and thus to miss the difference in class reproduction rate between ideal-typical systems of property closure and ideal-typical systems of credential closure.

12 Collins does of course include an important cultural element, in so far as symbolic power (the power to define the tasks of positions and organizations) is identified as an essential element of political labour and positional property (1979: 50, 57). But his notion of political labour is still ruled by an emphasis upon the imposition of control over the conditions of work and appropriation of the fruits that issue therefrom.

13 In order to avert a senseless priority battle around the concept of cultural capital, let me note that first formulations of it are encountered in anarchists such as Bakunin, Machajski, and Nomad, and that Karl Mannheim and Hendrik De Man already describe education and culture as new forms of capital (Mannheim 1968 [1929]: 138–9; De Man 1931: 79ff.; 1933: 139ff.). From about 1933, and manifestly inspired by Machajski and Nomad, Lasswell analysed the new phenomenon of 'skill politics' as announcing a world revolution of permanent modernization under the leadership of the 'symbol specialists' or intellectuals, whose primary capital consisted of their knowledge (1977: 152ff., 177, 297, 385).

14 Reputations may of course 'hold' as a result of positional property and the presence of credentials, even though the practical competences have faded.

15 Since Collins' distinction is an analytical one, any job may be apportioned between the two categories in varying degrees. The modern occupational order can then be conceived as a 'range of variations in the possession of "political" resources for controlling the conditions of work and appropriating the fruits of production, hence it can be seen as a range of mixtures of productive work with political work' (Collins 1979: 52–3).

16 We may also recall our earlier exposition of Marx's and Weber's dual conception of bureaucracy as simultaneously functionalizing expertise and enclosing it by way of the 'administrative secret'.

17 Cf. a typical generalizing statement such as the following: 'Ideology is *both* false consciousness *and* rational discourse' (Gouldner 1976: 38).

18 Gouldner's rather summary sketch of the old economic and political classes between which the new knowledge class elbows itself to historical prominence,

also lacks an elaboration of its own 'vertical' composition or its marginalized or excluded groups (its 'underclass'). The nearest Gouldner gets to a theory of internal conflict is his paired definition of 'intellectuals' and 'intelligentsia', whose juxtaposition is presented as a major requirement and asset of any *general* theory of the New Class. Even if one disregards the fact that this division concerns two elites within a larger class, the distinction is not clear cut, and is further impaired by the fact that the unity-in-contradiction of the CCD dialectic repeats itself here in terms of corporate sociological agents. The CCD is most proximately activated by *critical* intellectuals, although the technical intelligentsia has it 'in latency'. 'Intellectuals' is both the generic and the 'specially valued' social category; 'intelligentsia' both its specific difference and its degenerate form.

19 Bazelon likewise suggests that the truly productive 'property' is 'the utility of the person', which is not merely individual but social and political, since the person's skill entails that he or she can do something, but also that the person can relate what he or she does to what others do (1967: 309). McDermott argues that professional knowledges and expert techniques are owned both individually and collectively, because they are only exercisable within 'corporate form' and crucially depend upon membership in a certain profession (1991: 80, 129).

20 Cf. the close connection between property and the issue of credibility in Weimer (1997).

8 TOWARDS A THEORY OF INTELLECTUAL RIVALRY

1 Concepts such as 'capitalism', 'proletariat', and 'culture', Mannheim suggested early on, were 'directional' in the sense of embodying a specific normative-political 'stress' (*tensio*); all sociological thought was embedded in a drive for change (1982: 199–200, 203, 247; 1968: 3–4).

2 In this manner, Schmitt substantively anticipated Lukes' and Connolly's application of Gallie's notion of 'essential contestability' to political theory. For Connolly, contests about the concept of politics are indeed simultaneously part of politics itself (1974: 30, 36, 39).

3 A few years later, this *völkische* version of standpoint epistemology was repeated by Schmitt, who in no uncertain terms connected the achievement of objectivity to its 'existential rootedness' in the life of the (German) Nation (1935: 45).

4 On the American dispute over *Ideology and Utopia*, cf. especially Kettler and Meja (1995: 193ff.).

5 It is peculiar that a diligent historian of science such as Shapin misses this boundary work on the right flank, and traces the emergence of stricter demarcations between 'internal' and 'external' accounts of scientific change exclusively to the Marxist historiography of the 1940s and 1950s (Shapin 1992: 338–9).

6 Gallie himself had already linked contestability to a logic of conversion in religious, aesthetic, political, or moral fields (1955–6: 188). Garver appositely assumes that 'our ideas have political relations with each other, which are informed by the metaphors and presuppositions inherited from political relations' (1990: 266n.).

7 As a curious matter of detail, we may note Bourdieu's double misreading, in his later defence of Merton, against the presumed nihilism and reductionism of the Strong Programme and its radical offshoots. First, his repeated warning against 'short-circuit' explanations, which fail to recognize the inevitable refraction of

external social interests by the laws of the intellectual field, evidently misfires when it is critically addressed at the Strong Programme (Bourdieu 1990; 1995). Second, Merton is credited with a quasi-economic conception of intellectual competition which not only directly and explicitly paraphrases Mannheim's 1928 text (which Bourdieu ignores), but which is also interpreted in a far more 'agonistic' sense than Merton ever intended (cf. Merton 1973: 100–1; Pels 1996a).

8 It is somewhat questionable whether Bourdieu still maintains this radical position twenty years after the fact. Since 1975, he has (rather like Mannheim after 1930) toned down his early formulations, in order to approach a more academic and Mertonian conception of scientific competition, which increasingly insists on the scientificity of sociology, on a strong version of 'relational realism', and on the autonomy of the scientific community as informed by an ever more stringent opposition between the logic of the political and that of the scientific field (Bourdieu 1995; cf. Pels 1995a).

9 This episode is treated more extensively in Pels (1997).

10 By itself, of course, this repoliticization of non-humans and things once again demonstrates the essential arbitrariness of conventional associations which pair politics to persons and property to things.

11 This law of accumulation is similarly operative in the field of artistic production:

> Few social actors depend as much as artists, and intellectuals in general, for what they are upon the image that other people have of them and what they are. . . . For the author, the critic, the art dealer, the publisher, or the theatre manager, the only legitimate accumulation consists in making a name for oneself, a known, recognized name, a capital of consecration implying a power to consecrate objects (with a trademark or signature) or persons (through publications, exhibition, etc.) and therefore give value, and to appropriate the profits from this operation.
>
> (Bourdieu 1971: 166)

12 When touching upon the subject of religious dogma, Weber was likewise attracted by a proprietary metaphor: 'Sie sind kein "Wissen" im gewöhnlichen Sinn, sondern ein "Haben"' (1968: 611; 1970b: 154).

13 Taking over the basic parameters of Bourdieu's field theory of science, Latour and Woolgar nevertheless also criticized him (rather unfairly, it now seems) for his 'tautological' conception of interest and for not sufficiently attending to the 'contents' of scientific work (1979: 206).

14 Cf. Bourdieu's account of the magic of 'investiture', by which an institution delegates part of its (in this case, political) capital to a person, its representative, who is thereby consecrated into an 'official' of the institution. It is the institution which controls access to personal fame by, for example, controlling access to the most conspicuous positions (general secretary, official spokespersons) or to the places of publicity (press conferences, TV), although the person endowed with delegated capital can still obtain personal capital through a subtle strategy of distanciation from the institution (Bourdieu 1991: 195–6).

15 Cf. Gouldner:

> *Whomever* intellectuals represent and *however diverse* the latter may be, intellectuals also, and always, represent their *own* interests. More than that: intellectuals always represent the interests of other classes as they see, define, and interpret them; and their interpretations are selectively

mediated by their own social character and special ambitions as an historically distinct social stratum.

(1975–6: 11)

16 Styles of thought, Mannheim argued in his essay on 'Conservative Thought', tend to polarize and develop in very clear-cut extremes. Citing Oppenheimer's interpretation of Romanticism as an 'intellectual counter-revolution' against Enlightenment rationalism (and an *imitation par opposition* in Tarde's sense), Mannheim added that 'no antithesis escapes conditioning by the thesis it sets out to oppose' (1953: 89). Cf. his view of the 'productive one-sidedness' which is characteristic of every school of thought, which tends to hypostatize itself as 'thought as such' (1982: 155).

17 Cf. Knorr-Cetina's related view of the mechanism of 'affirmative negation' (1977: 683–4).

18 In an early text, Mannheim already singled out as a distinctive feature of intellectual history that

consciousness, which at first appears to be unitary, splits, and certain of its possible directions are borne at a given point by specific social groups, whose world project elaborates these directions and makes them into absolutes. The opposing groups for their part take up the remaining tendencies of thought.

(1982: 183)

19 In a similar vein, both Schelsky (1975) and Gouldner (1985) have commented on the maintenance of the 'old class' myth about the historical conflict between bourgeoisie and proletariat as a mystificatory strategy on the part of the New Class.

20 One recent variant is provided by Beck's idea that the 'unpolitical' bourgeois of welfare capitalism has turned into a *political bourgeois* in the new phase of reflexive modernity, and is presently obliged to 'govern' in his or her economic sphere after the logic and criteria of political legitimation (1993: 197ff.).

21 In an important sense, the converging drives for politicization of the economy (which ideologically dominated the 'radical' 1960s and 1970s) and for economization of the polity (which is currently dominant as a result of the neo-liberal turn), have both channelled and furthered a process of *professionalization* and hence of *intellectualization* of both domains, a process which tends to be obscured by the lingering conviction of an 'essentially' adversarial relationship between them.

22 This position resembles the one which induced Alvin Gouldner to take equal distance from both academic sociology and Marxism, because, as an involuntary 'outlaw sociologist' and a self-styled 'outlaw Marxist', he could comfortably live neither in the one nor in the other. This value-committed, partial, but also potentially synthetic position might be characterized as the neither–nor position which is typically occupied by the 'outsider' or 'stranger' (cf. Pels 1993a; 1998).

BIBLIOGRAPHY

Ackerman, B. (1977) *Private Property and the Constitution*, New Haven, CA: Yale University Press.

Alcoff, L. and Potter, E. (1993) 'Introduction: When Feminisms Intersect Epistemology', in *idem* (eds) *Feminist Epistemologies*, New York and London: Routledge.

Allen, M. P. (1976) 'Management Control in the Large Corporation: Comment on Zeitlin', *American Journal of Sociology* 81(4): 885–94.

Althusser, L. (1971) *Lenin and Philosophy and Other Essays*, London: New Left Books.

—— (1976) *For Marx*, New York: Vintage Books.

Anderson, P. (1974) *Lineages of the Absolutist State*, London: New Left Books.

—— (1992) *Zones of Engagement*, London: Verso.

Ansart, P. (1969) *Marx et l'anarchisme*, Paris: PUF.

Aristotle (1977) *Nicomachean Ethics*, trans. J. A. K. Thompson, Harmondsworth: Penguin Books.

—— (1979) *The Politics*, trans. T. A. Sinclair, Harmondsworth: Penguin Books.

Arneson, R. J. (1992) 'Property Rights in Persons', *Social Philosophy & Policy* 9: 201–30.

Aron, R. (1965) *Main Currents of Sociological Thought*, 2 Vols, Harmondsworth: Pelican Books.

—— (1986) '*Macht*, Power, *Puissance*: Democratic Prose or Demoniacal Poetry?', in S. Lukes (ed.) *Power*, Oxford: Blackwell.

Aschheim, S. (1992) *The Nietzsche Legacy in Germany 1890–1990*, Berkeley, CA: University of California Press.

Austin, J. (1954 [1832]) *The Province of Jurisprudence Determined*, London: John Murray.

—— (1885 [1861]) *Lectures on Jurisprudence*, London: John Murray.

Avineri, S. (1972) *Hegel's Theory of the Modern State*, Cambridge: Cambridge University Press.

Aylmer, G. E. (1980) 'The Meaning and Definition of Property in 17th-century England', *Past and Present* 86: 87–97.

Bakunin, M. (1972) *Staatlichkeit und Anarchie und andere Schriften*, Frankfurt a.M.: Ullstein.

Balbus, I. (1971) 'Ruling Elite Theory vs. Marxist Class Analysis', *Monthly Review* 23(1): 36–46.

—— (1982) *Marxism and Domination*, Princeton, NJ: Princeton University Press.

Ball, T. (1978) 'Two Concepts of Coercion', *Theory and Society* 5(1): 79–112.

287

—— (1988) *Transforming Political Discourse. Political Theory and Critical Conceptual History*, Oxford: Blackwell.

Baran, P. H. and Sweezy, P. M. (1968) *Monopoly Capital*, Harmondsworth: Pelican Books.

Barnes, B. (1974) *Scientific Knowledge and Sociological Theory*, London: Routledge & Kegan Paul.

—— (1988) *The Nature of Power*, Cambridge: Polity Press.

—— (1993) 'Power', in R. Bellamy (ed.) *Theories and Concepts of Politics*, Manchester and New York: Manchester University Press.

—— and MacKenzie, D. (1979) 'On the Role of Interests in Scientific Change', in R. Wallis (ed.) *On the Margins of Science*, Keele: Sociological Review Monograph.

Barry, A., Osborne, T. and Rose, N. (eds) (1976) *Foucault and Political Reason*, London: UCL Press.

Barry, B. (ed.) (1976) *Power and Political Theory: Some European Perspectives*, London: John Wiley.

—— (1991) *Democracy and Power. Essays in Political Theory*, Vol. 1, Oxford: Clarendon Press.

Bazelon, D. T. (1967) *Power in America: The Politics of the New Class*, New York: New American Library.

—— (1979) 'How Now, the New Class?', *Dissent* 26: 443–9.

Beck, U. (1992) *Risk Society*, London: Sage.

—— (1993) *Die Erfindung des Politischen*, Frankfurt: Suhrkamp.

——, Giddens, A. and Lash, S. (1994) *Reflexive Modernization*, Cambridge: Polity Press.

Becker, G. L. (1964) *Human Capital*, New York: Columbia University Press.

Becker, H. and Barnes, H. E. (1952) *Social Thought from Lore to Science*, 2 Vols, Washington, DC: Harren Press.

Becker, L. C. (1977) *Property Rights: Philosophic Foundations*, London: Routledge & Kegan Paul.

—— (1980) 'The Moral Basis of Property Rights', in J. R. Pennock and J. W. Chapman (eds) (1980).

—— and Kipnis, K. (eds) (1984) *Property: Cases, Concepts, Critiques*, Englewood Cliffs, NJ: Prentice Hall.

—— (1992) 'Too Much Property', *Philosophy & Public Affairs* 21(2): 196–206.

Beetham, D. (1977) 'From Socialism to Fascism: The Relation Between Theory and Practice in the Work of Robert Michels', *Political Studies* 25(1&2): 3–24, 161–81.

Bell, D. (1961) *The End of Ideology*, New York: The Free Press.

—— (1968) 'The Power Elite Reconsidered', in W. B. Domhoff and H. B. Ballard (eds) (1968).

—— (1976a) *The Coming of Post-Industrial Society*, Harmondsworth: Penguin Books.

—— (1976b) *The Cultural Contradictions of Capitalism*, New York: Basic Books.

—— (1979) 'The New Class: A Muddled Concept', in B. Bruce-Briggs (ed.).

Bellis, P. (1979) *Marxism and the USSR*, London: Macmillan.

Bendersky, J. W. (1987) 'Carl Schmitt and the Conservative Revolution', *Telos* 72: 27–42.

Benedict, R. (1935) 'Magic', *Encyclopedia of the Social Sciences*, New York: The Macmillan Company.

Benoist, A. de (1983) *Aus rechter Sicht*, Vol. 1, Tübingen: Grabert Verlag.

—— (1984) *Aus rechter Sicht*, Vol. 2, Tübingen: Grabert Verlag.

—— (1993) 'Democracy Revisited', *Telos* 95: 65–75.

Berger, P. L. (1986) *The Capitalist Revolution*, New York: Basic Books.

Berle, A. (1954) *The Twentieth-Century Capitalist Revolution*, New York: Harcourt, Brace & World.

—— (1959) *Power Without Property*, New York: Harcourt, Brace & World.

—— and Means, G. W. (1968 [1932]) *The Modern Corporation and Private Property*, New York: Harcourt, Brace & World.

Berman, P. (ed.) (1972) *Quotations from the Anarchists*, New York: Praeger.

Bevers, A. and Zijderveld, A. C. (1992) 'Unexpected Convergences: New Class, Market, and Welfare State in the World of Art', in H. Kellner and F. W. Heuberger (eds) (1992).

Bierstedt, R. (1970) 'An Analysis of Social Power', in M. Olsen (ed.) (1970).

Binns, D. (1977) *Beyond the Sociology of Conflict*, London: Macmillan.

Blackburn, R. (1965) 'The New Capitalism', in P. Anderson and R. Blackburn (eds) *Towards Socialism*, London: New Left Review/Fontana.

Bloor, D. (1991) *Knowledge and Social Imagery*, Chicago: The University of Chicago Press.

Bodin, J. (1962 [1606]) *The Six Bookes of a Commonweale*, Knolles translation, ed. K. D. McRae, Cambridge, MA: Harvard University Press.

Böhme, G. (1992) *Coping With Science*, Boulder, CA: Westview Press.

—— and Stehr, N. (1986) 'The Growing Impact of Scientific Knowledge on Social Relations', in *idem* (eds) *The Knowledge Society*, Dordrecht: Reidel.

Bookchin, M. (1980) *Towards an Ecological Society*, Montreal and New York: Black Rose Books.

—— (1982) *The Ecology of Freedom*, Palo Alto, CA: Cheshire Books.

—— (1986 [1971]) *Post-Scarcity Anarchism*, Montreal and New York: Black Rose Books.

—— (1990) *Remaking Society: Pathways to a Green Future*, Boston: South End Press.

Bordo, S. (1990) 'Feminism, Postmodernism, and Gender-Scepticism', in L. Nicholson (ed.).

Bottomore, T. B. (1966) *Elites and Society*, Harmondsworth: Penguin Books.

—— (1979) *Political Sociology*, London: Hutchinson.

—— and Nisbet, R. (1979) 'Introduction' to *A History of Sociological Analysis*, London: Heinemann.

—— Nowak, S. and Sokolowska, M. (eds) (1982) *Sociology: The State of the Art*, London: Sage.

Bourdieu, P. (1971) 'Intellectual Field and Creative Project', in M. Young (ed.) *Knowledge and Control*, London: Collier-Macmillan.

—— (1979) *La Distinction*, Paris: Minuit.

—— (1980) *Le Sens pratique*, Paris: Minuit.

—— (1981) 'The Specificity of the Scientific Field', in Ch. Lemert (ed.) *French Sociology: Rupture and Renewal since 1968*, New York: Columbia University Press.

—— (1986) 'The Forms of Capital', in J. G. Richardson (ed.) *Handbook of Theory and Research for the Sociology of Education*, New York: Greenwood Press.

—— (1988) 'Vive la crise! For Heterodoxy in Social Science', *Theory and Society* 17(5): 773–87.

—— (1989) *La Noblesse d'état. Grandes écoles et esprit de corps*, Paris: Minuit.

—— (1990) 'Animadversiones in Mertonem', in J. Clark, C. Modgil, and S. Modgil (eds) *Robert K. Merton: Consensus and Controversy*, London: Falmer Press.

—— (1991) *Language and Symbolic Power*, Cambridge: Polity Press.

✻ —— (1993a) *The Field of Cultural Production*, Cambridge: Polity Press.

—— (1993b) *Sociology in Question*, London: Sage.

—— (1994) *Raisons pratiques. Sur la théorie de l'action*, Paris: Seuil.

—— (1995) 'La Cause de la science', *Actes de la recherche en sciences sociales* 106/107: 3–10.

—— and De Saint-Martin, M. (1978) 'Le Patronat', *Actes de la recherche en sciences sociales* 20/21: 3–87.

—— and Wacquant, L. J. D. (1992) *Invitation to a Reflexive Sociology*, Chicago: Chicago University Press.

Bowen, R. (1947) *German Theories of the Corporate State*, New York and London: Russell & Russell.

Braidotti, R. (1994) *Nomadic Subjects*, New York: Columbia University Press.

Brandt, R. (1974) *Eigentumstheorien von Grotius bis Kant*, Stuttgart/Bad Cannstatt: Frommann-Holzboog.

Brenan, G. (1943) *The Spanish Labyrinth*, Cambridge: Cambridge University Press.

Breuer, S. (1991) *Max Weber's Herrschaftssoziologie*, Frankfurt and New York: Campus Verlag.

—— (1993) *Anatomie der Konservativen Revolution*, Darmstadt: Wissenschaftliche Buchgesellschaft.

Brint, S. (1984) '"New Class" and Cumulative Trend Explanations of the Liberal Political Attitude of Professionals', *American Journal of Sociology* 90(1): 30–71.

—— (1994) *In an Age of Experts*, Princeton, NJ: Princeton University Press.

Brubaker, R. (1985) 'Rethinking Class Theory: The Sociological Vision of Pierre Bourdieu', *Theory and Society* 14(6): 745–75.

Bruce-Briggs, B. (1979) 'An Introduction to the Idea of the New Class', in *idem* (ed.) *The New Class?*, New Brunswick, NJ: Transaction Books.

Buckle, S. (1991) *Natural Law and the Theory of Property. Grotius to Hume*, Oxford: Clarendon Press.

Burnham, J. (1945) *The Managerial Revolution*, Harmondsworth: Penguin Books.

—— (1963) *The Machiavellians: Defenders of Freedom*, Chicago: Regnery.

Burns, J. H. (ed.) (1988) *The Cambridge History of Medieval Political Thought*, Cambridge: Cambridge University Press.

Burris, V. (1986) 'The Discovery of the New Middle Class', *Theory and Society* 15(3): 317–49.

Butler, J. (1989) *Gender Trouble: Feminism and the Subversion of Identity*, London and New York: Routledge.

—— (1992) 'Contingent Foundations: Feminism and the Question of Postmodernism', in J. Butler and J. W. Scott (eds).

—— and Scott, J. W. (eds) (1992) *Feminists Theorize the Political*, New York and London: Routledge.

Callon, M. (1986) 'Some Elements of a Sociology of Translation: Domestication of the Scallops and the Fishermen of St Brieuc Bay', in J. Law (ed.) (1986).

—— and Latour, B. (1981) 'Unscrewing the Big Leviathan', in K. Knorr-Cetina and A. A. Cicourel (eds).

——, Law, J. and Rip, A. (eds) (1986) *Mapping the Dynamics of Science*, London and Houndmills: Macmillan.

Cannan, E. (1917) *Wealth: A Brief Exploration of the Causes of Economic Welfare*, London: King.

Canning, J. P. (1988) 'Intro: Politics, Institutions, Ideas', in J. H. Burns (ed.).

Carchedi, G. (1977) *On the Economic Identification of Social Classes*, London: Routledge.

Carling, A. (1986) 'Rational Choice Marxism', *New Left Review* 160: 24–62.

Carlyle, R. W. and Carlyle, A. J. (1928 [1909]) *A History of Medieval Political Theory in the West*, Vol. II, Edinburgh and London: William Blackwood.

Carroll, J. (1974) *Break-Out from the Crystal Palace. The Anarcho-Psychological Critique: Stirner, Nietzsche, Dostoevsky*, London and Boston: Routledge & Kegan Paul.

Carter, A. (1993) 'Towards a Green Political Theory', in A. Dobson and P. Lucardie (eds).

Cassirer, E. (1910) *Substanzbegriff und Funktionsbegriff*, Berlin: S. Cassirer.

Castells, M. (1989) *The Informational City*, Oxford: Blackwell.

Challenger, D. F. (1994) *Durkheim Through the Lens of Aristotle*, Lanham, MD: Rowman & Littlefield.

Chandler, A. D. (1977) *The Visible Hand: The Managerial Revolution in American Business*, London: The Belknap Press.

Chirot, D. (1977) *Social Change in the Twentieth Century*, New York: Harcourt.

Church, W. F. (1941) *Constitutional Thought in Sixteenth-Century France*, Cambridge, MA: Harvard University Press.

Claeys, G. (1986) '"Individualism", "Socialism", and "Social Science"', *Journal of the History of Ideas* 47(1): 81–93.

Clark, J. P. (1977) *The Philosophical Anarchism of William Godwin*, Princeton, NJ: Princeton University Press.

—— (1978) 'What is Anarchism?', in J. R. Pennock and J. W. Chapman (eds) (1978).

—— (1984) *The Anarchist Moment: Reflections on Culture, Nature, and Power*, Montreal and New York: Black Rose Books.

—— (1989) 'Marx's Inorganic Body', *Environmental Ethics* 11: 234–58.

Clegg, S. R. (1989) *Frameworks of Power*, London: Sage.

Cohen, G. A. (1978) *Karl Marx's Theory of History*, Oxford: Oxford University Press.

Cohen, H. E. (1937) *Recent Theories of Sovereignty*, Chicago: The University of Chicago Press.

Cohen, J. L. and Arato, A. (1992) *Civil Society and Political Theory*, Cambridge, MA: The MIT Press.

Cohen, M. (1978 [1927]) 'Property and Sovereignty', in C. B. Macpherson (ed.) (1978).

Coleman, J. (1988) 'Property and Poverty', in J. H. Burns (ed.).

Coleman, J. S. (1988) 'Social Capital in the Creation of Human Capital', *American Journal of Sociology* 94: S95–120.

Colletti, L. (1973) *Marxism and Hegel*, London: New Left Books.

Collini, S. (1979) *Liberalism and Sociology: L. T. Hobhouse and Political Argument in England 1880–1914*, Cambridge: Cambridge University Press.

Collins, R. (1979) *The Credential Society*, New York: Academic Press.

—— (1986) *Weberian Sociological Theory*, Cambridge: Cambridge University Press.

—— and Makowsky, M. (1972) *The Discovery of Society*, New York: Random House.

Commons, J. (1965 [1899–1900]) *A Sociological View of Sovereignty*, New York: Kelley.

Comte, A. (1852) *Système de politique positive*, Vol. II, Paris: Mathias.

—— (1970) *Écrits de jeunesse 1816–1826*, ed. P. E. de Berrêdo Carneiro and P. Arnaud, Paris: Mouton.

—— (1974) *The Crisis of Industrial Civilization: The Early Essays of Auguste Comte*, ed. R. Fletcher, London: Heinemann.

—— (1975a) *Auguste Comte and Positivism: The Essential Writings*, ed. G. Lenzer, Chicago: University of Chicago Press.

—— (1975b) *Cours de philosophie positive. Leçons 46 à 60*, ed. J.-P. Enthoven, Paris: Mouton.

Connolly, W. E. (1974) *The Terms of Political Discourse*, London: D.C. Heath.

Coser, L. (1960) 'Durkheim's Conservatism and Its Implications for his Sociological Theory', in K. Wolff (ed.) (1960).

Crespi, F. (1992) *Social Action and Power*, Oxford: Blackwell.

Cropsey, J. (1957) *Polity and Economy: An Interpretation of the Principles of Adam Smith*, The Hague: Martinus Nijhoff.

—— (1975) 'Adam Smith and Political Philosophy', in A. S. Skinner and T. Wilson (eds).

Crosland, C. A. R. (1963) *The Future of Socialism*, New York: Schocken Books.

Crowder, G. (1991) *Classical Anarchism*, Oxford: Clarendon Press.

d'Agostino, A. (1977) *Marxism and the Russian Anarchists*, New York: Germinal Press.

—— (1988) 'Machajski and the New Class: A Reply to Haberkern', *Telos* 77: 138–42.

Dahl, G. (1996) 'Will the "Other God" Fail Again?', *Theory, Culture, and Society* 13(1): 25–50.

Dahl, R. (1969 [1957]) 'On the Concept of Power', in R. Bell *et al.* (eds) *Political Power: A Reader in Theory and Research*, New York: The Free Press.

Dahrendorf, R. (1959) *Class and Class Conflict in Industrial Society*, Stanford, CA: Stanford University Press.

—— (1967) *Conflict After Class* Noel Buxton Lecture, London.

—— (1969) 'On the Origin of Inequality Among Men', in A. Béteille (ed.) *Social Inequality*, Harmondsworth: Penguin Books.

—— (1979) *Life Chances: Approaches to Social and Political Theory*, London: Weidenfeld & Nicolson.

—— (1988) *The Modern Social Conflict: An Essay on the Politics of Liberty*, New York: Weidenfeld & Nicolson.

Dautry, J. (1951) 'Introduction' to C.-H. de Saint-Simon (1951).

Davis, K. (1970) *Human Society*, New York: Macmillan.

Déat, M. (1930) *Perspectives socialistes*, Paris: Librairie Valois.

De George, R. T. (1978) 'Anarchism and Authority', in J. R. Pennock and J. W. Chapman (eds) (1978).

De Lauretis, T. (1990) 'Eccentric Subjects. Feminist Theory and Historical Consciousness', *Feminist Studies* 16(1): 115–50.

De Man, H. (1926) *De psychologie van het socialisme*, Arnhem: Van Loghum Slaterus.

—— (1931) *Opbouwend socialisme*, Arnhem: Van Loghum Slaterus.

—— (1933) *De socialistische idee*, Arnhem: Van Loghum Slaterus.

Derber, Ch., Schwartz, W. A., and Magrass, Y. (1990) *Power in the Highest Degree: Professionals and the Rise of a New Mandarin Order*, New York: Oxford University Press.

De Wit, T. (1992) *De onontkoombaarheid van de politiek*, Ubbergen: Pomppers.

Dews, P. (1987) *Logics of Disintegration*, London: Verso.

Disco, C. (1987) 'Intellectuals in Advanced Capitalism. Capital, Closure, and the "New Class" Thesis', in R. Eyerman *et al.*

Djilas, M. (1957) *The New Class: An Analysis of the Communist System*, New York: Praeger.

Dobson, A. (1990) *Green Political Thought: An Introduction*, London and New York: Routledge.

—— (1993) 'Afterword', in *idem* and P. Lucardie (eds).

—— and Lucardie, P. (eds) (1993) *The Politics of Nature: Explorations in Green Political Theory*, London and New York: Routledge.

Domhoff, W. B. and Ballard, H. B. (eds) (1968) *C. Wright Mills and the Power Elite*, Boston: Beacon Press.

Donahue Jr, Ch. (1980) 'The Future of the Concept of Property Predicted from Its Past', in J. R. Pennock and J. W. Chapman (eds) (1980).

Donzelot, J. (1979) *The Policing of Families*, New York: Pantheon Books.

—— (1984) *L'Invention du social*, Paris: Fayard.

Dronkers, J. (1983) 'Mythen over elites. De rol van het onderwijs bij de recrutering van directeuren van grote bedrijven', *Amsterdams Sociologisch Tijdschrift* 9(4): 606–46.

Droz, J. (1948) *Histoire des doctrines politiques en France*, Paris: PUF.

Duguit, L. (1920 [1912]) *Les Transformations générales du droit privé depuis le Code Napoléon*, Paris: Alcan.

Durkheim, E. (1958) *Socialism*, New York: Collier-Macmillan.

—— (1966) *Montesquieu et Rousseau. Précurseurs de la sociologie*, Paris: Marcel Rivière.

—— (1970) *La Science sociale et l'action*, ed. J.-C. Filloux, Paris: PUF.

—— (1972) *Selected Writings*, ed. A. Giddens, Cambridge: Cambridge University Press.

—— (1975) *Textes 1. Eléments d'une théorie sociale*, Paris: Minuit.

—— (1977) *Textes 3. Fonctions sociales et institutions*, Paris: Minuit.

—— (1982 [1895]) *The Rules of Sociological Method*, ed. S. Lukes, London and Basingstoke: Macmillan.

—— (1984 [1933]) *The Division of Labour in Society*, Houndmills and Basingstoke: Macmillan.

—— (1986) *Durkheim on Politics and the State*, ed. A. Giddens, Cambridge: Polity Press.

—— (1992) *Professional Ethics and Civic Morals*, London and New York: Routledge.

Easton, D. (1953) *The Political System*, New York: Knopf.

Eckersley, R. (1992) *Environmentalism and Political Theory*, Albany, NY: SUNY Press.

Eco, U. (1995) 'Ur-Fascism', *New York Review of Books* 22 June.

Ehrenreich, B. and Ehrenreich, J. (1979) 'The Professional-Managerial Class', in P. Walker (ed.) *Between Capital and Labour*, Hassocks: Harvester Press.

Elbow, M. H. (1953) *French Corporative Theory 1789–1948*, New York: Columbia University Press.

Elias, N. (1978) *What is Sociology?*, London: Hutchinson.

—— (1984) 'On the Sociogenesis of Sociology', *Amsterdams Sociologisch Tijdschrift* 11(1): 14–52.

Elster, J. (1976) 'Some Conceptual Problems in Political Theory', in B. Barry (ed.).

—— (1985) *Making Sense of Marx*, Cambridge: Cambridge University Press.

Engels, F. ([1847] 1972) 'Die Kommunisten und Karl Heinzen', *Marx-Engels Werke*, Vol. 4, Berlin: Dietz Verlag.

—— ([1878] 1972) *Herr Eugen Dühring's Umwälzung der Wissenschaft, Marx-Engels Werke*, Vol. 20, Berlin: Dietz Verlag.

Etzioni-Halévy, E. (1993) *The Elite Connection. Problems and Potential of Western Democracy*, Cambridge: Polity Press.

Eyal, G., Szelényi, I., and Townsley, E. (1997) 'The Theory of Post-Communist Managerialism', *New Left Review* 222, March/April: 60–92.

Eyerman, R. *et al.* (eds) (1987) *Intellectuals, Universities, and the State in Modern Western Societies*, Berkeley, CA: University of California Press.

Fennema, M. (1982) *International Networks of Banks and Industry*, The Hague: Martinus Nijhoff.

—— and Schijf, H. (1978–9) 'Analyzing Interlocking Directorates: Theory and Methods', *Social Networks* 1: 297–332.

Ferguson, A. (1966 [1767]) *An Essay on the History of Civil Society*, Edinburgh: Edinburgh University Press.

Filloux, J.-C. (1977) *Durkheim et le socialisme*, Genève: Droz.

—— (1993) 'Inequalities and Social Stratification in Durkheim's Sociology', in S. P. Turner (ed.).

Firestone, S. (1970) *The Dialectic of Sex*, New York: Bantam Books.

Fletcher, R. (1974) 'Introduction. The New Social System: From Criticism to Construction' in A. Comte (1974).

Forbes, D. (1966) 'Introduction' to A. Ferguson (1767).

Foucault, M. (1977) *Discipline and Punish*, Harmondsworth: Penguin Books.

—— (1978) *The History of Sexuality I: An Introduction*, London: Allen Lane.

—— (1980) *Power/Knowledge*, ed. C. Gordon, New York: Pantheon.

—— (1983) 'The Subject and Power', in H. Dreyfus and P. Rabinow (eds) *Michel Foucault: Beyond Structuralism and Hermeneutics*, Chicago: The University of Chicago Press.

—— (1985) *Ervaring en waarheid*, Nijmegen: Te Elfder Ure.

Franklin, J. (1973) *Jean Bodin and the Rise of Absolutist Theory*, London: Cambridge University Press.

Fraser, A. (1983) 'The Corporation as a Body Politic', *Telos* 57: 5–40.

Fraser, N. (1989) *Unruly Practices*, Cambridge: Polity Press.

Freidson, E. (1986) *Professional Powers: A Study of the Institutionalization of Formal Knowledge*, Chicago and London: The University of Chicago Press.

Freyer, H. ([1921] 1966) *Die Bewertung der Wirtschaft im philosophischen Denken des 19. Jahrhunderts*, Hildesheim: George Olms.

—— (1926) *Der Staat*, Leipzig: Ernst Wiegandt.

—— ([1930] 1964) *Soziologie als Wirklichkeitswissenschaft*, Stuttgart: Teubner.

—— (1931) *Revolution von Rechts*, Jena: Eugen Diederichs Verlag.

—— (1986) *Preussentum und Aufklärung und andere Studien zu Ethik und Politik*, ed. E. Üner, Weinheim: VCH.

—— (1987) *Herrschaft, Planung, und Technik*, ed. E. Üner, Weinheim: VCH.

Fried, F. (1931) *Das Ende de Kapitalismus*, Jena: Eugen Diederichs Verlag.

Friedmann, W. (1972) *Law in a Changing Society*, London: Steven.

Frisby, D. and Sayer, D. (1986) *Society*, London: Tavistock.

Furubotn, E. J. and Pejovich, S. (eds) (1974) *The Economics of Property Rights*, Cambridge, MA: Ballinger.

Galbraith, J. K. (1972) *The New Industrial State*, Harmondsworth: Penguin Books.

Gallie, W. B. (1955–6) 'Essentially Contested Concepts', *Proceedings of the Aristotelian Society* 56: 167–98.

Gane, M. (1992) 'Institutional Socialism and the Sociological Critique of Communism', in *idem* (ed.) *The Radical Sociology of Durkheim and Mauss*, London and New York: Routledge.

Garver, E. (1990) 'Essentially Contested Concepts: The Ethics and Tactics of Argument', *Philosophy and Rhetoric* 23(4): 251–70.

Geiger, T. (1949) *Die Klassengesellschaft im Schmelztiegel*, Köln and Hagen: Gustav Kiepenheuer.

Gerschenkron, A. (1962) *Economic Backwardness in Historical Perspective*, Cambridge, MA: The Belknap Press.

Gewirth, A. (1951) *Marsilius of Padua and Medieval Political Philosophy*, New York: Columbia University Press.

—— (1956) 'Introduction' to Marsilius of Padua (1324) *The Defender of Peace*, New York: Harper & Row.

Giddens, A. (1972a) *Politics and Sociology in the Thought of Max Weber*, London and Basingstoke: Macmillan.

—— (1972b) 'Introduction' to E. Durkheim (1972).

—— (1973) *The Class Structure of the Advanced Societies*, London: Hutchinson.

—— (1976) *New Rules of Sociological Method*, London: Hutchinson.

—— (1977) *Studies in Social and Political Theory*, London: Hutchinson.

—— (1979) *Central Questions in Social Theory*, London and Basingstoke: Macmillan.

—— (1982) *Profiles and Critiques in Social Theory*, London and Basingstoke: Macmillan.

Gierke, O. (1958 [1900]) *Political Theories of the Middle Age*, trans. with an introd. by F. W. Maitland, Cambridge: Beacon Press.

Gilbert, F. (1965) *Machiavelli and Guicciardini: Politics and History in Sixteenth-Century Florence*, Princeton, NJ: Princeton University Press.

Gilmore, M. P. (1967 [1941]) *Argument from Roman Law in Political Thought 1200–1600*, New York: Russell & Russell.

Godechot, J. (ed.) (1970) *Les Constitutions de la France depuis 1789*, Paris: Garnier-Flammarion.

Godwin, W. (1976 [1793]) *Enquiry Concerning Political Justice*, ed. I. Kramnick, Harmondsworth: Penguin Books.

Goldsmith, G. C. (1966) *Hobbes's Science of Politics*, New York and London: Columbia University Press.

Goodman, E. H. (1973) *The Socialism of Marcel Déat*, PhD thesis, Stanford University.

Gordon, C. (1987) 'The Soul of the Citizen: Max Weber and Michel Foucault on Rationality and Government', in S. Lash and S. Whimster (eds).

Gordon, S. (1991) *The History and Philosophy of Social Science*, London: Routledge.

Goubert, P. (1973) *The Ancien Regime: French Society 1600–1750*, New York: Harper & Row.

Goudsblom, J. (1977) *Sociology in the Balance: A Critical Essay*, Oxford: Basil Blackwell.

Gouldner, A. (1958) 'Introduction' to E. Durkheim (1958).

—— (1970) *The Coming Crisis of Western Sociology*, London: Heinemann.

—— (1975–6) 'Prologue to a Theory of Revolutionary Intellectuals', *Telos* 26: 3–36.

—— (1976) *The Dialectic of Ideology and Technology*, New York: Oxford University Press.

—— (1979) *The Future of Intellectuals and the Rise of the New Class*, New York: The Seabury Press.

—— (1980) *The Two Marxisms*, New York and Toronto: Oxford University Press.

—— (1985) *Against Fragmentation: The Origins of Marxism and the Sociology of Intellectuals*, New York: Oxford University Press.

Gray, J. (1983) 'Political Power, Social Theory, and Essential Contestability', in D. Miller and L. Siedentop (eds) *The Nature of Political Theory*, Oxford: Clarendon Press.

Gregor, A. J. (1969) *The Ideology of Fascism*, New York: The Free Press.

—— (1979a) *Young Mussolini and the Intellectual Origins of Fascism*, Berkeley, CA: University of California Press.

—— (1979b) *Italian Fascism and Developmental Dictatorship*, Princeton, NJ: Princeton University Press.

Grey, T. C. (1980) 'The Disintegration of Property', in J. R. Pennock and J. W. Chapman (eds) (1980).

Griffin, R. (1991) *The Nature of Fascism*, London and New York: Routledge.

Grint, K. (1995) *Management: A Sociological Introduction*, Cambridge: Polity Press.

Grossman, S. (1969) *Neo-Socialism: A Study in Political Metamorphosis*, PhD thesis, University of Wisconsin.

Gsovski, V. (1948) *Soviet Civil Law*, Ann Arbor, MI: University of Michigan Press.

Guérin, D. (1965) *L'Anarchisme*, Paris: Gallimard.

Gumplowicz, L. (1926 [1885]) *Grundriss der Soziologie*, Innsbruck: Universitäts-Verlag Wagner.

Gurevich, A. (1977) 'Representations of Property During the High Middle Ages', *Economy and Society* 6: 1–30.

Gurvitch, G. (1965) *Proudhon: sa vie, son œuvre*, Paris: PUF.

Haberkern, E. (1987) 'Machajski: A Rightfully Forgotten Prophet', *Telos* 71: 111–28.

Habermas, J. (1987) *The Philosophical Discourse of Modernity*, Cambridge: Polity Press.

—— (1992) *Faktizität und Geltung*, Frankfurt: Suhrkamp.

Hall, P. (1986) *Governing the Economy: The Politics of State Intervention in Britain and France*, New York: Oxford University Press.

Haraway, D. (1991) *Simians, Cyborgs, and Women*, London: Free Association Books.

Harding, S. (1991) *Whose Science? Whose Knowledge?*, Milton Keynes: Open University Press.

Harper, F. A. (1974) 'Property and Its Primary Form', in S. Blumenfeld (ed.) *Property in a Humane Economy*, LaSalle, IL: Open Court.

Harris, H. S. (1966) *The Social Philosophy of Giovanni Gentile*, Urbana, IL: University of Illinois Press.

Hartsock, N. (1983) 'The Feminist Standpoint', in S. Harding and M. B. Hintikka (eds) *Discovering Reality*, Dordrecht: Reidel.

—— (1990) 'Foucault on Power: A Theory for Women?', in L. Nicholson (ed.).

Haselbach, D. (1985) *Franz Oppenheimer. Soziologie, Geschichtsphilosophie und Politik des 'liberalen Sozialismus'*, Opladen: Leske & Budrich.

Haug, F. (1982) 'Frauen und Theorie', *Das Argument* 136: 168–73.

Hayek, F. A. ([1944] 1986) *The Road to Serfdom*, London: Routledge & Kegan Paul.

Hayward, J. E. S. (1960) 'Solidarist Syndicalism: Durkheim and Duguit', *Sociological Review* 8: 17–36, 185–202.

—— (1961) 'The Official Philosophy of the French Third Republic: Léon Bourgeois and Solidarism', *International Review of Social History* 6: 19–48.

Hearn, F. (1985) 'Durkheim's Political Sociology: Corporatism, State Autonomy, and Democracy', *Social Research* 52(1): 151–77.

Heilbron, J. (1995) *The Rise of Social Theory*, Cambridge: Polity Press.

Heinzen, K. (1846) 'Gegen den Kommunisten', *Der Opposition*, Mannheim: Heinrich Hoff.

Hennis, W. (1987) 'A Science of Man: Max Weber and the Political Economy of the German Historical School', in W. J. Mommsen and J. Osterhammel (eds) *Max Weber and His Contemporaries*, London: Unwin Hyman.

Herf, J. (1984) *Reactionary Modernism: Technology, Culture, and Politics in Weimar Germany and the Third Reich*, Cambridge: Cambridge University Press.

Hill, C. (1974) *The World Turned Upside Down*, Harmondsworth: Penguin Books.

Hirst, P. (1990) *Representative Democracy and Its Limits*, Cambridge: Polity Press.

—— (1994) *Associative Democracy*, Cambridge: Polity Press.

Hitler, A. (1969) *Mein Kampf*, London: Hutchinson.

Hobbes, T. (1841) *The English Works*, Vol. II, London.

—— (1968 [1651]) *Leviathan*, ed. C. B. Macpherson, Harmondsworth: Penguin Books.

Hobhouse, L. T. (1913) 'The Historical Evolution of Property, in Fact and in Idea', in Ch. Gore (ed.) *Property: Its Duties and Rights*, Oxford: Clarendon Press.

Hohfeld, W. N. (1978 [1919]) *Fundamental Legal Conceptions as Applied in Juridical Reasoning*, Westport, CT: Greenwood Press.

Hollowell, P. (1982) *Property and Social Relations*, London: Heinemann.

Honoré, A. M. (1961) 'Ownership', in A. G. Guest (ed.) *Oxford Essays in Jurisprudence*, Oxford: Clarendon Press.

Hont, I. and Ignatieff, M. (eds) (1983) *Wealth and Virtue: The Shaping of Political Economy in the Scottish Enlightenment*, Cambridge: Cambridge University Press.

Huber, E. R. (ed.) (1966) *Dokumente zur deutschen Verfassungsgeschichte*, Vol. 3, Stuttgart: Kohlhammer.

Hunter, J. D. and Fessenden, T. (1992) 'The New Class as Capitalist Class: The Rise of the Moral Entrepreneur in America', in H. Kellner and F. W. Heuberger (eds).

Iggers, G. G. (ed.) (1972) *The Doctrine of Saint-Simon: An Exposition*, New York: Schocken Books.

Ionescu, G. (1976) 'Introduction', *The Political Thought of Saint-Simon*, Oxford: Oxford University Press.

Jahn, T. and Wehling, P. (1991) *Ökologie von Rechts*, Frankfurt and New York: Campus Verlag.

Jakobs, O. W. (1965) *Eigentumsbegriff und Eigentumssystem des Sowjetischen Rechtes*, Cologne: Graz.

Jameson, F. (1988) 'Cognitive Mapping', in C. Nelson and L. Grossberg (eds).

Johnson, T. (1977) 'What is to be Known? The Structural Determination of Social Class', *Economy and Society* 6: 194–233.

Jünger, E. (1930) 'Die totale Mobilmachung', *Werke*, Vol. 5, Stuttgart: Ernst Klett Verlag.

—— (1932) *Der Arbeiter. Herrschaft und Gestalt*, Hamburg: Hanseatische Verlagsanstalt.

Kahn-Freund, O. (1949) 'Introduction' to K. Renner (1949).

Karady, V. (1979) 'Stratégies de réussite et modes de faire valoir de la sociologie chez les durkheimiens', *Revue française de sociologie* 20: 49–82.

Keane, J. (1988) 'Despotism and Democracy. The Origins and Development of the Distinction between Civil Society and the State 1750–1850', in *idem* (ed.) *Civil Society and the State: New European Perspectives*, London and New York: Verso.

Kellner, H. and Berger, P. L. (1992) 'Life-Style Engineering: Some Theoretical Reflections', in H. Kellner and F. W. Heuberger (eds).

—— and Heuberger, F. W. (eds) (1992) *Hidden Technocrats: The New Class and New Capitalism*, New Brunswick, NJ: Transaction Publishers.

Kettler, D. and Meja, V. (1995) *Karl Mannheim and the Crisis of Liberalism*, New Brunswick, NJ, and London: Transaction Publishers.

—— Meja, V. and Stehr, N. (1984) *Karl Mannheim*, London: Tavistock.

Kiernan, V. G. (1976) 'Private Property in History', in J. Goody *et al.* (eds) *Family and Inheritance: Rural Society in Western Europe 1200–1800*, Cambridge: Cambridge University Press.

Klingemann, C. (1996) *Soziologie im dritten Reich*, Baden-Baden: Nomos Verlag.

Knorr-Cetina, K. (1977) 'Producing and Reproducing Knowledge: Descriptive or Constructive?', *Social Science Information* 16(6): 669–96.

—— (1981a) *The Manufacture of Knowledge*, Oxford: Pergamon Press.

—— (1981b) 'Introduction' to K. Knorr-Cetina and A. V. Cicourel (eds) (1981).

—— (1982) 'Scientific Communities or Transepistemic Arenas of Research? A Critique of Quasi-Economic Models of Science', *Social Studies of Science* 12: 101–30.

—— and Cicourel, A. V. (eds) (1981) *Advances in Social Theory and Methodology*, Boston: Routledge & Kegan Paul.

—— and Mulkay, M. (1983) 'Introduction: Emerging Principles in Social Studies of Science', in *idem* (eds) *Science Observed*, London: Sage.

Kolakowski, L. (1981) *Main Currents of Marxism, Vol. 1: The Founders*, Oxford: Oxford University Press.

Konrad, G. and Szelényi, I. (1979) *The Intellectuals on the Road to Class Power*, Brighton: Harvester Press.

Korda, M. (1975) *Power! How to Get It, How to Use It*, New York: Random House.

Kraemer, P. E. (1966) *The Societal State*, Meppel: Boom.

Kriesi, H. (1989) 'New Social Movements and the New Class in the Netherlands', *American Journal of Sociology* 94(5): 1078–1116.

Kymlicka, W. (1990) *Contemporary Political Philosophy. An Introduction*, Oxford: Clarendon Press.

Laclau, E. (1975) 'The Specificity of the Political: The Poulantzas-Miliband Debate', *Economy and Society*, February: 87–110.

—— (1977) *Politics and Ideology in Marxist Theory*, London: New Left Books.

—— and Mouffe, M. (1985) *Hegemony and Socialist Strategy. Towards a Radical Democratic Politics*, London: New Left Books.

Lacroix, B. (1981) *Durkheim et le politique*, Paris: Presses de la Fondation Nationale des Sciences Politiques.

—— and Landerer, B. (1972) 'Durkheim, Sismondi, et les Socialistes de la Chaire', *Année Sociologique* 23: 159–204.

Lash, S. (1990) *Sociology of Postmodernism*, London and New York: Routledge.

—— and Urry, J. (1994) *Economies of Sign and Space*, London: Sage. ✳

—— and Whimster, S. (eds) (1987) *Max Weber: Rationality and Modernity*, London: Allen & Unwin.

Lasswell, H. D. (1958 [1936]) *Politics: Who Gets What, When, How?* New York: Meridian Books.

—— (1977) *On Political Sociology*, ed. D. Marvick, Chicago and London: University of Chicago Press.

—— and Kaplan, R. (1950) *Power and Society. A Framework for Political Enquiry*, New Haven, CT: Yale University Press.

Latour, B. (1984) *Les Microbes. Guerre et paix*, Paris: Fayard.

—— (1986) 'The Powers of Association', in J. Law (ed.) (1986).

—— (1988) 'Mixing Humans and Nonhumans Together: The Sociology of a Door-Closer', *Social Problems* 35: 298–310.

—— (1993) *We Have Never Been Modern*, Cambridge, MA: Harvard University Press.

—— and Woolgar, S. (1979) *Laboratory Life. The Social Construction of Scientific Facts*, London: Sage.

Law, J. (ed.) (1986) *Power, Action, and Belief. A New Sociology of Knowledge?*, London: Routledge.

—— (1989) 'Technology and Heterogeneous Engineering: The Case of Portuguese Expansion', in W. E. Bijker, T. P. Hughes, and T. J. Pinch (eds) *The Social Construction of Technological Systems*, Cambridge, MA: The MIT Press.

—— (1991a) 'Introduction: Monsters, Machines, and Sociotechnical Relations', in *idem* (ed.) *A Sociology of Monsters: Essays on Power, Technology, and Domination*, London and New York: Routledge.

—— (1991b) 'Power, Discretion, and Strategy' in *idem* (ed.).

Lawson, F. H. (1958) *Introduction to the Law of Property*, Oxford: Clarendon Press.

Lebovics, H. (1969) *Social Conservatism and the Middle Class in Germany 1914–1933*, Princeton, NJ: Princeton University Press.

Lee, D. (1980) 'On the Marxian View of the Relationship between Man and Nature', *Environmental Ethics* 2: 3–16.

✦ Lefort, C. (1986) *The Political Forms of Modern Society: Bureaucracy, Democracy, Totalitarianism*, Cambridge: Polity Press.

—— (1988) *Democracy and Political Theory*, Cambridge: Polity Press.

Lehmann, W. (1971) *Henry Home, Lord Kames and the Scottish Enlightenment*, The Hague: Martinus Nijhoff.

Lenger, F. (1994) *Werner Sombart 1863–1941. Eine Biographie*, Munich: C. H. Beck.

Lenski, G. (1966) *Power and Privilege: A New Theory of Stratification*, New York: McGraw-Hill.

Lepenies, W. (1985), *Die drei Kulturen. Soziologie zwischen Literatur und Wissenschaft*, Munich: Carl Hanser Verlag.

Levine, D. N. (1995) *Visions of the Sociological Tradition*, Chicago: University of Chicago Press.

Lévy, J.-P. (1972) *Histoire de la propriété*, Paris: PUF.

Lindenlaub, D. (1967) *Richtungskämpfe im Verein für Sozialpolitik*, 2 Vols, Wiesbaden: Franz Steiner Verlag.

Locke, J. (1975 [1690]) *Two Treatises of Government*, London: Everyman's.

Long, D. (1979) 'Bentham on Property', in A. Parel and T. Flanagan (eds).

Luhmann, N. (1982) *The Differentiation of Society*, New York: Columbia University Press.

Lukes, S. (1973) *Emile Durkheim: His Life and Work*, London: Allan Lane.

—— (1974) *Power: A Radical View*, London and Basingstoke: Macmillan.

—— (1982) 'Introduction' to E. Durkheim (1982).

Lundberg, F. (1968 [1937]) *The Rich and the Super-Rich*, New York: Stuart.

Lynch, M. (1993) *Scientific Practice and Ordinary Action*, Cambridge: Cambridge University Press.

Lynd, R. (1968) 'Power in the United States', in W. B. Domhoff and H. B. Ballard (eds).

Lyttleton, A. (ed.) (1973) *Italian Fascisms: From Pareto to Gentile*, New York: Harper & Row.

McClure, K. (1992) 'The Issue of Foundations: Scientized Politics, Politicized Science, and Feminist Critical Practice', in J. Butler and J. W. Scott (eds).

McDermott, J. (1991) *Corporate Society: Class, Property, and Contemporary Capitalism*, Boulder, CO: Westview Press.

McIlwain, Ch. (1932) *The Growth of Political Thought in the West*, New York: Cooper Square Publishers.

MacIver, R. (1947) *The Web of Government*, New York: Macmillan.

MacKinnon, C. (1982) 'Feminism, Marxism, Method, and the State: An Agenda for Theory', *Signs* 7(3): 515–44.

✦ Macpherson, C. B. (1962) *The Political Theory of Possessive Individualism: Hobbes to Locke*, London: Oxford University Press.

—— (1973) *Democratic Theory: Essays in Retrieval*. Oxford: Clarendon Press.

—— (1977) 'Human Rights as Property Rights', *Dissent*, Winter: 72–7.

—— (ed.) (1978) *Property: Mainstream and Critical Positions*, Oxford: Blackwell.

—— (1979) 'Property as Means or End', in A. Parel and T. Flanagan (eds).

Mandeville, B. (1970 [1705–24]) *The Fable of the Bees*, Harmondsworth: Pelican Books.

Mann, M. (1986) *The Sources of Social Power*, Vol. 1, Cambridge: Cambridge University Press.

Mannheim, K. (1952) *Essays on the Sociology of Knowledge*, London: Routledge & Kegan Paul.

—— (1953) *Essays on the Sociology of Culture*, London: Routledge & Kegan Paul.

—— (1968) *Ideology and Utopia*, London: Routledge & Kegan Paul.

—— (1982) *Structures of Thinking*, London, Boston and Henley: Routledge & Kegan Paul.

Manoïlescu, M. (1934) *Le Siècle du corporatisme*, Paris: Felix Alcan.

Marceau, J., Thomas, A. and Whitley, R. (1978) 'Business and the State: Management Education and Business Elites in France and Great Britain', in G. Littlejohn *et al.* (eds) *Power and the State*, London: Croom Helm.

Marshall, P. (1992) *Demanding the Impossible: A History of Anarchism*, London: Harper Collins.

Martin, B. (1992) 'Symbolic Knowledge and Market Forces at the Frontiers of Post-modernism: Qualitative Market Researchers', in H. Kellner and F. W. Heuberger (eds).

Martin, B. and Szelényi, I. (1987) 'Beyond Cultural Capital: Towards a Theory of Symbolic Domination', in R. Eyerman *et al.* (eds).

Martin, R. (1977) *The Sociology of Power*, London: Macmillan.

Marx, K. ([1843a] 1972) 'Bemerkungen über die neueste preussische Zensurinstruktion', *Marx-Engels Werke*, Vol. 1, Berlin: Dietz Verlag.

—— ([1843b] 1972) 'Zur Kritik der Hegelschen Rechtsphilosophie', *MEW*, Vol. 1, Berlin: Dietz Verlag.

—— ([1847] 1972) 'Die moralisierende Kritik und die kritisierende Moral', *MEW*, Vol. 4, Berlin: Dietz Verlag.

—— ([1852] 1972) 'Der achtzehnte Brumaire des Louis Bonaparte', *MEW*, Vol. 8, Berlin: Dietz Verlag.

—— ([1867] 1972) *Das Kapital*, Bd. I, *MEW*, Vol. 23, Berlin: Dietz Verlag.

—— ([1894] 1972) *Das Kapital*, Bd. III, *MEW*, Vol. 25, Berlin: Dietz Verlag.

—— (1973) *Grundrisse*, ed. M. Nicolaus, Harmondsworth: Pelican Books.

—— (1981) *Early Writings*, ed. L. Colletti, Harmondsworth: Pelican Books.

—— and Engels, F. ([1845] 1974) *The German Ideology*, London: Lawrence & Wishart.

—— and Engels, F. ([1848] 1972) 'Manifest der kommunistischen Partei', *MEW*, Vol. 4, Berlin: Dietz Verlag.

—— Engels, F. and Lenin, V. I. (1972) *Anarchism and Anarcho-Syndicalism*, Moscow: Progress.

Mason, T. W. (1995) *Nazism, Fascism, and the Working Class*, Cambridge: Cambridge University Press.

Mathie, W. (1979) 'Property in the Political Science of Aristotle', in A. Parel and T. Flanagan (eds).

Meek, R. (1967) *Economics and Ideology and Other Essays*, London: Chapman & Hall.

—— (1973) *Studies in the Labour Theory of Value*, London: Lawrence & Wishart.

—— (1976) *Social Science and the Ignoble Savage*, Cambridge: Cambridge University Press.

Meisel, J. (1958) *The Myth of the Ruling Class*, Ann Arbor, MI: University of Michigan Press.

Meja, V. and Stehr, N. (eds) (1982) *Der Streit um die Wissenssoziologie*, 2 Vols, Frankfurt: Suhrkamp.

Merriam Jr, Ch. E. (1900) *History of the Theory of Sovereignty Since Rousseau*, New York: Columbia University Press.

Merton, R. K. ([1941] 1968) 'Karl Mannheim and the Sociology of Knowledge', in *Social Theory and Social Structure*, Glencoe: The Free Press.

—— (1973) *The Sociology of Science*, Chicago and London: University of Chicago Press.

Meulenbelt, A. (1975) 'De economie van de koesterende functie', *Te Elfder Ure* 20: 638–75.

Michels, R. (1974 [1934]) *First Lectures on Political Sociology*, New York: Arno Press.

—— (1987) *Masse, Führer, Intellektuelle*, Frankfurt/New York: Campus Verlag.

Miliband, R. (1973) *The State in Capitalist Society*, London: Quartet Books.

—— (1994) 'Introduction' to *idem* (ed.) *Reinventing the Left*, Cambridge: Polity Press.

Miller, D. (1984) *Anarchism*, London and Melbourne: Dent.

Millett, K. (1969) *Sexual Politics*, New York: Avon Books.

Mills, C. W. (1951) *White Collar: The American Middle Classes*, London: Oxford University Press.

—— (1956) *The Power Elite*, New York and London: Oxford University Press.

—— (1963) *Power, Politics and People*, ed. I. L. Horowitz, New York: Oxford University Press.

—— (1969) *The Marxists*, Harmondsworth: Pelican Books.

Mohler, A. (1972) *Die konservative Revolution in Deutschland 1918–1932*, Darmstadt: Wissenschaftliche Buchgesellschaft.

—— (1988) 'Carl Schmitt und die "Konservative Revolution". Unsystematische Beobachtungen', in H. Quartsch (ed.) *Complexio Oppositorum. Über Carl Schmitt*, Berlin: Duncker & Humblot, 129–51.

Mommsen, W. J. (1974) *Max Weber und die deutsche Politik 1890–1920*, Tübingen: J. C. B. Mohr (Paul Siebeck).

—— (1989) *The Political and Social Theory of Max Weber. Collected Essays*, Cambridge: Polity Press.

Montesquieu, Ch. de (1969 [1748]) *De l'esprit des lois*, Paris: Editions sociales.

Moore Jr, B. (1966) *Social Origins of Dictatorship and Democracy*, Boston: Beacon Press.

Moriss, P. (1987) *Power: A Philosophical Analysis*, Manchester: Manchester University Press.

Mosse, G. (1981) *The Crisis of German Ideology: Intellectual Origins of the Third Reich*, New York: Schocken Books.

Mouffe, C. (1993) *The Return of the Political*, London: Verso.

Mulkay, M. J. (1977) 'Norms and Ideology in Science', *Social Science Information* 15(4/5): 637–56.

Muller, J. Z. (1987) *The Other God that Failed: Hans Freyer and the Deradicalization of German Conservatism*, Princeton, NJ: Princeton University Press.

—— (1991) 'Carl Schmitt, Hans Freyer, and the Radical Conservative Critique of Liberal Democracy in the Weimar Republic', *History of Political Thought* 12(4): 695–715.

Müller, H.-P. (1993) 'Durkheim's Political Sociology', in S. P. Turner (ed.).

Munzer, S. R. (1990) *A Theory of Property*, Cambridge: Cambridge University Press.

Murphy, R. (1988) *Social Closure: The Theory of Monopolization and Exclusion*, Oxford: Clarendon Press.

Narveson, J. (1988) *The Libertarian Idea*, Philadelphia: Temple University Press.

Nelson, C. and Grossberg, L. (eds) (1988) *Marxism and the Interpretation of Culture*, Houndmills: Macmillan.

Neumann, F. (1957) *The Democratic and the Authoritarian State*, Glencoe: The Free Press.

Nicholas, B. (1962) *An Introduction to Roman Law*, Oxford: Clarendon Press.

Nichols, T. (1969) *Ownership, Control, and Ideology*, London: Allen & Unwin.

Nicholson, L. (ed.) (1990) *Feminism/Postmodernism*, New York and London: Routledge.

Nisbet, R. (1966) *The Sociological Tradition*, London: Heinemann.

—— and Bottomore, T. (eds) (1979) *A History of Sociological Analysis*, London: Heinemann.

Nolte, E. (1965) *Three Faces of Fascism*, New York: Holt, Rinehart & Winston.

Nowak, L. (1983) *Property and Power: Towards a Non-Marxist Historical Materialism*, Reidel: Dordrecht.

Nozick, R. (1974) *Anarchy, State, and Utopia*, New York: Basic Books.

O'Brien, M. (1981) *The Politics of Reproduction*, New York: Routledge & Kegan Paul.

Olsen, M. (1970) 'Elitist Theory as a Response to Marx', in *idem* (ed.) *Power in Societies*, London: Collier-Macmillan.

O'Neill, J. (1986) 'The Disciplinary Society: from Weber to Foucault', *British Journal of Sociology* 37(1): 42–60.

Paine, T. (1969 [1791–92])) *Rights of Man*, Harmondsworth: Penguin Books.

Parel, A. (1979) '"Aquinas" Theory of Property', in A. Parel and T. Flanagan.

—— and Flanagan, T. (eds) (1979) *Theories of Property: Aristotle to the Present*, Waterloo, Ontario: Wilfried Laurier University Press.

Parkin, F. (1972) *Class Inequality and Political Order*, St Albans: Paladin.

—— (1979) *Marxism and Class Theory: A Bourgeois Critique*, London: Tavistock.

Parry, G. (1969) *Political Elites*, London: George Allen & Unwin.

Parsons, T. (1954) 'A Revised Analytical Approach to the Theory of Social Stratification', in *Essays in Sociological Theory*, New York: The Free Press.

—— (1967) 'On the Concept of Political Power', in *Sociological Theory and Modern Society*, New York: The Free Press.

—— (1968) 'The Distribution of Power in American Society', in W. Domhoff and H. B. Ballard (eds).

Pearce, F. (1989) *The Radical Durkheim*, London: Unwin Hyman.

Pels, D. (1977) 'De onfeilbare rechtvaardigheid van William Godwin', *De Gids* 7: 483–500.

—— (1983) 'Het project als object. Durkheim's kennispolitiek in relativistisch perspectief', *Amsterdams Sociologisch Tijdschrift* 10(1): 51–91.

—— (1984) 'A Fellow-Traveller's Dilemma. Sociology and Socialism in the Writings of Durkheim', *Acta Politica* 19(3): 309–29.

—— (1987) 'Hendrik de Man and the Ideology of Planism', *International Review of Social History* 32(3): 206–29.

—— (1988) 'Het socialisme in het niemandsland tussen staat en maatschappij', in S. Koenis and L. Nauta (eds) *Een toekomst voor het socialisme?*, Amsterdam: Van Gennep.

—— (1993a) *Het democratisch verschil. Jacques de Kadt en de nieuwe elite*, Amsterdam: Van Gennep.

—— (1993b) 'Hendrik de Man and the Fascist Temptation', *History of the Human Sciences* 6(2): 65–95.

—— (1993c) 'Missionary Sociology between Left and Right. A Critical Introduction to Mannheim', *Theory, Culture, and Society* 10(3): 45–68.

—— (1995a) 'Knowledge Politics and Anti-politics. Toward a Critical Appraisal of Bourdieu's Concept of Intellectual Autonomy', *Theory and Society* 24: 79–104.

—— (1995b) 'The Politics of Critical Description. Recovering the Normative Complexity of Foucault's *pouvoir/savoir*', *American Behavioral Scientist* 38(7): 1018–41.

—— (1996a) 'Karl Mannheim and the Sociology of Scientific Knowledge. Toward a New Agenda', *Sociological Theory* 14(1): 30–48.

—— (1996b) 'Historical Positivism', *History of the Human Sciences* 9(1): 113–21.

—— (1997) 'Mixing Metaphors: Politics or Economics of Knowledge?', *Theory and Society* 26(5): 685–717.

—— (1998) 'The Proletarian as Stranger', *History of the Human Sciences* 11(1): 49–72.

Pennock, J. R. and Chapman, J. W. (eds) (1978) *Anarchism: Nomos XIX*, New York: New York University Press.

—— (eds) (1980) *Property: Nomos XXII*, New York: New York University Press.

Phillips, D. (1977) *Wittgenstein and Scientific Knowledge: A Sociological Perspective*, London and Basingstoke: Macmillan.

Piccone, P. (1993–4) 'Confronting the French New Right: Old Prejudices or a New Political Paradigm?', *Telos* 98/99: 3–22.

Pipes, R. (1974) *Russia Under the Old Regime*, Harmondsworth: Penguin Books.

Pocock, J. G. A. (1985) *Virtue, Commerce, and History*, Cambridge: Cambridge University Press.

Polanyi, K. (1957) 'Aristotle Discovers the Economy', in *idem*, C. Arensky and H. Pearson (eds) *Trade and Market in the Early Empires*, Glencoe: The Free Press.

Pollock, F. (1981 [1941]) 'Ist der Nationalsozialismus eine neue Ordnung?', in H. Dubiel and A. Söllner (eds) *Wirtschaft, Recht, und Staat im Nationalsozialismus. Analysen des Instituts für Sozialforschung 1939–1942*, Frankfurt: Europäische Verlagsanstalt.

Pollock, F. and Maitland, F. W. (1899) *The History of English Law before the Time of Edward I*, 2 Vols, Cambridge: Cambridge University Press.

Poulantzas, N. (1974a) *Les Classes sociales dans le capitalisme aujourd'hui*, Paris: Seuil.

—— (1974b) *Fascism and Dictatorship*, London: New Left Books.

—— (1978) *Power, State, Socialism*, London: New Left Books.

Proctor, R. N. (1991) *Value-free Science? Purity and Power in Modern Knowledge*, Cambridge, MA: Harvard University Press.

Pross, H. and Boetticher, K. W. (1971) *Manager des Kapitalismus*, Frankfurt: Suhrkamp.

Proudhon, P.-J. (1923 [1846]) *Système des contradictions économiques ou philosophie de la misère*, 2 Vols, Paris: Marcel Rivière.

—— (1866) *Théorie de la propriété*, Paris: Librairie Internationale.

—— (1982) *Œuvres complètes*, 15 Vols, Geneva and Paris: Slatkine.

Rathenau, W. (1917) *Von kommenden Dingen*, Berlin: S. Fischer Verlag.

Reeve, A. (1986) *Property*, Atlantic Highlands, NJ: Humanities Press.

Reich, Ch. (1978) 'The New Property', in C. B. Macpherson (ed.) (1978).

Reinhold Noyes, C. (1936) *The Institution of Property*, London: Longmans, Green.

Rendall, J. (1978) *The Origins of the Scottish Enlightenment*, London and Basingstoke: Macmillan.

Renner, K. (1949) *The Institutions of Private Law and Their Social Functions*, London: Routledge & Kegan Paul.

Richter, M. (1960) 'Durkheim's Politics and Political Theory', in K. Wolff (ed.).

Riedel, M. (1975) 'Gesellschaft, bürgerliche', in O. Brunner, W. Conze, and R. Koselleck (eds) *Geschichtliche Grundbegriffe*, Vol. 2, Stuttgart: Klett-Cotta.

Roemer, J. (1982a) 'New Directions in the Marxian Theory of Exploitation and Class', *Politics & Society* 11(3): 253–88.

—— (1982b) *A General Theory of Exploitation and Class*, Cambridge, MA: Harvard University Press.

—— (ed.) (1986) *Analytical Marxism*, Cambridge: Cambridge University Press.

—— (1994) *Egalitarian Perspectives: Essays in Philosophical Economics*, Cambridge: Cambridge University Press.

Römer, P. (1978) *Entstehung, Rechtsform und Funktion des kapitalistischen Privateigentums*, Cologne: Pahl-Rugenstein.

Rootes, C. (1995) 'A New Class? The Higher Educated and the New Politics', in L. Maheu (ed.) *Social Movements and Social Classes*, London: Sage.

Rosenstock-Franck, L. (1934) *L'Economie corporatiste fasciste en doctrine et en fait*, Paris: Camber.

Routley, V. (1981) 'On Karl Marx as Environmental Hero', *Environmental Ethics* 3: 237–44.

Rubin, G. (1975) 'The Traffic in Women: Notes on the Political Economy of Sex', in R. Rapp Reiter (ed.) *Toward an Anthropology of Women*, New York: Monthly Review Press.

Runciman, W. G. (1963) *Social Science and Political Theory*, Cambridge: Cambridge University Press.

—— (1974) 'Towards a Theory of Social Stratification', in F. Parkin (ed.) *The Social Analysis of Class Structure*, London: Tavistock.

Rupnik, J. (1988) 'Totalitarianism Revisited', in J. Keane (ed.).

Russell, B. (1940) *Power: A New Social Analysis*, London: Allen & Unwin.

Ryan, A. (1984) *Property and Political Theory*, Oxford: Basil Blackwell.

—— (1987) *Property*, Minneapolis, MN: University of Minnesota Press.

—— (1994) 'Self-Ownership, Autonomy, and Property Rights', *Social Philosophy & Policy* 11(2): 241–58.

Sabine, G. II. (1968) *A History of Political Theory*, London: Harrap.

Said, E. (1983) *The World, the Text, and the Critic*, Cambridge, MA: Harvard University Press.

Saint-Simon, C.-H. de (1951) *Textes choisis*, ed. J. Dautry, Paris: Editions sociales.

—— (1964) *Social Organisation, the Science of Man and Other Writings*, ed. F. Markham, New York and Evanston, IL: Harper Torchbooks.

—— (1966 [1868–1876]) *Œuvres*, Vols I–VI, Paris: Maison d'Editions Anthropos.

—— (1976) *The Political Thought of Saint-Simon*, ed. G. Ionescu, Oxford: Oxford University Press.

305

Sargent, L. (ed.) (1986) *The Unhappy Marriage of Marxism and Feminism*, London and Sydney: Pluto Press.

Schäffle, A. (1894 [1874]) *The Quintessence of Socialism*, London: Swan Sonnenschein.

—— (1896) *Bau und Leben des sozialen Körpers*, 2 Vols, Tübingen: Verlag der H. Laupp'schen Buchhandlung.

Schelsky, H. (1975) *Die Arbeit tun die Anderen. Klassenkampf und Priesterherrschaft der Intellektuellen*, Opladen: Westdeutscher Verlag.

Schlatter, R. (1951) *Private Property: The History of an Idea*, London: George Allen & Unwin.

Schmitt, C. ([1922] 1934) *Politische Theologie*, Munich and Leipzig: Duncker & Humblot.

—— ([1923] 1926) *Die geistesgeschichtlichen Lage des heutigen Parlamentarismus*, Berlin: Duncker & Humblot.

—— (1931) *Der Hüter der Verfassung*, Tübingen: Mohr.

—— (1932) *Legalität und Legitimität*, Berlin: Duncker & Humblot.

—— (1935) *Staat, Bewegung, Volk*, Hamburg: Hanseatische Verlagsanstalt.

—— (1988) *Positionen und Begriffe im Kampf mit Weimar-Genf-Versailles*, Berlin: Duncker & Humblot.

—— (1993) 'The Age of Neutralizations and Depoliticizations', *Telos* 96, Summer: 130–42.

—— (1996) *The Concept of the Political*, ed. G. Schwab and T. B. Strong, Chicago and London: University of Chicago Press.

Schmitter, P. (1977) 'Still the Century of Corporatism?', *Review of Politics* 36(1): 85–131.

Schochet, G. H. (1975) *Patriarchalism in Political Thought*, Oxford: Blackwell.

Schüddekopf, O.-E. (1972) *National-bolschewismus in Deutschland 1918–1933*, Frankfurt: Ullstein.

Schwarz, H. P. (1962) *Der konservative Anarchist. Politik und Zeitkritik Ernst Jüngers*, Freiburg: Rombach.

Scott, J. (1979) *Corporations, Classes, and Capitalism*, London: Hutchinson.

—— (1996) *Stratification and Power: Structures of Class, Status, and Command*, Cambridge: Polity Press.

Shapin, S. (1992) 'Discipline and Bounding: The History and Sociology of Science as Seen Through the Externalism-Internalism Debate', *History of Science* 30: 333–69.

Shapiro, F. R. (1984) 'A Note on the Origin of the Term "Social Science"', *Journal of the History of the Behavioral Sciences* 20(1): 20–2.

Sharrock, W. W. (1974) 'On Owning Knowledge', in R. Turner (ed.) *Ethnomethodology: Selected Readings*, Harmondsworth: Penguin Books.

Shonfield, A. (1978) *Modern Capitalism: The Changing Balance of Public and Private Power*, London: Oxford University Press.

Simmel, G. (1990 [1907]) *The Philoso phy of Money*, ed. D. Frisby, London and New York: Routledge.

Skinner, A. S. (1970) 'Introduction' to A. Smith (1970 [1776]) *The Wealth of Nations*, Harmondsworth: Pelican Books.

—— (1975) 'Adam Smith: An Economic Interpretation of History', in *idem* and T. Wilson (eds).

—— and Wilson, T. (eds) (1975) *Essays on Adam Smith*, Oxford: Clarendon Press.

Skinner, Q. (1978) *The Foundations of Modern Political Thought*, 2 Vols, Cambridge: Cambridge University Press.

Sloterdijk, P. (1983) *Kritik der zynischen Vernunft*, 2 Vols, Frankfurt: Suhrkamp.

Smith, A. (1896 [1763]) *Lectures on Justice, Police, Revenue, and Arms*, ed. E. Cannan, Oxford: Clarendon Press.

—— (1976 [1776]) *An Inquiry into the Nature and Causes of the Wealth of Nations*, ed. R. H. Campbell, A. S. Skinner, and W. B. Todd, Vol. 1, Oxford: Clarendon Press.

Sombart, W. (1934) *Deutscher Sozialismus*, Berlin: Buchholz & Weisswange.

Sontheimer, K. (1978) *Antidemokratisches Denken in der Weimarer Republik*, Munich: Deutscher Taschenbuch Verlag.

Spencer, H. (1969 [1884]) *The Man versus the State*, Harmondsworth: Penguin Books.

Spengler, O. ([1919] 1934) 'Preussentum und Sozialismus', *Politische Schriften*, Munich and Berlin: Beck.

Spivak, G. C. (1988) 'Can the Subaltern Speak?', in C. Nelson and L. Grossberg (eds).

Stabile, D. (1984) *Prophets of Order: The Rise of the New Class, Technocracy and Socialism in America*, Boston: South End Press.

Stehr, N. (1994a) *Knowledge Societies*, London: Sage.

—— (1994b) *Arbeit, Eigentum, und Wissen. Zur Theorie von Wissensgesellschaften*, Frankfurt: Suhrkamp.

—— and Ericson, R. V. (1992) 'The Culture and Power of Knowledge in Modern Society', in *idem* (eds) *The Culture and Power of Knowledge*, Berlin and New York: De Gruyter.

Stein, L. von (1971 [1848]) *Der Sozialismus und Kommunismus des heutigen Frankreichs*, Hsg. M. Hahn, Munich: Wilhelm Fink Verlag.

Sternhell, Z. (1986) *Neither Right nor Left: Fascist Ideology in France*, Berkeley, CA: University of California Press.

—— Sznajder, M. and Asheri, M. (1994) *The Birth of Fascist Ideology: From Cultural Rebellion to Political Revolution*, Princeton, NJ: Princeton University Press.

Stirner, M. (1982 [1845]) *The Ego and Its Own*, trans. S. Byington, London: Rebel Press.

Svacek, V. (1976) 'The Elusive Marxism of C.B. Macpherson', *Canadian Journal of Political Science* 9(3): 395–422.

Sweezy, P. M. (1953) *The Present as History*, New York: Monthly Review Press.

—— (1968) 'Power Elite or Ruling Class?', in W. B. Domhoff and H. B. Ballard (eds).

Szacki, J. (1979) *History of Sociological Thought*, London: Aldwych Press.

—— (1982) 'The History of Sociology and Substantive Sociological Theories', in T. B. Bottomore *et al.* (eds).

Szelényi, I. (1982) 'Gouldner's Theory of Intellectuals as a Flawed Universal Class', *Theory and Society* 11(6): 779–98.

—— and Martin, B. (1988) 'The three waves of New Class theories', *Theory and Society* 17: 645–67.

Szirmaï, A. (1986) 'Social Stratification and Social Co-ordination', *Amsterdams Sociologisch Tijdschrift* 12(4): 710–52.

Taguieff, P.-A. (1993–4) 'Discussion or Inquisition? The Case of Alain de Benoist', *Telos* 98/99: 34–54.

Talmon, J. L. (1970) *The Origins of Totalitarian Democracy*, London: Sphere Books.

Tawney, R. H. (1920) *The Acquisitive Society*, London: Allen & Unwin.

Tenbruck, F. (1981) 'Emile Durkheim oder die Geburt der Gesellschaft aus dem Geist der Soziologie', *Zeitschrift für Soziologie* 10(4): 333–50.

Therborn, G. (1976) *Science, Class, and Society*, London: New Left Books.

Thomas, P. (1980) *Karl Marx and the Anarchists*, London: Routledge & Kegan Paul.

Tigar, M. E. and Levy, M. R. (1977) *Law and the Rise of Capitalism*, New York: Monthly Review Press.

Touraine, A. (1969) *La Société post-industrielle*, Paris: Editions Denoël.

Tribe, K. (1984) 'Cameralism and the Science of Government', *The Journal of Modern History* 56(2): 263–84.

—— (1988) *Governing Economy: The Reformation of German Economic Discourse 1750–1840*, Cambridge: Cambridge University Press.

Tully, J. (1980) *A Discourse on Property: John Locke and his Adversaries*, Cambridge: Cambridge University Press.

Turner, B. S. (1987) 'The Rationalization of the Body: Reflections on Modernity and Discipline', in S. Lash and S. Whimster (eds).

—— (1992) 'Preface to the Second Edition', in E. Durkheim (1992).

Turner, S. P. (ed.) (1993) *Emile Durkheim: Sociologist and Moralist*, London & New York: Routledge.

—— and Factor, R. (1987) 'Decisionism and Politics: Weber as Constitutional Theorist', in S. Lash and S. Whimster (eds).

Useem, M. (1982) 'Classwide Rationality and the Politics of Managers and Directors of Large Corporations in the U.S. and Great Britain', *Administrative Science Quarterly* 27: 199–226.

—— (1984) *The Inner Circle*, New York and Oxford: Oxford University Press.

—— (1985) 'The Rise of the Political Manager', *Sloan Management Review* 27: 15–26.

—— (1990) 'Business Restructuring, Management Control, and Corporate Organization', *Theory and Society* 19: 681–707.

—— and Karabel, J. (1986) 'Pathways to Top Corporate Management', *American Journal of Sociology* 51: 184–200.

Vanderjagt, A. (1988) 'Frans-Bourgondische geleerde politici in de 15e eeuw', *Theoretische Geschiedenis* 16(4): 403–19.

Van Parijs, P. (1993) *Marxism Recycled*, Cambridge: Cambridge University Press.

Veblen, T. (1898) 'The Beginnings of Ownership', *American Journal of Sociology* 4: 352–65.

Vernon, J. R. (1970) 'Ownership and Control Among Large Member Banks', *Journal of Finance* 25(3): 651–7.

Vernon, R. (1984) 'Comte and the Withering-Away of the State', *Journal of the History of Ideas* 45(4): 549–66.

Vincent, A. (1992) *Modern Political Ideologies*, Oxford: Blackwell.

Vinogradoff, P. (1961) *Roman Law in Medieval Europe*, Oxford: Oxford University Press.

Viroli, M. (1992a) 'The Revolution in the Concept of Politics', *Political Theory* 20(3): 473–95.

—— (1992b) *From Politics to Reason of State*, Cambridge: Cambridge University Press.

Voline (1974 [1947]) *The Unknown Revolution 1917–1921*, Detroit/Chicago: Black/Red & Solidarity.

Wagner, P. (1990) *Sozialwissenschaften und Staat: Frankreich, Italien, Deutschland 1870–1980*, Frankfurt: Campus Verlag.

Waldron, J. (1988) *The Right to Private Property*, Oxford: Clarendon Press.

Warren, M. (1992) 'Weber's Nietzschean Conception of Power', *History of the Human Sciences* 5(3): 19–37.

Wartenberg, T. E. (1990) *The Forms of Power*, Philadelphia: Temple University Press.

Weber, M. (1963) *Gesammelte Aufsätze zur Religionssoziologie*, Tübingen: J. C. B. Mohr.

—— (1968) *Gesammelte Aufsätze zur Wissenschaftslehre*, Tübingen: J. C. B. Mohr.

—— (1970a) *The Interpretation of Social Reality*, ed. J. E. T. Eldridge, London: Michael Joseph.

—— (1970b) *From Max Weber: Essays in Sociology*, ed. H. Gerth and C. W. Mills, London: Routledge & Kegan Paul.

—— (1971) *Gesammelte Politische Schriften*, Tübingen: J. C. B. Mohr.

—— (1978) *Economy and Society*, 2 Vols, ed. G. Roth and C. Wittich, Berkeley, CA: University of California Press.

Webster, F. (1995) *Theories of the Information Society*, London: Routledge.

Wegierski, M. (1993–4) 'The New Right in Europe', *Telos* 98/99: 55–69.

Weimer, D. L. (1997) 'The Political Economy of Property Rights', in *idem* (ed.) *The Political Economy of Property Rights: Institutional Changes and Credibility in the Reform of Centrally Planned Economies*, Cambridge: Cambridge University Press.

Weiss, J. (1963) 'Dialectical Idealism and the Work of Lorenz von Stein', *International Review of Social History* 8: 75–93.

Whelan, F. G. (1980) 'Property as Artifice: Hume and Blackstone', in J. R. Pennock and J. W. Chapman (eds) (1980).

Wieck, D. T. (1975) 'The Negativity of Anarchism', *Interrogations* 5: 25–55.

—— (1978) 'Anarchist Justice', in J. R. Pennock and J. W. Chapman (eds) (1978).

Williams, R. (1977) *Marxism and Literature*, Oxford: Oxford University Press.

Wilsher, J. C. (1983) '"Power Follows Property" – Social and Economic Interpretations in British Historical Writing in the 18th and Early 19th Centuries', *Journal of Social History* 16(3): 7–26.

Wilterdink, N. (1984) *Vermogensverhoudingen in Nederland*, Amsterdam: De Arbeiderspers.

Wiseman, H. V. (1972) *Politics: The Master Science*, London: Routledge & Kegan Paul.

Wittig, M. (1990) 'The Straight Mind', in R. Ferguson *et al.* (eds) *Out There: Marginalization and Contemporary Culture*, Cambridge, MA: The MIT Press.

Wolff, K. (ed.) (1960) *Emile Durkheim 1858–1917*, Columbus, OH: Ohio State University Press.

Wolff, R. and Resnick, S. (1986) 'Property, Power, and Class', *Socialist Review* 16(2): 97–124.

Wolin, R. (1992) 'Carl Schmitt. The Conservative Revolutionary Habitus and the Aesthetics of Horror', *Political Theory* 20(3): 424–47.

Woodhouse, A. S. P. (1938) *Puritanism and Liberty*, London: Dent.

Woolf, C. N. S. (1913) *Bartolus of Sassoferrato*, Cambridge: Cambridge University Press.

Wright, E. (1978) *Class, Crisis and the State*, London: New Left Books.

—— (1985a) 'A General Framework for the Analysis of Class Structure', *Politics & Society* 13(4): 385–423.

—— (1985b) *Classes*, London: New Left Books.

——, Levine, A. and Sober, E. (1992) *Reconstructing Marxism*, London: Verso.

Wrong, D. (1979) *Power: Its Forms, Bases, and Uses*, Oxford: Blackwell.

—— (1983) 'The New Class: Does it Exist?', *Dissent* Fall: 491–9.

Young, I. M. (1990) *Justice and the Politics of Difference*, Princeton, NJ: Princeton University Press.

Zeitlin, I. M. (1968) *Ideology and the Development of Sociological Theory*, Englewood Cliffs, NJ: Prentice Hall.

Zeitlin, M. (1974) 'Corporate Ownership and Control: The Large Corporations and the Capitalist Class', *American Journal of Sociology* 79(5): 1073–119.

—— (1976) 'On Class Theory of the Large Corporation: Response to Allen', *American Journal of Sociology* 81(4): 894–903.

——, Ewen, L. A. and Ratcliff, R. E. (1974) 'New Princes for Old? The Large Corporation and the Capitalist Class in Chile', *American Journal of Sociology* 80(1): 87–123.

Zeldin, T. (1979) *France 1848–1945: Politics and Anger*, Oxford: Oxford University Press.

INDEX